ICE SKATING

Reader

EDITED BY
MARSHALL DEUTELBAUM
AND **LELAND POAGUE**

IOWA STATE UNIVERSITY PRESS / AMES

ACKNOWLEDGMENTS

Jean Douchet's "Hitch and His Public" is reprinted from *Cahiers du Cinéma*, no. 113 (November 1960) by permission of the editors.

Maurice Yacowar's "Hitchcock's Imagery and Art" is reprinted from *Hitchcock's British Films* (Hamden, Conn.: Archon Books, 1977) by permission of the author.

Robin Wood's "Retrospective" is reprinted from the 1977 edition of *Hitchcock's Films* (South Brunswick and New York: A.S. Barnes) by permission of the author.

Leonard J. Leff's "Hitchcock at Metro" is reprinted from *Western Humanities Review*, vol. 37, no. 2 (1983) by permission of the journal and the author.

Lesley W. Brill's "Hitchcock's *The Lodger*" is reprinted from *Literature/Film Quarterly*, vol. 11, no. 4 (1983) by permission of the journal.

William Rothman's "Alfred Hitchcock's *Murder!*: Theater, Authorship, and the Presence of the Camera" is reprinted from *Wide Angle*, vol. 4, no. 1 (1980) by permission of the author and The Johns Hopkins University Press.

Elisabeth Weis's "Consolidation of a Classical Style: *The Man Who Knew Too Much*" is reprinted from *The Silent Scream: Alfred Hitchcock's Sound Track* by permission of Associated University Presses.

James McLaughlin's "All in the Family: Alfred Hitchcock's *Shadow of a Doubt*" first appeared in *Wide Angle*, vol. 4, no. 1 (1980); it is reprinted here (in a slightly longer version) by permission of the author and The Johns Hopkins University Press.

Thomas Hyde's "The Moral Universe of Hitchcock's *Spellbound*" is reprinted from *Cinemonkey*, no. 15 (1978) by permission of the editor.

Richard Abel's "*Notorious:* Perversion Par Excellence" is reprinted from *Wide Angle*, vol. 1, no. 1, revised and expanded (1979), by permission of the author and The Johns Hopkins University Press.

Robin Wood's "*Strangers on a Train*" is reprinted from the 1969 edition of *Hitchcock's Films* by permission of the author.

Robert Stam and Roberta Pearson's "Hitchcock's *Rear Window:* Reflexivity and the Critique of Voyeurism" is reprinted from *enclitic*, vol. 7, no. 1 (1983) by permission of the editor.

Robin Wood's "Male Desire, Male Anxiety: The Essential Hitchcock" first appeared as "Fear of Spying" in *American Film*, vol. 9, no. 2 (1983); reprinted here by permission of *American Film*.

Stanley Cavell's "*North by Northwest*" is reprinted from *Themes Out of School: Effects and Causes*, © 1984 by Stanley Cavell. Published by North Point Press and reprinted by permission. All rights reserved. An earlier version of the essay appeared in *Critical Inquiry*, vol. 7, no. 4 (1981). © 1981 by The University of Chicago. Reprinted by permission.

Ian Cameron and Richard Jeffery's "The Universal Hitchcock" is reprinted from *Movie*, no. 12 (1965) by permission of Ian Cameron.

Margaret M. Horwitz's "*The Birds:* A Mother's Love" is reprinted from *Wide Angle*, vol. 5, no. 1 (1982) by permission of the author and The Johns Hopkins University Press.

Raymond Bellour's "Psychosis, Neurosis, Perversion" is reprinted from *Camera Obscura*, no. 3-4 (1979) by permission of the journal and the author.

Barbara Klinger's "*Psycho:* The Institutionalization of Female Sexuality" is reprinted from *Wide Angle*, vol. 5, no. 1 (1982) by permission of the author and The Johns Hopkins University Press.

First edition, 1986

Library of Congress Cataloging-in-Publication Data

A Hitchcock reader.
 1. Hitchcock, Alfred, 1899-1980—Criticism and interpretation—Addresses, essays, lectures.
I. Deutelbaum, Marshall. II. Poague, Leland.
PN1998.A3H54735   1986   791.43′0233′0924   86-176
ISBN 0-8138-0891-X
ISBN 0-8138-0892-8 (pbk.)

Last number is the printing: 19 18 17 16 15 14 13 12 11

A Hitchcock Reader

A Hitchcock

For those other readers, Joyce and Gregory
— M.D.

And for Dennis Poague, master of hawk and handsaw
— L.P.

Contents

Preface

A Hitchcock Reader grew out of our desire as classroom teachers for a comprehensive anthology that could be used as a critical text in introductory or advanced courses devoted to the director's films. We believe, in addition, that many a general "Hitchcock reader" will find most of the essays in this collection exciting and thought provoking for, as they reveal, thinking about Hitchcock's films quickly leads to speculation about larger issues of filmmaking and film culture.

Apart from the occasional special journal issue devoted to Hitchcock, the only real precedent for the present volume is Albert J. LaValley's *Focus on Hitchcock,* now long out of print and compiled before the advent of many of the critical approaches that presently animate Hitchcock criticism. Despite their considerable merits, neither the available biographies of Hitchcock by John Russell Taylor and Donald Spoto, nor the extended, one-volume critical discussions of his films by Claude Chabrol and Eric Rohmer, Raymond Durgnat, and Donald Spoto, nor even the late François Truffaut's lengthy interview book could serve as a central text for the kind of Hitchcock course we have both wanted to teach. The recent rerelease of the five "lost" Hitchcock films — *Rope, Rear Window, The Trouble with Harry, The Man Who Knew Too Much, Vertigo* — further reinforces the need we have long felt for an updated Hitchcock anthology representing the rich variety of critical response his films have evoked over the years.

In addition to a book offering critical discussions of Hitchcock's major films and explaining the well-known motifs and themes that have long been associated with them, moreover, we envisioned a collection that, through its choice of essays, would also reflect something of the history of film criticism and theory over the past thirty years, moving from the initial auteurist claims for taking Hitchcock seriously to the more recent psychological, feminist, and Marxist theories that have lately been brought to bear on his films. Thus another goal of this book is to encourage students to become more aware of the traditions and assumptions underlying various perceptions of cinema — that cultural institution in which Alfred Hitchcock plays an historically crucial role. These interests guided us in both the selection and the organization of essays for the collection.

The essays in Part I, "Taking Hitchcock Seriously," for example, introduce readers to the director's visual style and working methods while asking them to ponder their own relationship to the images Hitchcock creates as he develops his abiding themes. The essays in the three sections at the center of the collection offer critical discussions of individual films to be read in conjunction with their screenings. Part V, "A *Psycho* Dossier," provides an extended consideration of one of Hitchcock's key films from a more thoroughly theoretical position. The Introduction that follows this Preface explains our aims and principles of selection in greater detail.

Because *A Hitchcock Reader* is designed for beginning as well as advanced courses, each of its five sections provides an introduction offering readers an overview of the essays that follow and a context for their consideration. Hitchcock's films are so visually and thematically provocative, however, that no one reading (or sequence of readings) of a given film is ever likely to be exhaustive. For this reason, extensive bibliographies appended to these introductions direct readers to other books and articles relevant to the material in each section. Thus while *A Hitchcock Reader* can be used as the sole text for a course on Hitchcock, these bibliographies suggest additional items that might serve as supplemental readings.

In addition to expressing our appreciation to our many contributors, we would like to thank our editors at the Iowa State University Press, Judith Gildner and Nancy Bohlen, both of whom labored diligently to bring this project to completion. No one labored more diligently or more deserves our thanks than Susan Poague who typeset nearly the entire manuscript on a personal computer. We are grateful as well to Janet Bergstrom and Thomas Hyde for helping us make important contacts in Paris. Terri Paul, Mary Beth Haralovich, Joseph Kupfer, Dan Miller, Mark Bracher, Rick Altman, William Cadbury, Kathy Sichi, and Dudley Andrew all contributed advice and encouragement. Marian Keane helped provide frame enlargements. Our indebtedness to many helpful journal editors is evident in our list of permissions; our personal thanks for their cooperation we tender here. Thanks also to Iowa State University Press Director Merritt Bailey for his sustained cooperation and support.

Finally, we would like to thank the anonymous reader who recommended the book's publication and whose editorial judgments proved crucial in helping to determine the final lineup of essays. The difficult task of selecting a small group of essays from the wealth of available material was made significantly easier because we had another opinion to factor in. Thanks again.

Marshall Deutelbaum
Leland Poague

Introduction

To speak of Alfred Hitchcock is to evoke a remarkable series of histories: the history of cinema generally, in which Hitchcock plays an exemplary role as a technical and stylistic innovator; a history of Hitchcock's films themselves, seen alternately as a matter of decline (for those who prefer his British films) or development (for those who champion his later American movies); a history of film criticism, especially given Hitchcock's status as a primary test case for the auteur theory which held that commercial films ("classical films" in the more current usage) can and should be discussed in the same terms as were previously reserved for "art" films; a history of contemporary film theory, understood at least in part as involving a return to more sociological concerns after the excesses of auteurism; etc.

A Hitchcock Reader has a double purpose relative to the history evoked by the name of Hitchcock — which is to say the book has (at least) two audiences. For Hitchcock scholars *A Hitchcock Reader* is a summary of some aspects of their field, and it continues or renews debate over various aspects of the subject. For students, our primary audience, *A Hitchcock Reader* is an introduction to the field, a map of what may well be for individual students a quite foreign territory. One goal of *A Hitchcock Reader* is to render the territory less foreign, to help students become Hitchcock scholars, as it were, to encourage their claims to membership in the community of those who have chosen to think long and hard about their relationships to Hitchcock's films and to "Film" more generally. A reader of Hitchcock as yet unfamiliar with the field might well begin with Part I, "Taking Hitchcock Seriously," where the question of whether Hitchcock deserves to be taken seriously is addressed. We presume he does, and want here to specify the principles by which our particular exploration of the field has been guided. We are well aware — given the enormous range of essays we considered — that any number of Hitchcock anthologies are possible. We are acutely aware of the ways in which the present volume changed in scope and character through the stages of the editorial process which brought it together. But those changes were accommodated within a fairly stable set of editorial principles which we feel obliged to acknowledge.

The most basic of those principles should already be clear: that film study is an *institutional* activity. College-level film courses are offered in a variety of departmental and interdepartmental circumstances, and within those circumstances from a variety of methodological vantage points. Film is taught as an art form; as an opportunity for cognitive exercise and intellectual development; as a form of mass communication; as a factor in the replication or contestation of cultural wants, needs, and ways of looking. Put another way, film study is not merely "study of films." Rather, like any other academic discipline, film study is defined less by its objects than by the questions which are asked of those objects and of our relationships to them. How do people use films? How do films use them? It is a mark of the intellectual maturity of film study that at present film scholars are far more overtly and consciously concerned with such questions than they once were. In that regard the institutional pressures of film study, especially those resulting from the explosion of semiotic and feminist film scholarship, have served us well for insisting that we reexamine our basic assumptions and canonical figures, among whom Hitchcock retains a certain pride of place. One goal of A Hitchcock Reader is to represent something of the variety and concern presently at work in the film studies discipline. Most of the essays included are of recent authorship; some are published here for the first time. And a broad range of individual perspectives is brought to bear, each representing a particular conception of the film-critical task. The space between the auteurist formalism of someone like Maurice Yacowar and the ideologically grounded feminism of, say, Michele Piso is considerable; it is an area repeatedly traversed and mapped out in the essays which follow, as questions of language, sexuality, and visual ethics are repeatedly posed, answered, and posed again.

A second consequence of looking at our editorial task in institutional terms involves the questions of audience and vocabulary. We take our primary audience to be college undergraduates, many if not most of whom have completed only one or two film courses before taking a junior/senior level class which focuses to a significant measure on Hitchcock. In our experience many of these students have not been introduced to the complexities of modern film theory; many are from humanities departments other than Speech or English (wherein most advanced film courses are offered). So it seemed unwise to make selections on the assumption that Lacanian semiotics and suture theory are common knowledge among our students. For that reason alone essays especially reliant upon Lacanian-Marxian terminology have been largely excluded, though essays which argue that essentially ideological perspective in more ordinary terms do play a major part in A Hitchcock Reader.

The primary exception to this rule is Raymond Bellour's seminal essay on Psycho, though here we have provided options for the teacher who does not wish to confront Bellour directly or unaided. Indeed, one reason we have felt free to pitch this collection toward the general undergraduate audience is the belief that many different courses can be taught from this book, and that how this book is taught remains, for that very reason, remarkably open. For example, only a relatively brief list of reserved readings stands between this book and a theoretically ambitious investigation of the Hitchcock cinema. We have constantly kept such options in mind in preparing our lists of suggested readings. Furthermore, it is very often the case that the best teaching results from a clash of teacher and assigned reading: teaching *against the grain* of an assigned essay puts students in the position of needing to work out on their own terms how they will view and think about the films at hand. For that reason we have not shied away from ideologically oriented criticism—as the pieces by McLaughlin, Piso, and Klinger demonstrate—however much such criticism may clash with our particular individual vantage points.

If we have allowed ourselves an overt editorial bias, however, it is one having to do with the relationship between formal and historical analysis, modes of approach which are often seen as opposing one another. We take this to be a false opposition, especially when history is understood to be synonymous with ideology, because we take any analysis of particular films (ideological or otherwise) to be logically dependent upon an historical perception of the formal resources of cinema. Noël Carroll has even suggested (in "Film History and Film Theory: An Outline for an Institutional Theory of Film,"*Film Reader,* no. 4 [1979]) that such an historical perception of film is an essential factor in answering the question of whether any given film should count as an artwork at all (those do, in Carroll's view, which can be interpreted as repeating, amplifying, or repudiating the traditions of the art form in question). Such perceptions may or may not be difficult to acquire, depending upon how historically precise one wishes to be. Some descriptions of "the classical narrative cinema," for example, are remarkably inclusive, denying, often under the rubric of "myth," any useful formal or ideological distinctions between films made in the early thirties (Thierry Kuntzel's reading of *The Most Dangerous Game* in *Camera Obscura,* no. 5 [1980] comes to mind) and those made only recently.

It is an underlying assumption of *A Hitchcock Reader* that finer distinctions need to be made. Thus we have taken history—of film generally, but also of film criticism and of Hitchcock's own career—as an organizing principle of *A Hitchcock Reader.* In director-oriented criticism there is always a risk of reducing every film to a single formal-thematic model, which often amounts to privileging certain texts or periods as the theme of which all other films are read as variations. But as Robin Wood pointed out long ago, Hitchcock's films evidence a remarkable quality of variety and difference: to go from *Vertigo* to *North by Northwest* to *Psycho* is to experience three distinct film-worlds. Indeed, all three films are arguably about the necessity of *distinguishing* among particular views of the world, and in each case that involves a coming to terms with a very particular history. No one in the world of *Vertigo* can profit from the picture of Norman Bates which emerges at the end of *Psycho* unless that picture can be related in its particularity to the picture which emerges in

Vertigo of Madeleine and Scottie, or of Judy and John. Indeed, it is for ignoring particular differences, of Judy from Madeleine, of Madeleine from Judy, that Scottie stands condemned at the end of *Vertigo*. We risk a similar condemnation in any failure to distinguish *Psycho* from *Vertigo* or either one from *Blackmail* or *Spellbound*. It is our hope that an anthology format, a variety of authors, and a largely chronological survey will encourage a genuinely historical, yet sustainedly particular view of Hitchcock's films and their possibilities.

Let us not be naive about history in all of this. There are many histories, many *theories* of history, just as there are many Hitchcock films; failure to distinguish among histories can be just as deadly as the failure to be historical at all (again, Scottie's failure in *Vertigo,* his capture *by* history — Carlotta's, Madeleine's, his own — is a model instance). There is a history of Hitchcock as an empirical individual; there is a history of his filmmaking which only partly replicates the former. There is a history of the cinema, again only partly coincident with Hitchcock. And there is a history of viewing and criticism as well — for individual viewers and for the film studies discipline as a whole.

Beyond all that there is a history of culture, to which film studies has shifted much of its focus in the last decade, especially via the Marxist analysis of culture as both cause and effect, as determined (by modes of material production) and determining (for replicating, for re-presenting those modes in and for individual subjects). Hence the great attraction for film studies, especially for the Marxist and feminist versions, of Lacanian psychology, which offers a concise model for the connection of large-scale social conditions and individual systems of behavior and belief.

And perhaps Jacques Lacan is a bit too precise, to judge by recent feminist objections. Lacan offers a model for the determination of states of mind which accords with our longings for explanation. What often seems lacking in Lacan (or at least in the version of Lacan most commonly at work in film theory) is a corresponding model of interpretation, or of re-interpretation, which will empower us to change our relationship to given films, if not to all of film-culture. At present the primary critical gesture is typically one of *exposure,* designed as much to show forth the mechanisms of the film/culture relationship as to change them. But even that "showing forth" is arguably a species of change, whether or not we accept the psycho-logic underlying particular readings. One may not be convinced by the Lacanian model invoked throughout Raymond Bellour's reading of *Psycho,* which concludes that "film and cinema" are "the very institution of perversion," as if *Psycho* were subject to, subjects *us* to, "the monolithic power of its ruling signifier," such that our only alternative is to embrace perversion, to be perverse in our turn. But one can hardly deny that, after reading Bellour, our view and experience of *Psycho* will never be, *can* never be, the same. Bellour's reading of *Psycho* may not explain it, but his claim to an understanding of the film is a powerful one resting largely on the quality of his formal analysis, his understanding of part/ whole relations. This ability of interpretation to induce change, to intervene in the history of the text, of its reception, and of the traditions it inherits, is an historical fact too often overlooked by those who claim history as an antidote to formal analysis. History *is* a species of formalism in that it orders data under explanatory (often narrative) principles and it depends on formal criticism tc provide data and to test its explanations.

It should be noted that the "hypothesis and testing" model cited above has guided not only our selection of essays, in that we have tried to include a variety of hypotheses for testing, but also our arrangement of editorial matter and additional references. Books which cover all of Hitchcock and articles which are similarly inclusive in scope are listed after the introduction to Part I, "Taking Hitchcock Seriously." Any journey through Hitchcock should begin here. References listed after the introduction to Part II, "Hitchcock in Britain," are limited to articles primarily relevant to that period of Hitchcock's career and similarly for references listed for Parts III and IV. References included in Part V, "Hitchcock and Film Theory: A *Psycho* Dossier," fall under two headings appropriate to the double title, one on "Film Theory," a second including additional references specifically "On *Psycho.*"

It is often remarked that film in general, and Hitchcock's films particularly, have a dream-like quality about them, occasionally to the point of nightmare. But, as Stanley Cavell urges in *The World Viewed* (Cambridge: Harvard Univ. Press [1979]), films differ from dreams in at least one crucial respect: other people have had the same dream, seen the same film, and can help you remember it by remembering it themselves (p. 16). The common responsibility for such remembering is another marker of the institutional nature of film study. In working through the essays included here, we have found a number of lapses of memory on the part of individual critics, though none are especially vital in the sense that their correction would genuinely modify basic arguments or attitudes.

As a pedagogical case in point consider the following instance from an exemplary essay, though an instance since caught and corrected by its authors. In their discussion of *Rear Window* as it originally appeared in *enclitic,* Robert Stam and Roberta Pearson identify the James Stewart character, L. B. Jefferies, as a kind of surrogate director for using a camera lens to define a series of views upon an external reality, the courtyard across from his own rear window. In thematic terms they read this voyeurism as a species of isolation, as a means of endistancing, and they read Jefferies's final fall into the courtyard as a kind of fall into community, into relationship with those "neighbors" who had thus far served as subjects of his vicarious gaze. In urging this reading they imply (very much in passing) that Hitchcock forsakes his usual cameo appearance in the film, leaving the director role completely to Jefferies. Yet Hitchcock does appear, and his appearance can be accounted for.

While Lisa prepares to serve the dinner she has brought for Jefferies from "21," Jefferies watches Thorwald serve dinner to his invalid wife. They quarrel. Jefferies then looks away, to the flat of the songwriter next door to his own apartment. Hitchcock stands at the mantle, screen left, winding a clock, after which he turns his head and speaks (soundlessly) to the songwriter who sits at the piano. Cut back to Jefferies and Lisa, the latter asking where the music comes from. Jefferies's reply describes the musician as living "alone," and probably as the result of "a very unhappy marriage." The line calls attention to the fact that the songwriter is not presently alone (Hitchcock is there) and also to Jefferies's own desire to be solitary, despite Lisa's presence. None of which really changes the general thrust of Stam and Pearson's fine and thoughtful reading of *Rear Window*. We just have that much more to ponder. Indeed, Hitchcock's presence in the film can be easily accommodated to the theme of "neighborliness" which Stam and Pearson elaborate. As Maurice Yacowar remarks in *Hitchcock's British Films* (Hamden, Conn.: Archon Books [1977]), Hitchcock "is helping the character find his right time, his rhythm," and in this serves both as director and as a citizen of the film's depicted world, indeed "the first character in that tenement to help another" (p. 276).

Such accommodation, of new facts to old readings, of competing readings one to another, is a basic exercise of film criticism, a reminder that we are all critics and are all responsible for checking interpretive hypotheses against the facts of the texts in question. For that reason, and also given the difficulty and futility of trying to catch every such error of memory or observation, we have not undertaken to edit out any but the most minor of discrepancies. We have silently regularized spellings, punctuation, and documentation formats. Some few pieces have been revised at the request of their authors. But beyond those sorts of changes the essays are reprinted as originally published.

A final note on "history." For brevity's sake we have not included an exhaustive Hitchcock filmography. Such are readily available elsewhere. A disadvantage to this decision is the risk we run of overemphasizing Hitchcock's artistic autonomy. Even the most dedicated auteur critic could ask no better an example of directorial authorship in the commercial cinema than Hitchcock. But Hitchcock hardly worked alone. Excellent testimony to this effect is found in Susan Schenker's "Plotting the Hitchcock Family" (*Take One*, vol. 5, no. 2 [1976]) which provides a listing by frequency of Hitchcock's collaborative relationships. Not surprisingly for someone whose films are so profoundly concerned with questions of sexuality and marriage, Hitchcock's most sustained collaboration was with his wife, Alma Reville, who received screen credit of several sorts (adaptation, screenwriter, assistant director), always under her maiden name, on 18 of Hitchcock's 53 films, from *The Pleasure Garden* (1925) to *Stage Fright* (1950). Next on the list, again not surprisingly, are two directors of photography, Robert Burks and Jack Cox.

To avoid misrepresentation, we have included screen credits for principal members of cast and crew for all the films discussed at length in this volume. All such entries are found immediately following the essay in question. Credits for *Vertigo* follow Wood's essay on the film; those for *The Birds* and *Marnie* are listed after "The Universal Hitchcock"; those for *Psycho* follow Bellour's chapter. The brief chronology at the back of the book lists all of Hitchcock's feature films and television shows, keyed as closely as possible to the order of release or initial broadcast. At the very least it stands as reminder of all that is *not* covered in this selection of essays; we hope it will also serve as encouragement to further viewing and thinking. Such is both the substance and process of film criticism.

PART ONE

Taking
Hitchcock
Seriously

Robin Wood began his landmark study, *Hitchcock's Films,* with a crucial question: "Why should we take Hitchcock seriously?" As Wood pointed out many paragraphs later, nothing less than his entire book could stand as sufficient answer to that question because claims of artistic or aesthetic seriousness are only as valid as the "detailed analysis" supporting them. Because critics have continued to ask the same question of Hitchcock and his films over the past twenty-five years, *A Hitchcock Reader* similarly serves to answer that question by illustrating the variety of reasons these critics have found to justify their abiding interest in the man and his works. Indeed, the way that Hitchcock has served as a critical touchstone during these years suggests that his films remain central to questions of cinematic practice and critical theory.

If Hitchcock was a crucial test case for the development of the auteur theory of film criticism in the 1960s, he and his films have recently become crucial texts in the development of psychoanalytic and feminist approaches to film study (see Part V, "Hitchcock and Film Theory: A *Psycho* Dossier"). Indeed, during the intervening years Hitchcock's importance has been underlined by the way in which numerous critics (Jean Douchet, Raymond Durgnat, Peter Wollen, Andrew Sarris, Leo Braudy, John Belton, Raymond Bellour, and Janet Bergstrom, among many others) have felt it both worthwhile and necessary to work through their relationship to Hitchcock, as if an understanding of his films were absolutely essential to their understanding of cinema. Their cumulative work has taught all of us to perceive the films more clearly. Their testing of themselves against Hitchcock's practice in this way suggests the underlying wisdom of Maurice Yacowar's assertion that "what seems to be a Hitchcock error is likely our failure to work out what he is doing."

Such an answer to Wood's question as Yacowar's, however, does not ex-

1

haust the question, in part because "taking Hitchcock seriously" is not limited
to a single context. Yacowar's approach is almost a given of formalist or aesthetic approaches to film. In the context of aesthetics, taking Hitchcock seriously and seeing him and his films positively are nearly synonymous. But
there has always been a second approach to Hitchcock, more sociological than
aesthetic, which takes him seriously precisely *because* his films are seen nega-
tively, as evidence of an almost sadomasochistic pact between auteur and audience.

An early and relatively mild instance of this is O. B. Hardison's essay on
"The Rhetoric of Hitchcock's Thrillers." Hardison distinguishes between Art,
which in Aristotle's terms provides the kind of pleasure which "comes from
learning" and "insight," and Rhetoric, which is "oriented toward the marketplace," its "governing concept" being that "the work produced must be adjusted to the mind of the audience," not saying something new or insightful
but "what the audience has secretly known (or wanted to know) all along" (p.
138). In Hardison's view Hitchcock's reliance on the "thriller" format amounts
to an indulgence of this desire to experience the already known, and Hitchcock's "rhetorical skill" is seen largely in his ability to render this fantasy "credi-
ble" on (at least) two interrelated accounts: (1) by means of his "mastery of
technique," which effectively "insulates the spectator from the implications of
the thriller plot" by assuring him or her that "no matter how terrifying the
present may seem, sanity will prevail in the end"; and (2) by the "Quality" and
"Precision" of his style, which effectively "separate" Hitchcock's films from
their more overtly banal or melodramatic kindred, rendering them less "crude"
and somehow "more 'real' than reality" (pp. 141–42). Hardison is not especially condemnatory in all of this; he concludes his essay by invoking the film/
dream analogy to suggest that "a culture is like an individual. It needs its
dreams as well as its waking periods." Dreams allow us to "avoid waking up"—
and Hitchcock is to be praised, in a world where "it is becoming harder to
dream," for "bending the formulas so that [dreaming] at least remains possible" (p. 151).

Similar in logic, if not at all in tone, are the essays by Charles T. Samuels,
William Pechter, and David Thomson listed below, of which Thomson's *Film
Comment* piece is the more recent and the more vehement. "Hitchcock's
mechanistic imagination," writes Thomson, "is all triggers, blades and lethal
traps: it is an eloquent example of the oppressed mind being driven in against
itself, of dictatorship generating self-loathing." And the self-loathing is not
Hitchcock's alone. Hitchcock may put "the audience through it as torturer, not
as moral scientist or teacher," but only with its "willing support" (p. 29). As
David Lubin remarks in his reply to Thomson, such a view of Hitchcock depends crucially, and illegitimately, on the evidence provided in interviews,
chiefly that preserved in Truffaut's *Hitchcock*; but such a reliance on interviews
(as opposed to relying on the films) is certainly consistent with an approach

which holds the films themselves to be exercises in "whiplash superiority and domineering mistrust" (p. 29). The less time spent viewing and thinking about the films the better, or so this view of them implies.

Most of the cruxes in Hitchcock scholarship are versions of two basic questions. First, how are we to read the relationship between Hitchcock's camera, the views it takes and their succession, and the world it inhabits and takes views of? In other words, how are we to understand the relationship between form and content, between the way Hitchcock envisions and presents the world and the world so represented? Answers to this question often stress Hitchcock's indebtedness to the traditions of Soviet montage and German expressionism, in each of which an aspect of film form is generally held to "impose" meaning on the world rather than allow the world to be meaningful in its own ontological terms (see Wood's "Retrospective" but also John Belton's "Dexterity in a Void" in his *Cinema Stylists*). Second, there is the question of "Hitch and his Public," as Jean Douchet has phrased it. That is, how are we to understand *our* relationship to Hitchcock, to the world his films project, to the camera which takes those views, and to the "absent one" who determines which views will be taken and projected? In other words, how far does Hitchcock's apparent willingness to impose his views on film entail a corollary desire to impose those views on the members of his audience? Can audiences be imposed upon?

Paradoxically, the most current answers to these two sets of questions leave little to choose, beyond a certain quality of empathetic admiration and tolerance, between Hitchcock's critics and his partisans. William Rothman's *Hitchcock—The Murderous Gaze,* for example, concludes with a remarkable and extended reading of *Psycho* which takes the film, at least in part, as Hitchcock's gesture of revenge, a full-blooded attack on those who withhold their recognition of Hitchcock's authorship. "In the creation of a work of art," Rothman writes, "the artist takes his own death upon himself. And his art has a murderous aspect as well. How could his impulse to create be separated from his desire to avenge himself on those who, beholding his creations, draw sustenance from them?" (p. 340). Few would accuse Rothman of underestimating Hitchcock's accomplishments, but the echoes of Thomson's critique are resonant, even in this brief passage. Hence the gap between criticism and partisanship has narrowed to the point where we can enlist Robin Wood, long known for his advocacy on Hitchcock's behalf, to represent the negative case, at least by contrast with Maurice Yacowar, whose conclusion to *Hitchcock's British Films* is arguably closer in spirit to the first edition of Wood's book than much of Wood's later scholarship, where the desire to specify Hitchcock's limitations is as strong as the desire to defend them.

Perhaps the question now is not "Should we take Hitchcock seriously?" but rather "Which Hitchcock are we taking seriously?" Is it the Hitchcock who seems obsessively trapped in his dedication to "pure cinema," who fears abnormality yet finds it irresistibly attractive? Or is it a knowing Hitchcock whose artistry involves a self-conscious critique of the ideological circumstances which give rise to gender-specific notions of normal and abnormal? Is it Hitchcock the victim and victimizer; or Hitchcock the seer, Hitchcock the prophetic "eye"? Are his films exercises in obsession or exorcisms of those very same and overtly destructive longings for certainty and fantasy?

And what do we mean by "Hitchcock" in all of this? By and large (and not illegitimately) the Hitchcock invoked in most film scholarship is that implicated or implicit in the films. But there was also an Alfred Hitchcock who lived and died and made a living as a film director. Whether or not these two Hitchcocks can ever be reconciled, can ever "marry" in Rothman's terminology, remains an open question, though the distance between them has long been a matter of considerable fascination, if not confusion. Robert Cumbow makes the case, for instance (in "Of Staircases and Potato Trucks: Fear and Fatness and Alfred Hitchcock"), that the fears and apprehensions that recur in Hitchcock's films, far from being universally applicable or significant, "represent the very particular anxieties and discomforts peculiar to the fat person" (p. 6)—to which it might well be replied that we are all, in some sense, "fat." A similar conflict between aesthetic and intentionalist approaches to Hitchcock marks the incredible gap of attitude and methodology between Donald Spoto's critical study of Hitchcock and his more recent popular (if not scandalous) biography of the man.

The uncertain relationship between artistic sensibility and finished film is complicated all the more by the workings of the Hollywood studio system, where economic pressures as well as the conflicting interests of many people invariably transform a director's intentions. Hitchcock yearned to establish an independent production company during the years he toiled under what he regarded as an onerous long-term contract with David O. Selznick. Though his own production company, Transatlantic Pictures, proved to be short lived, the dissolution of the studio system during the 1950s enabled Hitchcock to maneuver to his advantage in striking production deals with the still established, if tottering, studios. In "Hitchcock at Metro" Leonard Leff documents the director's struggle to control the production of what would prove to be *North by Northwest*. While Leff's essay sheds little light on the aesthetics of the film, "Hitchcock at Metro" offers us a case study of Hitchcock as a businessman, reminding us of the ways in which a film as an industrial product is inevitably subject to legal and economic constraints but also of the ways in which at least some directors are able to acquire the kind of "power and freedom" enjoyed by Hitchcock during what is arguably the most significant decade of his decadeslong career.

References and Suggested Readings

Bazin, André. *The Cinema of Cruelty*. New York: Seaver Books, 1982.
Belton, John. *Cinema Stylists*. Metuchen, N.J.: Scarecrow, 1983.

_____. "Reply to Samuels' Article on Hitchcock." *American Scholar*, vol. 39 (1970): 728–31. See Samuels (cited below).

Bogdanovich, Peter. *The Cinema of Alfred Hitchcock*. New York: Museum of Modern Art, 1963.

Braudy, Leo. "Hitchcock, Truffaut, and the Irresponsible Audience." In LaValley (cited below).

Buscombe, Edward. "Dickens and Hitchcock." *Screen*, vol. 11, no. 4–5 (1970): 97–114.

Carroll, Noël. "Toward a Theory of Film Suspense." *Persistence of Vision*, no. 1 (1984): 65–89.

Corey, David. *Fearful Symmetries: The Contest of Authority in the Hitchcock Narrative*. Ph.D. dissertation, New York University, 1980. On the British films and the Hollywood films through *Strangers on a Train*.

Cumbow, Robert. "Of Staircases and Potato Trucks: Fear and Fatness and Alfred Hitchcock." *Movietone News*, no. 25 (1973): 6–12.

_____. Review of Durgnat's *The Strange Case of Alfred Hitchcock*. *Movietone News*, no. 41 (1975): 3–8.

Douchet, Jean. "La Troisième Clé d'Hitchcock." *Cahiers du Cinéma*, no. 99 (1959): 44–50.

_____. "La Troisième Clé d'Hitchcock II." *Cahiers du Cinéma*, no. 102 (1959): 30–37.

_____. "Hitch et Son Public." *Cahiers du Cinéma*, no. 113 (1960): 7–15. Reprinted here.

Durgnat, Raymond. *The Strange Case of Alfred Hitchcock: Or The Plain Man's Hitchcock*. Cambridge: MIT Press, 1974.

_____. "To Catch a 'Hitch'." *Quarterly Review of Film Studies*, vol. 8, no. 1 (1983): 43–48. Review of Rothman's *Hitchcock—The Murderous Gaze* (cited below).

Dynia, Philip. "Alfred Hitchcock and the Ghost of Thomas Hobbes." In Richard Dyer MacCann and Jack Ellis, eds. *Cinema Examined*. New York: E. P. Dutton, 1982, 23–37.

Fieschi, Jean-André. "Alfred Hitchcock: II." In Richard Roud, ed. *Cinema: A Critical Dictionary*, vol. 1. London: Martin Secker & Warburg, 1980, 502–10.

Freeman, David. *The Last Days of Alfred Hitchcock: A Memoir Featuring the Screenplay of "Alfred Hitchcock's The Short Night."* Woodstock, N.Y.: Overlook Press, 1984.

French, Philip. "Alfred Hitchcock: The Film-maker as Englishman and Exile." *Sight and Sound*, vol. 54, no. 2 (1985): 116–22.

Giacci, Vittorio. "Alfred Hitchcock: Allegory of Ambiguous Sexuality." *Wide Angle*, vol. 4, no. 1 (1980): 4–11.

Haley, Michael. *The Alfred Hitchcock Album*. Englewood Cliffs: Prentice-Hall, 1981.

Hardison, O. B. "The Rhetoric of Hitchcock's Thrillers." In W. R. Robinson, ed. *Man and the Movies*. Baton Rouge: Louisiana State Univ. Press, 1967, 137–52.

Harris, Robert A., and Michael S. Laskey. *The Films of Alfred Hitchcock*. Secaucus, N.J.: Citadel Press, 1976.

Haskell, Molly. *From Reverence to Rape*. New York: Holt, Rinehart and Winston, 1973, 1974.

Higham, Charles. "Hitchcock's World." *Film Quarterly*, vol. 16, no. 2 (1963): 3–16.

Houston, Penelope. "The Figure in the Carpet." *Sight and Sound*, vol. 34, no. 4 (1963): 159–64.

_____. "Alfred Hitchcock: I," in Roud (cited above): 487–501.

Jameson, Fredric. "Reading Hitchcock." *October*, no. 23 (1982): 15–42. Review of Rothman's *Hitchcock—The Murderous Gaze* (cited below).

Jhirad, Susan. "Hitchcock's Women." *Cineaste*, vol. 13, no. 4 (1984): 30–33.

Kane, Lawrence. "Shadow World of Alfred Hitchcock." *Theatre Arts*, vol. 33, no. 4 (1949): 32–40.

Kaplan, George [Robin Wood]. "Alfred Hitchcock: Lost in the Wood." *Film Comment*, vol. 8, no. 4 (1972): 46–53.

Lambert, Gavin. "Hitchcock and the Art of Suspense." *American Film*, vol. 1, no. 4 (1976): 16–23.

_____. "Hitchcock and the Art of Suspense, Part II." *American Film*, vol. 1, no. 5 (1976): 60–67.

LaValley, Albert J., ed. *Focus on Hitchcock*. Englewood Cliffs: Prentice-Hall, 1972.

Lubin, David. "Buts & Rebuts." *Film Comment*, vol. 15, no. 3 (1979): 66–68.

McCartey, John, and Brian Kelleher. *Alfred Hitchcock Presents: An Illustrated Guide to the Ten-Year Television Career of the Master of Suspense*. New York: St. Martin's Press, 1985.

McConnell, Frank. *Storytelling and Mythmaking: Images from Film and Literature*. New York: Oxford Univ. Press, 1979, 168–78. Chiefly on *North by Northwest* and *Sabotage*.

Miller, Gavin. "Hitchcock versus Truffaut." *Sight and Sound*, vol. 38, no. 2 (1969): 82–88.

Monaco, James. "The Cinema and its Double: Alfred Hitchcock." *Take One*, vol. 5, no. 2 (1976): 6–8.

Munday, Robert. "Another Look at Hitchcock." *Cinema* (Cambridge), no. 6-7 (1970): 10-12.
Pechter, William S. "The Director Vanishes." In *Twenty-four Times a Second*. New York: Harper & Row, 1971, 175-94.
Perry, George. *Hitchcock*. New York: Doubleday, 1975.
Phillips, Gene D. *Alfred Hitchcock*. Boston: Twayne, 1984.
Poague, Leland. "Hitchcock and the Ethics of Vision." In William Cadbury and Leland Poague. *Film Criticism: A Counter Theory*. Ames: Iowa State Univ. Press, 1982, 91-155.
Rohmer, Eric, and Claude Chabrol. *Hitchcock: The First Forty-Four Films*. Trans. Stanley Hochman. New York: Frederick Ungar, 1979.
Rothman, William. "How Much Did Hitchcock Know." *Quarterly Review of Film Studies*, vol. 5, no. 3 (1980): 383-92. Review of Yacowar's *Hitchcock's British Films* and of Taylor's *Hitch* (both cited below).
_____. *Hitchcock—The Murderous Gaze*. Cambridge: Harvard Univ. Press, 1982.
Russell, Lee [Peter Wollen]. "Alfred Hitchcock." *New Left Review*, no. 35 (1966): 88-92.
Sallitt, Daniel. "Point of View and 'Intrarealism' in Hitchcock." *Wide Angle*, vol. 4, no. 1 (1980): 38-43.
Samuels, Charles Thomas. "Hitchcock." In *Mastering the Film and Other Essays*. Knoxville: Univ. of Tennessee Press, 1977, 69-84.
Sarris, Andrew. "The American Cinema: Directorial Chronology 1915-1962." *Film Culture*, no. 28 (1963): 1-68. Expanded as *The American Cinema: Directors and Directions 1929-1968*. New York: E. P. Dutton, 1968.
_____. "Alfred Hitchcock: Prankster of Paradox." *Film Comment*, vol. 10, no. 2 (1974): 8-9.
Silver, Alain. "Fragments of a Mirror: The Use of Landscape in Hitchcock." *Wide Angle*, vol. 1, no. 3 (1976): 52-61.
Spoto, Donald. *The Art of Alfred Hitchcock*. New York: Hopkinson and Blake, 1976.
_____. *The Dark Side of Genius: The Life of Alfred Hitchcock*. Boston: Little, Brown, 1983.
Stam, Robert. "Hitchcock and Buñuel: Desire and the Law." *Studies in the Literary Imagination*, vol. 16, no. 1 (1983): 7-27.
Take One, vol. 5, no. 2 (1976): "Alfred Hitchcock: A Friendly Salute." Special Hitchcock number.
Taylor, John Russell. *Cinema Eye, Cinema Ear*. New York: Hill and Wang, 1978.
_____. *Hitch: The Life & Times of Alfred Hitchcock*. New York: Pantheon, 1978.
Thomson, David. *Movie Man*. New York: Stein and Day, 1967.
_____. "The Big Hitch." *Film Comment*, vol. 15, no. 2 (1979): 26-29. Reprinted as "Alfred Hitchcock and the Prison of Mastery," in *Overexposures: The Crisis in American Filmmaking*. New York: William Morrow, 1981, 188-201.
Truffaut, François. *Hitchcock*, revised edition. New York: Simon & Schuster, 1984.
Weis, Elisabeth. *The Silent Scream: Alfred Hitchcock's Sound Track*. Rutherford: Fairleigh Dickinson Univ. Press, 1982.
Wide Angle, vol. 4, no. 1 (1980). Special Hitchcock number.
Wollen, Peter. "Hitchcock's Vision." *Cinema* (Cambridge), no. 3 (1969): 2-4.
_____. "The Hermeneutic Code." In *Readings and Writings: Semiotic Counter-Strategies*. London: Verso, 1982, 40-48.
Wood, Robin. *Hitchcock's Films*, 3rd ed. South Brunswick and New York: A. S. Barnes, 1977.
_____. "Hitchcock, Alfred." In Christopher Lyon, ed. *Directors/Filmmakers: The International Dictionary of Films and Filmmakers*, vol. 2. Chicago: St. James Press, 1984, 259-63.
Yacowar, Maurice. *Hitchcock's British Films*. Hamden, Conn.: Archon Books, 1977.

CHAPTER ONE

Hitch and His Public

Jean Douchet
TRANSLATED BY VERENA CONLEY

A reading of this article is forbidden to those who have not yet seen *Psycho*.[1]

Which does not mean that others are obliged to read it. It is, however, impossible to study the film without unveiling its secret. And to know that would deprive the reader, as a future spectator, of a major part of his pleasure. I know this from experience. During his last interview, Hitchcock told Domarchi and myself about his film, and he mimed it to us from one end to the other, in an extraordinary fashion.[2] For more than one hour we watched *Psycho* being born, sequence by sequence, and at times shot by shot. I truly say *being born*, since this took place in October of 1959 and Hitchcock did not begin to shoot until November. And now, in his screening room at Paramount, we had the impression of seeing the film for a second time. We were cut off from part of the terror that seized the other spectators.

A Magical Art.

But this terror is the primary, if not the ultimate goal pursued by Hitchcock. Even in his most inconsequential interviews he likes to reveal to what extent, for him, creation depends on an exact science of the spectator's reaction. Not for financial reasons (he was even quite sure that *Psycho* would be a failure), nor even for promotional reasons (though he admirably uses publicity, and we know, since *North by Northwest*, what he thinks of it), but because he attributes a mission to "suspense." And this mission is cathartic. The spectator has to "undo his repressions" in a psychoanalytical sense, confess himself on a logical plane, purify himself on a spiritual level. Hitchcock depends therefore on the active participation of the public.

The proof? *Rear Window.* It is there that Hitchcock elaborates his very concept of cinema (that is to say of cinema in cinema), reveals his secrets, unveils his intentions. James Stewart, a news photographer, is before everything else a spectator. This is one of the reasons why he is seen bound to his wheelchair. Through him, Hitchcock intends to define the nature of the spectator and, especially, the nature of a Hitchcockian spectator. The latter is a "voyeur." He wants to experience (sexual) pleasure (*jouir*) through the spectacle. What he looks at on the screen (in other words, what Stewart watches in the building on the other side of the courtyard) is the very projection of himself. Only the latter is capable of interesting him. In one way or the other, it is himself that he comes to see. A spectacle which, after all, would quickly become dull if some special matter, some mystery, would not happen to capture his attention entirely. From then on, his understanding is fixed on this idea which becomes an obsession. Reasoning and deduction are subordinated to subjectivity, to feelings of desire and fear. The more he desires or fears, the more his expectation will be rewarded and beyond all his hopes. Stewart so ardently desires that a crime take place that the crime does materialize and approach him. In a Hitchcock movie, the spectator creates the suspense. It does nothing but answer his own summons. (Remember, too, Doris Day, the spectator, in *The Man Who Knew Too Much*.) In other words, Hitchcock first excites vile and low feelings in his public and authorizes it through his spectacle to satisfy these urges. The impression of horror the spectator then feels brings forth other feelings in him, noble and pure, which alone are capable of destroying the initial urges. More than a therapy, cinema, here, is a truly magic art.

The Three Realities.

All of which sends us back to the intention of the author. Hitchcock intends to unveil reality and have us discover it in three ways. Three, like the three blinds which go up, one after the other, in the very first shot of *Rear Window*. The first reality, evidently, is that of the everyday world which is immediately recognizable by the spectator. Hence the care which Hitchcock accords it. Because it functions as a stable basis for his construction, the filmmaker has not ceased to depict reality with a great deal of truth. For him, the fake is intolerable. Even less the arbitrary. (We are far from Clouzot's *Diaboliques*.) Never, ever, does Hitchcock deceive the spectator. At times he lulls, sometimes willingly, the spectator's attention (the way he lulls Stewart at the moment the crime takes place in *Rear Window*), but he always leaves him information enough. The spectator can, if he desires it, reconstitute in his thoughts the events which have taken place. This observation is of the utmost importance for *Psycho* where everything, to the least detail, is explained clearly. Nothing is therefore less justified than the accusations of implausibility that some direct toward Hitchcock.

The second reality, the second set of blinds, opens onto the world of desire. It is thus that the building on the other side of the courtyard appears. Everything that takes place in the everyday world of Stewart's apartment inscribes itself there, projects itself as if on a screen. The apartment itself is shown in multiple examples, each populated by forms and animated by the forces which have brought them into being. These form-forces personify secret thoughts, mental attitudes, and especially the desires of our hero. And in this world they possess a real existence and an active power. Like an immense mirror, put up in front of the quotidian reality, the world of desire inverts situations as well as thoughts. Thus, the Kelly-Stewart couple (paralyzed) and the other, Raymond Burr and his bedridden wife. Thus also the existence of Stewart's latent desire to rid himself of Kelly, a desire which Raymond Burr acts out. These form-forces of desire constitute the primary element of any Hitchcock movie. A psychoanalyst will see in it the figure of culpability. However, never before *Psycho* had our filmmaker made it so evident. Here, the form is endowed with a terrifying force.

Finally, the third reality, the intellectual world. The latter is the main support beam of the Hitchcockian *oeuvre,* the perpendicular which links the two parallel universes and thus allows them to communicate. It is on this beam that the filmmaker relies for all his films. It is therefore via this intermediary world that Stewart, confined in his quotidian universe (and that is the reason why we do not leave his living room throughout the movie), is able to see through to the world of desire. As spectator, what does our hero see? What he believes to be the quotidian world, though it is only his own reflection. But the world of desire soon unveils his true nature. A horrible action takes place in it, one which the hero has not seen but suspects. From then on his attention is awake, his intellect at the service of his self-interest. If Stewart, on the basis of the slightest clues, leads his investigation according to the logical process of induction and deduction, it is not that he pursues a noble goal. To the contrary, he seeks less to reveal the light than to penetrate the darkness, the darkness in which the murderer envelops himself, though his presence is nevertheless betrayed by a cigarette. In brief, he examines the objective givens (*les données objectives*) only to please his own subjectivity, or even better, to satisfy an even sicker curiosity. (Understood from this perspective, the publicity about *Psycho* imagined by Hitch becomes a chief element in the movie: the public must want to feel fear.) Once this happens, the audience deprives itself of its most important weapon, lucid understanding. The audience is as unprotected as a savage, subject to great ancestral fears. Its reason voluntarily loses itself in the irrational, surrenders itself without defense (like Janet Leigh under the shower) to the almighty power of the occult.

In front of the menacing Shadow of the murderer who, having come from the world of desire, suddenly invades his quotidian universe, the flashes of the camera seem to Stewart laughably ineffectual. This purely material light cannot suffice to protect him. "Each is caught in his own trap," we hear it said in *Psycho.* The Hitchcockian spectator more than anyone else. Because of this intellectual distance (represented by the courtyard), Stewart, at the height of curiosity, wants Kelly to cross it. He then releases what occultists and magicians fear the most: the blow in return. Now, if the reader is willing to be convinced that *Rear Window* illustrates the very concept of Hitchcockian cinema, then he can summarize what precedes in these terms: Stewart is like the projector; the building opposite like the screen; then the distance which separates them, the intellectual world, would be occupied by the beam of light. If the reader also remembers that Stewart is first the spectator, he can conclude that the hero "invents his own cinema." But is that not the very definition of a "voyeur," the very core of morose gratification?

From Contempt to Complicity.

So? We have to push our investigation of this intellectual world even further. First of all, the more this investigation concentrates on an object of desire or fear, the more intense it becomes, the more the force of this intensity animates the form which it brought into being. At the same time, the force becomes more precise and grows stronger. Thus in *Psycho.* Assume that Stewart has descended from the screen of *Rear Window* to take his place in the theater, that he has become each one of us, a spectator. His voyeur's appetite finds nourishment in the opening of *Psycho.* Indeed, the camera penetrates indiscreetly into a room with lowered shades, in the middle of the afternoon. And in this room there is a couple on a bed, embracing, kissing, demonstrating a great physical attraction. From then on, he feels frustrated. He would like "to see more." Even if John Gavin's bare chest could possibly satisfy half the audience, the fact that Janet Leigh is not naked is hardly tolerated by the other half. This awakened desire must logically find its conclusion at the end of Janet's journey. She will be naked, completely, offering herself entirely. The sexual act which will be perpetrated on her will also be extreme — therefore, a wish fulfillment beyond all hopes.

But let us get back to the beginning of the movie. The spectator's feeling toward Janet is one of envy and contempt at the same time. A woman who accepts a sleazy hotel room in the middle of the afternoon in her own provincial town is not worthy of esteem. He may therefore ascribe to her his worst instincts — among others, his unconscious desire, which he does not dare to act out in real life, that of theft. Indeed, back at her desk, Janet witnesses an important transaction of cash. The spectator, who is beginning to get bored by these banal business scenes, wishes for something to happen. And precisely — why not? — that Janet Leigh take the money for herself. Since the transaction is irregular, there would be no proof, and the owner of the money is truly loathsome. Luckily, her boss has her carry the money to the bank. The amount is $40,000. In addition, the events take place on a Friday: the theft will not be noticed until the following Monday. So Janet takes the money. And here she is, on the road.

A cop stops her: a simple verification of identity. A disquieting feeling overcomes us. This feeling increases. The cop follows her. What does he want from her? Has the theft already been discovered? But from now on we ardently desire that she succeed. We are with her with all our heart. But this altruistic thought covers our very own crime which Janet Leigh has to assume. Under the guise of sympathy, it hides a vile desire—a desire which will be realized: the cop abandons his pursuit.

(Why did he abandon her? There are, of necessity, three explanations. One, psychological: this woman seems distraught; moreover, she is pretty. It is normal that a cop—who is nevertheless a man—hopes that she will ask him to help her. But she does not ask. Another logic: as a highway patrolman, the state of fatigue of Janet Leigh intrigues him. Professional reasons oblige him to observe her behavior for fear that she may provoke an accident. But, she provokes none. Finally another, an occult, reason. The very appearance of the cop, similar to that of the cops in Cocteau's *Orpheus,* belongs to the domain of the fantastic. He is both conscience and Angel of Order, sent for a last attempt at salvation. But he cannot save that which does not want to be saved. If the reader-spectator imbues himself with magical ideas, he understands that the hostile flow from the audience prevents the Angel from accomplishing his mission. Hence, in Hitchcock, the extreme importance of the call, the appeal, often symbolized by the telephone. That is how, in *Rear Window,* Stewart, seeing Kelly at the murderer's place, at the same time provokes and calls the latter. Inversely, the murderer calls Stewart before coming. In *Psycho,* the fact that the sheriff calls Bates in the second part of the film strangely illuminates what such calls represent in the occult order. One can converse only between equals, from man to man, from angel to angel, or from God to Satan (*North by Northwest*). By contrast, man may appeal to superior powers, whether good or evil. Teresa Wright in *Shadow of a Doubt.* Farley Granger in *Strangers on a Train.*)

Salvation being rejected by us, and therefore by Janet Leigh, she is given up to nocturnal powers, is incapable of enduring the radiance of light; from now on she falls prey to any delirium. Her state of fatigue makes us wish that she would stop. Hence our relief when she comes to a motel. But the unusual and mysterious aspect of the place and of its host provoke in us a mute anguish. We have the premonition of a danger, the more so as Janet Leigh is alone in this sinister place, alone in her room, with the window wide open, while she tries to hide her money (our money). And can't she find a better place to hide it than in plain sight, on the nightstand? From then on, we fear the worst. We fear that while she has dinner someone will steal the bank notes. And because we fear everything, her conversation with Perkins seems too long to us. We wish to see this fear verified. Our desire *to see* will increase even more: Perkins, like ourselves, is a voyeur and watches his client undress. Is there going to be a rape or a theft (*viol ou vol*)?

Neither one nor the other, but worse. Because our desire and our fear do not know yet in which object to invest, because they are still vague in our mind, the form they take is also vague—a kind of shadow, an ectoplasm. But exacerbated by our long wait, they are at the height of their intensity. Also, the force we have transmitted to this form will be of a terrifying power. The form-force then accomplishes its crime.

(Let no one tell me that I extrapolate. On the one hand, I describe only what one sees and what each spectator may have felt. On the other hand, I point out that *Psycho* was shot in forty-one days. But this scene itself, which only lasts forty-five seconds on the screen, took six days to film. Hitchcock has carefully explained the difficulties he and Russell, his director of photography, had in rendering this indefinite form. He wanted no special effects but insisted that the effects be the result of lighting itself. In short, he had a very precise idea about arriving at this indefinite form. Let us give him the benefit—which he claims vigorously elsewhere—of knowing what is needed and of not shooting anything that is not rigorously necessary).

A crime at one and the same time hallucinating and fascinating. A crime which Perkins tries to efface out of filial devotion. And while he does so, we enter completely into his thoughts. We witness his sordid household chores; we accept that Janet Leigh, wrapped in a transparent shower curtain, really becomes what she represented for us, a form. We are simply anxious for this operation to be over. Moreover, we fear that another driver, lost on this little-frequented road, will discover the crime. A fear heightened even more when Perkins, having made a rapid inspection of the room to see if he has not forgotten an object belonging to Janet, does not see *our* money.

(Which shows that Janet had found the best hiding place for it. "To appreciate *Psycho,* one needs a great sense of humor," states Hitchcock. Especially some Hitchcockian humor which consists, as we know, in reversing wishes, that is to say in realizing them in a way contrary to our expectations. Besides, is not inversion our filmmaker's favorite system?)

But Perkins retraces his steps, sees the package, and takes it. We hope that he will see the money and keep it, in short, that the murder will have its material justification. But since he also throws it into the trunk, together with the corpse and the other belongings of the victim, we feel at the same time relieved. Perkins pushes it all into the viscous, sleepy waters of a marsh. The car sinks halfway in. "Let us hope that it disappears," we think. At last it sinks completely, definitely. We utter a sigh of relief. Darkness—or our subconscious—has swallowed forever, we think, our complicity in the theft.

Return to the Everyday World.

But to arrive at that, we have become accomplices in a crime. We have gone up one step on the ladder of culpability. I do not think that it would be useful to summarize the rest of the film in detail. What is important to perceive above all is the process of Hitchcock's creative faculty: how Hitch uses the spectator for the internal progression of the film, how he plays on his desires and fears. To understand this, one need only analyze his own reactions at the moment when the private detective arrives. The viewer understands why the form-force, when it surges for the second time, will have become very precise, though it still remains mysterious. After this test, he has one desire only: to flee. To flee the motel and its inhabitants. But the machinery he himself has set in motion cannot be stopped. From now on, paralyzed, riveted to his chair, he reaches the limits of fear. The more so as he learns that the presumed murderer has been dead for ten years. This is the utter rout of his logical mind, the disturbance of his intellectual world. Henceforth, for the spectator, everything becomes a terrifying business. It is enough for him to see some simple thing, be it the most banal, to become afraid. Each new shot is an instrument of fear. He is left with one attitude only: that of prayer and blind faith. He hopes with all his might that Vera Miles, Janet Leigh's sister, come in search of her, will be saved. These noble and disinterested feelings, together with his fear which has reached the height of its paroxysm, make it necessary that the form-force be revealed at last, its true face in the light. It is vanquished.

Hence the necessity, after this trying incident at the end of the night, at the end of the world of desire, of returning to our quotidian world. This task may be incumbent only upon the intellectual world, but devoid of any passion, detached from subjectivity, freed of all unhealthy curiosity. In short, a task for scientific reasoning. This is the reasoning of the psychiatrist's discourse. From then on, freed, the spectator can contemplate the object of his fear, this form-force, which seems like a nocturnal bird, to be stuffed and fixed upon a wall. And then, it excites in him an immense compassion. Compassion which the form-force attempts to refute by making believe that he wants to provoke it. ("I am not going to move. They all look at me. This fly is going to continue to walk on my hand. And they will say, he is not even capable of harming a fly.") And our pity is perhaps the only chance for salvation for this form-force which appears to be forever damned, its possibility of returning from the dark, like the car that a huge chain pulls out of the black waters of the marsh.

The Ideal Vehicle.

Thus, after the example of *Psycho* and by adopting solely the point of view of the audience, it becomes easier to understand the multiple relations which exist, in Hitchcock's *oeuvre*, between the three realities. If the spectator belongs to the everyday world, it is evident that the screen unveils the world of desire. Is it not the screen's very property to be populated by forms animated by forces? These forms, though untouchable, possess a reality. So if the spectator finds on the screen the exact reflection of his quotidian universe, he immediately communicates with the latter. If he feels that appearances have not been falsified in order "to get" him, he cannot "pull away." He is carried off in a fatal movement. The more so as, on this screen, Hitch wants to provoke what

the spectator does not dare to do in his everyday reality. The spectator participates more and more intensely in these forms charged with assuming his impulses and secret dreams. He no longer looks objectively at the appearances of
everyday reality but receives them subjectively. However, these appearances do
not change intrinsically. It is the spectator who transforms them, who changes
their lighting. To the point where, at last, the screen becomes for him the sole
reality. His ultimate goal is to penetrate it.

The ultimate vehicle which links those two worlds and allows them to
communicate (the spectator with the screen, the quotidian world with the
world of desire) is evidently the intellectual world. In fact, for Hitchcock it is a
question of giving it a function of transmission. And the term "vehicle" seems
to be the only one to account for all the trains, planes, automobiles, skis,
boats, bicycles, wheelchairs, etc., which haunt his universe. We receive them
not only as a sign of passage from one world to the other but especially as a
sensation. A sensation of being carried off, of a skidding that nothing will be
able to stop anymore. They give the very impression of fatality. The reader will
have been quick to remember the multiple variants which Hitch loves to introduce into this theme which is so dear to him. But never, perhaps, has he so
completely and so well "dreamed" of it as in *Psycho*. The slow and wonderful
drive of Janet Leigh allows for the material and intellectual passage from one
world to the next. From objectivity to pure subjectivity. In general, in Hitchcock the human body is the first vehicle. (Hence the condemnation of dancing
which allows the body to slide and to be carried off—the Stork Club in *The
Wrong Man*, the dance at the afternoon tea in *Vertigo*, as well as the waltzes of
the merry widows in *Shadow of a Doubt*.) By extension, any vehicle which
contains a body becomes for the latter a new body. This is why Janet Leigh,
when changing cars, expresses her profound desire to change bodies, personali-
ties. She wants to save a love, pure in itself, from the sordid material circumstances which accompany it. But far from wanting to struggle to achieve noble
conditions for this love, she only looks for purely external expedients. Far from
trying to change herself, she believes that by changing the material wrapping
her wish will be granted.

A World of Harshness.

If I believe truly that the occult is at the basis of Hitchcock's universe, it is
not that I am impassioned with the esoteric nor even that I think that it is
fundamental for the director. But simply, it is a way of understanding which
permits the artist's imagination the greatest possibilities of revery. In addition,
as this doctrine does not contradict other systems of knowledge, it allows for an
extremely varied vision of the world adapted to the real temperament of the
creator. It is certain that one can content oneself with psychoanalysis in order to
comment on Hitchcock. I do not, however, believe that psychoanalysis suffices
to explain the invention of forms and their internal dynamics.

Hitchcock's work has always depicted in a certain manner the duel of Light and Shadow, therefore of Unity and Duality. The very first shot of *Psycho* which follows the abstract credits by Saul Bass uncovers a large plain surrounding a banal city in a very raw light. It seems that everything here is immutable and must give a feeling of eternity. Subtitles specify the place, the time, and the date. Opposed to this light, from the second shot on, is the absolute darkness of a room into which we penetrate with the camera to discover a bed and lovers in embrace. In two shots, Hitchcock expresses his purpose: *Psycho* will talk to us about the eternal and the finite, of existence and of nothingness, of life and of death, but seen in their naked truth. Nothing can please in *Psycho*, which is the inverse of *Vertigo*. The latter was built upon seduction, hence upon makeup, appearances, the joining of images, in short, upon attraction. Here, everything is based on crudity (and we are spared no detail in that regard), on faces without makeup, on the clash of montage (a montage, cutting like a knife). This trip toward death must produce only fear, and it must produce that fear through its harshness.

Notes

1. This article is the last in a series begun under the title: "The Third Key of Hitchcock," *Cahiers du Cinéma*, nos. 99 and 102.
2. *Cahiers du Cinéma*, no. 102.

CHAPTER TWO

Hitchcock's Imagery and Art

Maurice Yacowar

Of the twenty-three feature films that Hitchcock directed in his first fifteen years, none is without some interest and some lively personal character. Hitchcock was Hitchcock from the outset — perceptive, progressive, playful, in his mischievous machinations against the simple securities of his audience, yet profound in the implications of his ironic stance. The early films show the same thematic concerns for which his later work is known, and the same expertise.

As in his later work, Hitchcock often paralleled characters of ostensible innocence and guilt to dramatize the thin line that separates man from his pretensions to purity. Thus we have Patsy Brand contrasted to Jill Cheyne in *The Pleasure Garden*, the romantic policeman contrasted to the Lodger, and the two men of *The Manxman*. In *Easy Virtue, Rich and Strange, The Skin Game*, and *Jamaica Inn*, figures of simple innocence are inadvertently seduced into criminal complicity. These foreshadow the drama of Bruno and Guy in *Strangers on a Train*.

Often the Hitchcock innocent is drawn into evil by boredom, which functions as the image of moral lassitude. Thus we have the passionless marriages of *The Pleasure Garden, The Manxman*, and *Sabotage;* the premature marriages in *The Ring, Easy Virtue*, and *The Skin Game;* and the boredom which prompts the girl to flirt with the artist in *Blackmail*. Hitchcock realizes how dull morality is and how exciting sin is. His delight is to make his moral points through exciting fictions, reminding his audiences of the difficulties and pain of the moral life — albeit in his delightful way. These marriages foreshadow the cold, antiromantic situations that are developed in *Notorious, North by Northwest*, and *Topaz*.

Because innocence and guilt are so radically intertwined, a Hitchcock hero never enjoys a simple success. The innocent will die along with the guilty: the native girl in *The Pleasure Garden*, the pirate in *Rich and Strange*, Stevie Verloc in *Sabotage*, as later the children and Annie in *The Birds*, and Marion Crane will *after* she has resolved to surrender to police in *Psycho*. For man's laws fail in the allocation of justice.

In *Rope,* Jan asks playfully of a friend's description of her: "Did he do me justice?" Rupert replies sharply: "Do you deserve justice?" From the lovers of *The Pleasure Garden* through the murderers of *Family Plot,* Hitchcock's heroes are of at best a dappled virtue, and his villains of civilized elegance. Indeed, his villains are often extremely sympathetic people, as Verloc is, or Fane of *Murder!* Even the nasty Levet in *The Pleasure Garden* is allowed a death of charming civility.

Hitchcock's justice is tricky, poetic rather than legal. For his world is full of uncertainty. *Shadow of a Doubt* may seem to have a happy ending, but the killer is eulogized by the small town, and an innocent man was fed to an airplane propeller by mistake. Similarly in *Blackmail,* the murderers go free while a small-time blackmailer is killed in their stead. Even the happy endings, then, refuse the confidence of a secure order. No simple justice, no simple psychology, can be sustained in Hitchcock's world of quicksand insecurity. So almost all Hitchcock's films end on an uncertain image, from the new lovers in *The Pleasure Garden* to the mass of abiding doom at the end of *The Birds.* And in *Frenzy,* Blaney establishes his innocence by performing the crime for which he was wrongly sentenced; no matter that the woman he attacks in Rusk's bed is already dead.

Hitchcock often uses the X image to express his sense of man as a complex of innocence and evil. Thus in *The Pleasure Garden* we found the two women forming an X to suggest their equivalence in their lover's mind; the husband moves to kill his wife in order to complete the X, in response to his murdered mistress's imagined demands. In *Blackmail* a similar editing completes an X between the corpse's hand and the policeman's, where the plot develops the illegality of police activities and the criminal parodies justice. The X imagery is developed most fully, of course, in *Strangers on a Train.*

Perhaps Hitchcock presents two different concepts of man's makeup. First, opposite tendencies may unite to form a single, composite whole, as the ladies do in *The Pleasure Garden* and as the strangers on a train do. Here the X would represent the unity of opposite motions and values in human nature. Similarly, in *I Confess* an X variant, the cross, unites Father Logan and killer Keller in a criminal sacrament that costs them Alma (the soul in its earthly existence). But in the second image of human nature, opposite wholes are parallelled. Charlie and Uncle Charlie in *Shadow of a Doubt* are parallel opposites, albeit with such similarities as name, selfishness, vanity, and telepathic connection. They are not a unity. The good Charlie may have some flaws and the evil Uncle Charlie some elegant pretense to justice in his effect, but the characters are clearly separable and they diverge by the impulse of their respective wills. So too in *Psycho,* Norman Bates pretends to be an X with his mother, but she is innocent, misrepresented even after she was murdered by her spoiled, jealous son. Norman and his mother are antitheses who only intersect in Norman's malevolent rationalizing. The bantering and bickering lovers in Hitchcock's romances (*Champagne, Mr. and Mrs. Smith*) and in his thrillers (*The 39 Steps, Saboteur*, and on through *Marnie*) are spirited strokes who discover themselves fulfilled as Xs.

The other quintessential Hitchcock image is the staircase. Again the early films show ample use of this device for which his later work is known. Whether upward or down, Hitchcock's stairs take his characters and his audience to the fears, dangers, and rewards of self-discovery. The most common staircase shot is downward through a seeming spiral, which leaves the impression of stairs within stairs. One finds this shot from *The Lodger* through *Vertigo*. As an emblem it recalls Peer Gynt's onion, concentric layerings around a void, with the addition of the danger that height always means in Hitchcock.

The occasional round staircase, as in *The Pleasure Garden* and *Secret Agent*, also suggests a plunge through layers of one's self. There are even three staircases in *Waltzes from Vienna*: the rickety ladder down which Schani's rival carries the heroine in the opening fire scene; its parallel, the ladder the girl climbs at the end to save Schani from the duel and to reclaim him romantically; and the palatial staircase down which the Count rolls his valet to a piano riff, an image of their difference in privilege and station. In *Juno and the Paycock* the stairs provide a single straight and dark descent from the family warmth to the cold public funeral and to their dispossession.

In *Shadow of a Doubt* Charlie's home has two parallel staircases, the clean public front and the dangerous, steep, private back, the latter which Uncle Charlie uses to escape and to threaten Charlie. The two-staired house works as an image of the human psyche and as an image of a societal ideal, both of which project a front that is more attractive and safer than their hidden natures.

Stairs compel movement and, with it, fear, as in Constance's ascent to Murchison's office in *Spellbound*, and Arbogast's in *Psycho*. The camera (the maker) has a liberty over space and stairs that the character has not. Hence the open, expressionistic staircase in *The Lodger* and the brittle one in *No. 17*. Hitchcock's stairs image both man's composition and the rigors and fears of his rise or plunge to awareness. The danger that always lurks around the stairs is the anxiety that undercuts all confidence (in the Hitchcock vision), all sense of secure footing, and that provides both the central metaphor and title for *Downhill* and for *Vertigo*. The source of the latter was a novel titled *Between Two Deaths*, but "Vertigo" conveys Hitchcock's primary interest: man's uncertainty in stepping between two moments of living.

Hitchcock's art is based on the dramatic appeal of the insecure. In the first place, his characters are typically secure people whose footing is swept out from under them. Thus Patsy loses her independence in *The Pleasure Garden* and the hero loses his whole world in *Downhill*. Sanders loses his station in *The Ring* and the fisherman his bliss, friend, and wife in *The Manxman*. Love provides only a false sense of security in *The Pleasure Garden, The Farmer's*

Wife, The Manxman, and *Champagne,* where the reconciled lovers begin to quarrel anew over their marriage arrangements. And in *Mr. and Mrs. Smith* a marriage suddenly ceases to exist.

Nor is there security in the social contract. The processes of justice go awry in *Easy Virtue, Blackmail, Juno and the Paycock, Murder!* And in the thriller series from *The Man Who Knew Too Much* through *The Lady Vanishes* the individual's private life is shattered by the social processes that are supposedly functioning to protect him. Hence Hitchcock's frequent twist where the hero is threatened by the police as much as by the enemy: *The Lodger, Blackmail, The 39 Steps, North by Northwest, Psycho, Frenzy.* Virtue and Hitchcock's justice are endangered by the merely human law. Joe in *The Lodger* eventually subordinates his romantic interest to his public duty. But not until *Frenzy* will we have a Hitchcock policeman whose arrival at the truth is based upon his sense of the criminal potential within himself.[1] For the others, the police are sheep (*The 39 Steps*) or careless shots (*Strangers on a Train*). In *The Trouble with Harry* the springy villagers have but a single fear—discovery by the sheriff's deputy, a cold Puritan named Calvin whose resurrections are confined to antique autos.

Hitchcock usually presents his theme of man's limited freedom in society as a conflict between love and duty. The tension is between love and friendship (a personal duty) in *Downhill, The Manxman,* and *The Farmer's Wife.* In the policeman drama the hero must choose between what his job requires and what his heart (and the lady) deserve: *The Lodger, Blackmail, Young and Innocent, Sabotage, Stage Fright, The Paradine Case.* The spy thrillers adjust the love versus duty debate to the tensions of the cold war, where the hero must choose between his personal love and his international duty: *Foreign Correspondent, Notorious, North by Northwest, Torn Curtain, Topaz.* Another form of this debate is the conflict between privacy and public involvement. Although the fullest presentation of this theme is in *Rear Window,* it is fully developed in both versions of *The Man Who Knew Too Much, Secret Agent, Sabotage,* and *The Lady Vanishes.* Possibly its earliest statement, however, is in the scene of the switchboard operator in *Easy Virtue.*

But if love and citizenship are two areas in which Hitchcock afflicts his characters with insecurity, the most dramatic is the family relationship. Richard Roud relates the motif of parental tyranny to the espionage plots:

> Even his domestic dramas involve a kind of espionage in the sense that his characters, having discovered frightening realities buried beneath the surface, are obliged to turn spy themselves in order to discover the whole truth. Often it has something to do with the past, the past that comes back to confound the present, to compromise the future.[2]

Thus we find so many tyrannical parents in Hitchcock's work, as we have noted in our discussion of *Downhill.* Cruel fathers spring readily to mind:

Downhill, Champagne, The Manxman, Waltzes from Vienna. Then there are the treacherous father surrogates in *Sabotage, The Lady Vanishes,* and *Jamaica Inn* (particularly after Hitchcock's revision of the villain in the latter). Even where the parent figures are not oppressive or negative, the parent must be abandoned at least temporarily, as in *Young and Innocent.* The family is presented as a fragile, sometimes false and always vulnerable, unit in all Hitchcock's thrillers of the late thirties. In *Psycho* we have a pervasive feeling of parental oppression, by Marion Crane's mother, Sam's father, and the happiness-buying Texas daddy; but in the main thrust of the film, it is the sick son that projects his guilt and inhibitions upon his parental image. The parent is blamed for the child's violent weakness.

In this respect one of the key Hitchcock's films is his comedy, *The Trouble with Harry.* A little boy discovers a man dead in the forest; it's his stepfather, unknown to the boy. The dead Harry Warp harmonizes the entire community as each member assumes guilt for this death and they all combine to conceal him. In one shot the corpse is so arranged that his feet and legs seem to complete the body of the little boy (Jerry Mather), whom we see from the waist up. Later we see the Captain (Edmund Gwenn) dozing in his rocker; we see all but the Captain's feet, but on the wall behind him we see the shadows of the corpse's feet. These two shots prove Roud's point. The dead complete and shape the living, but the living can make their own use of the dead.

Thus we have the fatal "haunting" of Levet in *The Pleasure Garden,* the heroine's haunting by her past in *Easy Virtue* and in *Blackmail,* and the community's haunting by the past in *Juno and the Paycock* and *The Skin Game.* The individual can succumb to the pressure of his past — or blame it for his own weakness. But the haunting can work as a regeneration, as it does in *The Trouble with Harry.* In *The Farmer's Wife,* too, the dead wife's message provides a new lease on life for her husband, as the lovers' exile will in *The Manxman.* As Roger Thornhill emerges chastened and solidified by his false death in *North by Northwest,* Richard Hannay assumes a responsibility from the death of the strange woman at the start of *The 39 Steps;* so do Ashenden and his lady from Caypor's death in *Secret Agent.* Even in *Waltzes from Vienna,* Schani descends through the hell of the pastry cook, abandoned suitor, duelling rake, and disowned son to emerge an Orphic hero. Hitchcock's hero can prove himself by surviving the tribulations that befall him (or that he claims to inherit).

Even more than the insecurity of his characters, though, Hitchcock exploits the insecurity of his audience, hence his penchant for subjective shooting angles. His early films abound with attempts to depict the character's mind through what he sees. Hence, too, Hitchcock's penchant for expressionistic devices. The camera and printing tricks of *The Lodger,* the hallucinations of *The Pleasure Garden, Downhill,* and *The Ring,* the swoop in *Young and Innocent,* all serve as nonrealistic rhetoric to dramatize the character's state of mind. Hitchcock used images of the concrete to express the reality of the imagination. As Tom Ryall points out, "the openings from *The Lodger* (1926), *The Manxman* (1928), and *Blackmail* (1929) could be documentaries of the newspaper industry, the fishing industry and the police force respectively."[3] So too, Hitchcock's delirium sequences document the hot currents of the character's mind. Durgnat's distinction between Hitchcock's "piercing realism" and his "vibrant irrealism" is a merely formal distinction, for Hitchcock's basic interest has always been in how our perceptions reshape our world. His realism constantly shades off into the expressionistic imagery and extravagant technical devices by which he conveys the realism of the emotional state. So his aquarium explosion of Picadilly Circus in *Sabotage* ranks with the best documentary poetics of Vertov.

Hitchcock continually violates his viewer's expectations. Thus we have the romantic deflations in *The Pleasure Garden* and *Champagne* and the surprise of Drew's innocence in *The Lodger*. Where the genre requires a fight, Hitchcock will provide a comic fight, as in *Downhill, No. 17, Waltzes from Vienna*, and *The Lady Vanishes*, for there is no room in Hitchcock's world of vertiginous insecurities for the conventional fight, which makes its protagonists appear efficient.

And from time to time Hitchcock allows his comic spirit, the vision of an anarchic principle at the heart of the universe, to run free. So we get the chaotic consequences of the courtships in *The Farmer's Wife*, the fumbling villains of *The Man Who Knew Too Much*, and old Ben in *No. 17*. Of course, these comedies of chaos are only lighter versions of Hitchcock's essential vision that man's civilization is underpinned by chaos, as we have it in *The Pleasure Garden, Downhill, The Manxman, Champagne, Rich and Strange, Murder!, The 39 Steps*, and *Sabotage*. In his later work, Marion Crane must die *because* she is played by the star, Janet Leigh. For Hitchcock's films are a relentless assault upon the viewer's security, as well as his moral assumptions.

The English films also prove that from the outset Hitchcock's technical innovations were close to the thematic center of the work. The experimental devices of *The Lodger* and *Blackmail* served those films' basic themes, the preoccupation of the former with the misleading power of perception, and of the latter with the obscurities and difficulties of communication. Then, too, the scenes with off-camera orchestras in *Juno and the Paycock* and *Murder!* were the pivotal points in the psychological development of the narratives. This observation serves as well when we approach Hitchcock's later work.

For example, his massive orchestration of birds for *The Birds*, a staggering technical challenge, is an assertion of the power of the human enterprise in the face of the film's assault upon man's pre-Copernican arrogance. The technical challenge in *Lifeboat* is analogous to its political theme, the fatal isolation of the Allies and their need for a selfless unity. The continuous shooting of *Rope*, which Hitchcock calls his "abandonment of pure cinema" because it eschewed his normal dependence upon dramatic editing, grows out of both the title image—something continuous that will tie one up—and the main theme of the film—the continuity of word into deed; a murderous human reality is spun out of a musing that was considered safely theoretical.[4] The restricted isolation of the camera in *Rear Window* relates to that film's central concern: the distinction between respecting one's brother's privacy and meeting his needs for a keeper. What Durgnat calls Hitchcock's "calmly hermetic aesthetic satisfaction" might be better considered as his passionate synthesis of idea, irony, and technique.[5] In his achievement of the emotional idea and the intellectual image he meets the aim of that other great film editor, Eisenstein. By so brilliantly uniting idea, image, and emotion, Hitchcock has come to make our nightmares for us with a clarity and thrust no other filmmaker has commanded.

Hitchcock's ironic detachment also explains those moments in his work where we see the seams of his craft, where his technical work may seem to be rough. One lesson which the British films should teach us is that Hitchcock always knows what he is doing. His plots are carefully crafted. For example, he has Drexler rehearse the orchestra of Strauss Sr. so that their surprise performance of Schani's new waltz will not seem implausible. And where Hitchcock's technical work seems shoddy, what we really have is not a craftsman nodding but an artist extending his resources. Where Hitchcock's craft seems loose, we usually find his technique subserving his content, his literal realism shading off into vibrant metaphor.

To put it another way, it is safe to assume that what seems to be a Hitchcock error is likely our failure to work out what he is doing. In *The Lady Vanishes,* for instance, the palpably false opening shot and the unreal proportions of the departing train are typical of how Hitchcock extends his realism into expressionism—only to be charged with poor technique. This liberty came from the German cinema. Thus Fritz Lang inserts a jarring interlude of false scenery into a key moment of *Rancho Notorious.*

William Johnson describes Hitchcock's "failure" in *Marnie:*

> It so happens that there are certain departments in which Hitchcock has a patently blind eye. These include the phony backdrops that grate like TV commercials (especially in color), the bits of rapid montage that do not quite fit together, and the two-shots that are held so long that they almost ossify.[6]

The false backdrops in *Marnie* are a concise image of the heroine's predicament: she lives in dislocation from her surroundings and from her own past. The false backgrounds provide a physical expression of the disjunction in her mind. Thus the first false back-projection scene is her first scene aboard Forio, when she is enjoying an artificial respite from her alienation. A loud, rhetorical swell in the music coheres with the rhetoric of the false background. The second is the scene at her mother's home, where the ships' dock is flat and false behind the tenement. The painted ships loom larger than life and paler, imaging the phantom sailor unacknowledged from her past. The false register of both backgrounds moves the shots from setting to active symbol. A false front stands behind the Rutland building, a building stripped of its back, or, a foreground unsupported by an integrated backing, as Marnie is. Mark varies this motif by giving Marnie a $42,000 ring instead of a family heirloom; he wants her to "have something that never belonged to anyone before." The line jocularly refers to her thefts, poignantly recalls her childhood, without a bed of her own, and provides another instance of an object without a past, a foreground without an integrated background.[7] Similarly in *Torn Curtain* the palpable falseness of the garden path up which Newman leads Andrews (Hud leads Mary Poppins) undercuts the noble pretense of the hero's ambitious venture. And what Samuels finds to be the "contentless virtuosity" of *North by Northwest* is the heart of the film: the film's central theme/effect is that total dislocation which the complacent hero and the typically injudicious cinema audience share.[8] As the title tells us, the film deliberately pursues a fantastical course.

It is similarly wrong to consider Hitchcock a craftsman first and only secondarily, accidentally as it were, an artist. From his first feature on, even through that period of self-conscious "respectable" adaptation, Hitchcock's films had something to say, sometimes an obvious message (*Easy Virtue, Lifeboat*) but more often an integrated theme (*Pleasure Garden, Downhill*). Only because form is content can Hitchcock say "I am interested not so much in the stories I tell as in the means of telling them."[9] Structure is theme in *Psycho, Vertigo, The Trouble with Harry*, but also as early as *The Pleasure Garden, Downhill*, and *The Ring*.

The early films are also notable for their ambitious conception. Though working in an unacknowledged medium, Hitchcock showed himself a serious artist even then. For Hitchcock, popular film is art. His art is the manipulation of the audience's emotions and fantasy through a variety of felt dangers and thrills, to send his viewers out at the end, calm of mind, all smugness spent, ready to brave the hairline moralities of real life. In his early films Hitchcock also dealt with the responsibilities of the artist. The dance-floor meat markets of *The Pleasure Garden, Downhill*, and *Champagne* and the squared circle of *The Ring* are fairly tawdry arenas of human enterprise. But even in those settings it is possible for an individual to achieve art, to fulfill his own creative and expressive impulses, and to establish a community with an audience.

The laughing clown in *Blackmail* provides the neatest statement Hitchcock makes about art. Coherent with the fertility of silent montage, the portrait gains new meaning from each juxtaposition, each context, yet it maintains the same detached, ironic stance regardless of its changing set. When all about are noisy, loud, ambiguous, Hitchcock's mute jester remains silent. Yet the portrait is eloquent in its accusatory stare, its lively eye, its shameless traditional garb. Beyond the inflections of that painting in the story itself, Hitchcock devotes himself to a career of critical irony that will be independent of changes in mode and in medium. The jester retains his acrid independence even when stored in the vaults of the most conventional (the police station; the commercial bastions of light, diversionary cinema).

From *Murder!* we can infer why Hitchcock was never to stray into the esoterica of Bergman, late Godard, or even the Penn of *Mickey One*. For *Murder!* is the drama of an artist who takes his artistic skills and interests into the prosaic business of real life. In *Murder!* some fulfill themselves through art (the theater folk), some conceal themselves in their art (the transvestite trapeze artist), but the noblest and most gifted turn their art to the service of humanity (Sir John), to the discovery of truth and self-knowledge and the saving of lives—from prison and from boredom. The West End artist-aristocrat brings his style and sensitivity to the service of the hurly-burly world.

For Hitchcock, life is a matter of drawing art and reality together. In *Stage Fright,* Eve Gill comes from a separated family, a realistic but theatrical father and a whimsical but prosaic mother. Eve's salvation lies in ordinary Smith, a policeman who plays the piano, and in her own abilities at acting and setting scenes. The clues point to the guilt of the Marlene Dietrich figure, but as her song warns us, she is too lazy to be either criminal or moral. The real villain is the Richard Todd character. He is unable to distinguish pretense (art) from reality, so he kills for Dietrich and is ultimately prepared to kill Eve to prove his own insanity. As befits his unharmonized dichotomy, he is chopped in half by the safety curtain on the theater stage.

For Hitchcock, art is to come from life (*Waltzes from Vienna*). But often life emulates art, as in the film parodies in *Sabotage, Saboteur,* and *North by Northwest.* Art at its best will cultivate, free, and invigorate the human spirit, both the emotion and the will, as the cartoon does for Sylvia in *Sabotage.* Sometimes art will deliver a narrow truth, as Mr. Memory does, or deliver one from bondage, as the child is freed by song and by shot in the two versions of *The Man Who Knew Too Much.* But its deeper function is to free the emotions. So Hitchcock often sets up a theatrical situation to expedite a character's physical escape: *The Pleasure Garden, Downhill, The Ring,* the fashion show in *The Lodger,* the auction in *The Skin Game,* Roger Thornhill's auction in *North by Northwest,* the ballet in *Torn Curtain.* In *Vertigo* even more fully than in *Murder!* and *Stage Fright,* Hitchcock explores the corollary danger: losing one's self in the act of performance. Hence the penultimate image in *Psycho:* Norman Bates dissolves into the skull; the hidden reality overwhelms the muted, visible reality; the role overtakes the self. But like the Todd figure in *Stage Fright,* Norman Bates lost the sense of where lie and art were to be distinguished. Upon this distinction and interplay Hitchcock thrives for fifty years of splendid filmmaking.

Hitchcock's genius lies in his synthesis of mind, eye, and heart in the dynamic film experience. Some critics prefer the craft of the American period over the English or the profundity of the later American films over the earlier diversions. William Pechter prefers Hitchcock's detailed realism of the English thrillers and bemoans his loss of contact with his audience in the American period. But even in 1931 C. A. Lejeune was to complain of Hitchcock's lack of "the warm humanity of a director like Griffith" and "Pabst's psychological insight":

> His figures are photographic records of synthetic men, not men of flesh-and-blood translated into the medium of the motion picture. . . . The fault with Hitchcock's unreality lies in the fact that he has been essentially a director of realistic films; his subjects have been intimate, detailed and individual. He has dealt with one man, not with men.[10]

Pechter harkens back to the golden age of the thrillers and Lejeune cavils before them, but both find Hitchcock naturalistically unsatisfying. Nor could anyone accuse the golden thrillers of realism!

Surely the realism of Hitchcock ranges from the physical settings of *The Lodger* to the imaginative inner worlds of *Downhill* and *The Ring* and between those poles throughout his later career. Always he is a poet and always he is engaged with the moral and perceptual nature of man. The early films are full of emotionally charged scenes, it is true: the praying scene, the fevered kiss, the final killing in *The Pleasure Garden,* or the private reconciliation of old Strauss in *Waltzes from Vienna.* But there is a well of feeling in Lydia's scenes with the coffee cups in *The Birds* too. The films of Alfred Hitchcock are rich enough, varied enough, yet of a spiritual piece, to make their total enjoyment preferable to any arbitrary choice of preferences. One can watch Hitchcock's British films in order to come to a better understanding of the American ones. But also because they are so good in themselves, so moving, so thoughtful, and so much fun.

Notes

1. See Leland A. Poague, "The Detective in Hitchcock's *Frenzy,*" *Journal of Popular Film,* vol. 2, no. 1 (1973): 47–59.
2. Richard Roud; "In Broad Daylight," *Film Comment,* vol. 10, no. 4 (1974): 36.
3. Tom Ryall, "Durgnat on Hitchcock," *Screen* (Summer 1975): 123. Hitchcock told Leslie Perkoff: "I would like to make documentary films, because here you have states of action or movement which can easily [be] treated by photography and cutting. But a cataclysm in any film, for example, is akin to documentary material. It begins with the camera and goes directly to the cutting-room." This is in "The Censor and Sydney Street," *World Film News* (March 1938): 4. Hitchcock here yearns for the fantastical opportunities provided by documentary! He exploited them most obviously in the plot line and settings of *Rich and Strange* and in the opening scenes of *Champagne, Blackmail,The Manxman, The Wrong Man,* etc.
4. Peter Bogdanovich, *The Cinema of Alfred Hitchcock* (New York: Museum of Modern Art, 1963), 28.
5. Raymond Durgnat, *The Strange Case of Alfred Hitchcock* (London, 1974), 367.
6. William Johnson, "*Marnie,*" *Film Quarterly,* vol. 18, no, 1 (1964): 38–42.

7. David Thomson provides a more general interpretation of the device in *Movie Man* (London: Secker and Warburg, 1971), 72.

8. Charles T. Samuels, "Hitchcock," *Encountering Directors* (New York: Putnam, 1972), 301. Of course, Hitchcock is famous for the painstaking attention he gives his work before going on the set. See the following articles from *American Cinematographer* as evidence: Hilda Black, "The Photography is important to Hitchcock: *I Confess*" (December 1952): 524–25, 546–47, 549; Frederick Foster, "Hitchcock didn't want it arty" (February 1957): 84–85, 112–14; Charles Loring, "Filming *Torn Curtain* by reflected light" (October 1966): 680–83, 706–7; Herb Lightman, "Hitchcock talks about lights, camera, action" (May 1967): 332–35, 350–51.

   Hitchcock's famous preplanning and subsequent appearance of casualness about the actual shooting may have contributed to the ready disdain for his technical "sloppiness." It certainly alienated André Bazin (see his "Hitchcock vs. Hitchcock" in *Cahiers du Cinéma in English*, no. 2: 51–60).

9. Bazin, 55.

10. William Pechter, *Twenty-four Times a Second* (New York: Harper & Row, 1971), 175–94. C. A. Lejeune, *Cinema* (London, 1931): 11–12.

CHAPTER THREE

Retrospective

Robin Wood

One can usefully begin by considering the two major aesthetic influences on Hitchcock's work. In the early years of his career, when his creative personality was in the process of formation, he made two films (in fact, his first two completed films as director, *The Pleasure Garden* and *The Mountain Eagle*) in German studios; the contact seems to have confirmed an interest in the potentialities of Expressionism that was already present (he speaks, in the Truffaut interview book, of Lang's *Der mude Tod* as one of his first important cinematic experiences). A little later, he discovered the Soviet cinema, which confirmed for him the crucial importance of montage, its centrality to what he wanted to do. The Expressionist influence is already very plain in *The Lodger* (1926); the importance to Hitchcock of montage is also implicit there, waiting to be developed. The film was also Hitchcock's first suspense thriller and first great commercial success: the coincidence of all these factors was obviously crucial in determining the development of his career.

"Expressionism" evades simple definition, but a central impulse was clearly the attempt to "express" emotional states through a distortion or deformation of objective reality, "expression" taking precedence over representation. The continuing dominance of such an aesthetic aim in Hitchcock could be suggested by innumerable examples, of varying degrees of subtlety, from any of the films; it is enough here to mention the most obvious, the red suffusions in *Marnie*, which have nothing to do with representing "reality" and everything to do with communicating the heroine's subjective experience.

The importance to Hitchcock of Soviet montage theory is if anything even more obvious. The affinities become plain if one begins to analyze the Odessa Steps massacre in *Potemkin* as if it were a Hitchcockian suspense piece. Almost everything in the sequence works effectively in that way (and this partly accounts, of course, for its extraordinary emotional power): perhaps the most striking single example is the famous incident involving the baby's pram, where Eisenstein's fragmented editing is devoted to the buildup and release of tension on a basis of will-it-or-won't-it? All the techniques deployed in the

Odessa Steps sequence could be paralleled somewhere in Hitchcock, even the one potentially most disturbing to the audience's involvement on a "Realist" level, overlapping montage: in the sequence of the riding accident in *Marnie,* the camera covers (by a variety of technical means — both tracking and zooming) the same stretches of ground over and over again to convey the effect of time agonizingly "stretched" at a moment of supreme fear and anguish.

A central characteristic of Expressionism (as a cinematic movement) is the distortion of the "reality" the camera records or the creation of a world phenomenologically remote from the reality recognized by our senses; a central characteristic of montage theory is the creation of concepts that have no necessary phenomenological equivalents in what was actually presented before the camera. These two movements represent, in their very different ways, the two main lines of opposition to the notion of film as an inherently "realistic" medium: their emphasis is on artifice rather than representation. In Hitchcock's cinema, their "artificiality" is intensified by the fact that both techniques are divorced from their original ends. Expressionism was a "high art" movement rooted in a specific time and place, a specific *angst;* Soviet montage was associated with revolution and propaganda, with the task of making the principles underlying the revolution intelligible, cogent, and concrete. Hitchcock in a sense perverted both, employing their techniques (or his own modification of them) in the creation of popular bourgeois entertainment. Obviously, any innovation, its expressive possibilities established, becomes public property, a part of the complex apparatus of the cultural tradition, capable of being put to uses far beyond those that stimulated its evolution. Yet I find it significant — having in mind the whole Hitchcock *oeuvre* — that he should build the foundations of his style out of elements inherently "artificial," borrowed from cultures other than his own and detached from the conditions that originally gave them their meaning.

Doubtless, scholars more intimate than I am with Hitchcock's British period will be able to trace the process of absorption into his style and method of these major influences. For my purposes, to illustrate their fusion in his work and the purposes to which he put them, his first sound film, *Blackmail* (1930), offers a convenient and striking example. Consider the famous scene — it is repeatedly cited in textbooks on film history with reference to the development of sound — where the heroine, who has stabbed a would-be rapist to death, is forced to listen to a gossipy woman talking garrulously about the murder. The scene unites a number of thematic and stylistic elements central to Hitchcock's work: the bourgeois family involved in daily routine (in this case breakfast) contrasted with the extraordinary and disturbing, which exists nonetheless in their midst and for which one of them is responsible; the action presented through the consciousness (and to some extent the eyes) of the distraught heroine (who, like her successors through *Shadow of a Doubt* to *Psycho,* combines bourgeois "normality" with a romantic/dramatic situation, hence is an ideal identification figure); the knife on the breakfast table, to which the camera (i.e., the heroine's consciousness) obsessively returns; close-ups of the woman's lips moving as she chatters on; the gradual distortion of her voice to an unintelligible gabble out of which only the word "knife" emerges clearly, "cutting through" the scrambled sound track. Here montage combines with the Expressionist distortion of physical reality to communicate a character's subjective experience directly to the spectator; to involve us in that experience; to confirm what is already encouraged by the construction of the scenario, the empathic identification of spectator and character.

My use of the term "artificial" (intended as descriptive rather than evaluative — though I shall argue that the particular artificiality of Hitchcock's cinema carries with it certain weaknesses and limitations) inevitably raises many of those questions about "Realism" that haunt contemporary film criticism; here I can only touch on them in a way that I am aware leaves major theoretical issues unresolved. I will mention in passing, however, that the Realism debate seems frequently clouded by a failure to distinguish sufficiently two main ways in which the cinema can be spoken of as a "Realist" art form — the two being neither incompatible nor necessarily, beyond a certain primitive point, interdependent. The cinema derives from two major sources, the invention of photography and the nineteenth-century novel. From the former comes the simple, basic notion of film "Realism": the camera records the reality in front of it. From the latter comes a much more sophisticated and complex notion of "Realism," bound up not so much with literal visual representation as with the audience's involvement in the movement of a narrative, the illusion that we are experiencing "real life." The potentiality for confusion can be suggested by pointing out that the Odessa Steps massacre or the horse accident in *Marnie* is "Realist" in the former sense only in the most barely literal way but intensely "Realist" in the latter sense: the reality the camera records has very little to do with the illusion the audience experiences. Hitchcock's cinema is either the least or most "Realist," depending on which definition you are using.

In order to define its artificiality more precisely, I want to draw on certain key notions and motifs that recur almost obsessively in Hitchcock's interviews. His own statements about his work are — if one is ready to make connections and read between the lines — more illuminating than I used to give them credit for: both for what they reveal and for what they conceal, the two aspects being significantly related.

First, one cannot leave the question of Hitchcock's debt to the Soviet cinema without considering the importance he attaches (from his point of view, quite rightly) to the famous Kuleshov experiment. A close-up of the actor Mosjoukin was intercut with various objects which the editing implied he was looking at (a baby, a corpse, a bowl of soup); the audience is supposed to have admired his expressive acting, although in fact the same close-up was used each time and when the shot was taken the actor didn't know what he was meant to be looking at. Both the alleged results and the theoretical validity of the experiment have been called into question (notably by V. F. Perkins in *Film As Film*); what concerns us here is not what the experiment actually proved but what lessons Hitchcock drew from it. He drew two which are absolutely central to the development of his art. First, the Kuleshov experiment suggests the possibilities of editing for deceiving the spectator, for playing tricks with time and space. It is a lesson he could have learned equally from Eisenstein: witness, again, the Odessa Steps sequence, where the spatial relationships of the various characters are never clear (in fact, clearly didn't exist in terms of staged action), where the audience's sense of the length of the steps and the progress of the soldiers is consistently undermined, where the woman whose child falls *behind* her as they flee from the soldiers is subsequently shown going *down* the steps to retrieve his body. Spatial deception through editing is common practice in Hitchcock. For illustration, one needn't go to any of the famous set pieces. Consider the apparently simple moment in *Notorious* where Ingrid Bergman, having stolen Claude Rains's key from his key ring, is surprised by him as she holds it in one of her hands (we aren't allowed to be sure which). He, affectionate but gallant, wants to kiss her fingers; he uncurls one hand, and, after kissing it, makes for the other. She flings her arms round his neck, drops the key behind his back, and pushes it under a chair with her foot. Filmed by, say, Preminger, in a single-take long-shot from across the room, this simple action would be ludicrously implausible: Bergman would have, first, to crane her neck over Rains's shoulder to see where the key had fallen (and, short as the actor was, this would involve some craning); she would then have to wrap one leg around his body to maneuver her foot into position, then move the foot several inches to conceal the key (which would not be very effectively concealed anyway)—and all this, of course, without Rains noticing. Hitchcock breaks down the incident into a characteristically detailed and fragmented montage, culminating in a close-up of the foot pushing the key, both bodies out of the frame: it is doubtful, such is the tension and involvement generated by this admirable scene, whether any spectator at the time has questioned the plausibility of the action.

The other lesson is even more significant. The emotions Mosjoukin was felt to be expressing (tenderness, sorrow, hunger, or whatever) must obviously have been supplied by the spectator from his own fund of stock responses to babies, corpses, and bowls of soup: the principle of audience identification is already implicit in the Kuleshov experiment. Again, it is also implicit in Eisenstein, and a sequence such as the Odessa Steps (which supplies the audience with a careful selection of identification figures) suggests the relationship between the two "lessons": it is the spectator's emotional involvement that carries him over the deceptions and the artifice, making him ready to accept as "real" an action that patently isn't, even in the limited sense of being performed in spatial and temporal continuity. The relationship is in fact even closer: the

fragmentation of the Eisenstein sequence and the spatial/temporal disorienta-
tion (as in certain of Hitchcock's *tours de force* — the shower murder in *Psycho*,
where the blows are never seen actually to connect, the horse accident in
Marnie) actually *increase* the spectator's sense of confusion and panic.

The relationship between identification and the ready acceptance of
sleight of hand might be investigated through innumerable examples of Hitchcock's work. One general point emerges clearly: Hitchcock has grasped that the
identification principle can work in this elemental/elementary way only when
very simple and basic feelings are involved — often primitive feelings (especially
terror) rooted in direct physical sensation. Otherwise, identification (empathy,
as opposed to the kind of sympathy we may feel for the characters in, for
example, a Renoir film) is a doubtful and complicated phenomenon that has
to be built very subtly. There may be a reason beyond that of mere technical
obviousness why many people are so alienated by the artificial devices of *Marnie:* that, in the very nature of the central character and her predicament, total
identification is impossible. One can study the care with which Hitchcock
builds identification, when he can't rely on "primitive" emotions, in the first
scene of *Psycho,* where every stylistic decision and every step in the construction of the scenario can be seen as part of a process whereby Hitchcock prepares
for that identification with Marion Crane on which the effect and essential
meaning of the entire film depend (on whatever level of seriousness we feel it
as working). The opening is not a single take (as my own treatment of it might
seem to imply — an error perpetuated in Raymond Durgnat's interesting recent
book, *The Strange Case of Alfred Hitchcock*) but a series of shots linked by
almost imperceptible dissolves and one awkward cut (presumably from a location to the studio set) just before the camera moves in through the open
window. The captions identifying place, date (but not the year), and time of
day confirm the impression of "documentary" realism given by the location
work; the dissolves subliminally convey the sense of covering a lot of territory,
the progress towards the window seeming ambiguously arbitrary and purpos-
ive. The spectator (even if he missed the advance publicity) has been alerted to
expect some kind of horror movie by the title and by Bernard Herrmann's
opening music, but Hitchcock's insistence on the ordinary and "real" temporarily lulls him — under cover of which Hitchcock can begin at once to play
on his voyeuristic tendencies. As the camera takes us in through the open
window into the dark hotel bedroom, the lighting is subtly modified: the
effect is of our eyes becoming adjusted to the dark after the sunshine outside.
When Sam says, "You never did eat your lunch," Hitchcock cuts in a close-up
of the sandwich lunch on the bedside table: the shot is obviously superfluous
in terms of the conveying of information, but it corresponds closely to the
movement of our consciousness: if we were in the room and heard Sam say
that, we would instinctively glance at the lunch. When the lovers lie down
again on the bed, the camera moves in as though to lie down with them: from

being invisible spectators actually in the room, we are led to become participants. Then, when Marion springs up in recoil, the camera abruptly recoils
too, closely mirroring her movement: our participation begins to be given a
clear bias which is developed through the remainder of the scene. There are no
shots that are strictly subjective, but the camera repeatedly favors Marion and
her viewpoint. She is privileged with close-ups (notably on "I'll lick the
stamps," where the music also endorses our romantic sympathy for her position
and attitude) or shown in profile; we look at Sam, on the other hand, in
medium long-shot and *almost* as through her eyes (notably on his, "Well, all
right," as he surrenders to her demand for "respectability" with a submissive
gesture of the hands). In fact, the first clearly subjective shot in the film is
withheld until the moment when Marion's car is stopped at the traffic lights
and she sees her boss crossing in front of her — by which time the movement of
the scenario, the editing, the placement of the camera, the music, have thoroughly but unobtrusively determined our relationship to her and to the action.

Hitchcock's attitude toward actors — another, though seldom so explicit,
recurrent theme of his interviews — follows logically from the centrality to his
art of the Kuleshov experiment. One can make a broad distinction (and it is
intimately bound up with certain aspects of the "Realism" debate) between
directors who work collaboratively with actors and directors who use actors to
execute a preconceived plan or idea: Renoir, Hawks, McCarey against von
Sternberg, Antonioni, Hitchcock. To von Sternberg, actors were "puppets": he
claimed that every detail of Dietrich's performances in their films was created
by him, down to the smallest gesture or flicker of expression. Arthur Penn
aptly described the actors in Antonioni's films as "beautiful statuary." Hitchcock has denied saying that "actors are cattle": what he said was that they
should be *treated* like cattle. The former trio seek to discover what an actor can
give and then encourage him to give it, within the limits of an overall conception which is relatively loose: one knows, for example, that some of McCarey's
best scenes were improvised on the set, that *La Règle du Jeu* changed and grew
during the course of shooting, that Hawks and his cast more or less made up
Hatari! as they went along, within the loose framework of a hunting season.
The spectator won't find in a Hitchcock film (or only very rarely) the continuous invention of detail, the spontaneous bits of business, that make *La Règle
du Jeu, Rio Bravo, Once Upon a Honeymoon* so inexhaustibly alive; I find
that Hitchcock's films go "dead" on me more easily. The broad distinction is
between actor-centered cinema and image-centered cinema. The former implies a "humanist" philosophy and a certain form of "Realism." It also carries a
logical thematic extension: the characters of Hawks, Renoir, and McCarey experience and express at least a relative freedom (literally, of movement within
the frame; spiritually, of moral choice); the films of these directors are centered
on values of generosity and affection between people, on the possibility of
contact and reciprocal relations. In contrast, the characters of von Sternberg,

Antonioni, Hitchcock are, typically, trapped, isolated, unable to communicate; there is a strong emphasis on impotence (the word to be understood in its general sense, though its specifically sexual overtones are not inappropriate).

To define and exemplify Hitchcock's image-centered concept of cinema, one needn't adduce specimens of Kuleshovian editing: one needn't look beyond the first shot of *Marnie*. Its primary function is to arouse the spectator's curiosity/voyeurism, though it also introduces certain important thematic motifs; its method involves the virtual elimination of the actor or of acting. Each precisely calculated detail in the action, the *décor*, and the camera movement conveys a precise idea or represents a strategy in the Hitchcockian game of audience manipulation (at this stage of the film taking the form of teasing). The close-up on the yellow bag tells us the bag is significant without giving us any clue as to why; as the camera slows and the figure walks on, our chief desire is to see her face — a desire Hitchcock systematically frustrates until, like Michelange in *Les Carabiniers,* we want to climb in through the frame and run ahead to take a look. She has black hair, so it can't be Tippi Hedren; except that it is so very black, and so glossy, that it may be dyed, so perhaps it *is* Tippi Hedren after all. We want the camera to catch up with her again so that we can get a better look: perhaps she will stop and turn. Hitchcock accordingly slows the camera down even more, eventually stopping it altogether; then, just as she turns and we might see her face (even at a distance) in profile, he cuts. Our curiosity is increased by other factors in the scene which are revealed as she moves further from the camera: the time of day (apparently very early morning), the station platform (completely deserted, without even a porter in sight, so she will have to wait a long time for a train), the way she is walking very straight and precariously along a yellow line, like a girl balancing on a tightrope. The "corridor" pattern of converging, receding lines (tracks, empty trains, the edges of the platform), familiar from *Vertigo* and taken up recurrently later in the film (the hotel corridor, the honeymoon ship, Mrs. Edgar's street), has an immediately expressive impact with its suggestion of a trajectory, introducing the "journey" motif on which the film is built. There is no purer example of the Hitchcock shot: the execution of a complex of ideas, with audience response a crucial determining concern.

The characteristics of Hitchcock's cinema so far described make logical another recurrent theme of his interviews: the repeated assertions that he is not really very interested in the actual shooting because he knows, with the completion of the shooting script, shot by shot what the film will be like: the filming is merely the mechanical execution of a precise blueprint. One takes this with at least one pinch of salt. On the one hand, it helps to explain the unevenness of so many Hitchcock films, the process of shooting providing no compensation for a failure of interest at the planning stage. Were all those slack sequences in *Topaz* — that look as if they'd been shot and thrown together by a television crew during the director's absence — really planned shot by shot?

Perhaps so; the slackness could be accounted for by assuming that Hitchcock wasn't interested in them at the planning stage and, because he isn't a McCarey, could instill no life into them during shooting. On the other hand, one needs to account for the numerous superb performances in certain films where the acting quite transcends any Kuleshovian trickery. Hitchcock might, of course, have anticipated Grant's performance in *North by Northwest*, and even Bergman's in *Notorious*, from prior knowledge of the players. But Joseph Cotten in *Shadow of a Doubt?* Robert Walker in *Strangers on a Train?* Anthony Perkins in *Psycho?* One might account for them by the hypothesis that, because Hitchcock isn't interested in acting, certain actors, left to their own devices, are able to seize their chances and create their own performances independently; there is more reason to deduce that there are certain performances—or, more exactly, certain *roles*—which arouse in Hitchcock a particular creative interest.

Minor reservations apart, however, the films convincingly bear out the notion of detailed preplanning—especially the set pieces of what Hitchcock calls "pure cinema," a concept that invariably turns out to be based on the possibilities of montage. This accounts for Bazin's famous disillusionment when he visited Hitchcock on location for *To Catch a Thief* and found the *metteur en scène* apparently very little concerned with what was currently being shot. It is also the ultimate confirmation of our sense of Hitchcock's conception of cinema as an artificial construct—the most artificial, perhaps, short of animation (which something like the horse accident in *Marnie* strikingly resembles). This goes some way towards explaining the paradox that Hitchcock's cinema, dedicated so singlemindedly to the total entrapment of the spectator in an emotional experience, is also the easiest mentally to deconstruct. It is a truism that works of art can give pleasure on different levels, depending on a variety of factors: familiarity with the work, familiarity with its background and context, familiarity with its conventions; personal temperament; degree of intellectual awareness; the mood of the moment. The sorts of pleasure afforded by Hitchcock's films are unusually disparate, even contradictory: one might assume they would be mutually exclusive. There is the pleasure derived from experiencing the films in a state of total submission, carried through step by step in the scenario, shot by shot in the montage, in intense emotional participation; there is the pleasure of total awareness of how everything is done, the pleasure usually termed "aesthetic," wherein one delights in the skills of Hitchcock's technical mastery (when it works). Happily, the complexity of the human organism and its responses is such that even such seemingly opposed experiences can operate simultaneously (though each will modify the other). This is in fact implicit in my parenthesis above on Hitchcock's mastery ("when it works"): our intellectual awareness that something "works" (on which that apparently purely "aesthetic" delight rests) inevitably refers to an emotional level of response, the only level on which (at least in a Hitchcock movie) the concept of "working" can be validated.

* * * * * *

So far, this attempt at a more precise and concrete definition of the nature of Hitchcock's art than *Hitchcock's Films* originally offered might seem to lead logically either to the traditional rejection or denigration of it as the work of a skillful technician and manipulator or to the type of analysis favored by the semiological school of "materialist" critics which would bypass questions of individual creativity and personal response, seeing the films as part of a "social process." The latter, certainly, would produce its revelations: one looks forward (not without trepidation) to accounts of, say, *Vertigo* and *Psycho* along the lines of Stephen Heath's remarkable reading of *Touch of Evil* in the Spring 1975 issue of *Screen*. But it is my contention that, however completely "coded" a work of art can be demonstrated to be, at its heart (if it is alive) is individual creativity, and it is with the nature of the creative impulses embodied in it that we must ultimately be concerned. This is not to talk naively about "genius" in a way that suggests that works of art spring spontaneously out of the artist's head via some process of immaculate conception. That Hitchcock's American period is in general richer than the British (a proposition I see no reason to retract or modify) can doubtless be attributed as much to a complex set of interacting determinants as to personal development; similarly, a complete account of any one of the great Hitchcock films would have to see it as the product of an intricate network of influences, circumstances of production, collaborations, happy confluences. But at the center of that network is—must be—a particular creative personality. The *auteur* theory, concerned to trace relationships between films and between different aspects (style, structure, theme) of the same film, exaggerated the degree of individual determination in the process of making it possible to define it; the current swing of the critical pendulum overcompensates for this by seeking to deny the individual altogether.

As soon as one begins to contemplate Hitchcock's work thematically, it becomes evident that its technical elaborations, the manifest desire to control audiences, have a thematic extension: they are determined, in other words, not simply by conscious commercial strategy but by powerful internal drives and pressures of the kind that never operate exclusively on a conscious level. The desire to control, the terror of losing control: such phrases describe not only Hitchcock's conscious relationship to technique and to his audiences but also the thematic center of his films. The personal relationships that fascinate Hitchcock invariably involve the exercise of power, or its obverse, impotence; in many cases, a power drive that seeks to conceal or deny or compensate for a dreaded impotence, the perfect metaphor for which is provided by the "double" Norman Bates of *Psycho*: the young man terrified of women and the exaggeratedly "potent" monster wielding the phallic knife. This relationship-pattern, with its possible permutations and variations, links films as apparently diverse as *Notorious, Rope, Rear Window, Vertigo, Psycho,* and *Marnie:* on the whole, the more the plot structure allows it to dominate, the richer, more forceful, more fully achieved is the film. *Notorious*—one of Hitchcock's finest works, of which we still await an adequate account—derives its fascination from its complex shifting of power-and-impotence relationships, involving all four of the principle characters, and from certain suggestive Freudian overtones related to this: the key Ingrid Bergman steals from Claude Rains to give to Cary Grant, the bottle in the cellar which Grant discovers and which contains Rains's secret "potency" (in the form of uranium ore).

The scene of the party in Rains's house suggests the central importance in Hitchcock of a motif peculiarly appropriate to the cinema, the "look," and its relation to the power/impotence obsession. It also suggests that the common simplistic association of subjective camera with audience identification (which parts of *Hitchcock's Films* may have done something to encourage) needs careful qualification. During the early part of the scene, we are placed, in turn, in the positions of Bergman, Grant, and Rains as they watch each other across the room, through the throng of guests, each for his or her own reasons apprehensive; the spectator is led to participate in the tensions expressed through the pattern of interchanged looks rather than to identify with a particular character. The look expresses both dominance (the power of watching) and helplessness (the impotence of separation); by the use of subjective shots, Hitchcock at once makes the tension personal to himself (camera as the director's eyes) and transfers it to the audience (camera as eyes of the spectator).

The close connection between this and the voyeuristic tendencies so often noted in Hitchcock's cinema is obvious. Again, perhaps, the most vivid single instance is in *Psycho* (significantly, among the most intensely personal of all his films, and the one in which he was most singlemindedly dedicated to manipulating his audience): the close-up of Norman's eye as he watches through his peephole and the cut to a subjective view of Marion undressing, so that the eye becomes both ours and Hitchcock's. The whole of *Rear Window* can be seen as an elaboration of this principle, the James Stewart character combining certain aspects of the roles of spectator and *metteur en scène.* The notion of impotence is concretely embodied in the broken leg; the people Stewart watches are at once dominated imaginatively by his consciousness (like Marion, they don't know they are being watched) and forever beyond his control.

To trace the creative drives behind Hitchcock's films to sources in psychopathology (possible, after all, to some degree with *any* artist) does not necessarily invalidate the emphasis placed in my book on their therapeutic impulses: indeed, it could logically be felt to strengthen this emphasis by giving the therapeutic impulses a particular focus or motivation. I still feel that the Hitchcock films I most admire are centered on a movement towards health via therapy and catharsis. I have, however, become much more keenly aware of a need to insist on sharp discriminations—a need to stress the limitations of Hitchcock's art and to distinguish the work (a small proportion of the total *oeuvre*) that succeeds in transcending them.

The limitations are of two kinds, though perhaps not entirely unconnected. There is, first, the somewhat equivocal relationship between Hitchcock the artist and Hitchcock the showman-entertainer. Obviously, the two can never be cleanly separated, nor would it be desirable that they could be, as their interrelationship is in many ways crucial to the robustness of Hitchcock's work. One can, nevertheless, set up fairly obvious polar opposites: the intensely involved personal art of *Vertigo,* say, as against the businessman who lends his name to anthologies of largely trivial horror stories or the comic fat man who introduces the Hitchcock half-hour on television. Between the two, however, lie areas where the relationship becomes problematic. What concerns me here is the way in which some of Hitchcock's finest work is flawed by compromises that, in an artist free of "commercial" constraints, would appear neurotic, the result of a reluctance to allow certain disturbing implications to be fully explored, but which Hitchcock encourages us (sometimes, in interviews, explicitly) to regard as the result of external pressures, fears of alienating his audiences (the two motivations are not, of course, incompatible). There is a whole series of Hitchcock films which work magnificently up to a point, arousing complex and disturbing emotions, achieving a rich—and often very subversive—suggestiveness, and then evade their own implications by a sudden simplification. I have already touched in *Hitchcock's Films* on the two most striking instances, *Strangers on a Train* and *Torn Curtain.* The former offers the neatest example of all, because one can point to the exact moment where the film goes wrong (which is also where it departs most decisively from its source, Patricia Highsmith's novel)—the scene where Guy *doesn't* murder Bruno's father. Here and in *Torn Curtain* Hitchcock's reluctance to explore or acknowledge the disturbing implications of his hero's behavior results in a curious paralysis at the center of the film: neither one thing nor the other, the hero ends up nothing, and interest is displaced onto Bruno (in *Strangers*) and onto peripheral characters (in *Torn Curtain*). If in *Strangers* the simplification takes the form of trying to pass off Guy as a conventional hero, in *Shadow of a Doubt* it takes the opposite form of turning the film's most complex and ambivalently viewed figure (Uncle Charlie) into a mere monster for the last third. *Psycho* is much nearer to being a masterpiece (the first half, up to the point where Marion's car sinks into the swamp, is certainly among the most extraordinary achievements of the American cinema). Yet even here one cannot but feel a lapse to a lower level of interest, with conventional detective-story investigation, "flat" characters (Sam and Lila), and scenes (especially those

involving Sheriff Chambers) that could easily come from one of the less distinguished of Hitchcock's TV shows. (The film picks up again, superbly, with
Lila's exploration of Norman's home.)

The second limitation is more damaging: I would define it as the relative
weakness in Hitchcock's art of the normative impulse. That great art strives—
however implicitly—towards the realization of norms seems to me axiomatic,
though the principle I am stating is frequently misunderstood or misrepresented. It is not a matter of whether a work is "optimistic" or "pessimistic" and
certainly not a denial of the validity of a tragic vision of life. It is a matter of
the nature of the creative impulse, which, to flourish, must be rooted in a
sense of at least a *potential* normality for which to strive, values by which to
live. "Normality" here must not be understood in terms of the reaffirmation of
established values, least of all the norms of bourgeois society: Godard's *Tout va
bien,* for example, answers perfectly to my concept of "normative" art, though
its tone is not optimistic and it proposes no clearly definable solutions to the
problems it raises; if I place beside it, as another essentially "normative" work,
Bergman's *The Silence,* I shall perhaps sufficiently have safeguarded myself
against simplification and parody.

It is not really paradoxical that Hitchcock's art is usually at its most creative when his material permits or encourages the most complete immersion in
the abnormal. If creativity is, almost by definition, a striving towards norms,
this implies a process, a *moving through.* The problem with Hitchcock is that
the movement seems almost always blocked. His work typically equates "normality" with a bourgeois life in whose values the creative side of him totally
disbelieves but to which it can provide no alternative. The couple in *Rich and
Strange* pass through a series of disruptive experiences only to return, at the
end of the film, to precisely the sterile existence of the beginning: all they have
learned is to be afraid of the unfamiliar. The pattern established here is fundamental to Hitchcock's work: bourgeois "normality" is empty and unsatisfying,
everything beyond it (or, more importantly, *within* it, secreted beneath its
surface), terrifying. This explains why Hitchcock's most satisfying endings are
those that express catharsis without reimposing a defined "normality"—at
once, necessarily, the bleakest and most "open": the opening of the window
and firing of the gun at the end of *Rope*; the car being withdrawn from the
swamp at the end of *Psycho*; above all, the end of *Vertigo.* And if this last
remains, unchallengeably, Hitchcock's masterpiece, this is surely because there
the attitude to the unknown and mysterious is not simply one of terror but
retains, implicitly, a profound and disturbing ambivalence.

It is symptomatic that the most obvious legacy of Hitchcock's Jesuit education should be the lingering fascination with Hell and damnation, often
concretized in the detail of the films. When Uncle Charlie arrives in Santa Rosa
(*Shadow of a Doubt*), the whole image is darkened by the black smoke from
the train, and the character is thereafter repeatedly shown with smoke hanging

around him from his cigarette; when Bruno pursues Miriam through the Tunnel of Love (*Strangers on a Train*) his boat is named Pluto; when Marion Crane tells Norman Bates that she "thought she must have gotten off the right road," he replies that "Nobody ever comes here unless they've done that." It is to these "damned" characters (ambiguously lost souls or devils) that Hitchcock's strongest interest gravitates, giving us some of the most vividly realized performances in his films; one looks in vain for any compensating intimation of Heaven. Hitchcock seems interested in the "normality" presented by the films only when he can treat it satirically, as with the "society" party of *Strangers on a Train*. *Shadow of a Doubt* is especially interesting here, as it is one film in which Hitchcock is supposed to create small-town life affectionately. In fact, the family the film depicts consists of a collection of more-or-less caricatured individuals, each of whom inhabits a private, separate dreamworld, the mother nostalgic for her youth and her adored younger brother, the father living in a fantasy world of detective fiction and real-life crime, the younger daughter perpetually immersed in books. The film is rich in amusing detail, and the early scenes of Uncle Charlie's intrusion into the small-town world are genuinely disturbing and subversive; but it would be difficult to claim either that the family life presented offers much in the way of affirmation or that the film suggests any possible alternative that isn't corrupt or "evil." Uncle Charlie, characteristically, brings life and excitement into an inert world, but proves to be a devil who must be destroyed: the sense of emptiness with which one is left at the end is closely bound up with the film's association of excitement with corruption, with Hitchcock's habitual distrust of the forces of the Id.

If I were to undertake a revision of *Hitchcock's Films*, the chapter that would call for the most modification would be that on *The Birds*, a film about which my feelings continue to be both mixed and fluctuating. It seems in some ways Hitchcock's most important, most "serious" film: the film in which he is most overtly concerned to elaborate a view of the universe. What is ultimately wrong with it is not that the eye too easily penetrates the technical trickery but that, for all the audacity of the conception and the consistent interest of the execution, the characters and their relationships are too slight to sustain the weight of significance implicitly imposed on them, too slight ever adequately to represent humanity and human potential; and there is no sign that Hitchcock can conceive of human potential positively in more adequate terms. The development the film appears to offer—the stripping away of the veneer of complacent superficiality—never really materializes, at least not very impressively. One is left with a sense of discrepancy between the film's grand postulate—the threatened end of civilization and perhaps of humanity itself—and the actual created civilization and humanity presented in it. The weakness can be localized specifically in the perfunctory treatment of the children, in Hitchcock's notable failure to respond to the notion of renewed potential they and the school might have represented, his reduction of the concepts of education and childhood—the human future—to the automatic reiteration of an inane jingle. It is because the film fails to achieve the dimensions of tragedy (which depends on concepts of positive value) that it seems so perilously to border on the sadistic—the sadism directed ultimately, perhaps, at the audience. The film suggests, strongly, that the artificiality of Hitchcock's cinema, which I have attempted to define stylistically, has ramifications far beyond the "unnatural" surface of the films: he seems unable to create a "normal" life, whether actual or potential, of any richness or density, a point that holds whether one understands "normal" in the conventional, bourgeois sense or in my sense of "moving towards new norms."

CHAPTER FOUR

Hitchcock at Metro

Leonard J. Leff

Throughout the 1950s, journalists repeatedly freshened up Hollywood's obituary. Dual evils—television and the 1948 divorcement decrees that separated exhibition from production-distribution—had sickened the studio system, and Three-D, Cinerama, and CinemaScope seemed drugs calculated to sustain, not cure it. Like many well-established, previously profitable institutions, the motion picture industry seemed insufficiently responsive to change. By 1955, several once-healthy companies had reduced their production output by half, yet the enormous overhead of underutilized personnel and property continued to erode earnings. Defying this downward trend was United Artists, which financed and distributed films but did not produce them. With no physical plant and thus no significant overhead, United Artists moved easily into independent production, a strategy for surviving if not solving the industry's midcentury crisis. UA vice-president Max Youngstein said that the company offered "complete creative autonomy"; when this was linked to tax benefits and profit participation, few artists could resist: "We are appealing basically to a combination of pride, ego, and the desire for greater financial gain." By transferring control of motion picture production from executives to filmmakers, UA attracted many of the industry's best producers and directors. In return, the company hoped, men like William Wyler, Joseph Mankiewicz, and Otto Preminger (all of whom were associated wth UA in 1957) would produce the industry's biggest hits.

UA's overwhelmingly successful model was eventually emulated by all the major studios, most of whom grew to favor distribution over production. The period from 1955 to 1960 saw a small revolution within the politics of the industry. In just five years, for example, Metro-Goldwyn-Mayer increased its independent production from ten percent to eighty percent of its total output. Suddenly, studios that had formerly hired directors now found themselves working for them. The significance of this point has been obscured, however, because the era's independent artists, middle-aged and experienced, were not unsympathetic to the commercial bias of American cinema. Their films were sometimes original but usually "safe"; with profit participation, they too had an investment to protect and an ailing industry to minister to. As Billy Wilder said, their goal was "not to work for awards, but to make the pictures which will 'bring them back in,' which will recover the lost audience." Their films were, in the last analysis, studio films.

The Eisenhower years evoke an image of conservatism and accommodation. But in the 1950s, if relations between Hollywood directors and studios were placid on the surface, tensions pulsated beneath. Youngstein's "complete creative autonomy" had fine print: "The motion-picture maker went out and made the film," UA's vice-president said, only after "subject-matter, major cast, director, and budget were mutually settled." Yet the studio's imposition of boundaries and the filmmaker's demand for increasingly more artistic freedom were not always reconcilable. The fact that each recognized the legitimacy of the other's goals did not prevent the development of stress in the relationship, usually the result of one's testing the other's limitations in a new and evolving role.

As example, a case study of the artist in a 1950s corporate context in Hollywood might center on a director whose reputation warranted independence and a studio whose fiscal precariousness merited considerable caution in surrendering any control. To enhance the study, the designated studio should be rich in history, the director prominent and talented, and the film important. Metro-Goldwyn-Mayer, Alfred Hitchcock, and *North by Northwest* (1959) amply qualify. To many critics, *North by Northwest* is the culminant film in Hitchcock's canon, a conservative work financed and distributed by Hollywood's most conservative, once wealthiest studio. In the relationship of Hitchcock and MGM—an independent producer-director who sought absolute control and a studio struggling to survive a period of transition—lies a significant segment of American film history.

By fiat, Leo the Lion once ruled the MGM studios; by consensus, the entire movie kingdom. The envy of its peers, Loew's (MGM's parent company) had solid management, excellent distribution machinery, a fine worldwide theater chain, some valuable real estate in Culver City, California, a splendid film library, and perhaps the industry's best production facilities. Yet in the first quarter of 1956, it estimated earnings of only a nickel a share, a dismal record that would worsen in the years ahead. The March 1956 annual meeting was raucous. Though company executives pledged implementation of cost-cutting measures, stockholders stomped their feet and jeered. MGM, some charged, had inadequately responded to changes in the economic climate of Hollywood. Stalling on the Supreme Court's 1948 decision to separate exhibition from production, Loew's had seen its competitors—free of their theaters—concentrate on filmmaking and turn out superior products eagerly booked by the new independent exhibitors. Other studios were also actively engaged in television production. In 1949, when he had reportedly had the opportunity to join David Sarnoff in partnership with RCA's television enterprises, Loew's president Nicholas Schenck had declined; by the mid-1950s, MGM's involvement with television production was still relatively minor. Finally, MGM under Schenck had discouraged independent production. Studios like UA readily offered producers, directors, and actors lucrative profit participation, so as their MGM contracts lapsed, these newborn independents struck deals elsewhere. "Other studios played the reluctant giant," ousted MGM production head Dore Schary observed, "and M-G-M was the last of the stag line. A lot of dances had been booked by then."

In 1955 Arthur Loew, son of the company's founder, had reluctantly assumed the presidency of Loew's, but after less than a year in office, he suddenly quit. For two weeks, Loew's had no president; then, in October 1956, the Board appointed Joseph R. Vogel head of Loew's, Incorporated. A theater usher who had risen in the corporation, Vogel had run Loew's theater chain since 1954. He began his presidency by announcing the kind of cost-cutting measures that would characterize the early months of his tenure: development of a responsible cost accounting system, strict budget controls, and reallocation of significant studio resources for television rather than film production. Vogel must have approached the issue of feature film production apprehensively. Though MGM had facilities and staff to produce up to fifty films annually, it made only twenty-five in 1955, many of them box office failures. Yet features were virtually mandatory, if only to absorb some of the studio's enormous overhead. More films—better films—could come primarily from one source, the independent. Vogel's plan, announced retrospectively in *Time,* was to make a "succession of deals with Hollywood's independent producers to put M-G-M on a competitive par with its more alert rivals."

That MGM would approach Alfred Hitchcock is unsurprising. However eccentric he may have been socially, he was known as a dependable, fiscally responsible director. Some independents, like Fred Zinnemann and Elia Kazan, used their hard-won creative control to make deeply felt social problem films. Hitchcock, despite the thematic complexity that even some contemporary critics ascribed to his work, appeared to be a crowd pleaser, certainly not a director of "personal" films. *Rear Window* (1954), *To Catch a Thief* (1955), and *The Man Who Knew Too Much* (1956), all at Paramount, had earned high positions on *Variety*'s annual lists of top moneymaking films. As cake icing, television's *Alfred Hitchcock Presents,* a *coup de maître* begun in October 1955, inestimably publicized the director and his films. To a company looking for a safe director of box office hits, Hitchcock must have seemed very attractive. Ever since leaving David Selznick in 1948, though, Hitchcock had sought increasingly more independence. The question for MGM was clear-cut: how much control would Hitchcock want and how much could the studio relinquish?

In early 1957, MGM's Floyd L. Hendrickson began negotiating with

MCA's Edd Henry for Hitchcock's services as both producer and director of *The Wreck of the Mary Deare*, based on a novel that the studio owned. As Paramount had done, MGM would deal with the Hitchcock Production Company, a corporation that shielded Hitchcock from heavy personal income taxes. Certain points of accord were immediately reached: with approval of writer and principal cast members ceded to him (that in itself a major concession), Hitchcock would agree to produce and direct the *Mary Deare* for $250,000 and a percentage of the receipts. Interestingly, despite MCA's pressing questions on how Metro would figure its overhead on the film (which would ultimately affect Hitchcock's percentage), salary was never a serious point of contention. A Paramount executive told Hendrickson that Hitchcock's San Francisco tax attorney was "a competent, meticulous gentleman with whom it is a pleasure to do business," and the Hitchcock file at MGM suggests that the negotiations, though prolonged, were amicable. The only major impediment lay in a clause that Hitchcock originated. Although simply worded, it touched on a matter central to Hitchcock's personality and professional development, control: "Hitchcock," a tentative contract proffered by MCA read, "is to have artistic approval and approval of all elements of production of the picture."

Though Hitchcock had no signed contract with MGM, he began work on *The Wreck of the Mary Deare* in summer 1957. Bernard Herrmann, who had composed the music for *The Trouble with Harry* (1956) and *The Man Who Knew Too Much*, had introduced MGM screenwriter Ernest Lehman to Hitchcock, and a congenial relationship developed. Working at Hitchcock's home and then at Paramount, where Hitchcock was in preproduction on *Vertigo* (1958), the two men discovered in less than a month that *The Wreck of the Mary Deare* was not salvageable. Hitchcock soon recalled an idea offered him by journalist Otis Guernsey, Jr. Guernsey had told Hitchcock that during the Second World War two bored secretaries at the British embassy invented a fake master spy, complete with name and record; to their surprise, the Nazis "gobbled the bait" and began hunting down the nonexistent operative. Guernsey suggested that in a "movie melodrama" an ingenuous young American might accidentally have a false identity pinned on him. "He is on the spot," Guernsey wrote to Hitchcock; "the enemy is trying to capture and kill him and his friends cannot help him because they cannot afford to have their ruse exposed." Hitchcock felt that this situation could accommodate several attractive visual ideas: a dramatic scene against a floodlighted building, a murder on a Detroit automobile assembly line, a chase across Mount Rushmore; Lehman felt that it would allow him to write, as he desired, the ultimate Hitchcock film. So without notifying MGM, the two men began plotting what they originally called *In a Northwest Direction*.

At Loew's Incorporated, a different drama of intrigue was unfolding. Allying himself with Joseph Tomlinson, Loew's biggest shareholder, Loew's board member Stanley Meyer sought the corporation's presidency and probably the liquidation of its film production unit at Culver City. First, of course, he needed control of the board of directors. By threatening a proxy fight, he succeeded in reconstituting the Loew's board with six Tomlinson-selected men and one independent. At the February 1957 annual meeting, though, the board confirmed Joseph Vogel in his presidency. Throughout the spring of 1957 Tomlinson and Meyer, along with deposed studio head Louis B. Mayer, continued sniping at Vogel; however ill-founded, their attacks created within the financial community an aura of doubt about Loew's stability. The July resignation of two board members aggravated the problem. Though Vogel called for a special stockholders meeting to fill the positions, Tomlinson and Meyer quickly assembled a board quorum and elected former Paramount executive Samuel Briskin and Louis B. Mayer. Vogel termed the action "illegal," but only the courts could invalidate it.

As one of its principal decisions, the Tomlinson rump board tied Vogel's hands: it forbade him to sign contracts for more than one year's duration or in excess of $25,000 without board approval. This restriction, Vogel maintained, was costly. During midsummer, one broadcaster with a pending $3 million television licensing contract terminated negotiations, and one independent producer about to consummate "a very important deal" with MGM took his film to another studio; both feared that under Vogel, Loew's management had no legal authority to contract for the corporation. But if Hitchcock was concerned about Loew's stability, he gave no sign. Proceeding with *In a Northwest Direction,* Hitchcock and Lehman perhaps recognized that if their script was not made at MGM it could be made elsewhere. And by mid-August, it was more than a farrago of visual ideas. The characters in place included a hero named Roger Thornhill, a heroine named Eva, and a villain named Tomlinson.

By 21 August 1957, Hitchcock and Lehman had devised a working outline of the film's first act, moving Thornhill from his Manhattan office to a Long Island mansion, the decoy's hotel room, the United Nations, and a train. Although some incidents would be altered and a few scenes trimmed, the setting, characters, and motivations in the first act were virtually fixed. Less than a week later, Hitchcock informed MGM that he was "temporarily putting aside" *The Wreck of the Mary Deare* and assigning Lehman to develop an original story of "espionage and counterespionage in the United States with locales in New York, Detroit, Mount Rushmore and Alaska, among others." Without reading a script—which of course did not exist—MGM executives could not estimate the cost of this new film. They were, however, still negotiating Hitchcock's contract, and in an early draft of it was a clause that gave him artistic approval of all elements of production, with one exception: MGM "will be supplied with a maximum monetary limitation on the budget and negative cost as a control, and Hitchcock will be obligated to meet such limitation."

Since Lehman was already under a long-term MGM contract and since the studio ultimately intended to protect itself with a ceiling on expenses, it had no reason to discourage Hitchcock's change of plan. On the contrary, reflecting on the recent defection of one independent producer, MGM may have welcomed the support implied by Hitchcock's willingness to continue working at the Culver City lot. Furthermore, the popular director seemed to be offering MGM two films instead of one, *The Wreck of the Mary Deare* and *In a Northwest Direction*. Studio executives must have felt buoyant: earlier on the day of their meeting with Hitchcock, a state court had ruled the Tomlinson board and its action invalid. With an authority that may have seemed perceptibly stronger, MGM amended its "handshake deal" with Hitchcock and directed him to legally acquire Otto Guernsey's idea and proceed with his new story.

By 11 September 1957, Lehman had polished the outline of first-act scenes that had been drafted three weeks before. The remaining scenes—hopscotching from a cocktail party to an automobile assembly line, the Mount Rushmore monument, and an Alaskan missile site—bear little resemblance to the completed film; in fact, they suggest that chaos dominated both Thornhill's life and the work in progress that MGM was now calling *The CIA Story*. At this time, with two-thirds of the screenplay unfinished, Hitchcock left to begin filming *Vertigo*. Lehman felt that he needed a fresh perspective, so in October 1957 he flew east on a research trip. MGM carefully monitored his expenses: as he traveled, he kept an itemized accounting that included even phone calls, tips, and taxi fares under $2.00. Lehman resented the studio's close attention to economy, but Loew's precarious corporate health had mandated it. In New York, the screenwriter visited the St. Regis, the United Nations, the Glen Cove courthouse, and Yankee Stadium (for a sequence earlier planned but never written); he traveled by rail to Chicago and to Rapid City, South Dakota, where he spent a day at the Mount Rushmore monument, and then returned to Los Angeles. His first rough-draft screenplay was written in November, but writer's block still prevented its completion. By December 1957, Lehman's anxiety mounted; the last quarter of *Breathless* (the film's new title) was "unthought of and unwritten," yet Hitchcock had already begun casting.

With little hope of success but for good reason, MGM tried to persuade Hitchcock to cast Metro stars as his leads. The studio's choices, Gregory Peck and Cyd Charisse, were advanced even before a script was written and the characters set, perhaps in an attempt to make it difficult for Hitchcock to say no with finality. None too happily, Hitchcock had worked with Peck at Selznick Productions on *Spellbound* (1945) and *The Paradine Case* (1948); when some years later François Truffaut diplomatically suggested that Peck was not a "Hitchcockian actor," the director did not disagree. Peck was at least a star; Charisse, on the other hand, had primarily her temporary idleness at MGM to recommend her. Even the studio must have recognized her limits as a dramatic actress. Exercising his right of cast approval, Hitchcock immediately rejected them both.

   As Thornhill, Hitchcock cast Cary Grant, who had appeared in Hitchcock's *Suspicion* (1941), *Notorious* (1946), and *To Catch a Thief*. Both Englishmen, Grant and Hitchcock were consummate professionals, and though off the set Grant insisted on preferential treatment, on the set he contributed to the order and harmony that Hitchcock so desired during production. When agent Kurt Frings suggested Eva Marie Saint for Eve Kendall, Hitchcock screened *On the Waterfront* (1954) and *That Certain Feeling* (1956), two recent films in which she had appeared. (Hitchcock preferred not to screen-test or audition actors, for he disliked having to reject them.) Interested in Saint, Hitchcock invited her to lunch for an informal interview. Unaware of Eve Kendall's personality, Saint wore subdued beige and donned short white gloves, suggesting not a seductress but "Miss Priss." After lunch, however, she learned by telephone that Hitchcock had cast her. Yul Brynner and Martin Gabel, early choices for Vandamm, the film's suave villain (earlier named Tomlinson), gave way to James Mason. As Leonard, Vandamm's associate, Hitchcock cast Martin Landau, whom he had first seen in Los Angeles as the wiry antagonist in a road company production of *Middle of the Night*. Leo G. Carroll (with whom Hitchcock had previously worked five times) and Jessie Royce Landis filled out supporting roles. None of the principals, as it turned out, was under contract to MGM.
   With a suddenness that suprised both Hitchcock and Lehman, the idea of Eve's shooting Thornhill with blanks unblocked the screenwriter and throughout the winter of 1957–58 he finished the first-draft screenplay and began polishing it. Much of the repartee between the two romantic leads evolved at this time, but so did some astringent lines that helped deepen character. In dialogue written in 1958, Eve tells Thornhill: "Trouble is, you know everything and believe in nothing. You're the American dream gone sour, Thornhill—the successful man whose only cause is himself." Such dialogue, ultimately cut, clashed with the otherwise bright tone of what Lehman had temporarily titled *The Man on Lincoln's Nose*. Meanwhile, in spring 1958, as Lehman refined the dialogue and worked through the dramatic problems, Hitchcock began conferring with director of photography Robert Burks and production designer Robert Boyle about continuity sketches and sets. Though he had virtually completed his work on Paramount's *Vertigo*, Hitchcock was still operating under an oral contract with MGM.
   "Handshake deals" for Hollywood films sometimes resulted in signed contracts only after a movie was finished. Like the evolution of a screenplay, elements of an agreement were defined, redefined, polished, and then often withdrawn for reconsideration. During negotiation, each party took the measure of the other. For his part, Hitchcock was in no hurry. Selznick's experience suggests that Hitchcock and artists like him habitually dragged their heels in signing a contract: "It's the same old story," Selznick wrote to a business associate in late 1945, "months and months of negotiations, endless con-

versation, yackety-yackety, and no deals.' But MGM may also have stalled the contract talks. In April 1958, it insisted that Hitchcock budget the use of the studio art director, even though he had his own. According to Leonard South, Hitchcock's camera operator, Hitchcock regarded the duplication as a nuisance. He may also have regarded it as encroachment, the studio's subtle attempt to discover its limits in the area of artistic control. Rather than behaving insidiously, though, MGM probably acted chiefly to enhance its fiscal well-being.

Like an individual, a corporation may have a survival instinct, and although an expanded board of directors had given Vogel more support throughout the winter of 1957–58, Loew's was still struggling. According to Wall Street rumor, the corporation lost $1 million monthly on its Culver City operation and borrowed five times that to meet the payroll. In April 1958, for the third straight quarter, Loew's could declare no dividend. In one sense, however, MGM's imposition of an in-house art director—probably done to charge studio overhead to Hitchcock's film—may be construed as encroachment. With regard to the substantive issue of creative autonomy, Hitchcock's interest was pictures, MGM's was profits. To maximize the latter, the studio felt it necessary to control the former.

MGM knew that supervising Hitchcock would be difficult, for the director expected wide latitude during production. A Paramount executive had earlier told MGM's Floyd Hendrickson "that over the last ten years in making deals with Hitchcock [at Paramount], Hitchcock has been given increasingly greater control over every facet of the making of his pictures until now Paramount functions practically as a facility setup for him, and [MGM] should be prepared to give him everything." MGM did not intend to go that far. Paramount, for example, had allowed the rights to *Rear Window, The Trouble with Harry, The Man Who Knew Too Much,* and *Vertigo* to revert to Hitchcock eight years after their release. MGM, which called the arrangement "almost unheard of," maintained that since it assumed one hundred percent of the financing and risk, it retained all rights to its Hitchcock film. It also continued to press for a ceiling on costs. In a final revised written contract with Hitchcock, the studio offered the director "approval of all elements of production . . . provided he agrees that budget for photoplay shall not exceed _____."
But when offered the contract, Hitchcock demurred: he requested that the budget provision be deleted.

MGM's experience in independent production was relatively limited; furthermore, the motion picture unit was still draining profits from its corporate parent, Loew's. Giving an outsider carte blanche must have seemed foolhardy, perhaps even suicidal. In late May 1958, to determine whether its apprehension was justified—and to learn just what others had ceded to Hitchcock—Hendrickson spoke with Warner Brothers and again with Paramount. Since he had come to Warners after Hitchcock had already gone, Warner

Brothers' legal counsel was unaware of how much supervision the studio had exercised over Hitchcock; he knew, however, that Warner Brothers retained final approval of the first screenplay that Hitchcock made on the lot. Quickly scanning Hitchcock's seventy-five page 1948 contract, he also told Hendrickson that he found no "autonomous provisions as to cast, general artistic approval, story, script or editing." Talking again with Paramount, Hendrickson again was told that Hitchcock controlled the whole production and delivered a completed picture. On *Vertigo* and *The Man Who Knew Too Much,* however, Paramount retained the right of budget approval when estimated production costs exceeded $1.1 million. The budgets of both films must have topped that amount, and *North by Northwest* was figured at double it. MGM was beginning to realize that if it wanted Hitchcock, it might have to take him on his terms, including a flexible budget ceiling.

In early summer, MGM and Hitchcock neared completion of a written contract. The last major point of dispute involved, appropriately, a measure of control. MGM insisted on a morals clause, an option that allowed the company to release an employee for deviant behavior. Hitchcock, whose rectitude was Hollywood legend in the 1950s, objected both personally and professionally; in addition, through his agent he argued that Paramount had never inserted such a clause in his employment contracts. Despite Hitchcock's protest, an MGM executive recommended to Hendrickson in early July 1958 that "we should take the position that we will not delete or modify" the clause. The studio's firmness derived not from mistrust of Hitchcock but apparently from an unwillingness to establish a precedent in dealing with independent producers and directors. As a concession to Hitchcock, however, MGM relented. Eighteen months after opening negotiations and less than a month before production began, Hitchcock signed a contract with MGM.

For both the director and the studio, Hitchcock's MGM contract signaled a triumph. In the fall of 1957, *Fortune* had written a prescription for Loew's infirmity: "Vogel must, as quickly as possible, establish a climate at M.G.M. that will attract top creative talent — producers, writers, directors, and actors — and then surround and support their projects with businesslike practices in budgetary control, promotion, and distribution." Hitchcock represented the artist, Sol Siegel the businessman. After almost two years without an experienced production head, MGM hired Sol Siegel in April 1958 to fill the position left vacant when Dore Schary was terminated in 1956. But Siegel, the independent producer of one of the studio's few hits of the mid-1950s, *High Society* (1956), had little authority. By contract, Hitchcock exercised nearly exclusive control over his work at MGM.

The significance of the director's contract should not be underestimated. Over a period of years, Hitchcock had established a working relationship with Paramount that film by film had increased his creative autonomy. Now he had been afforded great freedom by a studio for whom he had never worked. His

MGM contract thus consolidated his independence: it implied that his control over production was absolute, that it could successfully be transferred from one studio to another, intact. Loew's, whose net earnings per share for 1957 had been a nine-cent deficit, could only hope that independence implied responsibility and promised success.

While in June 1958 associate producer Herbert Coleman, director of photography Robert Burks, and production designer Robert Boyle conducted a location search in the East and Midwest, MGM had its initial look at the first-draft screenplay. Its interests centered on budget, legal clearances, and potential Production Code violations. At this point, although the Rushmore sequence was only vaguely sketched, other narrative elements were sufficiently clear for executives to estimate the film's production cost at $2.3 million. Though an average film in 1958 cost $1 million, few studios produced average films: *The Ten Commandments* (1957), *Around the World in Eighty Days* (1957), and *The Bridge on the River Kwai* (1958) had demonstrated that big profits lay in blockbusters. With equanimity, MGM accepted the $2.3 million budget projection for *The Man on Lincoln's Nose*, a "big" film to be the studio's first in wide-screen VistaVision. To the $2.3 million figure, accountants added thirty percent for overhead, the maximum percentage allowed by Hitchcock's contract, and thereby established the film's total cost.

Part of the overhead involved the administrative expense of clearances and negotiation with the Production Code Administration. For Loew's attorneys, the script raised a host of small and large problems. From every institution or individual whose name, likeness, or image was to appear in the film — including the Greyhound Corporation, Northwest Airlines, Charles Addams — the studio requested formal permission to use the name, likeness, or image. Other legal problems were less routine, certainly larger. The United Nations had told MGM in 1957 that no motion picture company was allowed to film the building or premises. Though MGM had hoped to soften this position by donating color raw stock to the United Nations, it knew by June 1958 that the organization did not intend to cooperate. Its chief objection to the script lay in the murder of a man in the Delegates Lounge, implying a "lack of diligence" by the United Nations internal security force. Hitchcock told MGM that he was "very anxious" to retain the Delegates Lounge for its "beautiful dramatic appearance," but MGM, as a sop to the United Nations, persuaded Lehman to set the murder in the nonrestricted Public Lounge. The studio legal staff's research confirmed meanwhile that no federal or local statute could prevent anyone from photographing the building's exterior. Since requesting support from the New York Police Department — which Hitchcock had reportedly called "New York's Worst" — might result in the police seeking the secretariat's approval, thus tipping off the organization to the studio's plans, MGM recommended that Hitchcock use a candid camera to film exterior shots of the United Nations.

Hitchcock, whose vision of a chase across Mount Rushmore antedated even the film's plot, had projected his budget for sets on the assumption that he could shoot the film's climax at the monument, not the studio. But the South Dakota park authorities had objections. After the monument's superintendent read the first-draft script, still bearing the facetious title *The Man on Lincoln's Nose,* he denied MGM permission to film acts of violence on Mount Rushmore. So final seemed his response that one studio executive termed the situation "hopeless." But in August 1958, MGM location manager Charles Coleman wrote to the superintendent to argue that in the film the monument would thwart the enemy and save the protagonist: "We sincerely believe that it will be symbolically and dramatically satisfying to the people of the United States that this great national memorial, standing there in all its granite glory, becomes the very stumbling block of those who would undermine our country. In the end, the enemies of democracy are defeated by the Shrine of Democracy itself." With the superintendent apparently warm to negotiation, Coleman one month later wrote to promise that "no scene of violence is to show the sculpture [of the presidents] or talus slope [area between the heads] in the background." Per this agreement, the Interior Department gave its permission, and for the present, MGM's relationship with the Interior Department stabilized.

Like the federal government, the movies' own regulatory body would have to read and approve the script. While making *Rebecca* (1940), Hitchcock was first introduced to Hollywood's Production Code Administration. "The whole story of *Rebecca* is the story of a man who has murdered his wife," David Selznick observed; after the PCA altered it, he noted disgustedly, it became "the story of a man who buried a wife who was killed accidentally!" PCA involvement with a film based on an original script began when the producer submitted a first-draft screenplay and continued until the company presented its final release print. If at any point the PCA found a script or film unacceptable — for reasons that included its language, treatment of sex, or presumed offensiveness to a minority group — it so advised the studio; if it ultimately denied a film a Code Seal, most first-run theaters in major cities would refuse to exhibit the film, virtually destroying its profit potential. To distribute a film effectively, then, a studio had to insure that its product could pass the industry's gatekeeper, the PCA.

In his earliest negotiations with MGM, Hitchcock's agent told the studio that after submitting the preview cut of a film, Hitchcock was "not generally concerned with changes required because of censorship." This point, which applied primarily to the censorship laws of individual states and foreign countries, was later incorporated into Hitchcock's signed contract; but to avoid the possibility of expensive retakes or reediting, the studio hoped that Hitchcock would comply with changes as required. The PCA's first reaction to the script arrived in letters during August and September 1958. Though the Administration's concerns were minimal, a single violation of the code could prevent a film from receiving a Code Seal, so producers took every suggestion seriously. In its response to the script, the PCA focused on matters of sexuality. More specifically, it objected to aspects of Vandamm's relationship to Eve and to Leonard. Before the end of the film, the PCA said, MGM should provide "a proper denial" that Eve was Vandamm's mistress. Leonard, whom Lehman had characterized as "effeminate," constituted a more clear-cut problem: "if there is any flavor of homosexuality about the character of Leonard . . . we will not be able to approve the finished picture."

While Hitchcock was filming on location in New York, Chicago, and Mount Rushmore, MGM's Robert Vogel facilitated communication between the PCA and Hitchcock. For the few lines to which the PCA objected, Vogel instructed the associate producer and assistant director to see that protection dialogue was recorded. The MGM executive was more uneasy about the treatment of Leonard: lines could be overdubbed, but nuances in a performance were immutable. In October, Vogel wrote in a memorandum of record that he had "prevailed on Hitchcock to take out [Leonard's] most blatant line of dialogue," the use of the word "sweetie," and "scared [Hitchcock] into avoiding any excesses of movement, etc." Hitchcock's interpretation of what Vogel said would be invaluable here but is undocumented. More than likely, Hitchcock, who was loath to engage in confrontation, felt that the point at stake did not merit a sustained argument; in fact, by understating Leonard's part, the director could simultaneously serve the Code and enrich the character's sexual ambiguity. Searching for Leonard's raison d'être, Martin Landau had seized upon the homosexuality and urged Hitchcock to permit its subtle depiction, but Hitchcock, who had perhaps already conferred with Vogel, replied: "I don't make message movies, Martin." Hitchcock's response drove Leonard's sexuality further inside the character and perhaps served to deepen Landau's shrewd portrayal of a man sexually attracted to his employer, jealous of his mistress.

The last major Code problem centered on the implications of the film's conclusion. In early October the PCA counseled MGM that Thornhill's "reference to 'two ex-wives' seems gratuitous and should be omitted"; by midmonth, it asserted that in the scene in the Pullman upper berth, Thornhill and Eve must be "attired in day clothes" and their behavior must not in any way suggest "an imminent illicit sex affair." Vogel told the PCA that the scene would stress the comedy, not the sex. Privately, he then wrote to Hitchcock: "Believe I can 'con' them into accepting it even if the couple are not wearing full dress." But the PCA remained firm: it insisted that Thornhill and Eve be married in the last scene and that they be dressed for day, not night. When MGM approached Hitchcock about protection footage and alterations of content, however, he apparently proved evasive.

MGM, observing both the letter and the spirit of a contract that guaranteed Hitchcock artistic freedom, had not interfered with day-to-day production, but it grew apprehensive about whether Hitchcock was or was not implementing the PCA's suggestions. It is easy to imagine Hitchcock resorting to his noncommittal Buddha pose and thus further increasing studio paranoia. On one occasion — the PCA's objection to the term "bed down" applied to Eve and Vandamm — the studio first thought that Hitchcock had *not* filmed protection footage, then learned that he had; afterwards, Vogel by memorandum assigned an MGM employee to "make sure the footage isn't — mislaid." Hitchcock's apparent imperviousness to the PCA's recommendations about the film's denouement continued into January 1959. He had previously conceded certain points to the PCA; but as the relentless pace of shooting accelerated, he probably had little patience for such matters.

MGM, which wanted to meet the PCA's nonnegotiable objections as efficiently as possible, could reasonably imagine the following scenario: Irked by the Code Administration's attempted control of his work, Hitchcock might decide to hold out for the sexier ending of his completed film. He was not an Otto Preminger, who in 1955 had United Artists withdraw from the [Motion Picture] Association rather than honor Code regulations; but he might engage in a test of wills that took MGM down to the film's release date. And while Hitchcock stood off the PCA, Loew's would be paying high interest on an undistributed multimillion dollar investment. By the end of January 1959, the studio seemed very concerned: "Please explain to Hitch," MGM production head Sol Siegel wrote to Edd Henry, Hitchcock's representative at MCA, "that we will lose the [Radio City] Music Hall booking for this summer if we get a bad rating from the Production Code." Hitchcock, of course, knew what was at stake, and during postproduction in March 1959 he devised a final shot acceptable to the PCA and appropriate to the film. The playful conclusion, Eve and Thornhill's train racing into a tunnel, probably seemed to Hitchcock to mitigate some of the Code's injuries to the film's close, especially its two lovers' daytime dress. Six days after photographing the last shot, Hitchcock advised Vogel that he would approve all of the PCA's requested changes.

As Hitchcock's assistant Peggy Robertson remembers it, *North by Northwest* was "a perfect film." But during their production, very few Hitchcock films encountered major problems. The director surrounded himself with professionals and expected quality performance. Asked what he would do if someone carelessly ruined a take, Hitchcock replied: "I'd say 'cut,' look in the direction of the [crew member], and expect him not to be there." Hitchcock's definition of happiness was "a clear horizon," and as much as possible he tried to establish a conflict-free environment. In part, his formal dress and decorous relationship with his co-workers acted as a distancing mechanism on the set to keep problems at arm's length or, if they reached him, to defuse their inherent emotions. Hitchcock, for example, reportedly did not speak to extras; when in the auction scene of *North by Northwest* he saw a clump of them all wearing brown, he asked the assistant director to rearrange them. Protocol for him was a protective device. Likewise, his self-proclaimed boredom during filming was perhaps less indifference than its affectation to induce calm and discourage personal engagement.

For most productions, Hitchcock planned thoroughly. Though his $2.3 million budget for *North by Northwest* was high, expenses for all major films had taken quantum jumps in the late 1950s, and MGM was satisfied that Hitchcock, who reputedly knew what he needed and used what he asked for, was no wastrel. An anecdote that centers on a crane best characterizes the day-to-day relationship between Hitchcock and MGM during production. Hitchcock, fond of crane shots, had specified that his camera operator request a Chapman crane for use in New York's Grand Central Station. MGM's production supervisor told Leonard South, Hitchcock's operator, that although the studio did not own a Chapman, it would furnish the director with comparable equipment. But the Chapman was not merely Hitchcock's preference, it was the only crane that would work. When the MGM supervisor insisted that the studio's crane be used, South referred him to Hitchcock. The following day, MGM rented the Chapman from Paramount. This instance of conceded control typifies MGM's dealings with Hitchcock on *North by Northwest*. Despite a series of hand-wringing memoranda that urged the director to maintain the established budget (a reasonable desire given MGM's still uncertain fiscal health in the late 1950s), the studio never denied Hitchcock the materiel necessary to make the film that he envisioned.

On significant and insignificant budget items, MGM satisfied Hitchcock's needs. For Eve's romantic meeting with Thornhill after the mock shooting, Hitchcock wanted to duplicate a South Dakota woodland as he duplicated the United Nations lounge; thus, at the director's request, MGM bought one hundred ponderosa pines from a Rapid City nursery and had them shipped to Los Angeles and "planted" on a studio soundstage. (On film, ironically, the forest looks artificial.) A more expensive problem involved the movie's climax. The impracticality of filming on the monument necessitated the reconstruction of a fabricated Mount Rushmore at MGM, an expense that helped swell the line item for total set operation by sixty percent. But though astonished by the size and cost of the sets, MGM did not protest their construction. In fact, during the first two months of shooting, the studio communicated only once with Hitchcock about finance. In late October, Sol Siegel asked Hitchcock to have his film ready to distribute by 2 March 1959; thereafter, MGM was subject to California state personal property tax on any unshipped film. "To meet this schedule," Siegel wrote to Hitchcock, "will require a very substantial degree of assistance and cooperation from you, which I know we can count upon." Almost $75,000 was at stake on a single film, *North by Northwest*, and "in the aggregate a small fortune. . . ."

By early November, however, studio executives recognized that the film would not be finished in March. Furthermore, earlier predictions of "considerable overage due to additional set costs, complexities of scheduling, and lack of finished script" were proving accurate. At the studio and on location in New York and in Bakersfield, California (where the cropdusting sequence was photographed), Ernest Lehman said that he "worked and reworked over many scenes still unshot, trying to get them 'right'." Ultimately, he stayed with the film for two months beyond the beginning of principal photography, at an additional cost to the production. At the time Lehman went off the payroll, in October 1958, production began to lag. As the original sixty-day shooting schedule was stretched to seventy, perhaps even seventy-five days, the budget projections increased. When translated into overtime salary for expensive talent like Cary Grant, time was most assuredly money. And, to the studio's consternation, the film's cost and MGM's property tax liability rose in tandem. Sol Siegel's next memorandum to Hitchcock, written in early November after a new budget projection of $2.7 million had been announced, sounded a note of alarm and a plea: "I know that you are just as concerned as I am at the manner in which the costs are mounting on your picture. Certainly neither of us contemplated this kind of cost at the outset. Do you think there is anything you can do in the remainder of the work that would have the effect of reducing the indicated final cost?"

Hitchcock, a director known for his economy during production, was cost conscious; indeed, to some small extent his overruns were cutting into his own profit participation. In response to MGM's concern, he eliminated certain shots to be filmed on the monument; once he edited this sequence, he planned to photograph additional closeups only as needed: "These, naturally," he wrote to Sol Siegel, "I do not expect to be very many." Whatever Hitchcock saved at the end, he wished to use at the beginning. In late November, writing again to Siegel, he said that "a script deficiency" necessitated a prologue to clearly establish Thornhill as an advertising executive. As a proposed new main title, Hitchcock would open on Thornhill at work in his office; the camera would then discover rough layout cards in various stages of completion. Though similar to advertisements for *Life* magazine, they would actually be the film's main title sequence. (Interestingly, Hitchcock began his career in motion pictures as a designer of title cards; if photographed, this sequence might have appeared fresher than it seems in print.) But Siegel remonstrated against the idea: noting again in early December that "the final cost of the picture will be far more than we both anticipated," he urged Hitchcock to employ normal titles, as originally budgeted.

Loew's fiscal prospects were improving, yet the company's motion picture unit remained in debt and would need every dollar that *North by Northwest* could save in production and generate in distribution. Still, Hitchcock—a one- or two-take director—may have resented the fact that while Siegel pleaded conservation in Hollywood, the immoderate William Wyler was spending MGM money by the millions in Rome. By the end of 1958, *Ben Hur* had exceeded its original $10 million budget by at least forty percent. Perhaps to compensate for his apparent inability to control the runaway chariot abroad, Siegel tried to reign in expenses on *North by Northwest*. Hitchcock, who did persuade Cary Grant not to charge for his services on a new main title, was ultimately sensitive to MGM's concern; as he told Charles Thomas Samuels, he recognized in fiscal matters "a responsibility to the studios, which I obviously cannot, and would not, take advantage of." By January 1959, with cost overruns threatening to crest at a million dollars beyond original estimates, Hitchcock compromised. He told graphic artist and filmmaker Saul Bass that although *North by Northwest* had run out of money, it still needed a dynamic opening. Charging his friend a "ridiculously low amount," Bass salvaged footage of the company's Manhattan street scenes and created a montage of graphics and visuals in collision. Bernard Herrmann's fandango, like the remainder of his score, enhanced the effect. In the title sequence, then, the pressures of time and money worked to the film's advantage.

In early February 1959, MGM per its contracts with actors and others provided Bass with the wording and size of each title credit. Contemplated was one card that contained two statements: the standard qualifier about a coincidental resemblance between fiction and fact and the acknowledgment of Interior Department cooperation with the production. But executives, not having seen an assembly or rough cut and wary of asking the director to screen one, did not know whether Hitchcock had observed the studio's agreement with the Memorial's superintendent. To save money in case of a government objection, MGM decided to order a title card with and another without the acknowledgment to park authorities. In mid-February, Hitchcock invited Sol Siegel and other MGM executives to watch *North by Northwest*. The matte work on the Mount Rushmore sequence had still not been completed, but Hitchcock had conscientiously avoided depicting violence on the slopes and the heads. The effect of cutting together nonviolent shots on the memorial and violent shots off it, however, was of course to suggest that murder both attempted and accomplished occurred at Rushmore. Accurately, MGM predicted an adverse reaction from the Interior Department.

After the studio preview, Hitchcock told Sol Siegel that "an audience [will] tell us what else to cut." MGM, though, apparently had its own ideas. In March and April, Hitchcock worked more directly with Siegel, and as a result the paper file on *North by Northwest* becomes relatively silent about their relationship. Hitchcock told Truffaut, however, that MGM "put on a lot of pressure to have me eliminate a whole sequence at the end of the picture." Though the director refers specifically to Thornhill and Eve's meeting amidst the ponderosa pines, MGM may first have wanted Hitchcock to trim the Rushmore finale. The studio's anticipated alienation of the Interior Department was not its only concern. At well over two hours, the film simply seemed too long. Preview audiences gave it a preponderance of "excellents" (on a six-point scale, only "outstanding" stood above "excellent"); but virtually all of the negative comments focused on the Rushmore chase: its melodramatic flourishes, its loud music, its length. However effective the film, after two hours certain members of the audience had had enough.

Margaret Booth, MGM's supervising editor, recommended that the Rushmore sequence "should be cut more drastically. . . . We lose values by overriding the chase." Perhaps accepting Hitchcock's partiality to the sequence, MGM sought deletions elsewhere, namely the Thornhill-Eve rendezvous. When Hitchcock held firm, though, MGM did not press him. Ingenuously, Hitchcock told Truffaut "that, although I hadn't asked for it, they'd put in a clause giving me complete artistic control of the picture, regardless of production time, cost, or anything. So I was able to say politely, 'I'm very sorry, but this sequence must remain in the picture'." Hitchcock's statement subtly invokes the myth of the artist undermined by the studio; but documentation strongly suggests that MGM, sometimes against its better judgment, treated Hitchcock fairly. Writing to MGM's New York office, Story Department head Kenneth MacKenna accurately summarized his company's relationship with Hitchcock: "You should know that during our entire association with Mr. Hitchcock, it was the studio's policy to defer to him even when we had no legal obligation to do so in all possible ways." Paramount had told MGM to be prepared to give Hitchcock everything. Within reason, MGM had.

Several reasons account for MGM's deferential treatment of Hitchcock. First, like certain other directors of his generation, Hitchcock belonged to the film colony and shared its conservative philosophy. Since he was not an outsider, MGM probably sensed that it could trust him. In all likelihood, at least at this time, the studio would not have given Otto Preminger the same latitude; when it did hire William Wyler, another reputedly extravagant director, it selected script and cast, thereby trying to limit his control of *Ben Hur.* But MGM also respected Hitchcock's work. Coming from the exhibition wing of Loew's, Vogel must have appreciated Hitchcock's showmanship, his ability to produce an exploitable motion picture. He must have recognized, too, that Hitchcock had earned the right to be left alone. On those rare occasions when corporation executives threatened to overstep their bounds, the director probably leveled his murderous gaze at them. In stature and reputation, Hitchcock demanded respect. Finally, though, MGM understood that Hitchcock and his fellow independents, most of them responsible and popular filmmakers, had the freedom to move their profitable film productions from one studio to another. As much as possible, MGM executives wanted to maintain a good working relationship with the industry's best talent, for Hitchcock and others were guarantors of future success.

In spring 1959, Loew's corporation reported earnings of $1.08 a share for the period ending 12 March 1959, a 1,000 percent increase over the previous year. For stockholders who had not received a dividend in over eighteen months, the news signaled better days for the corporation. Loew's dramatic recovery derived from the fiscal success of MGM, its film-producing unit at Culver City, thus vindicating Joseph Vogel's determination not to liquidate it. A handful of successful 1958–59 films, stemming MGM's flow of red ink, undoubtedly improved company morale. Proudly, Loew's predicted even greater earnings from *Ben Hur,* its entry in the biblical extravaganza sweepstakes. Unlike *North by Northwest, Ben Hur* was not an independent but a $15 million studio production. Paramount's *The Ten Commandments* (1956) had demonstrated the box-office potency of such epics, and MGM stood to generate not only substantial gross receipts but also handsome profits: except for a six to seven percent of the net reserved for director William Wyler, Loew's owned the entire production. For the film, a $3 million promotional campaign was planned and in April 1959 already under way.

With honest but unfounded apprehension, Ernest Lehman feared that MGM's publicity department might undersell *North by Northwest.* "No picture of this size and cost that I know of has ever been such a well-kept secret," he wrote to Sol Siegel on 28 April 1959, no doubt exaggerating to make his point. "Hitch is off at Paramount. I'm here at Fox. We've done all we can. But [Publicity Department head] Howard [Strickling] is there at Metro. And our fate is in his hands. Millions of dollars worth of fate, in a shrinking, competitive market. Please?" MGM had no intention of burying a $3.3 million feature. Prior to its midsummer release, the studio purchased advertising for *North by Northwest* in *Life, True, McCalls, Cosmopolitan, Look, Redbook, Saturday Evening Post, Seventeen, True Story,* and numerous fan magazines. Many of the ads carried a photograph of Thornhill embracing and kissing Eve in their upper berth; through careful cropping well above the waist, this still had conformed to the Advertising Code Administration's demand that "the finished sketches [must] not look as though the man were trying to climb on top of the girl." (See, for example, the advertisement in *Life,* 22 June 1959, p. 17.) Observing in spirit its own agreement with the Interior Department, MGM in its copy carefully worded references to Mount Rushmore: the climax occurred not *on* the great stone face but *at* or *amid* the monument. Despite these restrictions, the advertisement suggested romance and adventure, well stirred by the prominently featured "Master of Suspense."

Ever willing to promote his work, Hitchcock and the Hitchcock persona figured conspicuously in the *North by Northwest* campaign. *Alfred Hitchcock Presents,* his CBS television program, ran a ten-second clip of the film as well as an announcement about it throughout the summer of 1959. MGM also tied into print advertising for Mercedes-Benz (early in the film, Thornhill "steals" a Mercedes); in photographs in national magazines, Hitchcock posed regally alongside Leo the Lion, MGM's mascot, in a shiny Mercedes. Though Hitchcock willingly traveled for the film, he clearly specified by contract the limits of his involvement. First, he would not appear on television, other than his own program. Second, he would speak to reporters only one at a time, not en masse. An MGM executive explained this "personal idiosyncrasy": Hitchcock "feels he can be charming and persuasive with one person, but he feels lost and uncommunicative when a group is present. In any case, this is what he wants and this is what he will have to get." Third, out of town he would stay only in first-class accommodations, with MGM paying his and his wife's expenses. Although the studio knew that the Hitchcocks "will not live cheaply," it again maintained a policy of noninterference. "I hope they will be reasonable," Marvin Schenck wrote to Loew's in New York, but "I don't think it would be good policy to try and pin [Hitchcock] down to a definite amount."

With Hitchcock and Eva Marie Saint on hand, *North by Northwest* premiered at Chicago's United Artist Theater on 1 July 1959. *The Chicago Tribune*, with a few reservations, called the movie "a frolicsome concoction." Seldom have "suspense, intrigue, comedy, humor" been "served up so delectably," *Variety* noted; "it should be top b.o." It was. MGM's man-in-Chicago wrote to Howard Strickling that *North by Northwest* "opened to the best business ever for an MGM motion picture at the United Artist theatre"; at the end of four weeks, it became MGM's biggest grossing release in Chicago for 1959. Running for seven weeks at New York's Radio City Music Hall, it also broke a house record for an MGM film in that theater. *North by Northwest* turned a profit in America, then went abroad. In Paris, according to Howard Strickling, it garnered excellent reviews and attendance. A few discouraging words were heard: the Interior Department requested that the studio remove the acknowledgment of Park Service cooperation, and *Motion Picture Daily* objected to "an open and unnecessary reference to homosexuality" (apparently Vandamm's assertion that Leonard is jealous of Eve). But audiences, critics, studio executives, and the film's creators shared in its critical and commercial triumph.

By the end of 1959, *North by Northwest* had become the year's sixth top-grossing film. Though the budget for it had reached $3.3 million, without overhead, the studio was satisfied to have a moneymaking hit. More important, after reluctantly ceding substantial power to a major director, MGM ended fiscal 1959 with earnings of $2.91 a share, the highest since just after the war. Hitchcock and a profitable *North by Northwest* had helped solidify the company's filmmaking unit within Loew's corporate structure and ease the studio's transition into independent production, the dominant industrial force of the 1960s. For his part, Hitchcock had won effective control of the means of production, exercised his creative autonomy judiciously, and produced a film that remained one of his happiest production experiences.

Why, then, did Hitchcock direct only one film at MGM? While working at MGM, whose ever-conservative management was even more cautious in the late 1950s, Hitchcock may have felt hampered, but certain factors suggest that studio and director saw eye to eye on important points. Talking with Philip Scheuer of the *Los Angeles Times* in December 1958, Hitchcock reflected on the rapacity of artists: "The male stars are practically running their own companies. They don't want salaries any more; they don't even want percentages; they want ownership of the negative." With a note of triumph Hitchcock concluded, MGM "is one company that won't agree to it." In his television persona, Hitchcock may have ridiculed the sponsor, but privately he respected it. Hitchcock himself was a conservative — in dress, in manner, in aesthetic. In all likelihood, though he wanted freedom to produce, he may also have wanted assurance that the studio could maintain the economic power necessary to confer that freedom. To a man with many fears, Loew's fiscal insecurity may unconsciously have been unsettling.

But to say that Hitchcock *left* MGM, rather than *went to* Universal, may be inaccurate. Universal was attractive in part because Lew Wasserman, Hitchcock's close friend, ran it; when the director had prepared his next project, Universal may also have offered him the best deal. It is doubtful, however, that it afforded him greater authority than he had enjoyed at MGM. According to John Russell Taylor, Hitchcock's biographer, Universal specifically forbade him, by contract, to make *Mary Rose,* a science-fiction tale that he especially wanted to produce. But circumstances at Universal, indeed throughout the motion picture industry as a whole, may by default have given Hitchcock and other directors more breathing room. In the 1960s, feature film production became secondary to the companies that controlled the studios; preoccupation with television, leisure parks, electronics, hotels, and other profit-seeking ventures must surely have affected management of the corporation's motion picture divisions and thus the nature and extent of its interests in any director's or producer's work.

In the 1970s, the letters that loomed above Sunset and Vine and spelled "Hollywood" seemed to be the film capital's last link with its past. MGM, for example, nearly went out of the motion picture business altogether; ironically, at its Las Vegas hotel, whose corridors were lined with giant photographs of former MGM stars, it mounted elaborate revues that celebrated the splendor of American movies. Chiefly a producer and packager of television programming, Universal distributed two Hitchcock films in the 1970s. Though *Frenzy* (1972) was critically praised, *Family Plot* (1976) — despite Ernest Lehman's witty script and some Hitchcock flourishes — met with only mixed reviews. Younger directors produced the decade's important work. Paramount's *The Godfather* (1972) became the industry's biggest financial success in its history, established the reputation of film school graduate Francis Ford Coppola, and ushered in a new generation of independents. Working in studios that had become almost exclusively distributors or lessors of sound stages, directors like Coppola, Martin Scorsese, Steven Spielberg, George Lucas, and Michael Cimino replicated the conventional work of their predecessors but occasionally used what freedom they had to discard formulas for more experimental or more personal films.

In the 1980s, when Coppola bought—and later sold—a studio and Lucas began building one, the so-called majors inched back into filmmaking. Though MGM, recently merged with United Artists, has not returned to full production, its lot is again active, and other studios that once worked for directors are now hiring them. Furthermore, as United Artists' belated control over *Heaven's Gate* (1980) illustrated, motion picture companies are reasserting a certain authority over the artists and products that they finance. In short, the revolution of 1955 to 1960 seems to have come full circle. One fact remains: filmmakers' desire for "complete creative autonomy" will continue to conflict with studios' demand for maximum fiscal control. The way out of this bind is north by northwest. As geographers and film scholars know, however, no such compass point exists.

Notes

The legal files on Alfred Hitchcock (6137), the writing of *North by Northwest* (7632), and the production of *North by Northwest* (1743)—all housed in the Thalberg Building, Metro-Goldwyn-Mayer, Culver City, California—provided key data used in the preparation of this essay. Specimen contracts, memoranda, working budgets, conference notes, letters, and other documents helped flesh out the relationship between studio and director. Without the interest and generous assistance of MGM's Michael Nathanson and Herbert Nusbaum, this essay could never have been written; the author thanks them both.

Numerous people associated with *North by Northwest* consented to be interviewed. In person: production designer Robert Boyle (7 August 1981), actor Martin Landau (1 July 1982), screenwriter Ernest Lehman (30 July 1981), production assistant Peggie Robertson (9 August 1981), actress Eva Marie Saint (28 June 1982), assistant director Robert Saunders (7 August 1981). By telephone: titles designer Saul Bass (27 July 1982) and camera operator Leonard South (13 July 1982). Their vivid memories of helping to create *North by Northwest* deepened my understanding and appreciation of their work.

Published interviews with and works about Hitchcock were helpful, especially *Memo from David O. Selznick*, ed. Rudy Behlmer (New York: Viking Press, 1972); Charles Thomas Samuels, *Encountering Directors* (New York: Capricorn Books, 1972); John Russell Taylor, *Hitch: The Life and Times of Alfred Hitchcock* (New York: Pantheon Books, 1978); François Truffaut, *Hitchcock*, trans. Helen G. Scott (New York: Simon & Schuster, 1967).

Information about the evolution of the script for *North by Northwest* derived primarily from conference notes and manuscript drafts in the Ernest Lehman Collection, Hoblitzelle Theatre Arts Library, Humanities Research Center, The University of Texas at Austin.

Information about the film's Production Code Administration clearance came from the MGM legal files and from the PCA files at the Motion Picture Association of America, New York City.

Consulted about Loew's Incorporated in the 1950s were financial data in *Moody's Industrial Manual* (1956–60) and numerous articles in *The Wall Street Journal, Business Week, Fortune, The New York Times*, and *Time*. Especially valuable were Emmet John Hughes, "M.G.M.: War among the Lion Tamers," *Fortune*, August 1957, 98–103ff.; "Loew's to Report Sharp Gain in Fiscal '59 Net," *The Wall Street Journal*, 3 September 1959, 19, cols. 2–3; Dore Schary, "Hollywood Fade Out, Fade In," *The Reporter*, 18 April 1957, 20–25; Robert Scheehan, "The Cliff-Hanger at M.G.M.," *Fortune*, October 1957, 134–35ff.; Colin Young, "The Old Dependables," *Film Quarterly*, vol. 13, no. 1 (1959): 2–17. Anecdotal but useful was Charles Higham, *Hollywood at Sunset* (New York: Saturday Review Press, 1972).

Finally, the clippings files and the knowledgeable staff of the Margaret Herrick Library, Academy of Motion Picture Arts and Sciences, Los Angeles, proved indispensable in tracking press coverage of Hitchcock, MGM, and *North by Northwest*.

PART TWO

Hitchcock in Britain

If critics refused for so long to consider Hitchcock as a serious artist, they merely reflected the pose of popular entertainer that the director carefully created for himself during the years he worked in the British film industry. Early in his career, Hitchcock appears to have realized that his own best interests lay in aligning himself—at least in words—with those who believed that the making of movies depended upon the production of entertainment, not art. As John Russell Taylor recalls in his biography of the director, Hitchcock "often said that one of the great misfortunes was when someone had the bright idea of calling the place that films were made a 'studio,' with all its artistic overtones, rather than a factory" (p. 41). This is not to suggest, however, that Hitchcock was indifferent to the aesthetics of the medium. Working in Germany on *The Blackguard* (1925) gave him ample opportunity to observe film production at the UFA studios at Neubabelsberg where he watched F. W. Murnau shooting the innovative *The Last Laugh*. Furthermore, Hitchcock attended screenings of other aesthetically innovative European films throughout the remainder of the decade as a member of the London Film Society. Thus even as a neophyte director, Hitchcock was in all likelihood well aware of the artistic issues and achievements which animated continental filmmakers as the silent film flowered into a supplely expressive medium.

As biographical evidence suggests, however, Hitchcock quickly learned that similar artistic aspirations on his part were a liability in the no-nonsense business of British film production. No one made this clearer than C. M. Woolf, the head of the company which handled distribution for Hitchcock's employer, Gainsborough Pictures. Woolf declared the first three films which Hitchcock directed to be uncommercial and shelved them. Though the films had received favorable reactions at press screenings, Woolf judged them too arty for general audiences. Thus while the major trade journal, *The Bioscope*, called *The Lodger* "a directorial triumph" in its 16 September 1926 issue, declaring that "it is possible that this film is the finest production ever made," Woolf withheld *The Lodger* from release to theaters until 14 February 1927. Only the intervention of Michael Balcon, the head of Gainsborough, made the film's release possible. He hired Adrian Brunel and Ivor Montagu, ironically two of the founders of the London Film Society, to work with Hitchcock in improving the film. Together, they eliminated many intertitles, added atmospheric title cards designed by E. McKnight Kauffer, and rephotographed a few sequences. Finally, six months after its press preview, *The Lodger* was released, to popular acclaim.

For the next six years, Hitchcock worked for British International Pictures, joining them in 1927 for a salary that made him the highest paid director in England. Despite his salary, Hitchcock lacked the authority to control his projects and the quality of his films varied greatly. In 1933 Hitchcock teamed again with Balcon and Montagu at Gaumont British Pictures for the first four of the thrillers which would securely establish his international reputation: *The Man Who Knew Too Much* (1934), *The 39 Steps* (1935), *Secret Agent* (1936), and *Sabotage* (1936).

Even at this late date, however, Hitchcock was not entirely free of the arbitrary control of distributors. His successful reunion with Balcon and Montagu for *The Man Who Knew Too Much* also reunited him with C. M. Woolf, who again acted as their distributor. Despite the success of *The Man Who Knew Too Much*, Woolf cancelled the production of *The 39 Steps* after reading the script prepared by Hitchcock and Montagu and tried to set the director to work, instead, on a musical called *The Floradora Girl*. Only Balcon's return from the United States managed to set *The 39 Steps* into production as he overruled Woolf.

Hitchcock appears to have realized fairly early in his career that his survival in the film industry depended upon both the commercial success of his films and the public's awareness of him as a director. The international success of his thrillers of the middle and late 1930s consolidated Hitchcock's reputation within the industry as a commercial director and attracted the interest of Hollywood producers. Since the later 1920s Hitchcock had also worked just as hard at making himself a household name for reviewers and the general public. Even the caricature profile by which Hitchcock is still known was invented by him for this purpose and mailed out to recipients in the form of a jigsaw puzzle as a Christmas greeting in 1927. In recalling Hitchcock's problems with C. M. Woolf during this time, Ivor Montagu told interviewers for *Screen* that it was only through such shrewd self-promotion that Hitchcock was finally able to gain some measure of control over his work by the late 1930s. As Montagu explained, Hitchcock designed his films to win good press notices so the public would quickly learn his name:

> The public did not generally know who directed the films they saw, but they had seen Hitchcock's name in the Press. The result was that every group that was floating a new company during the Quota Act wanted Hitch under contract in order to attract money. Hitch was able to go from company to company improving his position and contract each time. This is the way his career was made. (Wollen et al., p. 80)

While the public learned his name and face, Hitchcock made sure that neither they nor those for whom he worked would learn of his underlying artistic interests. These were increasingly hidden during the 1930s within the codes of the classical narrative film. Yet as the following six essays devoted to his English films attest, critics have come to recognize the abiding marks of Hitchcock's artistic concerns even if practical need eventually forced him to deny their existence. As Lesley Brill argues, Hitchcock's self-conscious manipulations of the thriller's conventions in *The Lodger,* along with his formalist experiments, encourage viewers to reflect upon the film's double status "as a work of art as well as a representation of life." Thus while Hitchcock finally may have learned to hide behind the public reputation of a popular entertainer in order to survive within the crudely commercial industry which viewed art with mistrust, critics have come to insist that he nevertheless inscribes himself as an artist, frame by frame, within the continuity of his films.

It should not be surprising, then, that these six essays repeatedly rely upon the close analysis of images and patterns of cutting to identify and discuss Hitchcock's artistry. At a thematic level, this artistry often defines itself through references to the stage and to acting, references which, as William Rothman suggests in his discussion of *Murder!,* permit Hitchcock to differentiate his interests from those of the established theatrical tradition. Thus in treating the stage as a subject, *Murder!* articulates "its reflection on its nature as a film."

As Hitchcock's repeated trouble with C. M. Woolf suggests, he was prudent to subdue his overtly self-conscious manipulation of the medium during these years. Elisabeth Weis's discussion of this process in relation to Hitchcock's use of sound in *The Man Who Knew Too Much* carefully explains how these formal experiments drew increasingly less attention to themselves as Hitchcock learned to motivate their innovative qualities within the framework of the classical cinematic codes. By so doing, Hitchcock could appeal to the mass audiences satisfied by a story told at breakneck speed, while rewarding at the same time the minority audiences who took pleasure from his testing of the medium's expressive possibilities.

Thinking about Hitchcock's films therefore invites a double awareness of his skills as both a commercial director able to entertain an international audience and, within these limits, as an original artist, actively engaged in exploring the narrative and stylistic possibilities of the medium. As Leland Poague argues in his discussion of *Blackmail,* a similar doubleness necessarily informs every interpretive endeavor as well, as each critic's personal interest in a particular film is shaped by and responds to the history of that film's critical reception. Thus in their respective essays on *The 39 Steps* and *The Lady Vanishes,* Charles L. P. Silet and Patrice Petro urge readers to look beyond received interpretations of these films to consider how both assert a place for feminist values in what many have taken to be Hitchcock's resolutely paternalistic films.

References and Suggested Readings

Anderegg, Michael A. "Conrad and Hitchcock: *The Secret Agent* Inspires *Sabotage.*" *Literature/Film Quarterly,* vol. 3, no. 3 (1975): 215–26.

Armes, Roy. *A Critical History of British Cinema.* New York: Oxford Univ. Press, 1978.

Barr, Charles. "*Blackmail:* Silent and Sound." *Sight and Sound,* vol. 52, no. 2 (1983): 189–93.

Bond, Kirk. "The Other Alfred Hitchcock." *Film Culture,* no. 41 (1966): 30–35.

Bordwell, David, and Kristin Thompson. *Film Art: An Introduction.* Reading, Mass.: Addison-Wesley, 1979, 239–43. On *The Man Who Knew Too Much.*

Browne, Nicholas. *The Rhetoric of Filmic Narration.* Ann Arbor, Mich.: UMI Research Press, 1982, 25–56. On *The 39 Steps.*

Camp, Jocelyn. "John Buchan and Alfred Hitchcock." *Literature/Film Quarterly,* vol. 6, no. 3 (1978): 230–40. On *The 39 Steps* and *North by Northwest.*

Everson, William K. "Rediscovery: *Easy Virtue.*" *Films in Review,* vol. 26, no. 5 (1975): 293–96+.

Goodwin, James. "Conrad and Hitchcock: Secret Sharers." In Michael Klein and Gillian Parker, eds. *The English Novel and the Movies.* New York: Ungar, 1981, 218–27. On *Sabotage.*

Kinder, Marsha, and Beverle Houston. *Close-Up: A Critical Perspective on Film.* New York: Harcourt Brace Jovanovich, 1972, 52–58. On *Blackmail.*

Linderman, Deborah. "The Screen in Hitchcock's *Blackmail.*" *Wide Angle,* vol. 4, no. 1 (1980): 20–28.

Low, Rachael. *The History of the British Film, 1918-1929.* London: Allen & Unwin, 1971.

McDougall, Stuart Y. "Mirth, Sexuality, and Suspense: Alfred Hitchcock's Adaptation of *The Thirty-Nine Steps.*" *Literature/Film Quarterly,* vol. 3, no. 3 (1975): 232–39.

Manville, Roger. "Revaluations (7): *The Lodger.*" *Sight and Sound,* vol. 19, no. 9 (1951): 377–78.

Noble, Peter. *Index to the Work of Alfred Hitchcock.* Supplement to *Sight and Sound,* Index Series no. 18, May (1949).

Ringle, Henry. "*Blackmail:* The Opening of Hitchcock's Surrealistic Eye." *Film Heritage,* vol. 9, no. 2 (1974): 17–25.

Stanbrook, Alan. "*The Lady Vanishes.*" *Films and Filming,* vol. 9, no. 10 (1963): 43–47.

Taylor, John Russell. *Hitch: The Life and Times of Alfred Hitchcock.* New York: Pantheon Books, 1978.

———. "The Last Great Silent Director." *Take One,* vol. 5, no. 2 (1976): 13–20.

Smith, John. "Conservative Individualism: A Selection of English Hitchcock." *Screen,* vol. 13, no. 3 (1972): 51–70.

Wollen, Peter, Alan Lovell, and Sam Rohdie. "Interview with Ivor Montagu." *Screen,* vol. 13, no. 3 (1972): 71–113.

Yacowar, Maurice. "The Best of the Earliest." *Take One,* vol. 5, no. 2 (1976): 42–44.

———. *Hitchcock's British Films.* Hamden, Conn.: Archon Books, 1977.

CHAPTER FIVE

Hitchcock's *The Lodger*

Lesley W. Brill

Following its director's lead, most critics identify *The Lodger* as the "first Hitchcockian" film.[1] In his third feature-length movie, Hitchcock made his first venture into what Maurice Yacowar calls the "genre of suspense," dealt with the theme of the unjustly accused innocent for the first of many times, and exhibited the conspicuous technical flash which has done so much for him at the box office. Despite its acknowledged importance as an early marker in Hitchcock's career, however, *The Lodger* has received little attention—a few short essays and the inconclusive remarks critics make as they bustle past it en route to the films they really want to talk about.[2] It deserves more careful scrutiny. Its significance in Hitchcock's career is underrated if it is regarded as little more than his first work of suspense. It displays, additionally, the mythic echoes, the complication of characterization, the self-conscious attitude towards its own formulae, and the social themes which run through Hitchcock's work for a half-century following.

The shaping mythic structure in *The Lodger* and in Hitchcock's films generally has gone virtually unnoticed. This aspect of *The Lodger* appears as a modern version of the Persephone (or Proserpine) myth; but as a broad tendency in Hitchcock's art, it is perhaps best called "romance," in the sense of a narrative genre strongly informed by folklore and fairy tale, classical myth, certain stories in the Bible, and the literary derivatives of all of them. The structures of comic romance in particular—with its sprawling quests, miraculous coincidences, fearsomely evil antagonists, and emblematic marriages—organize the narratives and imagery of most of Hitchcock's films.

Since Hitchcock has reworked the Persephone myth according to the conventions of a commercial film of 1926, it may be useful to review the original briefly before examining its metamorphosis in *The Lodger*. The daughter of Zeus and Demeter, Persephone is seized and carried down to Hades by Pluto while she is gathering flowers with her handmaidens. Demeter seeks her vainly until Zeus convinces Pluto to release her. But because she ate part of a pomegranate while in the underworld, Persephone is doomed to spend a portion of each year in Hades. She is thus associated mythologically with the appearance and growth of vegetation, especially flowers, in the spring and summer and with its dying and disappearance in fall and winter. It may be relevant to *The Lodger* that Persephone's abductor is invisible and not able to be propitiated by sacrifice.

In *The Lodger* Hitchcock changes the actors from gods into men and locates the action entirely upon earth. The essential features of the underlying myth are further obscured by the circumstance that the film starts in the midst of the story which it returns to complete only in a late flashback. By the end of the movie we understand the sequence of events in the Lodger's quest to be as follows. The Lodger is dancing with his sister at her coming-out ball when a mysterious hand turns off the ballroom lights. When they are turned back on, his sister is discovered to have been murdered in his arms. His mother has thereby suffered a shock that will send her to her death also, but before she dies she asks her son to promise to pursue "the Avenger," whose triangular mark and signature were found by the body of her murdered daughter. (All this information is imparted by the flashback.) The Lodger's sister proves to be the first of a series of golden-haired girls murdered by the Avenger, and the geographical pattern of these killings brings her brother to the neighborhood of the Buntings in anticipation of the next crime. He takes rooms in the Buntings's house where his suspicious behavior and his growing closeness to Daisy Bunting bring him under the scrutiny of a police detective suitor. He is arrested, escapes in handcuffs, and is nearly killed by a mob which believes him to be the Avenger; but the police detective learns just in time that the real Avenger has been caught and rescues him from the mob. He marries Daisy or becomes engaged to her—it is not quite clear—and takes her home to his magnificent mansion. There, in the last sequence, he entertains his awed working-class in-laws and embraces his bride while "TONIGHT GOLDEN CURLS" flashes in the London background as it did in the opening sequence.

The echoes of the Persephone myth are a bit confused, but suggestive. Like Demeter's daughter, the Lodger's golden-haired sister is assaulted, while in the company of an attendant crowd, by an assailant who seems to rise up from the underworld and disappear as abruptly as he came. The Lodger descends into the strange dark world of London (the film is subtitled "A Tale of the London Fog") and rescues another golden-haired girl with whom he returns to the bright and (socially) higher world of his home. The Demeter-figure, the Lodger's mother, has transferred her authority as searcher to her son, and the Persephone-figure is abducted in the person of his sister and recovered in the person of his new wife; but despite these and other alterations of the original myth, the outlines remain.

The imagery which dresses the plot is evocative of the mythic antecedent of the film. The ball at which the Lodger's sister is murdered is brilliantly lit and shot from predominantly low camera angles which make it appear to be a brighter, higher world than the dark, foggy London into which the Lodger descends on his quest. Darkness, as a mysterious hand that turns off the lights just before the murder of the Lodger's sister, erupts to seize the first Persephone-figure and the second is carried up from the persistently shadowy world of her parents' flat to the brilliant mansion in which she clearly belongs. The insatiability of the Avenger associates him with the unpropitiable king of the underworld. He commits his crimes in the darkness of Tuesday nights against golden-haired girls, emblems of the light (the flashing sign advertising "Golden Curls" is literally embodied in light). Daisy, in keeping with this imagery, is generally shot in bright light and shown full of gaity. Her name emphasizes her relationship to Persephone. In this very sparely titled silent, Hitchcock insists upon its significance with a pair of titles, at least one of which is entirely superfluous from a narrative standpoint, which say only "Daisy." The presence of her parents in the final sequence suggests that she, like Persephone, will have to return occasionally to a lower world; not a symbolic Hades, perhaps, but a place closer to the underworld than the Lodger's mansion. "All stories have an end" reads the title that introduces the last sequence. It thus emphasizes the formulaic quality of Hitchcock's film, the fact that it is a story somehow like "all stories." As it concludes, the golden-haired Daisy is in her lofty brilliant palace, the Avenger is out of business, and "TONIGHT GOLDEN CURLS" is again flashing in the background, but this time promising an imminent marital embrace rather than murder on a dark bridge over a symbolic Styx. "The End" is superimposed, significantly, on a shot of luxuriant foliage tossing in the wind. Summer has returned.

It is worth observing that the influence of the Persephone story may also account in part for one of the more puzzling details of *The Lodger,* its evocation of Christ on the cross when its hero is trapped on the spikes of an iron fence. The story of Christ, like that of Persephone, has to do with descent and return, death and resurrection. Its evocation in a narrative infused with those themes, then, seems consistent and appropriate. As I shall argue later, it is fitting for other reasons as well.

How the Persephone myth came to be embodied in *The Lodger* is a question that is beyond the scope of this essay. Several general points about its presence can be made, however. First, the mythic elements of plot and imagery are artifacts of the film only; they are not to be found in the novel by Marie Belloc-Lowndes on which the movie is loosely based. Second, the outcropping of such mythic bedrock recurs in Hitchcock's films throughout his career. Wicked stepmother figures in *Rebecca* and *Under Capricorn,* echoes of *Job* in *The Wrong Man* and of the fall from Eden in *Frenzy,* the romantic quests of *The 39 Steps* and *Sabotage* are a few among many examples. Third, the mythic component of the film clarifies the import of certain details—Daisy's name and the foliage behind the final title, for example—and solidifies the coherence of its plot.

When we turn to other aspects of *The Lodger* we again see that it often anticipates its director's later films. The almost schematic but nevertheless complicated treatment of characters is thoroughly Hitchcockian. The contrast between the Lodger and Joe, his rival, organizes the characterization of all the important figures. Ordinary looking, somewhat burly, and unmistakably middle-class, Joe carries himself with a rough cordiality against which the Lodger's dark, slim beauty and gentle reserve appear exotic. Though the camera is manipulated to give the Lodger an air of menace, his actions are characteristically protective. The scene in which he is discovered with Daisy in his arms after she has been frightened by a mouse typifies his solicitousness, as does his expression of distaste when he rushes into the hall after hearing a scream and finds Joe jocularly handcuffing Daisy to the newel post. Earlier Joe cheerfully declares, "After I put a rope around the Avenger's neck, I'll put a ring on Daisy's finger." As this remark and the handcuffing suggest, Joe extends his hunt-and-catch profession into his courtship. When he later puts handcuffs on the Lodger, he symbolically links Daisy and his rival as victims of his assaults. In contrast to Joe's rough clutching, Hitchcock sets a delicate symbol of the subtle intimacy growing between the Lodger and Daisy. During the scene in which they play chess, the Lodger and Daisy sit facing each other over a small table. Behind the table the arch of a fireplace rainbows between the two players and expresses, in contrast to the opposition of the chess game, a joining, a coming together. (Hitchcock was to use this symbol of lovers' concord again, for example, in *Secret Agent* [1936] when the arch of a bridge in the backgound pairs Mr. and Mrs. Ashenden as they confess their love for each other and in *Saboteur* [1942] when the lovers are framed at a crucial moment in their relationship by an arched door.)

Evidently somewhat older than Daisy, Joe seems to be associated as much with her parents as with her. The Lodger, on the other hand, is Daisy's age and has virtually no social contact with her parents, who are suspicious of him. Like Daisy's parents, Joe is solidly middle-class. The Lodger, for most of the film, has the air at once of a criminal and of a gentleman. He will prove to be the latter, of course, but for most of the story it is his equivocal status as much as his gentility which contrasts with the social clarity of the representative of law and order who is his rival. An indication of both their social status and the eventual outcome of their rivalry may be found in Hitchcock's characteristically symbolic use of stairs and interior levels. He generally shows Joe coming down the outside steps which lead from street level to the basement kitchen of Daisy's parents. There Joe visits Daisy and socializes with her parents. The Lodger's rooms are upstairs and, as a consequence, we usually see him ascending. Daisy's parents seem uneasy in that part of the house, and Joe is there only twice, both episodes of sharp hostility. Only Daisy appears to be a comfortable and welcome visitor to the second floor.

The association of Joe with downstairs and the parents and the Lodger with upstairs and Daisy has both social and archetypal consistency. If Daisy recalls Persephone, she also reminds us of Cinderella with the Lodger as her prince. The dress that the Lodger buys her serves as a glass slipper, a token of her suitability for a more refined world. The Lodger realizes while watching Daisy in the fashion show that she belongs in a mansion on a hill rather than a shabby flat along the Embankment. It is worth noticing that stories like "Cinderella" usually contain a female blocking figure—a stepmother, wicked witch, or jealous hag. Hitchcock mildly evokes such a figure in Daisy's mother, who distrusts and fears the Lodger and resists the budding affection between him and Daisy. Until the very end of the movie she favors Joe's suit almost to the point of collaboration. Daisy's father, though he is partly under his wife's sway, seems more inclined to trust the Lodger, and in the last scene he nudges his wife clownishly in the ribs to draw her attention to the tenderness between the two lovers. His action pointedly parallels an early scene in which Daisy's mother had nudged him during some amorous play between Daisy and Joe.

In general outlines the Lodger anticipates many of Hitchcock's protagonists at the outset of their careers. Somewhat isolated and under unjust suspicion, he is also attractive, unmated, of marriageable age, and inappropriately tied in some sense to family members whom he ought to be leaving for a spouse. (In the Lodger's case the ties consist of the memory of his dead sister and the promise to his mother; but the late flashback to his dancing with his sister suggests the mild retardation of development that Hitchcock often gives his main characters at the beginnings of his films.) Daisy, too, needs to escape her somewhat protracted dependence on her parents, while Joe serves as an early example of a typical Hitchcockian Mr. Wrong—wrong age (a little too old), wrong class, wrong style, wrong intuitions. Such is the stuff of Hitchcock's triangular configurations of characters: Sir John, Diana, and Fane in *Murder!* (1930); Robert Tisdall, Erica, and her father in *Young and Innocent* (1937); Jack, Charlie, and Uncle Charlie in *Shadow of a Doubt* (1943); Roger Thornhill, Eve Kendall, and Vandamm in *North by Northwest* (1959)—one could go on and on. Looking back across more than fifty films, one sees only a handful of exceptions to the disposition of characters which Hitchcock worked out in *The Lodger*. Joe must lose, the Lodger must triumph, and Daisy must find the arms of her proper gentleman prince.

Joe and the Lodger are rivals not only for Daisy but also in their pursuit of the Avenger. Their portrayal as hunters of the murderer involves them with the more general question of how society as a whole responds to the crimes. The reaction of London at large to the Avenger's crimes is the theme of the opening movement of the film. In the first shot the head of a light-haired young woman fills the frame; we see her scream. Immediately a crowd gathers to gape at the victim, newspaper reporters phone their central offices, presses roll, and distribution trucks rush into the streets. "Tuesday's my lucky day," crows a paper seller. Radio accounts are broadcast and eagerly consumed. For his amusement and to the alarm of a witness giving a statement to the police, a bystander at the scene pulls his coat across his face and pretends to be the murderer. Later we will see a young man play the same joke on a chorus girl in the show "Golden Curls"—ironically, for she proves to be the Avenger's next victim. The sequence that conveys society's response to the murders runs surprisingly long and gains emphasis from the repetition of several series of similar images.

Why this concern with social response? Part of the answer is, I believe, the obvious one: Hitchcock devotes the opening of the film—second in rhetorical importance only to its end—to social reactions because the murders have great significance for the whole society; they are not represented as an isolated aberration. Furthermore, the opening sequence establishes the extremes of an isolated individual and an unparticularized crowd between which the central concerns of *The Lodger* lie. First we see the face of a single woman, screaming for help that does not come; then we witness the social appropriation of her tragedy by crowds of people whose identities flow together as smoothly as the dissolves of the radio listeners' faces. Between the solitary victim and the crowds, and illuminated by both perspectives, are the central figures of the film.

London's response to the murders is to make of them entertainment, a source of titillation for the idly curious. Details both in the opening and in later sequences indicate that the amusement the people of London find in the Avenger's murders is related to the voyeurist pleasures they take in fair-haired young women more generally. The murders occupy an extreme place on a scale of entertainments, but the important point is that they are on a scale at all. The film does not portray them as socially incongruous acts. "Golden Curls," with its blond chorines, represents one aspect of the general fascination with fair young women; Daisy's job as a model is another. The pictures in the Lodger's rooms suggest that golden curls are consumed even in middle-class houses, and their sexy (in one case sadistic) renditions relate them to the Avenger's monstrous obsession. Even the Lodger is implicated. "Beautiful golden hair," he says, stretching his hand toward Daisy's head. The most suggestive indication that the Avenger's criminal passion has ordinary analogues occurs when the Lodger first kisses Daisy: the camera is very tight on Daisy's face, which is framed obliquely and lighted like the faces of the Avenger's victims.

Joe's attitude toward the Avenger is determined by both his public and his private interests. From the public viewpoint, as a police detective, Joe regards the Avenger with the amused interest of London at large. He bets Daisy's father that the criminal will be caught before the next Tuesday and is delighted to be assigned to such an entertaining and well-publicized case. But he has private interests as well, interests foreshadowed more clearly than he understands when he makes his remark about putting a rope around the

Avenger's neck and a ring on Daisy's finger. This personal interest climaxes with Joe's arrest of the Lodger. The Lodger and Daisy, out together despite the opposition of Daisy's mother, are confronted by Joe as they sit together on a park bench. Joe irritably claims that Daisy is *his* girl, the Lodger rises indignantly, and Daisy tells Joe that she never wants to see him again. She and the Lodger walk off, leaving a disconsolate Joe sitting on the bench alone. Head hanging, he gazes absentmindedly at the footprints of the just departed Lodger which (thanks to some deft lab work) begin to fill with inculpating images of his rival. Suddenly "on the track" of the Avenger, Joe rushes off to get a warrant for the search of the Lodger's rooms that leads to his arrest. The sequence makes the self-interest of Joe's suspicion unequivocal. Like the rest of London's citizens, Joe finds the Avenger murders a source of entertainment; and like the newspaper people and the radio broadcasters, he also finds in the crimes furtherance of his private interests.

Almost alone in London, the Lodger has an entirely serious interest in the Avenger's crimes. This fact, along with their contest for Daisy, brings him into conflict with Joe. For unlike Joe — and London at large — the Lodger expects no personal profit or pleasure from his pursuit of the Avenger. Already a victim of the Avenger through the deaths of his sister and mother, he will suffer again in his "crucifixion" by the tavern mob. From the social as well as the mythological perspective, then, the association of Christ and the Lodger is appropriate. The Lodger's sister is the first, and the Lodger himself is the last, to suffer from the Avenger's crimes. In his dedication to pursuing the criminal and in his near dismemberment by the mob, he may be seen as a redemptive figure, one who suffers not on his own behalf but in place of the truly guilty, the society which gave rise to the Avenger and is implicated by association in his crimes. The fact that the Avenger is apprehended at the same time the Lodger is arrested and attacked by the mob underscores the redemptive aspect of the Lodger's sacrifice. The explicatives in the detective's two titles during this sequence are perhaps more resonant than usual: "My God, he is innocent" and "Thank God I got here in time."

Joe, who incites the mob against the Lodger, also rescues him from them. As clearly as Hitchcock renders the contrasts between his central male characters, he does not make either one uniformly vicious or valiant. Not only does Joe, in an act of personal and professional integrity, save his rival but he is allowed to attract some empathy throughout. When Daisy returns Joe's cookie-dough heart and, more clearly, when she rejects him after he's discovered her with the Lodger on the bench, we are likely to sympathize with his disappointment even while finding it mildly comic. For all his rough edges, Joe behaves in a straightforward manner and has an unfeigned affection for the heroine of the film. The Lodger, on the other hand, carries a slight stain of the vigilante and outlaw, however just and gentle the main lines of Hitchcock's drawing show him.

The mild suggestions of tarnish on the hero of *The Lodger* must not be exaggerated, however, or the central themes of the film are rendered incoherent. It grossly deforms the tone of the Lodger's characterization to argue that "the Avenger is only doing on a larger scale what the hero, the avenger, would do."[3] One critic actually makes the Lodger more culpable than the Avenger: "He intends to kill the killer, and his crime — not of passion or a deranged mind . . . is a carefully premeditated act of hatred."[4] Such interpretations turn the diffident figure portrayed by Ivor Novello into something like Hawthorne's Roger Chillingworth, a revenge-obsessed monomaniac. We do not know, in fact, that the Lodger "intends to kill the killer"; he never says so, and his possession of a gun is hardly conclusive proof of such an intention. To equate the Avenger with the hero asks us to forget that the former is a madman who has killed innocent young women and the latter is the grieving brother of one of his victims.

Although she appears on first consideration to be the most clearly stereotyped figure in the film, Daisy's character nonetheless includes rich complications. A golden girl living below her natural station, she is surprisingly receptive to Joe's rather coarse attentions, especially early in the film. At the same time, she often retreats from him for no apparent reason. Her readiness for love precedes the arrival of its proper object, and her on and off responsiveness comes on the one hand from her desire and on the other from her intuition of the detective's unsuitability. When the Lodger arrives, Daisy immediately feels the pull of his attraction. Her prior involvement with Joe and her confusion about her own feelings lead to some intricate choreography. After Joe has angered her by playfully handcuffing her, for example, Daisy kisses him (in front of an approving mother) by way of forgiveness. Having done so, she immediately detaches herself and skips upstairs to the Lodger, leaving behind a puzzled detective and perhaps a puzzled film audience as well. Daisy's ambivalent interest in the two men lasts until nearly the end of the film. It is echoed by triangular composition within the film frame and by prominent details of the sets — repeated shots of the chandelier, for instance, with its three glass shades. Medium shots very frequently include three figures. The triangles which decorate the titles and the Avenger's triangular logo underscore the broad implications of the love triangle as a motive for the action of the film.[5]

Daisy is both the likely prey of the Avenger and the protector of the Lodger. Thus she is potentially victim and savior, a young woman murdered or a wife — only at the end of the film can we be sure which possibility will be realized. (The prolonging of suspense implies substantial similarity between two roles which coexist so persistently.) When Daisy finally goes home with the Lodger, she has found someone like her in the most crucial ways. She protects her protector and, a revitalizing-Persephone figure herself, marries another redemptive figure. At the risk of belaboring a point, Hitchcock's treatment of the relation between Daisy and the Lodger again anticipates his later films.

Love in Hitchcock's work is nearly always mutually healing and transforming. The gallant heroes who carry away their loves need to be lifted up and carried themselves; without each other, both lovers in most Hitchcock films are misplaced and alienated.

Without each other they are also endangered. The on-screen murders of the two fair-haired young women and the arrest of the Lodger dramatize the vulnerability of the unprotected to misdirected erotic energies. The second murder occurs, significantly, after the victim and her boyfriend have quarreled and separated in anger, leaving her exposed to the sexual madman who stalks the London fog. It is hard to judge how far to push the implications of the fact that the Avenger's first victim, the Lodger's sister, is murdered while dancing in her brother's arms; but the suggestions which arise from her "coming-out ball" seem clearer. *The Lodger* is concerned both with right courtship and marriage and with the dangers of growing up and going out. In *Easy Virtue* (1927), *Notorious* (1946), *Psycho* (1960), and *Frenzy* (1973) the theme recurs: men and women—especially women—face terrible dangers from the distorted amorous impulses of other people when they are away from or fail to find their proper mates. Daisy and the Lodger might well look gratefully heavenward as they stand in each other's arms at the end of their adventures.

Among other themes and motifs typical of Hitchcock's art is a clear sense of physical geography and an equally clear sense of social geography, class consciousness; both do a great deal to define the ambiance of *The Lodger*. Hitchcock's famously unenthusiastic view of the police appears clearly in this early film, as does his less well-known but more consistent demophobia. (In a Hitchcock film any group of people larger than roughly half a dozen registers as a mob—conformist, unimaginative, inhumane. A curious variant on this pattern occurs in *The Birds,* in which the peaceful intimacy of a pair of lovebirds is set against the mob frenzy of the flocks that attack Bodega Bay.) These themes do not appear as emphatically in *The Lodger* as they do in other Hitchcock movies, but their presence demonstrates again how early in his career he found his central concerns.

Equally typical and of considerably more importance in *The Lodger* is Hitchcock's self-conscious treatment of the mystery genre, the playfulness with which he treats its more conspicuous conventions and his systematic manipulation of the audience's expectations. As the subtitle promises, most of the photography is dismally atmospheric. The murders are portrayed by the stylized heads of screaming women and there is a memorable low-angle shot of a line of police marching through the night. Hitchcock relentlessly uses the conventions of the murder mystery to cast suspicion upon the Lodger. He appears first, shrouded in fog and masked by his muffler, on the Buntings's doorstep just after the gaslights have abruptly gone off in the house. The Buntings, of course, live at No. 13. His rooms are full of spooky shadows. He behaves eccentrically: sneaking outside in the middle of the night, carelessly leaving money lying about his room (an idea Hitchcock repeats in the opening of *Shadow of a Doubt*), and making oracular pronouncements about the concerns of Providence. Radical camera angles and suggestive cutting give innocent gestures an aura of menace. Obvious examples include the occasions when the Lodger reaches for a poker to stir the fire and when he tries the bathroom doorknob while Daisy is in the tub (another idea, the vulnerability of a bathing woman, that Hitchcock was to use effectively later in his career). The famous shot through the ceiling of the room below the Lodger's chambers casts further suspicion on him.

The obvious conclusion that these sequences show the unreliability of appearances has been drawn often enough. Equally, however, they show the unreliability of the conventions of the genre. In doing so they emphasize the self-consciousness of the film, its tendency to draw the viewer's attention to its status as a work of art as well as a representation of life. *The Lodger* gives its audience the sort of images they can easily recognize as conventional; Hitchcock did not invent the game, but he played it enthusiastically throughout his career. In *The Lodger* Hitchcock's manipulations of the conventions of the mystery-thriller enrich the other modes of the film. A modern mystery story encompasses the shape of an ancient myth; an entertainment based on Jack the Ripper portrays a society titillating itself with accounts of murders. There is a mild suggestion that such imitation and social appropriation help people to deal with the fear engendered by violent, random crimes. The two men who mimic the Avenger in the film both intend to produce the relief of laughter, though neither meets with overwhelming success. What is true of the social transformations of the Avenger's crimes within the film is true of the film itself. It too makes of murder an entertainment; it too transforms anxieties into stylized, distanced, cathartic representations. "The technique of art and the technique of life," as Sir John calls this mingling of real and fictional events in *Murder!,* blur and twine in *The Lodger.*

While the film, like the media it portrays, exploits the sensational appeal of homicide, it also brings to its subject a complex personal and social understanding quite unlike media accounts. The voyeuristic eyes suggested by the rear windows of the newspaper van represent only too well the public perspective on violent crimes, then and now.[6] But Hitchcock's early silent turns its eyes to the more human perspective of Joe, the Lodger, Daisy, and her parents. *The Lodger,* like most of Hitchcock's films for the next half-century, is a love story in which suspense and loss occasion resolution and marriage. It is, additionally, a self-conscious narrative turning its gaze inward at itself as well as outward at its characters and action. In doing so it asks, in contrast to the blankly staring eyes of the newspaper van, what it is and who is watching.

Hitchcock has complained that the presence of Ivor Novello as leading man compelled an exonerating ending for the film.[7] The changes he made in adapting the novel to the screen bring the narrative into a shape so characteristic of his later work, however, that I think we can discount as superficial the influence of the matinee idol on *The Lodger* as a whole. What Hitchcock changed, and kept, in Marie Belloc-Lowndes's novel shows clearly his characteristic romanticism, social concerns, and self-consciousness as a storyteller. The center of attention in the novel, and the source of most of its point of view, is the landlady, Mrs. Bunting; in the film the center of attention shifts to the three younger people; and the point of view, with a few interruptions, is objective. The film adds Daisy's job as a model, a change that emphasizes her natural nobility. It changes the Lodger from a sham to a real gentleman and from a murderer to the innocent pursuer of the Avenger. As it makes him into a type of Christ it also removes a theme of religious dementia which is prominent in the novel. From a few mild hints in the Lowndes story the film develops the involvement of Daisy and the Lodger, and it adds entirely the rivalry between the Lodger and Joe. Hitchcock kept most of the details which in the novel eventually reveal the Lodger's true identity as the murderer, but in the film they are used deceptively to suggest a spurious guilt. The film preserves almost unchanged from the novel the gossipy interest of media and populace in the Avenger's crimes, but it pushes the implications of that interest harder. The flashback to the sister's coming out exists only in the film, of course, as does the associated imagery invoking the Persephone myth. The changes that Hitchcock made in adapting the novel all incorporate the themes and motives that were to characterize his entire career. In Marie Belloc-Lowndes's story he found, not those concerns, but materials to be reshaped and converted. At age twenty-seven Hitchcock showed a remarkably secure grasp of what were to be his central artistic preoccupations for the next fifty years. His conceptions were clear, and he was confident enough to treat a popular novel by a well-known writer with extreme freedom. One might add in closing that such license with his sources is also characteristically Hitchcockian.

Notes

1. In François Truffaut, *Hitchcock* (London: Panther Books, 1969), 48, Hitchcock calls *The Lodger* "the first true 'Hitchcock movie'."
2. Since I wrote this essay, William Rothman has published *Hitchcock—The Murderous Gaze* (Cambridge, Mass.: Harvard Univ. Press, 1982) which includes an extended treatment of *The Lodger.* He is concerned largely to discuss "the relationship of author and viewers" in that film. His analysis thus overlaps only slightly the subjects of my discussion.
3. Maurice Yacowar, *Hitchcock's British Films* (Hamden, Conn.: Archon Books, 1977), 40.
4. Donald Spoto, *The Art of Alfred Hitchcock* (Garden City, N.Y.: Doubleday, 1976), 7.
5. Yacowar discusses "the contrast of circle and triangle shapes," 38.
6. Hitchcock discusses this shot in Truffaut, 50.
7. Truffaut, 48–49.

THE LODGER (Gainsborough, 1926). *Producer:* Michael Balcon, *Script:* Alfred Hitchcock, Eliot Stannard, from the novel by Marie Belloc-Lowndes, *Assistant Director:* Alma Reville, *Photography:* Giovanni Ventigmilia, *Editor:* Ivor Montagu, *Sets:* Wilfred Arnold, Bertram Evans, *Players:* Ivor Novello (the Lodger), June (Daisy), Marie Ault (Daisy's mother), Arthur Chesney (Daisy's father), Malcolm Keen (Joe). 100 minutes.

Criticism and/as History: Rereading *Blackmail*

Leland Poague

In the essay on *Psycho* which concludes this volume, I discuss a view of the relationship of a given artwork to its historical (genetic) context which assumes that a text (even a film text) has a "once-and-for-all existence, a once-and-for-all relationship to other texts which is marked and determined by the circumstances of its origin."[1] Once a regressive text, always a regressive text.[2] Such a view of art history or of history generally is remarkably and obviously problematic; disallowing significant change effectively disallows "history" at all. A hopeful response to this problem as it bears on film criticism is seen in the fact that film scholars have lately doubled the history question by acknowledging that at least two histories are involved in any interpretive act: the history of the text itself and the history of the reader or viewer. As Stephen Crofts has recently made the point in *Wide Angle:* "Not only the author and the text, but just as importantly, the reading must be seen as historically and culturally shaped. Time and place will, almost always, divide the moment of production from the moment of reading. The 'meaning' of any text will thus vary. . . ."[3]

A similar, though far more fully worked out model of this "dualistic" or "relational" view of art history (one I propose to explore briefly and very provisionally in the following remarks on Alfred Hitchcock's *Blackmail*) is that suggested in the "reception theory" of Hans-Georg Gadamer and Hans Robert Jauss. Crucial to the work of both is a view of interpretation as a process, an explicitly historical process, which mediates or holds in tension the two historical moments or perspectives ("horizons") which might otherwise be taken as mutually exclusive, the "present" of the work and the "present" of the reader. The underlying theoretical point is simple, however complex its implications may be: our sense of the past is always already influenced by our present understanding of the world (we see the past through the present); and yet our present understanding of the world is itself always already influenced and determined by the past (we see the present through the past). Among Gadamer's contributions to the debate over the relation of history to understanding is the suggestion that we need to see past and present as involved in dialogue with one another, hence his interest in the concept of "tradition" as the arena where such "conversation" takes place.[4] Each interpreter "speaks" from his or her own historically situated present, as does the past itself, but the cumulative presence of many "speakers" serves as a check on interpretation, as a means of insuring that no one interpretation is crippled by its own preconceptions or subjectivity, however unavoidable preconceptions must be. Jauss, then, extends Gadamer's notion of dialogue, which Gadamer applies to all interpretive contexts, to more explicit questions of literary history.

Without elaborating further on the precise nature of that extension (Jauss wishes to allow for criticism of the tradition, even to the point of forgetting it), I wish to extract from Jauss two key interpretive principles to guide the following discussion of Hitchcock's *Blackmail*. One involves the question/answer nature of the past/present dialogue "according to which the past work can answer and 'say something' to us only when the present observer has posed the question that draws it back out of its seclusion" in the past.[5] Each work is thought of as answering to some prior (historical) question; thus interpretation involves reconstruction of the question, though such reconstruction need not rely particularly on evidence external to the text beyond that implicit in its generic and linguistic circumstances (see Jauss, p. 24; also Gadamer, pp. 335–36). The second principle I would extract from Jauss is the crucial importance of the tradition of criticism itself as being nearly synonymous with the history of the work's "reception." Precisely because of its crucial status as an early instance of sound on film there exists a sustained tradition of commentary on *Blackmail*. By and large I see the present remarks as an extension and contribution to that tradition of reception—though my primary focus will be on elucidating two questions (and their implications) which *Blackmail* may be understood as answering. In the process I hope to make the degree of my critical (historical) indebtedness clear.

Discussion of *Blackmail* generally begins with the curious fact that Hitchcock shot the film twice—or at least in such a way as to produce two distinct versions (one silent, one sound) where only one had been initially authorized.[6] We might say that in filming *Blackmail* twice Hitchcock attempted to avoid the question which sound posed. But the sound-on-film version of *Blackmail* is so extraordinary—to the point of seeming retroactively "modernistic" after the advent of filmmakers like Jean-Luc Godard—that "avoidance" is hardly an appropriate characterization of Hitchcock's accomplishment. Indeed, *Blackmail* is often taken to be a sustained reflection on the possible relations of sight to sound, of visual to aural aspects of film style, and we can usefully discuss the film by exploring the view which takes *Blackmail* as Hitchcock's answer to the question of the meaning and uses of sound in the cinema.

At least to judge by the promises splashed across its original advertise-

ments—"The First Full Length All Talkie Film Made in Great Britain," "Our
Mother Tongue As It Should Be Spoken," "Hold Everything Till You've Heard
This One"—*Blackmail*'s original audience may well have approached the film
with an expectation of fullness, of plenitude, of transparence: no longer would
cinema be hampered by the partiality of its representation of the real, by the
divorce of voice from speaker. But Hitchcock promptly counters this expectation in the first reel, which depicts the apparently routine location and apprehension of a criminal by a Scotland Yard "flying squad." The sequence moves
(literally, many of the shots having been taken through the windshield of the
moving police van) with a freedom and speed characteristic of the late silent
period: there are sound effects, to be sure, and musical accompaniment, but
no effort is made to eliminate moments when conversation is filmed though
not recorded. Hitchcock even plays with the sound/silence distinction at the
end of the sequence when the film's heroine, Alice White, shares a whispered
joke with a police sergeant: we hear the resulting laughter, but cannot share in
it for having missed the joke, just like Frank, Alice's detective sweetheart, who
can do no more than join weakly in the laughter to cover his discomfort at
being excluded from the gag. This play with sound is not limited, however, to
the film's opening few moments. We can describe the film as having five
primary "movements" each of which is characterizable (at least in part) by
particular variations on the sound/silence relationship.

Part One: detection (directions are received by wireless as the flying squad
van is en route), apprehension and arrest, interrogation, incarceration, relaxation (as the detectives clean up at the end of their shift). Synchronized conversations are kept to a minimum in this section, and the conversations we do hear
(often spoken by characters with their backs to the camera) are partial or
indistinct. Here visuals carry the primary burden of information.

Part Two: Alice's date. She meets Frank in the lobby of Scotland Yard
headquarters (Frank and a colleague pass through glass doors to get to her, the
doors serving almost as a dividing line between silence and sound). Frank and
Alice quibble about Frank's being half an hour late. Leave the Yard. Ride the
underground to another section of London (Hitchcock makes his cameo appearance as a fellow passenger) and make their way to an upper floor of a
crowded restaurant. They argue about what to do for the evening: shall they
see a detective film (a "picture") or not? Frank in frustration (and self-confi-
dence) walks out on Alice, assuming (perhaps) that she will follow him and
apologize, only to see her leave the establishment on the arm of another man.
Alice's date then continues (what she and the second man do is unspecified)
and concludes at the man's flat, just around the corner from Alice's King's
Road home where her parents run a news agency and tobacco shop. The man,
an artist, invites her to see his studio. Alice hesitates. Crewe (the artist) speaks
briefly to a passerby. Alice and Crewe ascend to his flat. Drinks. Music. Attempted rape. Death.

Throughout this part of *Blackmail* synchronized sound and conversation are crucial to the development and understanding of the course of events. The dialogue, as often noted, verges on the banal, but that very banality is crucial to an understanding of character and action. The catch here, as in most of the film, is that dialogue works at several levels at once, banality at one level thus becoming significance at another. Example: Alice thrice changes her mind about going to the cinema. The third time Frank assumes she is being either flighty or playful, hence his theatrical exit. The viewer, by contrast, knows that Alice's playfulness is of a different, potentially more serious order. We have seen the note in Alice's purse, and the exchange of glances between Alice and Crewe. Visuals thus set dialogue in context; but the interaction is mutual — dialogue sets visuals in context as well, and as crucially.

Part Three: Alice's nightmare, the most frequently discussed section of the film. Here we find some of the most often cited instances of visual and aural distortion in all of Hitchcock: the neón cocktail shaker which Alice "White" ("Gordon's White Purity") sees transformed into a neon carving knife mechanically, repeatedly stabbing at the "cock" in "cocktail"; the chirping birds in Alice's bedroom upon her return home, their chirps increasingly amplified as Alice "wakes up" (Alice pretends to be asleep when her mother enters and uncovers the bird cage; Alice's bedclothes are printed in a tree branch motif, as if she were herself a bird); the word "knife," repeated over and over again by a local gossip discussing the prior evening's crime, amplified and abstracted from the surrounding conversation until it seems (to Alice, framed in close-up) a shout of accusation; etc. It all has a subjective, dream-like quality to it, a quality confirmed by the fact that the sequence may be said to begin when Alice emerges in her slip from behind the curtains of Crewe's bed; progresses for what seems a somnambulist's eternity as she walks from Crewe's flat to her own home (which she had earlier described as being just around the corner) and as she gets back into bed, reemerges, and goes down for breakfast; and concludes with the famous clanging doorbell, which announces the entrance of Frank and the beginning of the film's next-to-final section.

Intercut with Alice's sleepwalking is another sequence of events — the landlady's report of the crime (she seems completely unfamiliar with the telephone and can barely make herself understood) and the initial stages of the investigation, including Frank's discovery of Alice's glove on the floor beneath the cartoon nude she and Crewe had painted only hours before. Without doubting the "reality" of these events, it is also reasonable to see them as internal projections of Alice's fevered consciousness (akin to Marion Crane's "fine soft flesh" soliloquy in *Psycho*), which reading is confirmed by the cut from Alice screaming at the sight of a drunkard's arm to the landlady (similarly framed) as she screams at the sight of Crewe's dead body, as if the landlady were herself a figure of Alice's guilty conscience. Synchronous dialogue plays very little part in this section of *Blackmail*.

Part Four: Frank enters the shop to ask Alice about the glove, immediately followed by Tracy, the blackmailer, as if Tracy were shadowing him, as if Tracy were his shadow (as he had been earlier, of Alice: we see the shadow of his hat on the door of Crewe's flat as Alice leaves—which hat closely resembles Frank's). Tracy wants money for his silence (Tracy has the other glove, the twin of the one Frank found), though he couches his demand in terms of doing "business" (telling Frank and Alice they are fortunate he found the glove instead of someone else: "there are some men who would make money" but he "couldn't do a thing like that"). Tracy invites himself to breakfast. The police interrogate the landlady at Scotland Yard headquarters and decide to bring Tracy in for questioning ("Let's hear what he's got to say"). Frank receives a phone call in the booth inside Mr. White's shop—evidently, to judge by Frank's subsequent actions, instructions to arrest Tracy on the testimony of Crewe's landlady. Tracy threatens to implicate Alice ("She was there too"); Frank replies that his word, and Alice's, "are a bit better" than that of a jailbird. Tracy, desperate, bolts through a back window. The chase leads to the British Museum; Alice writes her confession. Tracy falls through the glass of the cupola over the museum's reading room.

Language, both written and aural, is perhaps more crucial to this section of *Blackmail* than to any of the other four segments, though its significance seems often to be overlooked. Partly this involves the necessary "indirection" of much of the dialogue, especially that connected with Tracy's blackmail scheme. But not all the dialogue in this section is indirect in the same manner. Consider, for example, the dialogue which follows Frank's phone conversation with Scotland Yard.

It is a commonplace of *Blackmail* scholarship that Frank and Alice turn the tables on Tracy, becoming blackmailers themselves in the process. But this is not what happens. The case against Tracy has nothing to do with Frank and Alice. Frank simply undertakes to carry out the order for Tracy's arrest. Tracy wants to escape before additional police arrive and threatens to talk. Frank offers no payment in return for Tracy's silence, nor does he request payment in return for his (he refuses Tracy's offer to return Frank's initial payment); Frank simply offers threat for threat, sound for sound, his word as opposed to Tracy's. Moreover, at this point, Frank does not rule out testimony from Alice (she will "speak at the right moment"), though he perhaps assumes, falsely, what her testimony will be. Indeed, Frank's guilt and Tracy's are far more a matter of things not said, of things elided or presumed, than the contrary. Perhaps Frank's greatest failing is not his "holding back" of evidence (if Frank were not Alice's sweetheart we would simply have, at least to this point, an instance of a cop collecting evidence, part of his job, and confronting a suspect, i.e., Alice, with it). Rather, Frank's most overtly culpable gesture is his willingness, with only a moment's hesitation, to pay the blackmail price Tracy asks, as if he believed all along that Alice was indeed guilty. Yet all he really has to go on is the fact of Alice's glove and the memory of Alice and Crewe departing the restaurant in high good spirits.

Tracy's case (our reading of his case) depends even more upon ellipsis and inference than Frank's. His anxious response to the threat of arrest far exceeds the obvious gravity of the situation confronting him. He still has Alice's other glove, has witnesses to his "friendship" with Alice and Frank, has considerable evidence that Alice herself will awaken from her trance and tell the truth (as she tries to do). So what is he trying to hide? We never know for sure, but it is clear that his relationship with Crewe significantly predates the evening of Alice's visit to Crewe's flat (the landlady tells Crewe that Tracy had called several times; Crewe seems to know Tracy when hailed on the steps of his apartment building). Perhaps Tracy is already in the blackmail business, even before Crewe takes Alice up to his flat. So we cannot simply say that it is the silence of Frank and Alice which drives Tracy to his death. Indeed, his death is directly coincident with his own attempt to turn tables: he pauses in his flight to accuse Frank, cringes as his pursuers rush toward him, and breaks through the glass of the dome. (Again the figure of ellipsis: Hitchcock's framing here, as later in *Vertigo,* makes it impossible to determine whether Tracy really trips or whether the glass merely gives way as Tracy shifts his weight.)

Part Five: After writing her confession, Alice stands up into the noose-like shadow cast by the window next to her. Dissolve, then, to the Scotland Yard plaque, after which Alice enters and asks to see the chief inspector. She is required to fill out a form, waits until an escort arrives to lead her to the inspector's office, and is finally shown into the presence of Frank and his superior. Frank attempts to stall her confession, asking if it is "worthwhile" (given the Yard's presumption that Tracy was the murderer); Alice herself delays a moment by saying how hard it will be to speak the truth—at which point the phone rings and the inspector turns Alice over to Frank, who then escorts her to the outer lobby. En route Frank pockets her note (the form she filled out), and she confesses that she "didn't know" what she was doing the night of Crewe's death. In the lobby the police sergeant jokes once again with Alice, aloud this time rather than in a whisper: if she told Frank who did it (in the sense of solving the mystery rather than of confessing to the crime) then Scotland Yard will soon have women detectives. And the joke is clinched when Alice sees Crewe's "Laughing Harlequin," along with the cartoon nude of her which she and Crewe had painted the night of his death, carted together, back to back, into the silent depths of Scotland Yard.

How can we construe the forgoing sequence of cinematic events as offering an answer to the question of the value of sound on film for the development of film language or of Hitchcock's particular ideolect or form of film speech? Two kinds of answer to this question are commonly available in the tradition of reception of *Blackmail*. One is to assert that Hitchcock's play with the silence/ sound relationship in *Blackmail* amounts to an idictment of "the limitations of verbal communication" (hence of the expectation that sound would be "all talking" and hence "all answering").[7] In this respect Hitchcock can be compared (as Marsha Kinder and Beverle Houston have done) to Crewe's "Laughing Harlequin" — both remain essentially silent, but in their silence they mock the expectation "of poetic justice and the effectiveness of verbal communication" (p. 58). Such an answer, we might say, depends upon seeing Hitchcock as the cause and *Blackmail* the effect, so that the unconventional or unexpected use of sound is taken primarily as a token of authorial autonomy and control. Another kind of answer takes the opposite tack and assigns causality to character subjectivity, as if film sound were only partially, at one remove, under directorial control. In *Hitchcock's British Films,* for example, Maurice Yacowar draws an insightful analogy between the workings of language in the world of *Blackmail* and the workings of the law: each depends upon the characters who use it, rather than upon the director per se. Thus Alice's personal association of the word "knife" with her stabbing of Crewe "corrupts the function of 'knife' in social language, as Frank's personal twist will corrupt the social function of justice later."[8] A third kind of answer to the question of Hitchcock's valuation of sound combines the first two, again by means of analogy.

Rather than see sound as more or less exclusively at the mercy of Hitchcock's authorial will or as subordinate to or determined by the lives and actions of characters in the depicted world of the film, we can have it both ways (as Deborah Linderman does) by pressing the analogy between Hitchcock and Crewe's "Harlequin" or, at least, between Hitchcock and Crewe. Both are artists who use the language of cinema, of visual and aural representation (Crewe both paints and sings), which language is itself a kind of law (at least in the scenario provided by Lacanian psychology), to pervert or deny the full (if unspeakable) humanity of Alice White — just as Frank, at film's end, denies her the opportunity to redeem herself through confession. In part what *Blackmail* represents *is* silence, if not of the audience, at least of Alice White. In this view the distance between Crewe's (apparently failed) attempt at rape and Frank's (successful) attempt to silence Alice is minimal. And the difference between Hitchcock and Crewe is only a little less so. The key difference here is that Hitchcock is himself confessing (knowingly or not) to the coercive power of his art, including its power, via an illusory expectation of visual and aural plenitude, over him. At best the film is a species of joke or witticism, *re*pressing by *ex*pressing: "The film perpetuates with great wit an intertextual ethos of repression of the feminine by raising the sophistication of its own level of desire whereby the ultimate blackmail is that proffered by the text to its proper character."[9]

One needn't concur with (or, for that matter, fully comprehend) the Lacanian logic invoked by Linderman's essay on *Blackmail* to find it intriguing and suggestive, though her emphasis on the question of Alice's confession seems somewhat skewed if Alice has nothing to confess, i.e., if Alice is to be seen as so thoroughly a product of the "male gaze" as to be nothing more than a (scandalous) token of "difference." But Linderman's "doubling" of the notion of authorship (as if the scene in Crewe's apartment has two authors, Crewe and Hitchcock, each of whom ultimately succumbs to the seductive power of his art) raises a second question to which *Blackmail* may be read as answering, though neither the film nor this particular reading of it can stand as a final or complete answer, that is, the question of the relationship of public to private as mediated by the notion of art.

The question comes to mind under the influence of Fredric Jameson's lengthy and thoughtful review of William Rothman's *Hitchcock — The Murderous Gaze*, itself a thorough and thoughtful reflection upon the nature of Hitchcock's artistic and cinematic accomplishments. Neither Rothman nor Jameson is easily summarized, but what I would take from both relates to the notion of "doubleness" urged above in connection with Gadamer and Jauss. Briefly put, Jameson understands Rothman as offering an "allegorical" reading of Hitchcock which depends on the very nature of the medium itself, almost on its "historical" nature, as figured for both Rothman and Jameson by the fact of the camera itself, which always exists in two worlds at once — the real world, wherein "the camera is the instrument of a real relationship between author and viewer," and the film world, in which "the camera has the power to penetrate its subjects' privacy, without their knowledge or authorization."[10]

Each film always takes place in both worlds, thus always tells two stories, one involving the relationships of characters to each other, the other involving our relationship as viewers to Hitchcock as the author-in-the-text; hence "the content of the film is an allegory of the latter's form, or to be more precise, the events within the film are an allegory of the latter's consumption."[11] Jameson doubles all this one step further by offering a "genealogical" reading of Hitchcock which he means to stand as corrective to Rothman. That is, Jameson wants to ask the question of the historical "conditions of possibility" in which such films could be made or, once made, could be read as Rothman reads them. And that condition of possibility, for Jameson, is late-stage capitalism, especially urban capitalism, wherein human relationships and functions (even within particular individuals) are divided, differentiated, alienated. Thus Jameson cites the later Metz ("The Imaginery Signifier") to confirm the almost schizophrenic character of the film-viewing experience (equally active and passive) and correlates this with the equally schizophrenic character of modern urban living, wherein so many of our actions and perceptions seem just as automatic, just as "material and anonymous," as the experience of film viewing itself, as if each (capitalism, cinema) called forth the other. Only under such circumstances, or so I take Jameson to imply, can the question of the relation of public to private be asked. I believe that Hitchcock asks it in *Blackmail*.

The relationship of public to private in *Blackmail* is especially complicated. For example, the film's opening sequence, the arrest and interrogation of some sort of criminal, seems on first viewing a remarkably "public" event— indeed, the intrusion of public authority into a private life. But through the course of the film the whole sequence takes on a very "private" quality via its relationship to Frank, who seems at first simply an actor in the public drama but for whom the drama takes on an increasingly private and personal significance. Partly this has to do with the resonances established retroactively with later scenes: Frank's pocketing of the criminal's gun recalls (and vice versa) the moment when he pulls Alice's glove from his coat pocket in the phone booth of her father's shop; his helping the crook to get dressed recalls his deference to Tracy while Tracy has the upper hand; the rock thrown through the window anticipates Tracy's exit through the window of the White's dining room—not to mention the criminal's addictions to newspapers and cigarettes (Alice's father runs a news agency and tobacco shop). But mostly it has to do with the degree of Frank's displeasure when Alice refuses to take an interest in the detective film he looks forward to seeing. He may be confident the filmmakers will get the details wrong, but Frank takes an obviously personal interest in the film nevertheless, as if it were a genuine token of himself. Perhaps it will be a silent film about the arrest and interrogation of a dangerous criminal. Perhaps we have just seen it.

A similarly private addiction to cinema can be seen to motivate Alice as well. One reason she gives for wishing to skip "Fingerprints" is the contention that she has "seen everything worth seeing." Her father's tobacco shop, moreover, is literally awash in what might well be fan magazines; and the walls of Alice's bedroom are covered with male pinups or publicity photos, presumably of film stars (among which the photograph of Frank in his Bobby uniform seems decidedly dour and out of place; indeed, it hangs on a different wall, by itself). Alice does not seem especially interested in Crewe as a sexual partner or life mate. Indeed, as Frank is on the verge of leaving their table at the restaurant she offers a sincere apology, as if not wanting really to offend him. But once he is gone, the prospect of acting out the flapper role seems irresistible and relatively harmless—hence her departure with Crewe, hence her willingness to go up to his flat. Once there, furthermore, it is the prospect of being pictured, of being sketched, which catches her fancy; she becomes the "Miss Up To Date" of whom Crewe sings.

Artist or no, Crewe is also caught up in the scenario. After he first kisses Alice, Crewe seems alternately encouraged and slightly disgusted with himself (recall the way he jams his hands into his pockets), the remorse recalling Alice's apology to Frank in the restaurant. But, again like Alice, Crewe cannot resist "playing" along. He returns to the piano and grabs Alice's dress from the dressing screen, eventually tossing it away (it lands, apparently, on the painting of the "Laughing Harlequin," as if to confirm Alice's secret desire to be framed or Crewe's desire to frame her). The catch, for both of them, is that such a "private" use or abuse of art is self-destructive. They play a scene on the screen provided by the draw curtains of Crewe's wall bed; but the scene is too private, too intense, yet also too much under the sway of public models which don't seem private enough, for misrepresenting each person's better self, or for disallowing its representation at all. Perhaps what they need is an audience beyond each other. The real nightmare, as both Frank and Alice learn at film's end, is not having an audience which will listen or can be trusted.

A major thread of Rothman's general case on Hitchcock is exactly concerned with the question of audience, of Hitchcock's need to elicit its recognition, of him and of its own complicity in the institution of cinema, as if his "privacy" behind the camera were both a privilege and a burden, a burden made somehow easier to bear "in public," on the screen. No absolute resolution of the public/private dilemma seems possible. However "public" a film like *Blackmail* may be, nothing disallows a view which construes it as symptomatic of Hitchcock's "private" obsessions. Nor is it a matter of an absolute split between artist (privacy) and audience (publicity). Alice and Frank are clearly identified as "viewers"; even Frank's gestures of control toward Tracy and Alice are directed by superiors (in each case a phone call from or to headquarters does the job). But Crewe is an instance of an artist enthralled by his own art (as if the cartoon nude of Alice were a factor in his arousal); and Hitchcock's cameo appearance, on the one hand a token of his artistry, depicts him as a reader, not as a writer. Perhaps the ideal circumstance (for Jameson, Rothman, and Hitchcock) is a world wherein everyone is both reader and writer, both viewer and director, where public and private are not two sides of an absolute antithesis. The world of *Blackmail* is not that world. But within that world (and within our own) it counts for something that Hitchcock willingly inscribes a version of himself on screen, facing us directly, and as one of us, as a reader: indeed, as someone who reads in public. By contrast Crewe's tokens of artistry, his paintings, are singular, in that sense destined for private (capitalist) consumption — and his posture toward his audience is neither direct (he faces away from Alice as she changes behind the screen, though the screen itself betokens the fact that he could confront her more directly, more honestly) nor is it self-conscious in a sense analogous to that evinced by Hitchcock. Crewe does not stand to his paintings as Hitchcock stands to Crewe, which is to say that Crewe takes little note of the negative implications or consequences of his actions, for himself or for Alice, his audience, apart from the private workings of his own desire. Let's say he has no sense of history, of inference, of narrative: his world is static, like the mask on the wall of his flat which silently, blindly, gazes over the scene of seduction — or like the equally static (if gigantic) Egyptian head which gazes past the fleeing Tracy in the British Museum. It is not running which kills Tracy, after all, but stopping. Movies move, with or without sound, and minds with them: that's the heart of the matter. In *Blackmail* Hitchcock refuses to be stopped by sound, though he welcomes it as an additional source of cinematic complexity, to be thought with, and thought about.

Perhaps the anxiety of criticism—the disquiet in many quarters at the thought of endless interpretation—follows from exactly this insight: movies move, time passes, views change. The literary/historical work of Gadamer and Jauss, appropriated here to the context of film criticism, offers us a perspective on the process of change which acknowledges the obligation we have to account for both difference (the sense in which a film answers as much to its own questions as to ours) and identity (the sense in which our reading is always *our* reading).[12] We discharge that obligation, or so I take them to imply, by means of a properly historical reading. In a curious way such a reading, if this "rereading" of *Blackmail* is any test, involves a chronological reversal. The "present" of my own reading is my confrontation with the immanent facts of *Blackmail*, with "the film itself," though the film has a past inscribed within its very structure of issues, in the questions it addresses. The background or "past" of my reading, by contrast, is provided by the efforts of other critics, many of them my contemporaries, whose efforts serve as both encouragement and corrective to my own, which in turn may serve as encouragement and corrective to theirs. In other words, one cannot *avoid* living historically: every reading is always situated, always takes place in particular circumstances. To "read historically" encourages one to become more aware of those circumstances, though history teaches us that such awareness can never be final or complete. Perhaps we should think of the desire for completion, the desire to give a particular text a once-and-for-all meaning, as a form of historical blackmail, blackmailing history, soliciting its silence—of which *Blackmail* teaches us to be wary.

Notes

1. Tony Bennett, *Formalism and Marxism* (New York: Methuen, 1979), 69.
2. On the denial of history see Kristin Thompson and David Bordwell's critique of Noël Burch in "Linearity, Materialism and the Study of Early American Cinema," *Wide Angle*, vol. 5, no. 3 (1983): 4–15.
3. Stephen Crofts, "Authorship and Hollywood," *Wide Angle*, vol. 5, no. 3 (1983): 21.
4. Hans-Georg Gadamer, *Truth and Method* (New York: Crossroad, 1975), 331, 345. An excellent summary of Gadamer is that by David Couzens Hoy in *The Critical Circle: Literature, History, and Philosophical Hermeneutics* (Berkeley: Univ. of California Press, 1978).
5. Hans Robert Jauss, *Toward an Aesthetic of Reception*, trans. Timothy Bahti (Minneapolis: Univ. of Minnesota Press, 1982), 21.
6. On the production history of *Blackmail* see Charles Barr, "*Blackmail*: Silent and Sound," *Sight and Sound*, vol. 52, no. 2 (1983): 189–93.
7. Marsha Kinder and Beverle Houston, *Close-Up: A Critical Perspective on Film* (New York: Harcourt Brace Jovanovich, 1972), 53.
8. Maurice Yacowar, *Hitchcock's British Films* (Hamden, Conn.: Archon Books, 1977), 106.
9. Deborah Linderman, "The Screen in Hitchcock's *Blackmail*," *Wide Angle*, vol. 4, no. 1 (1980): 28.

10. William Rothman, *Hitchcock—The Murderous Gaze* (Cambridge: Harvard Univ. Press, 1982), 102.

11. Fredric Jameson, "Reading Hitchcock," *October*, no. 23 (1982): 38.

12. On the notions of "identity" and "difference," see Fredric Jameson, "Marxism and Historicism," *New Literary History*, vol. 11, no. 1 (1979): 41–82.

BLACKMAIL (British International Pictures, 1929). *Producer:* John Maxwell, *Script:* Alfred Hitchcock, Benn W. Levy, Charles Bennett, from the latter's play, *Photography:* Jack Cox, *Editor:* Emile de Ruelle, *Sets:* Wilfred C. Arnold, Norman Arnold, *Music:* Campbell and Connely, arranged by Hubert Bath and Henry Stafford, *Players:* Anna Ondra (Alice White), Joan Berry (Alice's voice), Sara Allgood (Mrs. White), John Longden (Frank Webber), Charles Paton (Mr. White), Cyril Ritchard (Crewe), Donald Calthrop (Tracy).

CHAPTER SEVEN

Alfred Hitchcock's *Murder!*: Theater, Authorship, and the Presence of the Camera

William Rothman

Murder! is, arguably, the masterpiece of Hitchcock's early work. The philosophical dimension implicit in such films as *The Lodger* and *Blackmail* becomes explicit in the arguments between Sir John, the playwright protagonist, and the cunning and articulate Handell Fane, against whom he is pitted. *Murder!*'s philosophical concerns are those of all of Hitchcock's films and include the conditions of human identity; the relationships among love, desire, murder, dreams, madness, and theater; and the nature of views, visions, and fantasies. Underlying the film's arguments, and manifest in them, are its reflections on its nature as a film. The arguments between Sir John and Handell Fane about the conditions of art, and the film's testing of those arguments, are placed within a series of invocations of theater, which in turn are performed in the context of *Murder!*'s insistence on its own decisive separation from theater.

This essay will focus on *Murder!*'s extraordinary climax and conclusion. Through a close and reflective "reading" of this passage, we may begin to appreciate how the film declares itself as a film, how it poses and addresses its central question, *What is it one views or makes when one views or makes a film?* And perhaps this reading may also help us to learn a lesson about the seriousness of the thinking that some works of "classical cinema" have inscribed within their forms and the seriousness with which films like Hitchcock's call for being viewed if their thinking is to be acknowledged and not falsely reduced to a set of "codes."

Before we begin this detailed reading, it will be helpful to offer a brief synopsis of the film up to its climax. Edna Druce, an actress, is found murdered, an empty brandy glass beside her. All evidence suggests that the murderer is Diana Baring, a rival actress. At her trial Diana offers no defense other than that she remembers nothing. The scene shifts to the jury room, where those jurors inclined to believe in her innocence are persuaded, one by one, to change their votes. Reluctantly, Sir John too agrees to go along with the guilty verdict. At home in his bathroom, however, musing in a celebrated stream-of-consciousness voice-over, he berates himself for failing to convince the other jurors of Diana's innocence. The thought strikes him that the real murderer is the man who drank the brandy. He vows to embark on his own investigation, intending to expose this villain.

Sir John's project embeds a characteristically Hitchcockian nest of ambiguities and ironies.[1] Sir John's passionate struggle with his own dark double is also his investigation of Diana's mysterious nature and his courtship and seduction of her. But if Sir John desires Diana as his lover and bride, he also eyes her as a man of the theater would: he wishes to make her the star of his next production, to cast her *on stage* as the woman he loves. Sir John is swept up within a chain of events which would make a perfect piece of theater, a play which could be called "The Inner History of the Baring Case." Sir John is an actor in these events, but he also undertakes to assume, in effect, their authorship. But within the world of *Murder!*, "The Inner History of the Baring Case" is not merely an imaginary play: as the film unfolds, it gradually becomes clear that Sir John actually *is* immersed in writing a play that follows the events surrounding the murder point by point. When the film ends with a view of the curtain falling on a performance of Sir John's new play, we take this to *be* "The Inner History of the Baring Case" itself.

Sir John's investigation leads to the discovery of a crucial clue, the murderer's cigarette case. Sir John visits Diana in prison, hoping that, confronted with this object, she will break her silence and speak the name of the murderer. This "Prison Visit" scene is followed by a brilliant passage which might be called the "Play Scene," in which Sir John invites Handell Fane, the man named by Diana, to audition for the part of the murderer in his new play. Sir John and Handell Fane are locked in a struggle that is, at one level, a struggle for authorship of "The Inner History of the Baring Case."[2] At another level, it is a struggle for superiority as artists. When Fane does not break down as he reads the incriminating lines Sir John has written for him, Sir John is momentarily bested: he is reminded that he is powerless to make events come out as he wishes, powerless to write the ending of his new play without Fane's collaboration. The "Play Scene" sets the stage for the film's climax, in which the struggle between Sir John and Handell Fane is decided.

The scene shifts to the circus where Fane has returned to his former job as a most singular trapeze artist. Accompanied by Markham (the stage manager of Diana's theater company who acts as Dr. Watson to Sir John's Sherlock Holmes throughout the investigation), Sir John enters Fane's dressing room. Fane puts the finishing touches on a letter, seals it, and rises in welcome. Spotting a bottle of brandy on the table, Sir John says, with an undercurrent of accusation, "I suppose you find brandy steadying for the nerves." But he cannot comprehend the secret meaning in Fane's reply ("Mine's very nervy work, you see, Sir John. You never know what may happen"), for Sir John indeed does not know what "nervy work" Fane's performance is destined to be.

In the first part of Fane's performance, he exhibits himself as a spectacle of sexual ambiguity, making a series of theatrical entrances. He enters, in succession, the camera's field of vision, Sir John's view, and the "stage" of the circus ring.

A large black region momentarily eclipses all else in the frame. Almost immediately, this "shadow" reveals itself to be a figure in a huge feather headdress. As this figure — it appears to be a woman — walks into the depths of the frame, blackness consumes less and less of the screen. The effect is that of the raising of a curtain.[3] Finally, "she" turns and we recognize this figure to be Handell Fane.

The second entrance follows immediately. An elephant parades from background to foreground, screen left to screen right, blocking Fane from our view. As Sir John steps into the frame, the elephant moves by, repeating the "curtain raising" effect. Fane now turns, making his theatrical entrance into Sir John's view.

As the band starts up its haunting refrain, Sir John takes a step toward Fane, who turns away disdainfully then steps forward into the circus ring, presenting himself to the audience at large. This third entrance sets up the climax of the first part of Fane's performance: he opens his cloak and displays himself, a man/woman (and, in his feathered costume, also a man/bird).

Fane's form of theater is solitary. It does not consist in the enactment of roles but in theatrically displaying *himself*. He is a creature whose unfathomable sexuality condemns him to live and die outside the human community, a Hitchcockian "Wrong One."[4] Fane's performance is a ritual in which he exhibits his condition theatrically and seals his cursed fate. In *Murder!*, Fane's kind of theater stands opposed to the performance of which Diana Baring dreams.[5] It is rather kin to the death-in-life, the madness, represented by Diana's imprisonment. Fane is condemned to the cruel, inhuman gaze of his audience.

In the second part of Fane's performance — his high-wire act — Hitchcock intercuts shots of Sir John and Markham, Sir John and Markham placed within the audience at large, and the audience's views of Fane (these last represent both the general audience's views and Sir John's private views from his special place within the larger audience). The key to this sequence, which establishes a Hitchcockian paradigm, is that it images Fane's act in sexual terms.[6] This passage reveals Fane's passion and ecstasy as, absorbed in his performance, he appears as if on the threshold, then in the grips, of orgasm. The quasi-sexual performance on the trapeze culminates the self-exhibition of the first part of Fane's act. His "nervy work" calls for him to get "all worked up" before a heartless audience.

The climax of Fane's performance takes place only after he completes a series of feats which compose the main body of his act. First, he climbs the high pole. This accomplished, he looks down. We cut to the circus ring from Fane's point of view, then to Sir John and Markham attentively watching. Fane drops his feather headdress, dries his hands, grasps the bar, and begins swinging. Twin spotlights cast pools of light, with Fane appearing as a shadow in each pool, creating the image of a pair of watching eyes.[7] This part of the sequence ends with Fane soaring through the air, to ringing applause.

On this sound, Hitchcock cuts to Fane. He is swinging, but remains stationary in the frame, while the world, as an out-of-focus backdrop, passes first downward then upward before our eyes. This vertiginous effect signals the loosening of the world's grip on him. In his ecstasy, he turns inward and at the same time looks triumphantly into the camera.

From Sir John and Markham looking on uncomprehendingly, Hitchcock cuts to a closer view of Fane, the world again passing vertiginously through the frame. His face now registers great tension and anguish: his ecstasy is also a passion. We cut again to Sir John and Markham, still oblivious to Fane's condition, then back to Fane. His face is in dark shadow, but as the world rises up through the frame, it becomes lit by harsh glare. At this decisive moment, the camera penetrates Fane's subjectivity and frames a series of three visions.

In the first, we see Sir John in close-up, looking slightly off to the left, superimposed on the world passing through the frame. (At one point, a string of lights momentarily crosses his face, creating an image of a death's head grin. This effect anticipates the ending of *Psycho,* when the dead mother's and Norman's grins are momentarily superimposed.)

Do we take it that, in his anguish and ecstasy, Fane literally *sees* Sir John's face before him? We may be tempted to say that this is a superimposition of what Fane hallucinates (Sir John's face) and what he literally sees (the world passing before his eyes). The hallucinatory aspect of this image is what leads me to call this a *vision* rather than a *view*. But perhaps Fane suffers no hallucination at this moment, the image of Sir John's face corresponding to nothing that Fane either sees or imagines. Perhaps this superimposition simply serves Hitchcock as a conventional shorthand for indicating that, at this moment of inwardness, Fane is haunted by Sir John, transfixed by his image. Then again, perhaps this shot represents a real view of Sir John at this moment—this view the camera's, and corresponding to the view of no one within the world of the film—superimposed over Fane's real view. Then this shot would correspond to no "private" experience of Fane's at all but only serve as Hitchcock's reminder to us that, while Fane has turned inward, Sir John is still watching.

The status of this frame and its relation to Fane's subjectivity are precisely ambiguous. This may be an "inner vision" projected *from within* Fane's imagination, or this frame may itself be projected *onto* Fane's imagination, Fane being subjected to this image as we are. We cannot say whether, in effect,

Fane's imagination subjects us to this image or is subjected to it. But then again, we do not really know who or what the figure of Handell Fane represents, what his subjectivity comes to. What *is* Fane's relationship to the camera (to the film's author and viewers)? Who is subject to whom? And in a frame which contains a vision, whom or what does the camera represent?

One fact at least is clear. Whatever Sir John is envisioned as looking at, he is not envisioned as looking at the camera. In this oblique framing, his gaze does not confront the camera and poses no threat to it. Fane envisions Sir John as having no power to confront his gaze, having no power to penetrate or possess him with his gaze. In Fane's vision, Sir John's powers are inferior to his own.

From the first vision, we cut back to Fane, wide-eyed, his face half in light and half in shadow. Then we are presented with Fane's second vision: a close-up of Diana looking into the camera, her face likewise superimposed over the world passing through the frame.

In his second vision, Diana comes to Fane as a goddess who compels men's gaze. In Fane's first vision, Sir John was looking off, his eyes averted from the camera. In retrospect, we take it that Sir John, as envisioned by Fane, is held spellbound, like Fane himself, by a vision of Diana. But also, Diana looks right into the camera: within Fane's vision she penetrates his gaze as if she possessed the inner world of his imagination. Fane's vision of Diana appears as if it were a projection of the gaze of this goddess, as if it were she who conjured this vision of herself into being. But through what agency does this apparition really come to Fane? If it is projected from within his imagination, he is also subjected to it. And is it possible that Diana's powers really are magical, as Fane imagines them to be? After all, when the camera earlier penetrated the privacy of her prison cell, Diana looked up at it, violence in her eyes, as if confronting what disturbed her absorption: when we viewed her through the cell window, she appeared to possess the power to imagine, to penetrate, even to conjure, our views. What powers are natural for a being framed by the camera who is attuned to, and may be in league with, the agency that presides over that framing?

When we cut back to Fane, his eyes are almost completely shut, as if entranced by the voice of a siren. If he now abandoned himself completely to his vision, of course, he would fall to a violent death. But he does not black out. He opens his eyes and again looks up at the camera. But does this gesture break the spell cast by Diana's gaze as Fane envisions it, or does he bid his visions to continue? Does he look into the camera in defiance of Diana or at her bidding?

In the following frame, nothing is superimposed on Fane's vertiginous view of the world. Does this mean that this shot represents no vision at all? I prefer to think of this frame as representing a vision of nothingness. It is not simply devoid of a superimposed human countenance; the blurred images that pass before Fane's eyes are charged symbolically, and admit of a reading, like a dream. The shadowy pole; the curious bell-like hanging lights (suggestive both of death bells and wedding bells, and also invoking sightless eyes); the death's head grin; finally, the blurred image of a couple: this vision is charged with signifiers of the realm of human sexuality from which Fane is irrevocably estranged and charged as well with images of death.[8]

This vision of nothingness sums up Fane's nature in his own eyes and—as he imagines—in Diana's eyes. This vision of nothingness is also Fane's vision of his own fate. Death is Fane's mark: in the world, Fane spells death, and only his own death can release him from his curse.

The series of Fane's visions now complete, Hitchcock cuts to an "objective" view. Fane lands on the high platform, relinquishes his grip on the bar, passes a rope through his hands, and turns to acknowledge his audience. The second part of his performance is successfully completed, but his strength is spent. His hands hang limp, and he seems to be suffering overpowering vertigo. Can he go on?

If Diana died in Fane's place, he would be responsible for her death. His vision of Diana is a guilty one. Since it is, in effect, as a ghost that she appears to him, her death would not free him from her gaze but condemn him to being forever haunted. His vision of Diana brings home to him that his desires can never be satisfied and mocks his nothingness. It is as if Diana's envisioned gaze represented Diana's own revenge against him. It corresponds precisely to Diana's nightmare visions of her guards, which were central to the design of the "Prison Visit" sequence. Diana's imprisonment is the death-in-life of madness, but Fane, condemned to and by his visions, is also imprisoned, also mad, also already dead. Release from prison promises Diana a cure, while Fane's curse can be lifted only if his visions relinquish their hold on him.

Fane cannot bear his guilty vision of Diana, but this vision also arises out of his desire. He does not wish to be freed from it. I imagine him unwilling, for example, to confess and put himself at the mercy of a court, for I take it that he cannot abide bearing witness to the union of Sir John and Diana. Only through suicide can he keep faith with Diana without denying his desire. Death is the fulfillment of his calling.

First and foremost, Fane's suicide is a private act, admitting no audience. We might think of Diana as Fane's real audience, but the "Diana" Fane envisions as bearing witness to his death and the "Fane" who is possessed by this vision of Diana are not separate beings who could stand in the relationship of audience and theatrical performer. For this Diana is also within Fane, and this Fane within Diana. Diana's possession of Fane's act, which her gaze indeed also calls forth, does not make it a piece of theater, does not mitigate against its essential privacy. Diana can no more really sit in Fane's audience than we can.

On the other hand, Fane does perform his suicide in the most theatrical way possible and in a public arena before an audience that is hushed and waiting for the death-defying climax of his act. Fane's private act of tying the noose with spellbinding deliberateness, slipping it over his neck, and jumping off the platform is also a consummate piece of theater which brings down the house. True, we can imagine that Fane must "work himself up to it," overcoming his fear of death as though it were stage fright. Nonetheless, when Fane grabs the rope and passes it slowly through his hands, hardly appearing to attend to it, giving no sign of awareness that he is in the presence of an audience, the theatrical effect is stunning. But insofar as Fane's private act is also theater, who is its intended audience? We comprehend what is about to happen only an instant before Sir John does. At precisely the moment when it appears that Sir John has finally understood, Hitchcock cuts to Fane, who only now openly discloses that he is tying a noose. It is as though he defers this revelation until his obliviousness first impresses itself on Sir John, then addresses this revelation directly to him. When we now cut to Sir John, it is apparent that Fane's masterful theatrical stroke has its intended effect. Fane's suicide, at one level a completely private act, is also a demonstration, directed to Sir John, of the power his art holds over him. Sir John has taken his place as a spellbound member of Fane's audience. Fane has demonstrated that his theater is superior. Fane's art is triumphant.[9]

From Sir John, taut with anticipation, we cut back to Fane. He tightens the noose around his neck and jumps. Hitchcock (tactfully? theatrically?) holds this framing so that the rope swings back and forth across an empty frame as Fane dies offscreen. If Fane's suicide is addressed specifically to Sir John, it is also addressed to the circus audience at large, the audience within which Sir John has assumed a place. To this audience and to Sir John within it, Fane's gesture says: "All along, what you have really wished to view is my death. Your monstrous desire for the sight of blood is what drew you to the spectacle of my degradation. Here is the authentic climax of my act. Are you ready to confront your real desire?" In a rapid montage, Hitchcock details the audience's reactions of shock and ecstasy. Fane's audience breaks down, running amok. No one present can claim to be his superior. Fane's case is proved.

Fane's gesture is the dramatic climax of *Murder!*. Handell Fane is a figure of heroic stature who dwarfs Sir John, and his suicide casts a pall over the film. Even if *Murder!* ended with an unambiguous image of Diana freed and united romantically with Sir John, it would not have the feeling of a conventional happy ending. The film does not end in this way, however. Rather it presents an image of Sir John and Diana embarked on living happily ever after, then decisively draws back from that image, framing it and disavowing its reality.

After a brief transitional passage in which Sir John reads out loud Fane's suicide note, which fills in the gaps in his understanding of the mystery, we dissolve to the prison gate. This dissolve creates an air of unreality, in part due to the framing's invocation of a stage set viewed from across the barrier of the proscenium. The sense of unreality is also due to this image's clear repetition of the shot which opens the "Prison Visit" sequence. The effect is uncanny when Sir John enters this frame from below and walks into its depths. It is as if he crosses the barrier separating the stage from the world. He passes from the region of the camera, the region where *his* view and *ours* are one, to enter a space still haunted by his gaze. It is as if he were a dreamer who awakens and passes into the world of his own dream. In the depths of this charged frame, Sir John and Diana join in an embrace.

There is a slow dissolve to a much closer view of the couple locked in an embrace, the new view placing them in the back seat of a limousine. We can sum up one effect of this dissolve by saying that we do not know whether there are two embraces or only one.

The dissolve underscores the discontinuity between these scenes even as it smoothly bridges them, denying their real separation. The dissolve also calls attention to itself, on the one hand by its extreme slowness and on the other by its invocation of the passage in which the camera penetrated the privacy of Diana's prison cell.

Diana is in tears. They are tears of thankfulness: she is sitting beside her hero, in freedom. But to whom does she give thanks? And does she also weep for Handell Fane, whose love was responsible for her ordeal but who finally sacrificed himself, allowing her to assume this place? In any case, we recognize this as the conventional moment for Sir John to declare his love and propose marriage.[10] But what Sir John says is, "Now my dear, you must save those tears. They'll be very useful — in my new play."

By referring to it simply as his, Sir John claims sole authorship of this play. But if this play is indeed "The Inner History of the Baring Case," Sir John claims responsibility, not only for a work of theater, but for the conclusion to the real events surrounding the murder. Claiming sole authorship of this double conclusion, Sir John fails to acknowledge Handell Fane — fails to recognize the significance of Fane's final gesture and his own need for Fane's collaboration. This failure, I take it, confirms that he is not, finally, Fane's equal. Nor is he Diana's equal, in his continuing failure to acknowledge her. And if Sir John also means by his "new play" their *marriage,* then Diana will surely need all the tears she can muster for it. Like Alice at the end of *Blackmail,* Diana is condemned to a relationship which denies her freedom and from which there is no escape. Alice bears the brunt of mocking laughter and knows that the joke is on her, but Diana is cut off at this moment from our privileged vantage and does not yet know her condition of bondage. She weeps tears of joy, although she is imprisoned in a relationship with a man who claims to be her master; who subjects her to the dictates of his imagination, confining her within its frame; and who directs her to serve his art and his desire.

Sir John takes Diana's hand. As she gazes happily at him, he rests his face

against her, pressing his lips to her hair. Looking right into the camera, he gives
a half-smile, in a shot precisely echoing the ending of *The Lodger*. His open
eyes and smile reveal that Diana's complete absorption in this present moment
is not his own. His smile expresses his self-satisfaction in completing his project, and it shows him looking ahead to enjoying the fruits of his success. But
we cannot say whether his look is addressed to the camera, or whether he is
blind to the presence and agency it represents. Does his look acknowledge that
he knows we are watching, or is he so absorbed at this moment, not with
Diana's real presence, but with the scene he is imagining (whether or not it is
Diana's erotic proximity that intoxicates him, freeing his fantasy), that he can
look right into the camera without recognizing it? Is Hitchcock, and are we, his
coauthors in the scene that is about to be enacted, or do we bear witness, with
Hitchcock, to his continuing *hubris?*

From this intimate view, Hitchcock dissolves to an extreme long shot of
Sir John. As harmonious music plays, Markham — dressed as a butler — opens
the door to the room. Diana makes her entrance, attended by Dulcie Markham
in a maid's uniform. Sir John holds out his hand and Diana steps'toward him.
He takes her hand, the Markhams looking on.

The dissolve suggests that this is precisely the scene Sir John imagines
when he looks up at the camera, smiling. We take it that this is a tranquil coda
set in the future, when Sir John and Diana are husband and wife and the
Markhams are impressed into a nonthespian service more in line with their
talents. As Sir John kisses Diana's hand, the camera begins to track out. At
first, this movement strikes us as a gracious and tactful acknowledgment of this
couple's wish for privacy. The suggestion is that we are viewing the prelude to
an act of lovemaking and that we have arrived at a conventional happy ending.
Sir John and Diana appear poised for the kiss that signifies that they are
destined to live happily ever after, their blissful future to commence forthwith
in privacy. An implication of this suggestion is that Sir John's half-smile is
retroactively revealed to have been in anticipation of this ending and in particular the scene about to take place out of the camera's purview.

However, as the camera continues moving out, it crosses the barrier of a
proscenium and stops only when the proscenium emblematically frames the
view that a moment before had filled the screen. Within this frame-within-
the-frame, Sir John and Diana, tiny figures in the distance, kiss. The curtain
rings down to applause from an unviewed audience, the image fades out, and
a title announces the end of the film.

This scene that we took to be real is retroactively revealed to be staged.
Nor is this just *any* scene: it is, we take it, the final curtain of "The Inner
History of the Baring Case." The implication is that Sir John's half-smile was in
anticipation of the completion, production, and performance of his new play.
This play ends with the perfect fulfillment of Sir John's wishes, but what does

the ending of his play signify in reality? How do events really end within the world of the film? Does this staged kiss correspond to a real kiss, one which anticipates a real act of lovemaking? Yet no real kiss could coincide with this kiss performed in the public space of Sir John's theater, under his direction. The kiss in reality is the stuff from which Sir John creates his play's ending. The real kiss, on the other hand, is at the service of the staged kiss, which presents itself to its audience as at the service of nothing outside itself. Within the play, the final kiss signifies the lovers' mutual acknowledgment of their love and their equality in marriage. But the real kiss serves an art which Sir John claims as his alone, not acknowledging Diana as his partner. In completing "The Inner History of the Baring Case," Sir John completes his creation of himself as a character fated for the heaven-on-earth of marriage to Diana. But in finishing his play, Sir John also completes his break with that character. Sir John's play ends with the lovers joined in an embrace that is forever, but Hitchcock does not claim that the "real" events of his narrative end that way. *Murder!* disavows Sir John's ending as the film's own. Then what is Hitchcock's ending, and why does he close his film with this disquieting camera movement, rather than, for example, a direct dissolve from Sir John and Diana in the limousine to the stage with the camera from the outset beyond the proscenium?[11]

An answer that suggests itself is that this camera movement declares that all our views of the world of the film have really been views of scenes staged by Sir John. That is, perhaps at every moment the camera could have pulled out to reveal the proscenium of Sir John's theater. Perhaps Sir John's highbrow shocker/blood-and-thunder melodrama/aerial act/Shakespearean tragedy/romantic comedy *is* the film we have just viewed. Perhaps Sir John's and Hitchcock's authorships are really one and we are seated in the phantom audience whose applause resounds as the curtain rings down.

But we have already pointed out that Sir John's and Hitchcock's endings do not coincide. If there is any gesture within the world of the film that calls for comparison with the camera's final gesture or the series of gestures it culminates, it is performed by Handell Fane, not Sir John. *Murder!* acknowledges Fane's suicide in its ending, as "The Inner History of the Baring Case" cannot, because nothing in Sir John's play corresponds to Hitchcock's camera. Sir John's authorship is not Hitchcock's authorship. The audience for "The Inner History of the Baring Case" is not in our position, as *Murder!*'s viewers, to acknowledge an author in the camera's framings. *Murder!*'s invocations of the stage are framed by, and frame, a succession of views that can be identified with no piece of theater, real or imagined. In the camera's gestures, Hitchcock's authorship is declared and our acts of viewing acknowledged. *Murder!* ends with a gesture that is its most decisive declaration that what Hitchcock has made, and we have viewed, is not a piece of theater but a *film*. *Murder!* leaves its viewers with the question, What is it that one views or makes when one views or makes a film?[12]

Notes

1. In certain ways, Sir John's project is modeled on the protagonist's project in *The Lodger.* Hitchcock, I take it, is always attentive to the ironies in the relationship between his "characters'" projects and his own authorship.
2. In his doctoral dissertation, "Fearful Symmetries," submitted to the N.Y.U. Cinema Studies Department in 1979, David Corey studies the roles played by struggles for authorship within Hitchcock's narratives.
3. This "curtain raising" effect, already employed in *The Lodger,* becomes a staple Hitchcockian technique.
4. The concept of the "Wrong One" is developed in *The Murderous Gaze.* I adopt this chilling term from a number of Hitchcock films, most notably *The Wrong Man* and *Psycho* ("Did she look like a Wrong One to you?") and the teleplay "The Breakdown."
5. *Stage Fright* follows *Murder!* in the central importance it gives to this dialectical opposition between contrasting forms of theater.
6. Compare, for example, the climactic struggle between the two Charlies in *Shadow of a Doubt,* the fight on the merry-go-round at the end of *Strangers on a Train,* and the shower murder sequence in *Psycho.*
7. This is a modified form of a "joke" first used in *The Lodger.* A truck carrying bales of newspapers drives into the depths of the frame. Two heads, visible through the oval windows in the back of the vehicle, swing back and forth, providing the van with a pair of watching eyes.
8. This shot exemplifies an important Hitchcockian mode of symbolic representation. The presentation of Sebastian's discovery of Alicia's betrayal in *Notorious* is one of the most prominent examples of this mode. When the camera pans across the floor of the wine cellar until it frames the tell-tale stained drain, our view represents Alex's literal one, but it is also a symbolically charged vision. Through its veiled sexual references, it invokes a scene of love-making between Alicia and Devlin that Alex imagines or fantasizes or dreams. The climax of *Vertigo,* with Judy/Madeleine's vision of the black-robed nun, is another example. Cf. my "Alfred Hitchcock's *Notorious,*" *The Georgia Review,* vol. 29, no. 4 (1975). Readers might find it edifying to compare this essay with Richard Abel's essay on *Notorious* which appears in *Wide Angle,* vol. 1, no. 1 revised and expanded (1979).
9. The theatrical gesture as instrument of instruction plays a crucial but rarely recognized role in the characteristic Hitchcock film. This is a point developed at length in *The Murderous Gaze.*
10. Precisely this occurs in *North by Northwest,* although with a singular twist.
11. This camera movement echoes the one that closes *The Lodger* and anticipates the ending of *The 39 Steps. The 39 Steps* ends with Mr. Memory's death, the Professor's damnation, the union of Hannay and Pamela, and society's indifference as it turns its attention to the chorus line. But we might also say that it ends with a movement of the camera, by which it pulls out to hold its final framing. When the camera pulls out at the end of *Murder!,* it discloses that the lovers locked in an embrace are really on stage, acting. Their "union" takes place in the sight of society, although society is present, not as witness and celebrant, but only as audience. *The 39 Steps* reverses this. Hannay and Pamela are not revealed to be acting on stage in front of an audience. We alone view their embrace. Our view is conjoined with theirs as they step back to take in the moving spectacle of Mr. Memory's death. Our condition as viewers is joined with theirs. Their final embrace is no piece of theater. The camera's final gesture calls upon us to reaffirm our bond with Hannay. If we affirm our community with Hannay and Pamela, we exempt ourselves from Hitchcock's indictment of the unviewed audience within the hall and fulfill our calling.

   We cannot be satisfied when Handell Fane dies unacknowledged and Sir John persists and prevails in his *hubris.* But while the ending of *The 39 Steps* is not that of traditional comedy, its melancholy aspect in no way prevents it from giving us pleasure. There is justice in this world's fate. Hitchcock too must be satisfied with the fate of his subjects in this world: the

Professor's challenge to his authorship has been defeated and punished, and those who acknowledge his higher power have been saved. The camera's final movement in *Murder!* confronts us with our continuing failure to acknowledge the film's author. But the final gesture of the camera in *The 39 Steps* grants us satisfaction. Why should Hitchcock not give his blessing to those who "identify" with Hannay, who join in affirming this film's author?

12. This question identifies one of the main burdens of *The Murderous Gaze* as a whole: the task of articulating the answer to this question that is inscribed within Hitchcock's *oeuvre*.

MURDER! (British International Pictures, 1930). *Producer:* John Maxwell, *Script:* Alma Reville, Alfred Hitchcock, Walter Mycroft, from the novel and play *Enter Sir John* by Clemence Dane [Winifred Ashton] and Helen Simpson, *Photography:* Jack Cox, *Editors:* René Harrison, Emile de Ruelle, *Sets:* John Mead, *Players:* Herbert Marshall (Sir John Menier), Nora Baring (Diana Baring), Phyllis Konstam (Dulcie Markham), Edward Chapman (Ted Markham), Esmé Percy (Handell Fane). 102 minutes.

CHAPTER EIGHT

Consolidation of a Classical Style: *The Man Who Knew Too Much*

Elisabeth Weis

In a generally favorable contemporary review of *The Man Who Knew Too Much* (1934), Forsyth Hardy observed that "with *Murder!* in mind, the surprise of the film is the absence of any expressive use of sound."[1] If by "expressive" sound Hardy is referring to virtuoso effects, then he is right; there is nothing equivalent to the choric chanting in *Murder!* or the knife sequence in *Blackmail*. However, Hitchcock is still very much experimenting with sound in *The Man Who Knew Too Much*—in less obvious ways. With this film Hitchcock finds a successful formula that will enable him to develop his concerns with the deeper impulses of human behavior without resorting to noticeable expressionistic devices. It is the first film in the classical style that will characterize such films as *Young and Innocent* (1937), *The Lady Vanishes* (1938), *Foreign Correspondent* (1940), and *Mr. and Mrs. Smith* (1941).[2]

The classical method requires Hitchcock to manipulate his sounds within a realistic context. On the stylistic level this means that he has to provide a literal pretext for any exaggerated use of sound. On the thematic level, the method requires the incorporation of the aural effects into the plot itself, so that they are so obvious and so essential that they do not jar with the style of the rest of the film.

One means of amplifying a sound with a literal source is to find a plausible second sound that provides an aural correlative for the original sound. This substitution technique is akin to the use of "objects as visual correlatives" that Andrew Sarris has observed in Hitchcock's films.[3] In *The Man Who Knew Too Much*, vases serve this function during a shootout at the spies' hideout at Wapping. The director wants to show that the spies are gradually being overcome by the police who are firing at them through the windows, but he does not want to eliminate his few spies too soon lest he also eliminate the suspense.

He therefore uses vases, which line the room's shelves, as a visual substitute for and aural extension of the destruction being sustained. Hitchcock presumably does not want to actually depict the violence of the spies' deaths; not only does Hitchcock prefer implication but also Hollywood's gangster films had recently created a revulsion in England against excessive violence. He was able to suggest the impact of the bullets by showing the shattering and toppling of vases (just as Howard Hawks had shown Gaffney's murder through indirection in *Scarface* two years earlier by having the camera follow a bowling ball released by the murdered man to its target, where a last pin wavers and finally topples). Similarly, the sounds of gunshots from down the street, even if realistic (at this time sound-effects recordists had to find substitutes for the sounds of shots because recording the real sound would have blown out their sensitive equipment), were multiplied and amplified by the sounds of numerous vases shattering and crashing to the floor. In much the same way, Hitchcock uses crockery during a donnybrook in *Young and Innocent* and balloons during a birthday party in *The Birds* to intensify the effects of destruction.

The other way to manipulate sounds within realistic limitations is to carefully control the use of ambient noise, that is, the sounds that might occur naturally in the background of a given location. Background noises can be juggled quite extensively before the audience will notice them. Hitchcock was fond of saying that a "decisive factor" in *The Man Who Knew Too Much* was "the contrast between the snowy Alps and the congested streets of London," which he told Truffaut was a "visual concept [that] had to be embodied in the film."[4] For the transition between the Swiss and the British scenes Hitchcock dissolves from snowy mountains to a night shot of Piccadilly Circus and from the jingle of sleigh bells to the noise of traffic. Otherwise, he barely indicates any visual congestion of London. He depends much more on sound for ambience.

For instance, when the film's two heroes, Lawrence and Clive, first arrive at Wapping, the sound track is busy with boat whistles, hand-organ music, car horns, and traffic, but we see little activity. (Of course, this is the more economic way of creating ambience in a tightly budgeted studio.) As the men walk upstairs and wait outside a dentist's office that is a front for espionage activities, Hitchcock keeps up the level of ambient noise. However, while we wait outside with Lawrence once Clive has gone into the office with an unsavory-looking dentist, Hitchcock eliminates all but a few token exterior noises to focus our concentration on the closed door. Our expectations are rewarded with a scream (Clive's), which confirms our fears about both assassins and dentists. (An earlier association between the assassin and dentistry is suggested when Lawrence's daughter observes that she does not like the assassin because he uses too much brilliantine and has too many teeth.) It is important to the film that Wapping is the kind of seamy location in which a scream goes unheeded. The plausibility of its going unnoticed by the outside world has been increased by the introduction of that world as a noisy location.

In Hitchcock's American remake of *The Man Who Knew Too Much*
(1956), it is the first setting (in this version, Marrakesh) that is noisy and
London that is quiet.[5] Hitchcock emphasizes the congestion of Marrakesh by
staging the murder of the spy in the marketplace. Contrasted with the noisy
setting is the placidity of the Jimmy Stewart character—Hitchcock has specifically described his character to Truffaut as "an earnest and quiet man" (p. 170).
The manipulation of the ambient noise to underline this contrast is done with
great care. For instance, there is a scene in a police station in which Stewart and
his wife talk with a police officer. The shots alternate between the couple's view
of the policeman, which includes a view through the window of the busy city,
and the policeman's view of the couple, who are sitting across from him before
a blank wall. Although the ambient noise should theoretically not vary, in fact,
Hitchcock raises the traffic noise when we see the city and lowers it significantly
when we are looking at Stewart. I have described this detail to distinguish
between the early and later appearances of the classical style. The manipulation of ambient noise is already present in the 1934 film but in relatively crude
form. Later versions of Hitchcock's techniques are almost always more refined.

If the technical aspects of the classical style are superior in the second
version, however, those thematic aspects which the films share are already fully
developed in the first. That is to say, Hitchcock has so neatly incorporated his
thematic elements into the plot and characterization that they are all but
invisible to the viewer who does not want to look for them. The point where
the themes all coalesce is the famous Albert Hall sequence, in which a diplomat is to be assassinated. The spies plan to have the sound of the assassin's
gunshot at the concert hall be masked by the sound of cymbals crashing, so
that the structural climax of the film corresponds with the musical climax of a
dramatic cantata being performed. At the concert is a woman, Mrs. Lawrence,
who knows about the plot but has been warned that her intervention would
mean the death of her kidnapped daughter. Thus her last-second scream,
which saves the diplomat, is also the thematic climax of a film whose moral
dilemma has been a couple's choice between the life of their daughter and that
of a famous diplomat, between the family and the state, between love and
duty. The choice between screaming and remaining silent is related to one of
the film's major concerns: the contrast between silence and oral expression that
differentiates the spies from the heroes of the film. Furthermore, the concert
sequence creates a conjunction of music and murder, the one a sign of order,
the other a sign of chaos. The silence-versus-expression antinomy operates on
an individual level. The music-versus-murder antinomy operates on a social
level. These two antinomies merge at the concert sequence, which poses in
concrete terms the central tension of this and other Hitchcock films: the problem of how to reconcile the need for social order with the need for personal
expression. As my analysis will show, on the social level Hitchcock is more or
less on the side of control; on the personal level he is more or less on the side of
expression.

The silence-versus-expression motif is developed through contrasts of characters. *The Man Who Knew Too Much* is the first of Hitchcock's films to suggest that for criminals to be effective they must work quietly, a concept that is most fully and literally developed in *Family Plot,* where the kidnappers always remain mute in their dealings with lawmen. In both films, silence is associated with single-minded dedication to one's task. Noise and talking reveal espionage activities and must be avoided at all costs. The spies would not have known that the Lawrences "knew too much" in the first place if Lawrence had not talked too loudly about it in a hotel hall in Saint Moritz. Even shooting is to be avoided if possible. The spies battle Lawrence and Clive in their church with chairs rather than guns because they do not want the police to hear. During the brawl the woman spy tells the organist to play a hymn to cover up the sound of the scuffle. The spies engage in the final shoot-out with the police only because their hideout has been discovered. Thus it is altogether appropriate that their assassination attempt involves their concealing a gunshot under the sound of crashing cymbals. Similarly, it is appropriate that their kidnapping involves keeping the Lawrences quiet. Despite the film's title, it is not the Lawrences knowing too much, so much as their telling anyone, that concerns the spies. The idea of "keeping your mouth shut" is literalized by Hitchcock, who has Lawrence tell Clive to do precisely that after Clive has had his tooth extracted in the cause of their search for the daughter.

The most efficient, and the quietest, character in *The Man Who Knew Too Much* is the woman spy, who, even after being shot, dies without a sound, and who spends a good deal of time trying to prevent her brother, Abbott, the spy ringleader, from getting side-tracked from his work. Talking too much is Abbott's fatal flaw. It is also what gives him (as played by Peter Lorre) his personality because it humanizes him. He likes to chat, to make puns, and to laugh. He is so identified by his musical Swiss watch that, when Lawrence is searching for him in the hideout-church, his presence can be revealed by the sound of the watch chiming while he is still offscreen.

Keeping quiet involves controlling one's emotions. Abbott tells Lawrence, "You should learn to control your fatherly feelings and not drop things on the floor," and challenges the father not to give away his feelings when he is reunited with his daughter in the spies' hideout. That reunion sequence is matched later against the scene of the woman spy's death, in which Abbott cannot entirely suppress his despair.

In *The Silent Scream* I have suggested that silence is a symptom of moral paralysis; in *The Man Who Knew Too Much* it is also a sign of emotional paralysis. For Hitchcock implies that always keeping quiet requires the unhealthy suppression of emotions. Unlike the spies, the Lawrences are talkers. Volubility is a sign of emotional life, of spontaneity, of irrepressibility. In the second scene of the film, the skeet-shooting finals between Mrs. Lawrence and Ramon (who, it will turn out, is the spies' assassin), the Lawrence daughter spoils her mother's shot by talking too much. The mother remarks, "Let that be a lesson to you not to have children." Like most jokers, she is partly serious, although her actions for the rest of the film show that she prefers life, and having a daughter, to winning. (She does win in the "contest" that involves a life, rather than just winning an artificial game.) A moment later it is the mother who is shushed by the crowd for talking too much (as she is saying that she will "disown the child" if she loses), and the assassin wins the championship. There is a structural connection linking the first two confrontations between these two sharpshooter-antagonists. At the skeet-shooting match the daughter's speaking makes the mother miss a shot. At Albert Hall the mother's screaming makes the assassin miss.

Thus the concert sequence, which is usually considered merely a clever device for producing suspense, is related to the tension in the rest of the film between keeping quiet and revealing one's feelings. (More obviously, the concert sequence is also a confrontation between the good and evil forces.) At the concert the mother is torn between two forms of behavior—one trained, one instinctual. The audience sympathizes with both. One choice is not to disturb a concert, not to make a fool of oneself in public—a behavior pattern that has been instilled in us from an early age. The other choice is the impulse to cry out at a moment of danger. When the mother screams in the nick of time to prevent the assassination, she is not so much going against maternal instinct (by risking the life of her child) as responding to the more immediate instinct of wanting to save the ambassador's life. Thus her behavior here is one and the same healthy expression of emotion as her daughter's talking at the shooting match, and both are opposed to the unnatural repression of emotion typical of the spies.

The two screams elicited by the spies at different points in the film provide a measure of the extent to which anarchic forces have intruded into civilization. The spies' threat moves from an isolated room in a seamy suburb to an Albert Hall concert at the political and cultural center of British society. If a scream goes unheeded when emitted from a slum dentist's office, it is altogether conspicuous and inappropriate at a concert, and that is why it is an effective means for Mrs. Lawrence to save a diplomat's life.

The whole notion of staging the film's climax at a concert is particularly useful because Hitchcock can work with the concept of musical order in two ways, stylistic and thematic. A comparison of the role of music in both versions of the film reveals once again that, while both thoroughly develop the thematic associations of music, the second is a decided improvement on the first in its stylistic use of music. Hitchcock has said that "the first version is the work of a talented amateur and the second was made by a professional" (Truffaut, p. 65). He was, as usual, assessing his films only according to their craftsmanship, and in that area he is certainly right. In both films the stylistic function of the music is to create suspense. Music is such a useful tool for Hitchcock because a piece of music has its own structure, a preestablished order against which he can time the struggles of his characters.

Truffaut and Hitchcock together have quite thoroughly analyzed the improvements in the second version of the concert sequence itself (pp. 63–65). They have not so thoroughly discussed the preparation for the sequence, however. In the British version of the film Hitchcock gives us little chance to hear the musical phrase during which the shot will be fired. A considerable portion of the piece ("The Storm Cloud Cantata" by Arthur Benjamin) is played under the opening titles, but it stops short, just before the last four notes that make up the crucial phrase. The four notes in isolation are first heard just before the concert as Abbott plays them for the assassin (really for the audience, of course) on a record player. The American version is much more sophisticated aurally and visually in acquainting the audience with the music so that the suspense can be milked. Just a look at the scene in which the spies play the record reveals the added clarity of Hitchcock's later version—a clarity evidently based on a greater self-awareness of the elements of his own style. In the later film the spies provide the context of the musical phrase, and they play the record twice. In the first version the playing of the record is photographed in deep focus, so that we may watch the expressions of the father and daughter in the center and depth of the image, with Abbott and the assassin less conspicuously located on either side of the frame and nearer the camera. In the second version Hitchcock simplifies the shot (the three spies in it are all looking at the phonograph; the hostages are not seen), thereby forcing us to pay closer attention to the music. There is no emotional distraction.

Formal considerations aside, Hitchcock established with the first *Man Who Knew Too Much* the thematic role that classical music would usually play from then on in his films; the concert is a staid ritual of refined society. During the film's violent confrontations the spies use music to cover their activities. Their first assassination is that of a British spy in Saint Moritz who is shot while he is dancing with Mrs. Lawrence. Hitchcock does not emphasize the point, but this assassination, too, is concealed by music. The gunshot occurs on a musical beat, and the sound heard is not of a bullet but of window glass breaking. Even the victim himself looks down with surprise, after not noticing for a moment that he is wounded. As noted above, the spies try to cover the noise of the brawl in their church with music. At the end of the hymn, the organist plays a solemn amen. Church music is, of course, even more staid than choral music, and so we experience a frisson of pleasure when Lawrence earlier gets the chance to "naughtily" sing false words to a hymn while he is trying to warn Clive of their danger. (It is the same antiauthoritarian pleasure we get out of seeing grown men and women fighting in church.) Their disregard for the normal lyrics of the hymn may be seen as a foreshadowing, like the daughter's talking during the match, of the mother's "naughty," antisocial scream during the concert. The disrespect for music by the so-called moral forces in the film is continued, in a minor way, even during the final shoot-out, when two police-men, commandeering one citizen's parlor, use his piano as a barricade after the first policeman has scolded his younger partner for playing a few notes by saying, "This is a scrap, not a . . . concert."

The evil forces cover their activities with a front of respectability (religious and cultural). By contrast, the good side has to be disrespectful to cultural institutions to preserve them. The conjunction of music and murder is one of Hitchcock's many ways of showing that evil lurks very near the surface of respectability. Just as the attachment of Mrs. Lawrence's knitting to the coat of someone about to be killed juxtaposes "the domestic and the sinister," so the interruption of music by assassinations suggests that domestic and national security are very fragile illusions—as tenuous as a thread of yarn that breaks when a man dies; that security and control are gained at the cost of repressing natural instincts; and that a scream may be more civilized than a cantata.[6]

Notes

1. Forsyth Hardy, "Films of the Quarter," *Cinema Quarterly,* no. 3 (Winter 1935): 119.
2. Films that combine classical and subjective techniques in varying proportions include *The 39 Steps* (1935), *Sabotage* (1936), *Saboteur* (1942), *Lifeboat* (1943), *Dial "M" for Murder* (1954), *To Catch a Thief* (1955), and *The Man Who Knew Too Much* (1956).
3. Andrew Sarris, *The American Cinema* (New York: E.P. Dutton, 1968), 58.
4. François Truffaut, *Hitchcock* (New York: Simon & Schuster, 1967), 61; originally published as *Le cinéma selon Hitchcock* (Paris: Robert Laffont, 1966).
5. In the American version the characterizations of the heroes are more complex, and there is an added subjective component. See Elisabeth Weis, *The Silent Scream: Alfred Hitchcock's Sound Track* (East Brunswick, N.J.: Fairleigh Dickinson Univ. Press, 1982), 163.
6. Raymond Durgnat, *The Strange Case of Alfred Hitchcock* (Cambridge: MIT Press, 1974), 123.

THE MAN WHO KNEW TOO MUCH (Gaumont-British, 1934). *Producers:* Michael Balcon, Ivor Montagu, *Script:* A. R. Rawlinson, Charles Bennett, D. B. Whyndham-Lewis, Edwin Greenwood, Emlyn Williams, *Photography:* Curt Courant, *Editor:* H. St. C. Stewart, *Sets:* Alfred Junge, Peter Proud, *Music:* Arthur Benjamin, *Players:* Leslie Banks (Bob Lawrence), Edna Best (Jill Lawrence), Peter Lorre (Abbott), Nova Pilbeam (Betty Lawrence), Hugh Wakefield (Clive), Pierre Fresnay (Louis Bernard), Frank Vosper (Ramon). 84 minutes.

CHAPTER NINE

Through a Woman's Eyes: Sexuality and Memory in *The 39 Steps*

Charles L. P. Silet

The 39 Steps is often credited with being the first really successful "Hitchcock" film, the one which brought together for the first time all of those dramatic elements for which Hitchcock became justly famous: the innocent man pursued by both police and criminals, the Hitchcockian blonde who educates the hero in the ethics of sexuality, the foregrounding of art via themes of theatricality.[1] Indeed, William Rothman's discussion of the film in his recent *Hitchcock — The Murderous Gaze* gains much of its considerable force by simultaneously confirming and denying the typicality of *The 39 Steps* — seeing it as Hitchcock's first real seriocomic "thriller" but explicitly contradicting the commonplace which reads Richard Hannay, the film's hero, as an early version of the Cary Grant figure whom Hitchcock both condemns and redeems in the series of films stretching from *Suspicion* through *Notorious* and *To Catch a Thief* to *North by Northwest*. In *The 39 Steps*, as Rothman reads it, the series of awakenings which Hannay undergoes do "not add up to a conversion. There is no article of faith he comes into or loses. He receives no edification, but then again he stands in need of none: Hannay is perfectly all right as he is."[2]

Rothman is not literally accurate here: Hannay has much to learn if he wishes to clear himself of the charge of murder lodged against him after "Annabella Smith" is found knifed to death in his London flat. He needs to learn who lives at Alt-na-Shellach, for example; he needs to learn that Professor Jordan is the ringleader of "the 39 steps" spy organization; he needs to learn that the police who arrest him at the political rally are not police but Jordan's henchmen; he needs to learn where and how Jordan will pick up the Air Ministry secrets which he plans to spirit out of the country. But Hitchcock presents us with a kind of "MacGuffin" or displacement in *The 39 Steps* which makes it difficult to see the relationship between the film's overtly political intrigue and its primarily sexual thematic matrix. We might say that education in *The 39 Steps* is construed less in terms of self-criticism, as in *North by Northwest*, than as a matter of memory, such that it is less what Hannay says than what he remembers (or can remember) which counts; and what he has to remember is primarily a series of male/female encounters which mark the progress of his redemption from a charge of woman-killing to his implied union with Pamela, as if Hitchcock were thereby acknowledging the value of women on behalf of a (male) society which treats women, and especially marriages between men and women, as traps to be avoided.[3]

The opposition between sexual equality and the values of the dominant culture is first sketched out in the music hall scene which opens *The 39 Steps*, though the opposition between what are essentially masculine values and sexual honesty is repeated throughout the film in a series of scenes which invariably turn on or have recourse to overtly sexist jokes or assumptions—the scene between Hannay and the milkman, for instance, or that with Hannay and the corset salesmen on the Highland Express. The music hall scene is especially important, however, for happening twice, at the film's beginning as well as, in a modified or displaced form, at its conclusion. And its first instance, together with the following scenes between Hannay and Annabella Smith, provides clear evidence of the displacement of sex by politics (and vice versa) which structures the film.

Thus the first question put to Mr. Memory in the initial music hall scene is asked by a woman—"where's my old man been since last Saturday"—though the overt honesty, even anger, of her question is met with deaf ears. "A serious question, please," replies Mr. Memory. More "serious" questions follow—most of them having to do with British sporting events—though one of those, asked *by* a woman, effectively reasserts the link between private facts of sexuality and more public forms of knowledge: "Who was the last British heavyweight champion of the world?" She receives three answers: Henry VIII, "my old woman," and Bob Fitzsimmons, the latter of whom defeated Jim Corbett in October of 1897. The first two answers are offered as boisterous jokes; taken together they envision sex as a kind of national/dynastic battleground. Indeed, it is a repeatedly unanswered sex question—"How old is Mae West?"—which initiates the drunken brawl which Annabella's pistol shots then accelerate into a panic. And the sense in which Mr. Memory's species of sexual propriety (the questions he will not answer) is representative of the culture of his audience is indicated by the master of ceremonies, who boasts that Mr. Memory has willed his brain to the British Museum, as if it were a national treasure, part and parcel of the nation's larger recall of itself.

A similar pattern of sexual jokes and unanswered questions—leading again to sexual violence—is evident in the scenes leading from the music hall to Hannay's flat and finally to Annabella's death. Once outside the music hall Annabella asks Hannay if she can go home with him (so as to evade pursuit by

Jordan's henchmen). In a bemused tone Hannay replies "it's your funeral" —
not knowing that the violence jokingly hinted at in the sex/death commonplace will soon come back to haunt him. As they board the bus to go back to
Hannay's flat, and we catch a glimpse of Hitchcock walking by, we can also see,
if we are careful, a sign on the bus which reads "Cooperative Permanent."
Hannay clearly at this point sees Annabella's companionship as a very temporary affair. But the subsequent course of events—her hiding in the shadows
of Hannay's sitting room, her request that Hannay turn the mirror to the wall,
her insistence that Hannay not answer the incessantly ringing telephone, her
tale of espionage and a nation at risk which Hannay brushes off as a "spy story,"
the symptom of "persecution mania," cautioning her to be more careful in
choosing her gentlemen friends—makes of Annabella a very "permanent"
companion, an indelible fixture of Hannay's memory. Indeed it is for remembering his own response to Annabella—a memory which takes the form of
Annabella's ghostly presence in Hannay's field of vision: "The police would not
believe me any more than you did"—that Hannay decides to flee London, to
take Annabella's task upon himself, to become her "co-operative."

Hannay thus begins his journey with a sense of urgency and danger. It will
be a matter of life or death before he is through—and a matter of sexuality,
marriage, and women as well. Significantly, Hannay's next encounter with a
woman follows almost immediately upon his departure from the company of
the joking underwear salesmen whose compartment he has shared on the
Highland Express—as if in rejecting their sexual ethics he were fated henceforth to depend upon women and their world for his survival. Out in the train
corridor Hannay is stopped by a uniformed porter who inquires if he will take
tea in the dining car. Hannay replies that he will, but in replying notices police
moving through the train. Desperate, Hannay enters a compartment not his
own, sits down next to its only occupant, a blonde young woman reading a
book, whom we later recognize as Pamela, takes her into his arms, and rather
forcefully kisses her. During the kiss the woman's glasses slip between the
embracing couple and disappear. The police in the corridor pass by the couple
as one of the uniformed Bobbies cracks that "someone in there is getting a free
meal." The remark carries a double meaning, and the other police*men* smile at
the off-color joke. The remark also brings back to mind the cluster of associations of meals, domesticity, sex, marriage, and couples which have already
passed in the film. Particularly important here is the disappearance of the
glasses, perhaps suggesting that Pamela will be barred from reading about the
murder as the salesman had done and will need to draw her own conclusions
when she encounters Hannay again. Another possibility has to do with the
whole idea of Hannay's education and awakening. By the end of the film
Hannay will be forced to see the film world clearly, especially its underlying
sexual dynamics, which he accomplishes in (metaphorical) part by borrowing a
pair of women's opera glasses in the Palladium sequence (our kinship with

Hannay throughout the film will be confirmed by our sharing his point of view here). The single image we take away from the kissing scene is a vivid one of Pamela's right eye expressing a sense of fear while Hannay's head obscures the rest of her face. It is an image which will haunt both *Vertigo* and *Psycho.*

Hannay immediately apologizes for his actions, once the police have passed by, confesses that he is in danger, and pleads with Pamela not to betray him. The police return at this moment to ask if either of them have seen a man pass by. The man in front of her is the one they are seeking, Pamela tells them. Providentially, the railway porter enters at this moment to announce that tea is served. It is all the diversion Hannay needs to open the exterior door of the compartment and swing himself to the outside of the train. In the chase which follows, the police stop the train, allowing Hannay to get off and hide among the girders of the bridge spanning the Firth of Forth.

Hannay's next encounter with a female, the crofter's wife, begins by seeming chance, as did the first two. Hannay hikes down a hill and meets John, the dour crofter, who agrees to put him up for the night. For a second time Hannay pays for assistance; the milkman, while verbally refusing the pound note Hannay offers to borrow his white hat and coat, neatly takes, folds, and pockets the bill while announcing that he may need the same sort of assistance some day. The association of money with escape also brings it into a relationship with sex and marriage. John goes beyond the amiable banter of the milkman as his avarice is linked with his strangely obsessive jealousy. One might ponder the rather odd attraction afforded to him by bringing a handsome outsider into contact with his young and impressionable wife. After all, he could easily refuse to harbor Hannay: the money seems slight enough reason when one considers the extremity of his jealousy. There is obviously something more to his motives.

According to Hitchcock this whole scene was derived from an off-color story which was a favorite of his. In his interview with the late François Truffaut he tells the joke about the old, black-bearded, extremely austere South African Boer and his sex-starved wife. The latter slaughters a chicken and bakes her husband a chicken pie for his birthday, only to be scolded for killing the bird without his permission. The night is stormy and suddenly a stranger arrives at the door and requests shelter. The man is let in and offered some of the pie, but the Boer won't let him have very much. The woman, in Hitchcock's words, is "hungrily eyeing the stranger, wondering how she can get to bed with him." The husband suggests that the stranger sleep in the barn; the wife insists that all three get into bed together. Finally the woman sends the husband out to check the rest of the chickens and tells the stranger "Come on, now's your chance." And the stranger hops out of bed and gulps down the rest of the chicken pie.[4]

The point of the dirty story is to show how both the sex-starved wife and her grasping husband get their comeuppance at the hands of a stranger. By contrast with the crofter, however, Margaret is not the cartoon caricature of the joke merely brought to life on film. She seems genuinely compassionate and even is willing to risk her husband's wrath, which she has surely experienced before, in order to help the stranger escape. There are parallels in this scene to the one between Hannay and Annabella. Margaret prepares a meal of fish for Hannay, as he had for Annabella; both strangers confess their involvement in something mysterious; both seem exotic to their host/hostess and bring the latter a break in the monotony of their lives. In both scenes there is an implied sexual element, seen in Annabella's initial proposition and in Hannay's rather uncharacteristic attempts to manipulate Margaret's obvious loneliness and longing to his benefit. Also like Annabella, Hannay withdraws the sexual suggestion as he genuinely learns to appreciate Margaret's unselfish coopera- tion, even to the point of helping him escape. Hannay thus plays both roles — host/guest, male/female — and learns from the women in both instances. An- nabella teaches Hannay to attend to what people say: her warnings prove accurate, the spies are indeed dangerous, and Hannay does have to watch out. Margaret teaches Hannay a certain humility, as she willingly sacrifices herself for his well-being.

Rather than being an illustrated dirty joke, then, the scene at the crofter's becomes an object lesson in a bad marriage and provides a counterpoint for the Hannay/Pamela scenes later on. The crofter and his wife are truly chained together in a terrible sort of bondage. The cavalier quips of the milkman and the badinage of the traveling salesmen on the train become the horror of the Margaret/John relationship; it is the worst example of a marriage we will see in the film.

After the three retire for the night, Margaret and John to their marriage bed, Hannay to the box bed, the police arrive. For the second time in the film Hannay is awakened by a woman and sent on his way. The pattern which emerges here is not only that women (especially Annabella) alert Hannay to the dangers of the world but also that they are capable of saving him from danger altogether, as we later see in Pamela's case. In a final gesture Margaret gives Hannay her husband's overcoat because Hannay's jacket is "so terrible light." The coat provides an image of her protectiveness, her desperate need to care for someone. As Hannay leaves he kisses her and tells her that he will never forget her. After the door has closed on his exit, Margaret turns slowly toward the camera as Hitchcock lovingly captures her gentleness and goodness in a silent-screen image worthily reminiscent of Murnau or Griffith.

Hannay's subsequent flight from the crofter's cottage takes him over more ragged countryside to the door of the Professor's house, the goal of his journey so far, where Hitchcock provides him yet another object lesson in sexual poli- tics.

It is instructive that the most English of couples in the film are the spies, the Professor and his wife.[5] Even as he conveys his annoyance at Hannay's

sudden appearance, which might jeopardize his upper-class cover, Professor
Jordan notes in his civilized way that he doesn't know what his wife and
daughter would think. Just as the Professor is handing Hannay a gun and
suggesting that he might want to blow his brains out for the sake of convenience, Mrs. Jordan sallies in, irritated that she and the other guests are being
kept waiting at the dinner table. Glancing quite calmly at the gun in Jordan's
hand, she asks if Hannay will be staying for lunch. The Professor doesn't think
so. The husband/wife relationship here raises the question of marriage as a
kind of screen or cover and opens the possibility of seeing below the surface of
another relationship. If Margaret and John hid their feelings, they were nevertheless right below the surface. The Professor and his wife demonstrate how
layers of refinement can disguise depths of evil.

The conclusion of the sequence at Jordan's mansion—the "death" of
Hannay—jerks us both backward and forward. The Professor shoots Hannay to
eliminate the risk of disclosure; the film cuts to John and Margaret as she
confesses she gave the stranger his coat with the Bible in the pocket, a confession which earns her his abusive blows in return; the sound track delivers
laughter as we cut to the police station and a close-up of the Bible with the
Professor's bullet lodged in it. The sheriff's joke about some of those hymns
being powerful hard to get through also provokes the ironic realization that
John's religion has done some good after all, though only through Margaret's
intercession. Indeed, the contrast of Margaret and Annabella, to this point,
indicates that women may function as sources of liberation as well as of confinement or entrapment. This zigzagging between these seemingly contradictory states, freedom and bondage, will continue throughout the film with
Pamela finally uniting the two themes by providing freedom *through* confinement.

The next significant male/female encounter in the film follows Hannay's
escape from the sheriff and his participation, handcuffs and all, in a Salvation
Army parade. Once he has left the marchers he ducks into a doorway labeled
"Assembly Hall" to elude the police. As he does so, Hannay is promptly seized
by a woman who announces that they have been waiting for him and pushes
him out onto a stage where another woman beckons him to be seated. After a
mumbled introduction by another man and with some prompting from the
woman seated next to him, Hannay finally rises to make a speech. However, as
he is beginning to say how pleased, and perhaps relieved, he is to be on that
stage before this audience, the blonde from the train enters the hall in the
company of a man, presumably the politician whom Hannay has been mistaken for.

Both Hannay and the woman seem surprised to see each other. Hannay
continues to speak—to the effect that as long as he is on this stage he is
delivered from the cares, and also the dangers, of the day; about his ride on

the Highland Express; about the bridge at the Firth of Forth, in the process recalling (to his mind and ours) the location of his first meeting with the blonde woman. Meanwhile Pamela starts up the side aisle to get help—at which point she encounters two of the Professor's men. Mistaking them for policemen (though they most resemble Gestapo agents with their long leather coats), she confides to them that Hannay is an escaped criminal. They follow her back up the side aisle while Hannay, seeing this, becomes all the more impassioned about banishing cruelty and fear and oppression and of knowing how it feels to have the whole world against you. It is a compilation/distillation of Hannay's experience so far and suggests a change in his perspective. His world has widened and he has been made aware, as have we, of something missing in his life—passion and commitment. He now accidentally dangles the loose handcuff (the sheriff only managed to close one of the manacles before Hannay bolted) as an image of his incompleteness, of his need of another. As he finishes the speech he tries to exit through the front of the hall, but the pressing crowd pushes him back into the waiting arms of the Professor's thugs. Desperate, Hannay turns to Pamela, imploring her to call the High Commissioner of Canada, thus unwittingly implicating her (as Annabella had more knowingly implicated Hannay) in the effort against Jordan. The "police," accordingly, ask Pamela to come along as well.

And again it is a woman who helps Hannay to escape. Angry or not, haughty or not, Pamela is far more observant than Hannay (the result of prior experience—of memory?) in noticing first that the car has passed the local constabulary. Her saying so forces their captors to fabricate a story about having to take them to Inverary, and it is Pamela who precipitates Hannay's decision to run for it when she subsequently notices the signpost indicating that the car is not heading in the direction of Inverary at all. Hannay is quick to pick up on the implications of her observations and asks to see the warrant for his arrest—at which moment he begins to whistle the Mr. Memory tune from the first Music Hall sequence. In spite of the fact that he has been among the spies before, it isn't until he is with Pamela that he begins the process of unraveling the mystery of their "39 steps" organization. The reappearance of this little music hall tune symbolizes the beginning of what proves to be Hannay's final awakening. It is vitally important that the first appearance of it should be with Pamela—as if she were responsible for his memory.

Hannay follows up his original request to see the warrant by betting Pamela that the police are not police at all, that they work for a man whose little finger, right hand, is missing something. Hannay gets slugged for his trouble (like Margaret for hers?). As Hannay says "I win," Pamela looks at him in shock (as if she too had been slugged?). She is now consciously aware that things are not always what they seem. Hannay reintroduces the joke motif as the car skids to a stop amid a flock of sheep. Lots of detectives he quips.

Getting out of the car to clear the road, one of the spies fastens the other handcuff to Pamela's wrist, remarking that she is now a special constable and that Hannay will stay with her. Or go with him, Hannay says, exiting the other side of the auto.

This brilliant stroke of handcuffing Hannay and Pamela brings together a number of themes associated with sex and coupling and marriage which have become established features of the film.[6] The comic spectacle of two adults of the opposite sex handcuffed together, especially the subsequent episode of Pamela removing her hosiery, suggests both the dirty joke motif as well as the issue of eroticism as previously represented by the Mae West reference, by Annabella's come-on to Hannay, by the brassiere / girdle images associated with the salesmen on the train, by the crofter's sexual possessiveness and voyeurism, etc. It also brings forward once again the many direct references to marriage — the milkman's, the salesman's "my wife — burr," John and Margaret, the Jordans — all people tied or chained together. The loose cuff, shiny and circular, suggests a wedding ring, as well as whatever level of commitment and bond goes with it — or should.

The escape scene also recalls Hannay's earlier flight as he drags Pamela over waterways and across terrain resembling that which he encountered after fleeing the crofter's. The most important section of this sequence takes place as Hannay and Pamela walk along the fog enshrouded road. Hannay whistles the Mr. Memory tune; Pamela tells him to stop. Throughout this scene she snaps back at Hannay, suggesting her mettle and independence of spirit. She asks him why he is doing all of this if he can't possibly escape; Hannay tells her to keep such questions for her husband. The implication is strong by film's end — given the film's underlying concern with sexuality generally and marriage especially — that he will indeed become her husband, so the remark here is both appropriate and prophetic, like the remark to Annabella about her funeral. Hannay now mentions that the two men who captured them were not police, and Pamela asks when he noticed — to which Hannay replies that she too should have seen that they were impostors: it was right under her nose, he tells her, suggesting that she needs to observe things more carefully. While criticizing her, he also compliments her on her observation that they were not going in the right direction, which he admits he hadn't seen. When he now tells her the spy story for the third time, she responds as before by comparing his confession to an espionage thriller. As if on cue, Hannay tries a new tack and becomes menacing, taking on a melodramatic stance reminiscent of Annabella's death scene in which her choking and overacting followed soon upon Hannay's remark that *her* explanation sounded like a spy story. Hannay's allusions to archfiends and defenseless women elicits Pamela's mildly unconvincing assertion that she is not at all frightened — at which point she sneezes, breaking Hannay's theatrical moment and pose. Genuinely exasperated at Pamela's refusal to believe him, Hannay seizes her by the coat and tells her seriocomically to do everything he tells her to, and quickly. In the last line of the scene Hannay confesses that, after all, he likes her pluck. He then begins to whistle the Memory tune as the scene fades.

Two important points about this encounter stand out. One is that Pamela is not much put off by any of Hannay's ruses, being neither scared, nor convinced, nor even very angry at him—all of which points to their growing relationship of commitment. Secondly, Hannay openly admits to Pamela that he admires her spirit, an admiration grounded in Hannay's experience and memory. He has been surrounded by assertive women all along; Annabella is a spy whose financial cynicism seems more assumed than real; Margaret in her quiet way shows enormous daring by defying John; even Mrs. Jordan snaps at the Professor for keeping lunch. Pamela's grit becomes attractive to Hannay here because he has encountered other women with similar toughness and because Pamela is both desirable and unattached. Hannay's remark, then, is more than incidental. It sets up the sequence at the inn where Pamela will finally believe Hannay and acknowledge her love for him.

The next woman on Hannay's itinerary is the innkeeper's wife and we are asked to judge whether or not she is as perceptive as the rest of the women in the film in her assessment of the lovers, despite their quite evident antagonism. There are several occasions when the landlady sees through the obvious. For example, when Hannay and Pamela feign coziness in front of the fire as the landlady brings in the tray of food, Hannay remarks that they are "warming" themselves—to which the landlady replies "I can *see* that." What she "sees" is the young couple warming themselves in a sexual way. Perhaps this explains why the promised nightgown never appears: the landlady assumes Pamela won't really need it. In the landlady we also have another instance of someone who finds humor in sex—though not of the smirking variety seen elsewhere in the film. Her humor is more knowing and romantic in tenor. Hers is a woman's view of sexuality and its awkwardnesses which recalls especially Margaret's impassioned naivete about beautiful women and painted toenails. Where men seem incapable of dealing with their sexuality except through crude, even brutal joking, women in *The 39 Steps* learn to accept sexuality with understanding. When finally told by Hannay that he and Pamela are a runaway couple on their wedding night, a story he fabricates to cover Pamela's gaff in recalling the landlady as she is about to leave the room, the landlady responds by saying that she knew it all along.

What the landlady understands as a question of intimacy in marriage, Pamela understands as a more immediate question of sex. It is instructive that she never appears to fear for her life from Hannay but is terrified of spending the night sleeping with him. Sex is a more powerful fright than death (cf. the crofter's relief at learning that Hannay is wanted for murder and is not seducing his wife). The sex question finds visual expression when Hannay drags Pamela upstairs at the inn. As they enter the room, framed in the doorway, their arms outstretched but manacled together, they frame the double bed between them. Once inside the room there is also the question of how they will sleep. As with Annabella and later at the crofter's, Hannay will sleep fully clothed, but there is a good deal of banter in this later scene about Pamela's taking off her wet clothes. Pamela refuses all suggestions that she remove her wet skirt, though Hannay assures her of his indifference: "I don't mind." It is a throwaway line which rather succinctly sums up the ambivalence of this scene. Hannay *really* doesn't mind. He is man of the world enough not to be shocked by female nudity but is also tired enough and gentleman enough not to have any sexual designs on Pamela. At least not on this particular night. Given his previous behavior and the calming effect his gestures of concern have on Pamela, we have to trust his good manners here.

Witness, for example, the rapid change in attitude Pamela undergoes in the scene where she does remove her stockings. In part, the scene's impact reinforces the erotic references in the film and reminds us of the joke-like ridiculousness of the spectacle of two adults handcuffed together. Pamela's awkwardness in removing her stockings with Hannay's cuffed hand trailing across her bare legs is both comic and erotic. Hannay's limp hand, only once showing any interest in Pamela's knee, is ample visual proof of Hannay's sincerity about not being a sexual threat. And when Hannay helps her hang up the stockings, her thank you is much quieter and more heartfelt than her no thank you was when he offered to help remove her hose. The change in mood here is remarkable; Pamela has seen something which will prepare her for the bantering scene on the bed and the final revelation disclosed by the conversation she later overhears as the spies phone Mrs. Jordan from the bar below.

When Hannay suggests going to bed, Pamela once again reacts according to type, though he quickly soothes her by declaring a truce, to the battle of the sexes presumably, and announcing that all he wants is a good night's sleep. The truce allows both of them to enjoy the long and rather amusing story Hannay tells about his life of crime. Pamela even has to suppress a laugh at one point to keep Hannay from realizing that she is enjoying the story and thereby relaxing in his company. The jokes about the Cornish Bluebeard remind us again of the sex/death/joke connection and highlight the series of "stories" Hannay has been telling since he began his flight. The sad tale of his life apparently puts Pamela to sleep, and as they both settle down the film fades to the scene of Professor Jordan's oddly emotional and moving farewell to his family as he departs for London.

The departure of the Professor takes us back to the inn and Pamela's escape from Hannay. Once Pamela awakens, she turns her attention to removing her hand from the cuff, which she does with some pain. As she is about to put on her hose, preparatory to leaving the room and the sleeping Hannay, she hears a noise downstairs in the bar. Stealing out onto the landing she overhears the phone call from the spies to Mrs. Jordan, a portion of which confirms

Hannay's story. As the garrulous barkeep is about to reveal the whereabouts of Hannay and Pamela, his wife appears and like an avenging angel whisks the inquiring spies out into the night, declaring that there'll be no after hours drinking. And warming to her husband as she closes the door, she smiles and coos to her "old fool" about not wanting to give away the young lovers, to which he also smiles and looks heavenward. Overhead, Pamela hears all this and returns to her room a changed woman, now protective in her turn rather than combative—as if having suddenly seen all of Hannay's previous actions anew, in a new light, an act of memory, the precedent for which we have already seen in Hannay's memorial envisioning of Annabella after her murder. Smiling down at the sleeping Hannay, Pamela now pulls the blanket over him. She then settles herself on the bench at the foot of the bed, thus reversing the sleeping arrangement of Hannay and Annabella earlier.

When Hannay awakens the next morning he glances at the empty hand-cuff, then to the open door. He smiles to himself, unconcerned if not philo-sophical about Pamela's escape; the smile almost betokens admiration. As he glances to the foot of the bed, however, Pamela sits up and returns his smile in full measure. He is puzzled. "What's the idea? How did we get out of these?" "*We* didn't, I did" she replies, maintaining the tone of verbal give and take which has characterized their relationship all along. Pamela tells Hannay how she discovered the truth and of her decision to stick around. Her volunteering to stay with him and help him constitutes a commitment on her part which Hannay will acknowledge and accept in the final frames of the film. She also, for the second time, supplies him with information which will aid him to expose the spies and clear himself. She also confesses that she has been a fool and apologizes for doubting him, a gesture he humbly accepts by telling her that it really is all right. The mood of companionship and mutual acknowledg-ment continues as Hannay gently suggests they get moving if they are to get ahead of the spies whom he thinks are still asleep at the inn. When Pamela says that they left last night, however, Hannay explodes and becomes his old self again, calling her a "button-headed little idiot" for failing to understand the gravity of the situation. Hannay's outburst here reminds us that love will not entirely alter these characters we have come to know. It is also an assurance that one of the strengths of their relationship is their ability to remain individ-uals within it, even though Hannay still has a murder charge hanging over his head—as he points out to Pamela. Her response, like Hannay's to Annabella, is to suggest they contact the police rather than take personal responsibility for foiling Jordan's espionage scheme.

The scene shifts to London where it is Pamela's turn to discover the futility of dealing with the police, and specifically with their inability to believe her story. It is as if they can't take her seriously—as Mr. Memory would not take seriously the woman who first rose to question his authority, his knowledge, in the film's opening scene.

The final sequence of *The 39 Steps,* at the Palladium, brings the film full circle. The laughing, smoking "Crazy Months" audience, although more genteel than their Music Hall predecessors, still recalls, if only by virtue of what its members choose to view and laugh at, the earlier crowd. Again we follow a central character into the theater, only this time it is Pamela, not Hannay, and she is also followed by police (as Annabella followed Jordan's thugs). At first Pamela cannot find Hannay, but by going to the balcony she spots him from above, as we first saw Annabella in a shot from above. Furthermore, Hannay is sitting pretty much in the same location as earlier. Except this time he is not just observing but looking for something specific. He borrows a woman's opera glasses, as if to signify his adoption of a woman's vantage point, through which (and only through which) he espies the stunted maleness figured in Professor Jordan's little finger. Pamela arrives and asks Hannay what he will do, just as Mr. Memory's tune strikes up. The puzzle is complete. That's what he has not been able to get out of his head: the tune, Annabella, the Music Hall, . . . the memories come in rapid succession. Again Hannay raises the woman's opera glasses. What he sees is the Professor signaling to Mr. Memory with a pocket watch, suggesting it is time to go and implying, perhaps, that Mr. Memory's memory has fallen under an hypnotic spell. "I've got it," Hannay announces, just as police storm down the side aisle (recalling Pamela at the political rally). Confronting the police, Hannay tries one last time to tell his story. Again, disbelief follows upon propriety. In desperation Hannay charges back into the audience and challenges Mr. Memory to explain "the 39 steps," which, after brief hesitation, he starts to do. Again shots ring out; Mr. Memory is hit; Jordan leaps from the balcony; again an audience panics. The police—brought there unwittingly, though providentially, by Pamela, as if to witness Hannay's redemption from guilt—close in on Jordan as the curtain falls.

The delicacy of the film's concluding sequence is hard to capture in words. On the one hand, Mr. Memory's backstage, confession-like recitation of the Air Ministry secrets redeems Hannay and confirms the liberating power which the exercise of memory can have, and almost off-handedly resolves the "spy" plot. As if to confess and confirm their own memories—Hannay's of all the women he has encountered, Pamela's of Hannay—each quietly seeks the other out, their hands entwining as the image fades. Hannay and Pamela thus come together voluntarily, without the restrictions which manacle the other couples in the film, a fact symbolized by the now dangling and useless handcuff which hangs between them as they stand together, backs to the camera.[7]

On the other hand, as William Rothman points out, the recollections invoked in the final shots, specifically those connotations clustered around the initial Music Hall sequence, carry decidedly negative implications, evidenced chiefly by the line of high-stepping, barely clad chorines visible in the background while Mr. Memory confesses to Hannay. Their presence is intended to calm panic and to reassert the Music Hall norm, sexuality as gag or display, as something not serious, which replaces or displaces the life or death drama just enacted (it literally takes the place previously occupied by Mr. Memory and Professor Jordan). Thus it matters tremendously that in the film's last frame Hannay and Pamela displace the dancing chorines in our field of vision. What we remember of them, what they might be remembering of themselves, stands literally opposed to the vision of women on view to the world of the film. Hannay and Pamela embody the secret of sexual equality and acknowledgment represented by the memories they bear and bear witness to. And whether they are members of another world or worldview, ours perhaps, depends on us, on the views we take and find memorable. In the words of William Rothman: "The camera's final gesture calls upon us to reaffirm our community with them. If we do so, we exempt ourselves from Hitchcock's indictment of the unviewed audience within the hall. We fulfill our calling as viewers" (p. 172).

Notes

1. This essay is a shortened version of a longer work on *The 39 Steps* currently in preparation.
2. William Rothman, *Hitchcock — The Murderous Gaze* (Cambridge: Harvard Univ. Press, 1982), 125. The contents of this essay as well as its form owe much to Rothman's excellent chapter on *The 39 Steps*.
3. Maurice Yacowar touches on this theme lightly in his discussion of the film in *Hitchcock's British Films* (Hamden, Conn.: Archon Books, 1977), 185 and passim.
4. François Truffaut, *Hitchcock* (New York: Simon & Schuster, 1967), 66.
5. Donald Spoto briefly deals with this point in his analysis of *The 39 Steps* in *The Art of Alfred Hitchcock* (New York: Hopkinson and Blake, 1976), 42–43.
6. See also Raymond Durgnat's ideas on handcuffing in *The Strange Case of Alfred Hitchcock* (Cambridge: MIT Press, 1978), 129–30.
7. Stuart Y. McDougall writes about some of these same ideas, although his main point is to compare the adaptation of Hitchcock's film from the John Buchan novel, cf. "Mirth, Sexuality and Suspense: Alfred Hitchcock's Adaptation of *The Thirty-Nine Steps*," *Literature/Film Quarterly*, vol. 3, no. 3 (1975): 232–39. For an additional essay on the theme of adaptation see also Jocelyn Camp, "John Buchan and Alfred Hitchcock," *Literature/Film Quarterly*, vol. 6, no. 3 (1978): 230–40.

THE 39 STEPS (Gaumont-British, 1935). *Producers:* Michael Balcon, Ivor Montagu, *Script:* Charles Bennett, Alma Reville, Ian Hay, from the novel by John Buchan, *Photography:* Bernard Knowles, *Editor:* Derek N. Twist, *Sets:* Otto Werndorff, Albert Jullion, *Music:* Louis Levy, *Costumes:* J. Strassner, *Players:* Madeleine Carroll (Pamela), Robert Donat (Richard Hannay), Lucie Mannheim (Annabella Smith), Godfrey Tearle (Professor Jordan), Peggy Ashcroft (the crofter's wife), John Laurie (the crofter), Wylie Watson (Mr. Memory). 87 minutes.

Rematerializing the Vanishing "Lady": Feminism, Hitchcock, and Interpretation

Patrice Petro

I.

Whose desire does narrative speak? Does classical film narrative solely produce pleasure for the male spectator? Is all representation of female desire hopelessly caught within relations which situate man as bearer of the look, as the active and desiring viewer, and woman as merely the passive object of his gaze?

Ever since Laura Mulvey advanced this reading of classical cinema in "Visual Pleasure and Narrative Cinema," feminist theorists have returned to Hitchcock's films in an effort to address the question—and discern the possibility—of female desire in narrative.[1] This is not to suggest, however, that feminist theorists have reached any agreement about Hitchcock, narrative, or visual pleasure; indeed, the polemics which continue to rage on these issues, in and of themselves, raise further questions about the very function of feminist interpretation. Raymond Bellour, for example, agrees with Mulvey that Hitchcock's films inevitably reduce woman to the passive object of the male gaze. In his interpretation of *Marnie*, Bellour maintains further that Hitchcock's fascination with woman's image characterizes Hollywood cinema in general, where the "man-subject-behind-the-camera" guards against the disturbing fact of sexual difference by producing images of woman that define her desire in terms of his own. Reformulating the question Freud posed long ago ("What do women want?"), Bellour asks:

> What is orgastic pleasure for woman? What is the nature of her desire?
> . . . This question is raised in two movements. . . . The first of these
> movements consists in the activation of an irreducible difference: "the dark
> continent of female sexuality" for Freud, the privilege granted to woman
> with respect to pleasure for Lacan (with its reverse side of ignorance . . .);

in Hollywood cinema [this movement involves the] extreme condensation of sexuality in the woman's body image. The second movement effects a calculated reduction of this magnified difference based on a single element: of which the woman's sexuality . . . constitutes, for the man, a visible reversal, the mirror image.[2]

Where the representation of female desire effectively "vanishes" from Bellour's thinly veiled auteurist analysis of visual pleasure, it rematerializes in Tania Modleski's appropriation of a different practice and a different question for feminist interpretation. Countering Bellour, she argues that in order for woman to mold her image according to man's desire, "she must first ascertain what that desire is. And given the complex and contradictory nature of male desire, it is no wonder that women become baffled, confused. . . . Although women have not had the chance to articulate the problem as directly as men have, they could easily ask Freud's question of the opposite sex: what is it they want?"[3] Rather than construct classical film narrative as monolithic or invariant, Modleski seizes upon its contradictions which allow female desire to "speak," however tentatively or provisionally. To be sure, Modleski does not deny the force of Bellour's analysis of male power and pleasure in the cinema and in culture. Yet, rather than reproduce male Oedipal narratives in her own critical analyses, she interprets classical films differently so as to forge and identify a place for female subjectivity. As Modleski suggests: "Current film theory tends to agree with Roland Barthes that all traditional narratives reenact the male Oedipal crisis. . . . While I do not mean to underestimate the strength of this position—we do, after all, live in a patriarchal society—I believe that we occasionally encounter a film which adopts a feminine viewpoint and allows the woman's voice to speak (if only in a whisper), articulating her discontent with the patriarchal order" (p. 34).

Such a film, for Modleski, is Hitchcock's *Rebecca* (1940). But in my view, a much more forceful and less equivocal example of a female Oedipal (even anti-Oedipal) narrative is the film directed by Hitchcock two years earlier, *The Lady Vanishes* (1938). Despite the interest *The Lady Vanishes* might hold for feminists, and despite its canonical status as Hitchcock's penultimate British film, it has, of yet, received little critical attention. To date the most sustained and interesting close reading of the film is Raymond Durgnat's. While suggestive in his remarks about the film's maternal register—implicit in aspects of the Miss Froy/Iris relationship—Durgnat chooses to emphasize the film's historical and political import for its contemporary British audience.[4] He clearly acknowledges the questions and enigmas raised by *The Lady Vanishes* and attempts to interpret them without reducing their significance to a single or coherent meaning. Nevertheless, his contention that the film's secret tune is merely an element of the film's overall "musical atmosphere" and his suggestion that none of the characters (and particularly Iris) undergo any profound change in the narrative are two readings my own analysis will contest.

If the title of *The Lady Vanishes* raises the question of woman, it also seems to suggest an inevitable narrative resolution: the "lady," the woman, the secret support of narrative and symbolic order must vanish from representation in order for the narrative to contain the threat she poses by virtue of her sexual difference. While a feminist analysis cannot entirely dismiss such a resolution, it is also important to stress that the film does not present the heroine's progression towards Oedipus and heterosexual union in a straightforward or inevitable way. Instead, *The Lady Vanishes* explores female desire both within and on the margins of Oedipal/paternal relations, occasioning a textual movement through which affectual desire is activated for the spectator by focusing upon the heroine's search for the mother and for what rapidly becomes the lost object of her original desire.

This affectual or original desire, it must be emphasized, is not exclusively a function of the spectator's identification with the heroine or of the heroine's desire for reunion with the mother. As Julia Kristeva explains, desire is never simply desire for an object (whether that object be the mother or the father) but also for an experience that precedes object choice and sexual differentiation (a desire rooted not in identification but in its dissolution).[5] The heroine's desire for that which exists on the boundaries of the Oedipus complex might be said to carry with it both the pleasurable experience of rhythm and movement as well as the threat of horror, fear, and psychosis that follows upon the dissolution of identification and representation. This double desire—desire for an object and desire for desire itself—is set into play for both the heroine and spectator of *The Lady Vanishes* through a musical theme. And quite appropriately, for music carries with it perhaps the least obvious reference to objects and the strongest reference to emotion and affect, serving to mark the heroine's erotic development and to foreground the role of the nonrepresentational (affect, rhythm, movement, drive) in addition to the representational (*mise en scène,* characters, plot) in the desiring process that is cinema. That this music is ultimately portrayed as lending fundamental support to the film's depicted (symbolic, economic, and political) order cannot be denied. It is nonetheless significant that the heroine never violently repudiates the maternal figure (as the Joan Fontaine character repudiates Mrs. Danvers in *Rebecca*) but activates the emotive power of maternal psychic energy in order to resist patriarchal definitions which seek to deny both her vision and her memory.

II.

Over the credits that open *The Lady Vanishes* is the musical strain associated with Miss Froy, a phrase later identified as the secret tune carrying important information for European security. The camera reveals a serene mountain landscape, then passes over the results of a recent avalanche before the image dissolves to the chateau and then to the chateau lobby. The first human to interfere in the tranquility of this landscape is Miss Froy, the film's maternal figure, although she is soon forgotten in the pace of events which follow. After checking in at the desk, Miss Froy exits: two men enter and announce that an avalanche has blocked the railway lines, with the result that all passengers will be stranded at the chateau overnight. The composed *mise en scène* and melodious sound track give way to a cacophony of languages, sounds, and movements—to spatial and aural confusion. Miss Froy could thus be said to disturb the narrative's previously established order. And, indeed, what follows upon her departure is a rather fragmented introduction to the sexual "deviations" of the various characters: Caldicott and Charters, the two British gentlemen who bicker like a stereotypical married couple, are terrorized by the sexuality of the maid whose room they must share; "Mr. and Mrs." Todhunter, a couple who are involved in an extramarital affair, have lost the passion and intimacy they once had; Iris and her two girlfriends, whose bodies are displayed in a fragmented, specular series of shots, discuss the limitations of Iris's upcoming marriage to a British blue blood (Iris announces, "I shall take the veil . . . and change my name to Mrs. Charles Fotheringale. . . . I've no regrets. I've been everywhere, done everything. . . . What is there left for me but marriage?"—to which one of her friends responds, "Couldn't you get him to change *his* name instead?"); and Gilbert, a professional musicologist recording the ancient folk music of Central Europe, who interrupts the guitar serenade that enraptures Miss Froy and soothes Iris, both of whom occupy rooms directly beneath his.

Gilbert's music is, importantly, quite different from the music associated with Miss Froy. Serene, dangerous, and mysterious, Miss Froy's music carries with it what Kristeva has termed "abjection," the threat of horror, silence, and death as visualized in the strangulation of the lone guitarist who first performs it. In contrast, Gilbert's rendition of the ancient folk music of Central Europe is in no way natural, expressive, or evocative: he forces the rather reluctant servants to engage in a dance routine which he alone orchestrates and manipulates. His intent in performing this music is articulated, moreover, as a desire to preserve and promote the "ancient" sexual/social relations of patriarchal culture (the dance Gilbert orders up, he explains to the chateau manager, is "the dance they danced when your father married your mother"), and thus Gilbert is implicated in what Kristeva in *Powers of Horror* calls the desire "to know everything, to know, in particular, what seems to be lacking in his mother or could be lacking in himself" (p. 34). Explicitly represented as competing with the guitar serenade, Gilbert's music so annoys Iris that she reports Gilbert to the management. In retaliation, Gilbert forces himself into her room, tosses his cane onto her bed (only after he kisses it), and challenges her to get rid of him. As representative of the patriarchal order, Gilbert's music (not to mention his rather obnoxious behavior, noisily singing, brushing his teeth, and running the bathwater) sets up a strong polarity between himself and Miss Froy, respectively distinguishing and identifying the paternal and maternal registers of the film.

These different registers in *The Lady Vanishes* are explored both in image and in music, which is to say, in both representational and nonrepresentational ways. Iris's initial resignation in the face of Oedipal imperatives, her apparent need to aspire to heterosexual union as expressed in her conversation with her girlfriends, is in fact reinforced by the accompanying images that abstract and fragment her body in erotic display (a display, it may be added, which even embarrasses the manservant when he delivers a rather large bottle of champagne that punctuates her image). This visual fixing of the female figure is nevertheless disrupted by the musical strains associated with both Gilbert and Miss Froy. And yet rather than identify initially with the musical values associated with Gilbert (values which attempt to fix female positions in a hierarchical and paternalistic fashion in a way not unlike the images that fragment Iris's body), Iris will choose instead the maternal strain associated with Miss Froy. To be sure, Iris's choice for the maternal register is already anticipated by her relationship with her two girlfriends (she kisses them on the forehead and says, "Goodnight, my children"); she will nonetheless opt for maternal identification only after meeting Miss Froy again and sharing with her the experience of a different time and, indeed, a different desire.

Once the avalanche has been cleared and the passengers are able to proceed to London, yet another dislocation, again initiated by Miss Froy, disrupts narrative and spatial order. As Iris bids farewell to her friends, Miss Froy interrupts to ask if anyone has seen a piece of her luggage. Receiving only a quizzical response, Miss Froy walks away. Iris suddenly discovers that Miss Froy has inadvertently dropped her glasses and in returning them to her is struck on the head by a falling window box apparently intended for Miss Froy. (As a sign of female subjectivity, the glasses might be said to emphasize the risks involved when woman appropriates the gaze, especially when that woman is named "Iris.") Unable to delay the train's departure so that Iris might regain composure, Miss Froy assures Iris's friends that she will look after their companion and the two women board the train together. Now guided by Miss Froy, Iris embarks on a journey that leads her away from Oedipal desire and towards a desire characterized by delirium, displacement, and the threat of madness.

Iris's unsteady vision, evoked through a superimposed image of train wheels, smoke, and faces, suggests an aberration in her mental processes and calls into question for the spectator the "reality" of the sequence that follows. Significantly, this is the sequence where Iris and Miss Froy introduce themselves and share a conversation over a cup of tea. Iris introduces herself by situating her identity within the terms of patriarchal relations ("My name is Iris Henderson. I'm going home to get married"). Miss Froy, by contrast, introduces herself as a governess, but a train whistle drowns out her voice as she speaks her name. Struggling to make herself heard, Miss Froy pronounces her name precisely, but when Iris mistakes the assonance of "Froy" for "Freud," Miss Froy rhymes her name explicitly with "joy." Unmarried yet still maternal, joyful yet facing the constant threat of death as a secret agent, Miss Froy's identity is cast, not within patriarchal relations, but on their margins. Her recommendation to Iris that she have children may therefore be understood as a plea for a nonpatriarchal definition of motherhood, since Miss Froy herself performs a maternal function outside of marriage. Indeed, her very inability to speak her name situates her identity within a maternal realm that borders the unnameable, where subject identities exist, but only barely so.

This sequence of their meeting, the memory of which will later haunt Iris, is also rendered in ambiguous terms, bounded as it is by shots of train wheels that introduce, close, and reintroduce narrative action. As I have suggested, the first shot of train wheels is relayed from Iris's point of view: a superimposed image of smoke, faces, and train wheels, coded to be read as dreamlike, is followed by a shot of Iris waking from sleep. The shot of train wheels that closes the sequence is, by contrast, not superimposed and not coded as "unreal," and yet, like the first, it is followed by a shot of Iris waking from sleep. The organization of this sequence suggests the possibility that Iris has only imagined her encounter with Miss Froy, and that only upon waking from (her second) sleep does she regain "proper" consciousness. The dreamlike quality of their meeting is thereby reinforced cinematically, visualized as an intersection between the glimpse of a real object and an hallucination. Only the trace of Miss Froy's name on the dining car window will reactivate the truth of their encounter for Iris (and by extension for the spectator), serving to verify not only Miss Froy's existence but Iris's perception as well.

That Iris's desire for and identification with Miss Froy takes place on a train suggests a further variation in the film's maternal register. The temporality of the train ride, in addition to representing a "male" register of time as linear, progressive, and teleological, also initiates a kind of rhythm that provides for Iris's entry into an earlier psychic realm, a realm of undifferentiated sexuality and temporality.[6] (Indeed, even when Iris is brought back into line with the paternal symbolic system, that is, even when she transfers her focus of desire from Miss Froy to Gilbert, the train is again dislocated and driven off the main rails. Male authority, it seems, must assert itself far more forcefully if narrative closure or resolution is to be enacted.) Where the chateau is somewhat static, confining, and baroque, the train allows for movement and rhythm. And where the artificial architecture of the chateau contributes to the representational potential of the characters, individuating them from their environment, the rhythm of the train serves as the site for Iris's projection of her desire, where what is repressed at the level of the narrative (the representation of Iris's desire for the mother) reemerges through the *mise en scène* as hallucination, revealing Iris's desire to be analogous to that which psychoanalytic theory attributes to an inaugural loss (the loss of sexually undifferentiated affectual feelings that exist prior to maternal or paternal object-choices), a loss upon which desire, language, and meaning are subsequently founded.

In direct opposition to Mulvey's and Bellour's analysis of visual pleasure in the cinema—where desire is understood to be rooted in a hierarchical system in which the man is the bearer of the look, the woman the object of his gaze—Iris initiates the investigation into Miss Froy's disappearance and controls through her gaze the narrative search for the lost object which is also a woman. Although Iris's attempt to account for Miss Froy is clearly mistrusted by the other characters within the fiction, read symptomatically her look offers resistance to the assertion that woman's status in the cinema is to be objectified as spectacle according to the masculine structure and motive of the cinematic gaze. In fact, Dr. Hartz's attempt to produce such a reading of Iris's investigating gaze, that is, his attempt to name female subjectivity as a sign of illness ("There was no Miss Froy," he tells her, "only a vivid, subjective image") is likewise rendered suspect in the narrative. Not only is Dr. Hartz sinister, associated with the menace to international security, his theory is also understood by other characters (and, indeed, by the spectator) to be overly indulgent and dismissive of Iris's real experience. (When Iris tells him that one of the passengers has remembered Miss Froy, he replies, "My theory was a perfectly good one—the facts were misleading." The "facts" of woman's experience, it seems, are all too frequently passed over by psychoanalysis.) And when the doctor, in collaboration with the magician, substitutes Mme. Kummer for Miss Froy, Iris not only refuses to accept the substitution as a valid representation of the real object of her desire, but she also rejects the attempt to dematerialize her vision, to explain it away: she remembers and describes Miss Froy's dress exactly, down to the small blue handkerchief in her breast pocket.

Iris's refusal nevertheless carries with it the possibility of terror, where the lack of a signifiable object (Does Miss Froy exist? Is she an illusion?) calls attention to the basis of desire in that which exists prior to the selection of an object for desire. Iris's vision of Miss Froy is projected onto the faces of the other passengers, transforming her desire into an apparition materialized in the environment. The environment itself thus becomes threatening, causing Iris to temporarily suffer despair, isolation, and mental enclosure. Iris's state of delirium lasts only a short time, for she immediately pulls back from the threat of madness, from a desire which has foundered on drive and affect. Joining Gilbert, who advises her to make her mind "blank," she desperately tries to repress her memory and her vision. Gilbert's incessant talk about his father ("it's surprising how many great men began with their fathers")—that is, his attempt to bring her into line with the paternal order—leaves Iris unmoved. She returns to the topic of Miss Froy and lapses into hysteria when Miss Froy's name reappears on the dining car window. Importantly, this hysteria is attributed, not to her confusion about the boundary between subject and object, self and other, but to her conviction that a real object actually exists. Aggressively seizing control of the situation, Iris demands that the group take immediate action and pulls the emergency brake to halt the train when no action is forthcoming. With that gesture, she faints.

The potential danger of the female look is contained from this point on as Iris's return to "mental health" becomes dependent on her alliance with Gilbert, to whom is delegated the gaze. Significantly, Iris's alliance with Gilbert does not follow the pattern of *Marnie,* where the female character ultimately aligns herself with the person functioning in the role of psychoanalyst.[7] Gilbert adopts the posture, not of the psychoanalytic interpreter, but of the quintessential British investigator: he plays Holmes to Iris's Watson and appropriates the investigating gaze while she remains the less privileged, if still inquisitive, sidekick.

Now constituted as a team, Gilbert and Iris search the train together for Miss Froy and stumble across Signor Doppo's "Vanishing Lady" apparatus. A mysterious figure whose presence seems weakly motivated in terms of the central narrative enigma, Signor Doppo, or perhaps more precisely his apparatus for dematerializing the female figure, nonetheless serves a crucial function in realigning Iris's desire. After "disappearing" into the magician's apparatus, Iris emerges only to be subdued (explicitly cast by Gilbert in the Watson role) and brutalized (she tumbles to the ground and is attacked by birds!). As a metaphor for the cinema itself, Signor Doppo's "Vanishing Lady" apparatus effects an inversion of Iris's previous image: her investigating gaze is made passive, her desire is transformed according to patriarchal definitions of female sexuality. The title *The Lady Vanishes,* and the narrative's substitution of various female figures (Mme. Kummer for Miss Froy, the "nun" for a counterspy), could in fact be read as a self-conscious reference to the Méliès 1896 substitution-trick film, *The Vanishing Lady,* where the theatrical magician's attempt to master the threat posed by woman by making her vanish via the techniques of cinematic reproduction points to a fundamental relationship between the absence of woman and visual pleasure.[8] This magical aura of cinematic reproduction, when joined with the interpretive power of psychoanalysis in *The Lady Vanishes* (Signor Doppo works with Dr. Hartz in abducting Miss Froy), seems to suggest an even more insidious relationship between technologies which attempt to erase female desire or subjectivity by excluding it from representation.

It would be a mistake, however, to take this reading at face value and to assume the narrative logic of *The Lady Vanishes* (or classical narrative cinema in general) to work simply to recuperate female desire and make it submit to male authority, for a number of disturbances continue to riddle the film's portrayal of gender relations long after Iris transfers her desire from Miss Froy to Gilbert. To be sure, Iris's brush with madness, the result of Dr. Hartz's reading of her symptoms, renders her susceptible to psychoanalytic suggestion. (When Dr.

Hartz says he has poisoned their drinks, Iris passes out and Gilbert merely feigns sleep. When Gilbert discovers that the drinks were perfectly harmless, it is Iris alone who becomes the object of ridicule, engaging as she does in strenuous exercises to keep from falling asleep, a state she associates with madness.) Gilbert, moreover, clearly initiates all further narrative action: it is he who risks death by climbing through the train window to silence Mme. Kummer and he who steers the train back to the main line. Points of female resistance to male authority nonetheless remain, notably in the figure of the "nun" whose high-heeled shoes counter her saintly and servile image and whose muteness serves, not as a sign of (female) hysteria or aphasia, but instead as a disguise that allows her to assume a degree of control and narrative mastery.

Most important, however, is the presence of Miss Froy, who, despite the machinations of doctors, magicians, and self-centered British travellers, refuses to disappear. Entrusting Gilbert with protecting and transmitting crucial narrative information musically encoded in a tune, she attempts to transform the paternal register of the film by bringing it into contact with a distinctly maternal realm. Miss Froy, a governess and a music teacher, and Gilbert, a professional musicologist, are thereby linked through the song that opens and initially disrupts symbolic order. Fittingly enough, Gilbert forgets the tune once he consummates his union with Iris; that is, once Iris "vanishes" from her fiancé's sight and affirms her desire for Gilbert, Gilbert loses the memory of the maternal realm passed on to him. Quite appropriately, he can only reproduce the "Wedding March" at the foreign office. Nonetheless, the maternal strain is reactivated in the final sequence of the film, and again by Miss Froy, only this time she does not simply hum or listen to it but plays it on the grand piano in Whitehall. Maternal psychic energy, in the service jointly of patriarchy and the "mother country," thereby emerges as the ultimate—and no longer secret—support of both narrative and symbolic order.

III.

The guiding question that opened this essay—Whose desire does narrative speak?—was meant to raise the issue of psychoanalytic and cinematic discourses in relation to the theorization of female subjectivity. The received psychoanalytic interpretations of cinematic identification and visual pleasure leave no doubt that desire in narrative is fundamentally masculine. And yet, as my analysis of *The Lady Vanishes* suggests, narrative can—and often does—produce a place, however provisionally, for woman to tell her story and speak of her desire. Iris's initial refusal to accede to Oedipal imperatives by focusing her desire on Miss Froy instead of Gilbert, for example, sets into play the terms of her identification with maternal psychic energy—an identification that has the effect of interrupting her Oedipal "normalization" and revealing a desire rooted, not in repression, but in resistance. That is to say, Iris's desire for the mother is not a desire for the utilitarian, social, and symbolic aspect of mother-hood as defined by patriarchy but for the negating side of her symbolic posi-tion. It is significant, therefore, that Iris's brush with madness, her movement away from the maternal and towards a state of undifferentiated (that is, as yet unsexed) desire, does not situate her desire outside of Oedipus and representa-tion. On the contrary, it leads her to confront the patriarchal symbolic order and to refuse its definitions, which exclude a place for her identity, her expe-rience, and her memory. While not entirely "progressive" in its representation of female desire (Iris does, after all, shift her erotic attachment from the maternal to the paternal figure and relinquish her aggressive and investigating gaze), *The Lady Vanishes* nevertheless opens up a space where female desire can be articulated, where the female figure can exercise some of the narrative control traditionally denied to her.

References to magic, cinema, and psychoanalysis in *The Lady Vanishes* also expose the discursive mechanisms whereby the female subject is conven-tionally reproduced. *The Lady Vanishes* can therefore be read as rendering visible those discourses and modes of analysis which assume female subjectivity to be illusory and static rather than culturally and materially produced by a number of specific textual, discursive, and institutional practices. While the narrative development of *The Lady Vanishes* clearly works to fix and center traditionally patriarchal female and male positions, it also explores the nega-tive side of this Oedipal paradigm—the maternal power to refuse, withdraw from, and disturb the symbolic space. Miss Froy, for example, while never exceeding the boundaries of symbolic relations as defined by patriarchy, none-theless offers resistance to them, impeding Iris's erotic development by putting into play through her own ambivalent maternal function the possibility of a different desire.

My own interpretation of *The Lady Vanishes*, I must emphasize, should not be taken as a neutral or even exhaustive reading of the film (even if such a thing were possible). Indeed—and this must be kept in mind when consuming or producing textual criticism—there are political implications in every in-terpretive act, whatever meaning that interpretation seeks to bestow. This is not meant to suggest, however, that all readings should be regarded as of equal value, for readings can only be assessed politically in terms of their conse-quences in and for the present. Durgnat's interpretation of *The Lady Vanishes*, for example, is decidedly not a feminist reading of the film. While he certainly raises a number of interesting and clearly useful ideas for feminist criticism, his own position remains markedly idiosyncratic and less concerned with those issues that a feminist criticism would—indeed, must—seize upon.

Furthermore, in contrast to Mulvey's and Bellour's negative appraisal of the possibility for female desire to speak in narrative, as a feminist critic I prefer to follow the interpretive procedure outlined by Modleski and recently expanded upon by Teresa de Lauretis.[9] Their view that psychoanalysis and the cinema can and do address the experience of the female subject (even if they often will not or do not) and their contention that feminist practice must construct that experience in criticism and in narrative are, for me, absolutely uncontestable tenets for feminist interpretation. Rather than assume systems of signification (whether classical narrative, psychoanalytic theory, or cinematic reproduction) to be fixed in relation to female subjectivity and rather than attempt to place woman somewhere outside of narrative or representation, feminist criticism would do better to disrupt the prevailing array of discourses so as to produce new subject identities and, above all, new forms of political alliance through which moments of historical rupture might be constituted. It goes without saying that, in following through with such an interpretive project, feminist criticism would also have to bypass debates over the inherent meaning of Hitchcock's films for women; the point is that meanings do not inhere in texts alone nor can they be prescribed or assured for once and all time.[10] The notion I have entertained throughout my analysis of *The Lady Vanishes*—namely, that its narrative and visual organization reflects upon and transforms representational and theoretical discourses (the cinema and psychoanalysis respectively) so as to reveal and reconstitute them—must therefore be qualified and restated. That is to say, it is not cinematic narrative alone but feminist criticism which reveals and reconstitutes the cultural and ideological discourses that texts refer to and engage. Because a text's political effects are only produced in acts of viewing, analysis, and interpretation, feminist critics must therefore attend to the experiences of women as spectators and adopt an active position toward textual phenomena. It seems to me that the task of rematerializing the "vanishing lady" has to begin by wrenching so-called "classical" films from the ways in which they are customarily received so as to mobilize them in different, and more politically relevant, directions.

Notes

1. Laura Mulvey, "Visual Pleasure and Narrative Cinema," *Screen*, vol. 16, no. 2 (1975): 6–18.
2. Raymond Bellour, "Hitchcock, The Enunciator," *Camera Obscura*, no. 2 (1977): 85–86.
3. Tania Modleski, "'Never to Be Thirty-Six Years Old': *Rebecca* as Female Oedipal Drama," *Wide Angle*, vol. 5, no. 2 (1983): 38.
4. Raymond Durgnat, *The Strange Case of Alfred Hitchcock* (Cambridge: MIT Press, 1974), 142–63. Maurice Yacowar, in *Hitchcock's British Films* (Hamden, Conn.: Archon Books, 1977), also discusses the "maternal" implications of Miss Froy in *The Lady Vanishes*, but he conflates maternity and "family" and finds the latter notion altogether unproblematic; hence my own reading of the film cuts directly against the grain of his.
5. Julia Kristeva, "Something To Be Scared Of," in *Powers of Horror: An Essay on Abjection* (New York: Columbia Univ. Press, 1982), 32–55. See also her "Ellipsis on Dread and the Specular Seduction," *Wide Angle*, vol. 3, no. 3 (1979): 45–46.
6. Julia Kristeva, "Women's Time," *Signs*, vol. 7, no. 1 (1981): 16. See also Tania Modleski's discussion of time and memory in her "Time and Desire in the Woman's Film," *Cinema Journal*, vol. 23, no. 3 (1984): 19–30.
7. For an interesting analysis of *Marnie* see Mary Ann Doane, *The Dialogical Text: Filmic Irony and the Spectator*, Ph.D. dissertation, University of Iowa, 1979.
8. See, for instance, Lucy Fischer, "The Lady Vanishes: Women, Magic, and the Movies," *Film Quarterly*, vol. 33, no. 1 (1979): 30–40; and Linda Williams, "The Film Body: An Implantation of Perversions," *Cine-Tracts*, vol. 3, no. 4 (1981): 19–35.

Quarterly, vol. 33, no. 1 (1979): 30–40; and Linda Williams, "The Film Body: An Implantation of Perversions," *Cine-Tracts*, vol. 3, no. 4 (1981): 19–35.

9. See Teresa de Lauretis's discussion of "Semiotics and Experience" in *Alice Doesn't: Feminism, Semiotics, Cinema* (Bloomington: Indiana Univ. Press, 1984), 158–86.

10. I am indebted to Tony Bennett for this formulation. See his "Marxism and Popular Fiction," *Literature and History*, vol. 7, no. 2 (1981): 138–65.

THE LADY VANISHES (Gainsborough, 1938). *Producer:* Edward Black, *Script:* Sydney Gilliatt, Frank Launder, Alma Reville, from the novel *The Wheel Spins* by Ethel Lina White, *Photography:* Jack Cox, *Editors:* Alfred Roome, R. E. Dearing, *Sets:* Alec Vetchinsky, Maurice Cater, Albert Jullion, *Music:* Louis Levy, *Players:* Margaret Lockwood (Iris Henderson), Michael Redgrave (Gilbert), Dame May Whitty (Miss Froy), Paul Lukas (Dr. Hartz), Cecil Parker (Mr. Todhunter), Naugton Wayne (Caldicott), Basil Radford (Charters). 97 minutes.

PART THREE

Hitchcock in Hollywood

It is arguable that Hitchcock never left Britain entirely behind him. As Philip French observes, Hitchcock continued to rely on British (and French) novels or stories late into his Hollywood career: *Stage Fright, The Trouble with Harry, The Birds, Frenzy, Family Plot* all derive from English literary sources. And Hitchcock never hesitated to cast his films—even those set primarily in America—with British actors: Claude Rains and Cary Grant in *Notorious*; Leo G. Carroll in *Spellbound, Strangers on a Train,* and *North by Northwest*; Cary Grant and James Mason in *North by Northwest*; Sean Connery in *Marnie*; etc. Yet Hitchcock's move to Hollywood seems in retrospect an inevitable step in his development. He had done as much in Britain as he could. Indeed, the successful series of films from *The Man Who Knew Too Much* through *The Lady Vanishes* threatened to lock him forever into the comedy-thriller format. Moreover, Hitchcock got his start in cinema working for the London office of Famous Players–Lasky ("You might say I had an American training," as Hitchcock put it in the Truffaut interview), and he obviously reveled in the technical opportunities which working in Hollywood made available to him. But more than technology was involved in Hitchcock's decision to leave Britain. As Philip French remarks, "America was a place of reality and dream for Hitchcock. . . . He saw in the freer, larger, more dangerous, more socially mobile American society the possibility of discovering the objective correlatives for his powerful feelings about violence and sexuality" (p. 117). Only in Hollywood, or so French implies, could Hitchcock's agonized Britishness find its full expression.

At least initially, however, Hitchcock found himself no less restricted in Hollywood than he had been in England. While his contract with David O. Selznick was handsome enough, he soon realized that his new employer took as much interest in his day-to-day work as had his English producers. It made little difference that Selznick genuinely meant well in his concern about every detail for the production of *Rebecca* (1940), Hitchcock's first Hollywood effort. Selznick rankled Hitchcock by forcing him to adhere to a script as close to Daphne Du Maurier's novel as the censor's office would permit and by his protracted search for the actress to play the title role. Hitchcock responded to Selznick's intrusive supervision by slowing down the speed at which he worked and shooting only enough footage to insure that the film could only be cut together as he wished. Selznick, who had been used to having alternate takes to cut together, found himself stymied. Yet for all of this, Selznick's inter-ference was far less than it might have been had he not been so busy attending to the final details of *Gone with the Wind*, which occupied most of his atten-tion during this time.

Worse than his intrusions, Selznick finally failed to provide the stability that Hitchcock had hoped for. In 1940 Selznick began to dismantle Selznick International Pictures as part of a plan to minimize the taxes he would have to pay on the extraordinary profits from both *Gone with the Wind* and *Rebecca*. Then, worn out from the demands of the business, he finally closed his studio at the end of 1941 and gave up active production for three years. He retained, however, some personal contracts with performers and directors, including Hitchcock, for his new company, David O. Selznick Productions. So began a series of lucrative loan-outs as Selznick made deals for Hitchcock to work elsewhere. Thus while he made *Rebecca* directly for Selznick, Hitchcock was loaned out to Walter Wanger for *Foreign Correspondent* (1940), to R.K.O. for *Mr. and Mrs. Smith* (1941) and *Suspicion* (1941), to Universal for *Saboteur* (1942) and *Shadow of a Doubt* (1943), and to 20th Century–Fox for *Lifeboat* (1944) before actually working for Selznick again on *Spellbound* (1945).

While these loan-outs gave Hitchcock the welcome opportunity to famil-iarize himself with the superb technical facilities of the industry, he was not always able to develop the scripts for these films in advance or do as much preproduction planning on each project as he would have liked. In addition, he came to resent the profits Selznick made by hiring him out to others, often for twice his own salary. All of these inconveniences continued even during his final two films for Selznick. *Notorious* (1946) was sold as a package to R.K.O. with its script virtually complete, while *The Paradine Case* (1947) was shot entirely under Selznick's aegis. As had been the case with *Rebecca*, Hitchcock chafed under Selznick's constant supervision, though it too might have been more oppressive had the producer not been preoccupied with making *Duel in the Sun*.

In December 1947 Hitchcock ended his association with Selznick to be-come his own independent producer. Together with his trusted English friend Sidney Bernstein, he established Transatlantic Pictures and directed *Rope* (1948) and *Under Capricorn* (1949), both of which were distributed by Warner Brothers. Though he would not work with Selznick again, Hitchcock later

alluded to his unhappiness with him by making Lars Thorwald, the killer in
Rear Window (1954), resemble Selznick and by having Roger Thornhill in
North by Northwest (1959) reflect upon how his middle initial, "O," meant
nothing—an allusion to Selznick's decision early in his career to adopt "O" as
his middle initial in the belief that it would make his name sound more
distinguished. Yet however unhappy Hitchcock may have been during these
years because of Selznick's policies, the fact remains that this was a period of
great personal growth for him as he tested the technical facilities of the industry, extended his exploration of the formal properties of the medium, and
immeasurably deepened the implications of his recurrent themes.

Often Hitchcock spoke freely about the technical means available to him
in Hollywood for heightening effects, repeatedly explaining, for example, how
he managed to put a light bulb in a glass of milk in *Suspicion;* or devised the
elaborate crane shot in *Notorious* which ends in a close-up of the wine-cellar
key clutched in Alicia Huberman's hand; or constructed for *Rope* an intricate
series of rheostats which smoothly modulated the New York City backdrop
from late afternoon sunshine, to dusk, to a darkness set off by the miniature
lights of studio skyscrapers. He discussed his continuing formal experiments in
the medium less frequently, however, merely acknowledging *Lifeboat* as a
problem in filming in a restricted set, describing the Dali-designed dream
sequence in *Spellbound* as an attempt to render a dream in a hard-edged style,
or categorizing the long takes of *Rope* and *Under Capricorn* as problems in
coordination and execution. The more subtle details of these experiments he
left unmentioned.

Thus, while Hitchcock might discuss the obvious patterns of parallel lines
in *Spellbound* or the patterns of doubling established by cutting in *Shadow of
a Doubt* and *Strangers on a Train*, the formal resemblance between Johnny
Jones's paper cutouts at the beginning of *Foreign Correspondent* and the
windmill blades which betray the spies, or the contrast between the lattice-
work shadows of the Aysgarth house in *Suspicion* which bespeak Lina's fantasies about her husband's guilt and the right angles of the windows and wain-
scoting of the McLaidlaw house which reflect her parents' rationality were not
commented upon. Yet as suggested by several recent essays—e.g., Kristin
Thompson on the dishonest flashback in *Stage Fright* (1950) and Marshall
Deutelbaum on the visual design program based upon the Statue of Liberty in
Saboteur—critics are beginning to recognize the high degree of Hitchcock's
unspoken artfulness in his Hollywood films.

One can clearly see the need to go beyond Hitchcock's own guarded words
about his work in the case of a film like *Rope*. Though Hitchcock dismissed his
attempts at filming it in reel-long, ten-minute takes as a "stunt" in his discussion of the film with François Truffaut, the extraordinary care he takes to
explain how he attempted to make the film's continuity appear seamless by
using a close-up of an actor's jacket to hide the reloading of the camera be-

tween reels opens a series of questions for any student of cinema about the
basic principles of the classical Hollywood style. If only because such long takes
preclude the shot/reverse-shot cutting that is its mainstay, Hitchcock's practice
in *Rope* deserves closer scrutiny for what it may reveal about alternative systems
of *mise en scène*.

In fact, disguising the end of one reel and the beginning of the next in
the manner Hitchcock describes happens only part of the time in *Rope*. Not
only does an undisguised straight cut early in the film move viewers directly
into the apartment at the moment of the strangulation murder, but reel openings later are used to supply important reverse-shots which the long-take format otherwise denies. In one instance, the opening of a new reel suddenly
isolates Mrs. Wilson as she begins to clear the chest in which the body has been
hidden. The audience is left to wonder whether anyone will notice her before
she can lift the chest's lid. More importantly, the opening of a new reel coincides with the key dramatic moment when Rupert Caudell (James Stewart)
realizes that Philip is lying about never having wrung the neck of a chicken.
One reel ends focused on Philip as he denies the action; the next begins as
essentially a reverse-shot of Rupert's reaction as he realizes that Philip is lying
and begins to be suspicious of him. In this, as in its method of valorizing
different areas of the apartment at different times through its *mise en scène*,
Rope merits closer attention for what its formal properties can reveal to us
about the making and reading of cinematic narratives.

As the essays in this section reveal, the growing formal sophistication of
Hitchcock's Hollywood films is accompanied by a deepening of their thematic
resonances as well. Thus in writing about Bruno and Guy in *Strangers on a
Train* (1951), Robin Wood identifies one essential Hitchcockian theme—"that
ordered life depends on the rigorous and *unnatural* suppression of a powerfully
seductive underworld of desire"—which is easily as applicable to the lesson
young Charlie learns from her same-name uncle in the earlier *Shadow of a
Doubt*. Similarly, James McLaughlin reads out from young Charlie's experience the recurring motif of later films in which powerful women are punished
for desiring autonomy. As Richard Abel demonstrates through a sensitive structural reading of *Notorious*, such large-scale parallels between Bruno and Guy
and the two Charlies are also illustrative of the more particular dynamics of
cinematic coding and *mise en scène* which Hitchcock employs to establish and
play upon the echoing psychological relationships among an individual film's
cast of characters.

Indeed, this close relationship of psychological theme and symbolic visual
form in Hitchcock's forties films reaches a culmination of sorts in *Spellbound*,
where questions of visualization and displacement, of guilt conjured up and
denied—questions which will eventually inform such films as *Rear Window*
and *Vertigo*— become overt subject matter. Even here Hitchcock both disguises
and declares his artistry: disguises it by engaging Salvador Dali to design the

film's most overtly "artistic" sequence, John Ballantine's "dream" recollection of the murder of Dr. Edwardes, as if thereby to efface or downgrade his own authorship; but Hitchcock also quietly declares his authorial autonomy by rewriting the popular Freudian scenario of the "talking cure" to suit his own thematic ends. As Thomas Hyde observes in his discussion of the film, "the cure for John's amnesia is not found on the analyst's couch but rather emerges from a series of experiential trials culminating in John's physically reenacting the episode which originally triggered his disturbance." Freudian psychoanalysis, at least in *Spellbound*, provides Hitchcock less a master system than yet another metaphoric framework through which to explore the visual and moral dynamics of the world he puts in view.

Though the relative commercial failures of *Rope* and *Under Capricorn* as the 1940s ended cost Hitchcock his own production company, the popular success of *Strangers on a Train* in 1951 assured him of another successful decade as an independent producer. In the films he directed after 1951 he would develop these themes and continue his explorations of the medium's formal properties and possibilities in even more striking ways.

References and Suggested Readings

Abel, Richard. "*Stage Fright:* The Knowing Performance." *Film Criticism*, vol. 9, no. 2 (1985): 41–50.

Behlmer, Rudy, ed. *Memo from David O. Selznick*. New York: Viking Press, 1972.

Belton, John. "Alfred Hitchcock's *Under Capricorn:* Montage Entranced by Mise-en-Scène." *Quarterly Review of Film Studies*, vol. 6, no. 4 (1981): 365–83. On *Rope* and *Under Capricorn*.

Bordonaro, Peter. "*Dial 'M' for Murder:* A Play by Frederick Knott/ A Film by Alfred Hitchcock." *Sight and Sound*, vol. 45, no. 3 (1976): 175–79.

Bordwell, David. "Alfred Hitchcock's *Notorious*." *Film Heritage*, vol. 4, no. 3 (1969): 6–10+.

Brown, Royal S. "Hitchcock's *Spellbound:* Jung versus Freud." *film/psychology review*, vol. 4, no. 1 (1980): 35–58.

Chabrol, Claude. "Hitchcock Confronts Evil." *Cahiers du Cinema in English*, no. 2 (1966): 67–71.

Christ, Ronald. "*Strangers on a Train:* The Pattern of Encounter." In Albert J. LaValley, ed. *Focus on Hitchcock*. Englewood Cliffs: Prentice-Hall, 1972, 104–11.

Deutelbaum, Marshall. "Seeing in *Saboteur*." *Literature/Film Quarterly*, vol. 12, no. 1 (1984): 58–64.

Doane, Mary Anne. "*Caught* and *Rebecca:* The Inscription of Femininity as Absence." *enclitic*, vol. 5, no. 2/vol. 6, no. 1 (1982): 75–89.

––––––. "The Film's Time and the Spectator's Space." In Stephen Heath and Patricia Mellencamp, eds. *Cinema and Language*. Frederick, Md.: Univ. Publications of America, 1983, 35–49. Remarks on *Spellbound*.

French, Philip. "Alfred Hitchcock: The Film-maker as Englishman and Exile." *Sight and Sound*, vol. 54, no. 2 (1985): 116–22.

Haskell, Molly. "*Stage Fright*." *Film Comment*, vol. 6, no. 3 (1970): 49–59.

Haver, Ronald. *David O. Selznick's Hollywood*. New York: Knopf, 1980.

Heath, Stephen. "Droit de regard." In Raymond Bellour, ed. *Le cinéma americain*. Paris: Flammarion, 1980, 87–98. On *Suspicion*.

Kehr, Dave. "Hitch's Riddle." *Film Comment*, vol. 20, no. 3 (1984): 9–18. Discussion of *Rope*, among other of Hitchcock's "lost" films.

Kindem, Gorham Anders. *Toward a Semiotic Theory of Visual Communication in the Cinema*. New York: Arno Press, 1980. Lengthy discussion of all Hitchcock's color films from *Rope* onward.

Miller, Gavin. "Hitchcock versus Truffaut." *Sight and Sound*, vol. 38, no. 2 (1969): 82–87. Includes remarks on *Saboteur.*

Miller, Mark Crispin. "Hitchcock's Suspicions and *Suspicion*." *Modern Language Notes*, vol. 98, no. 5 (1983): 1143–86.

Modleski, Tania. " 'Never to be Thirty-Six Years Old': *Rebecca* as Female Oedipal Drama." *Wide Angle*, vol. 5, no. 1 (1982): 34–41.

Perkins, V. F. *"Rope."* In Ian Cameron, ed. *The Movie Reader.* New York: Praeger, 1972, 35–37.

Ranvaud, Don. *"Rebecca." Framework*, no. 13 (1980): 19–24.

Reisz, Karel, and Gavin Miller. *The Technique of Film Editing.* 2nd ed. London: Focal Press, 1968, 232–36. Discusses two examples from *Rope* illustrating how the film's commitment to long-take denies the dramatic impact constructed by standard editing practices.

Renov, Michael. "From Identification to Ideology: The Male System of Hitchcock's *Notorious.*" *Wide Angle*, vol. 4, no. 1 (1980): 30–37.

Rothman, William. "Alfred Hitchcock's *Notorious.*" *The Georgia Review*, vol. 29, no. 4 (1975): 884–927.

Scheib, Ronnie. "Charlie's Uncle." *Film Comment*, vol. 12, no. 2 (1976): 55–62. On *Shadow of a Doubt.*

Thompson, Kristin. "The Duplicitous Text: An Analysis of *Stage Fright.*" *Film Reader*, no. 2 (1977): 52–64.

Truffaut, François. "Skeleton Keys." *Film Culture*, no. 32 (1964): 63–67; reprint *Cahiers du Cinema in English*, no. 2 (1966): 60–66. On *Shadow of a Doubt.*

Van Wert, William F. "Compositional Psychoanalysis: Circles and Straight Lines in *Spellbound.*" *Film Criticism*, vol. 3, no. 3 (1979): 41–47.

Waldman, Diane. " 'At last I can tell it to someone!': Feminine Point of View and Subjectivity in the Gothic Romance Films of the 1940s." *Cinema Journal*, vol. 23, no. 2 (1983): 29–40. Remarks on *Rebecca* and *Suspicion.*

Wood, Robin. "Ideology, Genre, Auteur." *Film Comment*, vol. 13, no. 1 (1977): 46–51. On *Shadow of a Doubt* and *It's a Wonderful Life.*

Yacowar, Maurice. "Hitchcock's *I Confess.*" *Film Heritage*, vol. 8, no. 2 (1973): 19–24.

CHAPTER ELEVEN

All in the Family: Alfred Hitchcock's *Shadow of a Doubt*

James McLaughlin

> So fruitful of conjecture is the text of the family.
> —ELIZABETH HARDWICK, *Sleepless Nights*[1]

"This family has just gone to pieces." With those words, Charlie, the eldest daughter of Mr. and Mrs. Joseph Newton of Santa Rosa, California—she's eighteen years old and named after her uncle—recumbent in her bedroom in that very position described by Freud as being so conducive to the relaxation of the ego's vigilance over the unconscious, begins her grievance against a family that provides her with everything, not the least of which is disgust.[2] The idea of the family is a very important one in the films of Alfred Hitchcock; so is the idea of disgust. What we find is that the two ideas are very much related. Like everything else in Hitchcock, the family is not innocent: besieged by malevolent forces from without, it also engenders murderous feelings from within, and these two phenomena are intimately linked. The image that accompanies this obsession with the family and its filthy dynamics is, of course, that of the house. The facade of the Newton family home in *Shadow of a Doubt* is composed of sweetness and sunshine; behind it, however, lies, in the words of Uncle Charlie, "a foul sty."

Both Charlie and her uncle are introduced in the film in exactly the same manner: after a few introductory shots of their respective towns, Santa Rosa and Philadelphia, the camera cranes in on their bedroom windows and, after a cut, continues tracking in to approach their reclining figures on their beds. In this cinema of the bedroom that Hitchcock's films often turn out to be, this camera movement, in its Peeping Tom way, allows a nearness of observation that watches, that spies, that comes closer in order to see better. The camera's indiscreet curiosity creates suspicions of illegitimacy—the suspicion that the two houses are hiding something vaguely sinister, which must be exposed. The

Philadelphia boardinghouse shelters Uncle Charlie, who, we learn, more than vaguely sinister, is actually suspected of murder by two cops who subject him to relentless surveillance. The Santa Rosa home shelters Charlie (along with the rest of her family), who becomes, in the obscure equation proposed by the insinuating camera movement, a criminal too. The exact nature of her "crime," however, is not immediately apparent and is never explicitly stated. Yet the film provides numerous hints from which we can construe the reason for Charlie's association with criminality. In these early scenes, this coupling of the two characters lying in beds separated by a continent is the most striking indication of the relationship that exists between them; there is a sly hint that what Charlie and her uncle are thinking about while lying in bed is of the other in bed, i.e., of being with the other in bed. Incest is a barely suppressed presence in the film whose unconscious enactment certainly incriminates Charlie; and incest is a metaphor that conveys precisely the transgressive power of Charlie's fierce attachment to desires of which her uncle, as we will see, is the emblem.

The union of Charlie and her uncle is impugned as unhealthy from the start. The two characters are thought to be "sick." In the Philadelphia sequence, the landlady of the boardinghouse asks Uncle Charlie: "You look kinda tired to me. Are you sick?" On the train that carries Uncle Charlie to Santa Rosa, the porter and the passengers speak of how ill he is. When he alights from the train with the assistance of his fellow passengers onto that irremediably unpopulated Santa Rosa train station, Charlie is the sole person who sees him—she asks him if he's sick. When the Santa Rosa sequence begins, Charlie's father, Joe, in his first communication with his daughter, asks her if she's feeling well. (This occurs before Charlie complains about the ills of her family, which she thinks is sick.)

The intense togetherness of uncle and niece is registered then in fantasies of incest and illness and identity of name. Yet the insistence on their closeness goes still further. "We're more than an uncle and niece," Charlie says at one point, "we're sort of like twins." Hitchcock is fond of characters who resemble one another—twins, doubles, cases of mistaken identity pervade his work. It's as if he were mocking all bourgeois conceptions of the individual as a single, solitary self. For Hitchcock, the individual is often a charismatic organization of two.

Yet the charismatic becomes problematic—by becoming vividly vampiristic. "We have the same blood," is Charlie's arresting phrase, and her uncle's resemblances to the most famous of all vampires, Count Dracula, abound in the film. Like Dracula, Uncle Charlie comes from "the East." Like Dracula, he possesses a fearsome grip—Charlie twice complains that he hurts her when he grabs her.[3] Like Dracula, he is associated with the dead and the dark. (There are those great stretches of night in *Shadow of a Doubt,* those realms of darkness which haunt the day without yielding an hour and disappear eventually only in the new night of death.[4]) When Uncle Charlie speaks to the landlady of the boardinghouse, he sounds barely alive, indeed looks barely alive, until she pulls down the window shade. We see the darkness cover his face. Thereupon, Uncle Charlie springs up from the bed with a startling automatism and throws his glass against the wall: the darkness, with its magnetic obscurity, attracts and provides him with an explosive revivification. Like Dracula, he can mysteriously disappear. When the detectives pursue him in the beginning of the film, he eludes them and we see him watching them from the top of a building. Later, when the detectives visit the Newton home posing as "pollsters" sent by the National Public Survey to interview "the representative American family," one of the detectives bets Charlie that her uncle is not in her bedroom where she thinks he is. The detective is correct: Uncle Charlie unexpectedly enters the second floor through the doorway from the outside staircase. This phantom-like quality of Uncle Charlie is emphasized again in the shot where we see only his reflection on his niece's graduation picture — as if he were a disembodied spirit. There is even a direct reference to Dracula in the film. One of the detectives requests that Ann, Charlie's bibliophilic younger sister, tell Saunders "the story of Dracula."

His most important similarity to Dracula, however, is that Uncle Charlie is summoned by his niece. Charlie stresses the fact that her uncle "heard" her, that there is a kind of mental telepathy between them. She wanted him to come and, miraculously, he came. "To be in tune with another person who is on the other side of the country — it's all mental," she states. Similarly, Dracula does not invite one into his castle; one must make the first move and cross the threshold. The presence of Dracula is unconsciously wished for by the other characters in the novel. Dracula also communicates telepathically with women and has strong affinities with children and madmen.

> Dead, but still with us, still with us, but dead.
> —DONALD BARTHELME, *The Dead Father*[5]

Charlie's monologue in her bedroom in the presence of her father about the stagnation of family life continues thus:

Charlie: It's been on my mind for months. You sort of go along and nothing happens. It's in a terrible rut. What's going to be our future?

Father: Well, I just got a raise at the bank.

Charlie: How can you talk about money when I'm talking about souls? We eat, we sleep, and that's about all. We don't really have any conversations. We just talk.

Father: And work.

Charlie: Poor mother. She's not an ordinary mother. We ought to do something for her.

Father: And what do you propose to do?

Charlie: Nothing I suppose. We'll have to wait for a miracle.

Mother appears.

Mother: My, those back stairs sure are steep.

There is then a short exchange between the mother and father about Charlie's health. Then,

Charlie: I'm going to send a telegram. There's only one person who can save us. A wonderful person who will come and shake us all up. . . .

Charlie's summoning of her uncle is a way, she hopes, of curing the Newtons of the debilitation induced by the inertia of family living in small-town America: the endless repetition of mundane events, the joyless perform-ance of ever so quotidian tasks. It is also a way of "doing something" for her mother. There is a very interesting equation established between Charlie's desire to cure her family and her desire to "do something" for her mother — it is as if the two desires were one and the same thing. Charlie's notion of the family is conflated with the mother, not the father; she seems to think her family would be better off without him. "What destructiveness is implied in our desire to make life extraordinary," writes Philip Rieff, and Charlie's destruc-tiveness is aimed, like a gun, at her father.[6] Her wish for the presence of her uncle is another shot, more subtle but also more damaging than the first, at her father, who is vulgarly concerned with money, not with "souls." The impli-cation is that her father just doesn't "do" enough for her mother, while her uncle will. There is an undeniable tug underlying Charlie's remarks, with a hint of the father's inadequacy, sexual and otherwise.

So the serene surface of the Newtons' family life is disturbed by an under-tow of Charlie's unmistakable, barely conscious, hostility directed at her father, which is why, I think, Joe is such an insignificant figure in the film, a real cipher. The daughter's repressed rage radically diminishes the stature of the father. In addition, a slighter, more overt hostility, in the form of insult, is directed at Joe by the other female members of the household and by Uncle Charlie. Ann tells her father when he returns home from the bank carrying a digest of detective stories titled *Unsolved Crimes:* "Here I am only a child and I wouldn't be caught reading the things you do." After dinner, Mrs. Newton (Emma) gives her brother her husband's newspaper and pillow and the best chair. Uncle Charlie doesn't heed Joe's advice not to throw his hat on Charlie's bed. He also usurps Joe's position at the dinner table and treats him like one of the children. Joe receives his gift from Uncle Charlie at the same time the children receive theirs, while the mother and Charlie are regaled with a much more elaborate presentation. Uncle Charlie also embarrasses Joe in the bank in which he works by talking very loudly to him about embezzlement, and he further mortifies Joe by intimating in the presence of the bank's president that Joe is "looking out" for the latter's job.

The father becomes the presence that is really an absence. When Uncle Charlie arrives in Santa Rosa — preceded by ominous clouds of black smoke emitted by the train that carries him — and first meets his sister Emma, he declares: "Stop. You're Emma Spenser Oakley, not Emma Newton, of 46 Burnham Street. . . . The prettiest girl on the block." (Those vapors of Uncle Charlie, the billowing clouds of smoke and gas—obscure, opaque, shadowy— permeate this film so insidiously and resemble, with their elusiveness and their delicacy, the singular strength of their progenitor.) Joe doesn't exist for his brother-in-law, nor does the reality of his marriage to Emma. Charles strips his sister of her marital status and attempts to return to the world of their child-hood. He even presents Emma with photographs of their parents taken in 1888. "It was a wonderful world. Everybody was sweet and pretty then," he says, and it is this world he is trying to re-create. This sense of returning, at least in fantasy, to a golden age by visiting Santa Rosa is also conveyed by Uncle Charlie's voice when he speaks to the telephone operator. It is his voice-over of "Santa Rosa," pronounced in a tone of exquisite elegiac yearning, that begins the Santa Rosa section of the film: he is, in a sense, giving us Santa Rosa, a Santa Rosa without Joe Newton.

However, the superior transgression against the father occurs when Uncle Charlie takes Joe's newspaper to construct a house in order to hide from the Newtons a report that might reveal his culpability in the murder of three rich widows. Each of the children mention that their uncle is destroying "father's paper." This paper house is an exemplary image of the institution of the family whose fragility is guaranteed by dad's flimsy materials. The image also suggests a criminality concealed in the family's very construction.

Two other remarks further suggest that Joe is an absence, a lack, a big hole in the Newton family edifice. His neighbor Herb tells him, after some prank involving soda in Joe's coffee: "For all you knew, you might just as well be dead now." Charlie, at another point, irate at her father's conversation with Herb, screams: "Can't you two stop talking about killing people?"—to which Joe responds: "We're not talking about killing people. I'm talking about kill-ing him and he me."

The rich widow weeps with one eye and laughs with the other.
— PROVERB[7]

The father then is "dead," a soft murder for which Charlie's wish for her uncle's appearance is primarily responsible. And we have Uncle Charlie aching to take his place. Charlie's wish for the presence of her uncle is enough to create the reality—mental states produce physical events—but the reality so summoned appears in not quite the way that is expected, since the wish for it is strongly mixed with a good dose of guilt over the anger she feels toward her family, especially her father. Uncle Charlie is far from being the "wonderful person" she thinks. He does kill, and this time not in fantasy, what are called "merry widows." Now why are they labelled that and why do they disgust Charles so much that he feels compelled to murder them? One resonant scene occurs in the bank president's office. The wife of the bank president, accompanied by her widowed friend, Mrs. Potter, visits her husband's office to ask him for money. "One good thing about being a widow, Mr. Oakley," Mrs. Potter says to Uncle Charlie, "is that you don't have to ask your husband for money." What makes this widow "merry," and threatening, is her independence, financial and otherwise, from her husband. Uncle Charlie, in his diatribe against these "fat, faded, wheezing animals," distinguishes between "town women" and "city women" (shades of *Sunrise*), the latter being "useless women." (Charlie protests: "They're alive. They're human beings!" "Are they, Charlie?," her uncle responds.) "Their husbands dead, made so much money." Their widows are now "eating the money, drinking the money, they stink of money." These women, in other words, are enjoying an "unheard-of totality of pleasures—a [real] banquet."[8] Charles delivers his jeremiad in extreme close-up by which he acquires an exceptional ferocity. It is this pronounced fear of women with money, of women with any kind of power, which is essentially a fear of women's sexuality, that reverberates throughout and indeed structures so many of Hitchcock's films. (It similarly structures Bram Stoker's novel, *Dracula*.) It is a fear of, at once, wide scope and terrible specificity: a fear marking every gesture, undermining every speech, permeating every shot, and haunting every scene.

Charlie Newton exhibits qualities shared by those famous hysterical patients of Freud. Freud described those women as follows:

> I have described the patient's [Elisabeth von R.] character, the features which one meets with so frequently in hysterical people and which there is no excuse for regarding as a consequence of degeneracy: her giftedness [*"She's got brains," Joe says of Charlie*], her ambition, her moral sensibility, her excessive demand for love which, to begin with, found satisfaction in her family, and the independence of her nature which went beyond the feminine ideal and found expression in a considerable amount of obstinacy, pugnacity and reserve.[9]

Freud's psycho-moral prescription for women and his polite misogyny are apparent in this passage; Hitchcock's are no less apparent in his films, with the difference that Hitchcock's misogyny is hardly polite. Charlie also seeks to go "beyond the feminine ideal," the ideal embodied by that "town woman," her mother. She wants to escape the stultifying routines of family life in small-town America. In fact, what she is really after is the independence and power of the "merry widow." Her uncle consecrates those wishes by placing on her finger the ring of the widowed woman he has murdered.[10] This unhealthy, unholy union—it's as if they are getting married—of her and her uncle, of her feminine and masculine halves, must be broken in order to allow the holier one of her and Graham. The masculine half of Charlie's personality seeks those "masculine" traits of independence and power; and it is this phallic, striving half which is really the cause of the aggression unleashed against her family and, ultimately, herself. The unconscious guilt she feels over the "destruction" of her family eventually deflects the course of her anger and redirects it toward herself. Charlie's wish to escape the family and its mediocrity is, as the progress of the film makes quite clear, a death wish. The masculine desires which gnaw at her, feed off her, vampiristically suck her blood ("How's your throat?," a friend of Charlie's asks her in one scene), and almost kill her are those desires she eventually overcomes by pushing her uncle off his train to land in front of an oncoming one. The moment of their abolition occurs on that powerful, moving, black vehicle that brought Uncle Charlie to Santa Rosa and now brings him to his death.

Single women with money (or some kind of power) are deadly in Hitchcock; they provoke uncontrollable anxiety in men, which turns to murderous rage. They are regarded as inhuman and unnatural, unhinging both the social and natural orders. Those famous Hitchcock heroines who appear in the films made after *Shadow of a Doubt,* like Alicia Huberman (*Notorious*), Miriam Haines (*Strangers on a Train*), Judy Barton (*Vertigo*), Marion Crane (*Psycho*), Melanie Daniels (*The Birds*), Marnie Edgar (*Marnie*), and Brenda Blaney (*Frenzy*), are "mature" women; i.e., they possess the independence and power of the "merry widow," for which Charlie merely yearns and certainly does not possess. (That lack in Charlie constitutes her youth and "innocence." Innocence in quotes because even to yearn for independence is enough to contaminate any woman in Hitchcock's world.) This maturity makes them all, so to speak, notorious, i.e., criminal: in essence, to be a woman is a crime. And the punishment for that crime calls forth an impressive array of disciplinary techniques: Alicia is punched in the face and poisoned; Miriam is strangled; Judy is dragged to the top of a church bell tower off which she falls and dies; Marion is stabbed to death; Melanie is attacked by birds and pecked until she's unconscious (Annie Hayworth is pecked until she's dead); Marnie is tormented psychologically; and Brenda is strangled. Charlie is herself gassed, tripped down a flight of stairs, and almost thrown in front of a speeding train. And the "merry widows," of course, are murdered.

Uncle Charlie, the embodiment of his niece's phallic desires, lands in front of an oncoming train; Charlie herself, in the final scene of the film, lands on that pedestal upon which "Averageness"—her mother—has been firmly enthroned throughout the course of the film. (In the last shot of the film, Graham is looking up at Charlie.) "Average families are the best," Graham tells Charlie at one point. The film is a chart of her progress from rejection of her family and her premonitions of her future status within it to wholehearted acceptance of her mother's position. The repressed violence implicit in her desire for freedom and independence not only "kills" her father but thereby converts her mother into a "widow." As I suggested earlier, Charlie's remarks imply a world without the father, which would be the world of the merry widow, a world of unheard-of pleasures. This is the world she wants for herself and her mother. In fact, this world of incredible pleasures is obtained when she exists alone with her mother; it is equivalent to the bliss obtained in that golden age of the pre-Oedipal. Such is the nature of the extraordinary life Charlie seeks.

At the same time, however, that Charlie converts her mother into a "widow," she also prepares her mother for death at the hands of the "merry widow murderer," her uncle (i.e., her phallic desires). She learns to her horror that by "killing" her father she would also be "killing" her beloved mother. It is her uncle's closeness to her mother that terrifies Charlie—"Keep your hands off my mother," she warns him—and motivates her attempts to drive him out of town. Her love for her mother proves stronger than her love of independence and reconciles her to her mother's position. The ambivalent nature of Charlie's phallic wishes—that they kill both the father (desired) and the mother (undesired)—is reflected in the contradictory makeup of Uncle Charlie himself, who not only embodies Charlie's phallic yearnings but also voices the fears that those yearnings provoke.

Needless to say, Emma does not share her daughter's perception of family life as stagnant and hardly aims to suppress the presence of her husband. Yet an obscure vision of the world of the "merry widow" nevertheless also motivates Emma to a limited extent: she participates in the demeaning of her husband and is brought to tears at the departure of her brother. At one point she addresses Joe and Charles, standing side by side, as "the two men in my life," a remark which attests to the strength that Charles has in her life, as strong as that of her own husband. (Charles eventually leaves her, however.) Though Emma has become too much of a "town woman" for her to treat her daughter's unrest too seriously, she still betrays traces of that unrest, as, by implication, does every woman.

Yet the last scene of the film is so maliciously ambiguous. In medium-shot we see Charlie on the right, Graham on her left, standing a bit behind her so that he is looking up to her. There is a church in the background. We hear organ music and the voice of an off-screen priest extolling the character of Uncle Charlie during his obsequies.

Priest: Santa Rosa has gained and lost a son. A generous, kind. . . .

Charlie: (whose voice overwhelms that of the priest) He hated the whole world. He said people like us had no idea of what the world is like.

Graham: It's not as bad as all that.

Priest: . . . their sterling characters. . . .

Graham: Sometimes, the world needs a lot of watching. It goes a bit crazy now and then, like your Uncle Charlie.

Priest: . . . the beauty of their souls, the sweetness of their characters live on with us forever.

Hitchcock is not only convicting civilization of its illusoriness—the priest, stalwart representative of society's moral values, eulogizes a murderer—but is

also, in effect, marrying Graham and Charlie. There they stand, the redoubt-
able couple, churched and together, the detective and his recently "cured"
wife, with all contaminating traces of her uncle's influence, i.e., of her own
disturbing desires, expunged; she is (they hope) clean. Yet their "marriage"
occurs during a funeral. Is the implication that wedlock really is deadlock? Are
Charlie's fears about the killing mediocrity of family life being ever so under-
handedly confirmed? Those desires of independence and freedom almost do
kill her; yet she rids herself of them only to land in the tomb of marriage and
family life—so she really hasn't escaped death after all. Hitchcock, like God,
loves a joke; and divine jokes, as the Greeks knew so well, are often the
cruellest.[11]

Hitchcock's indictment of the family as a trap, if not a tomb, is suggested
in another way. When Graham proposes marriage to Charlie in an earlier
scene, the door of the garage in which they are standing slams shut. Hitchcock
also indicts the family as a fount of criminal mischief. In this last scene,
Graham and Charlie are a couple formed by a kind of secret complicity in the
death of her uncle; they achieve a composure at once silent and sinister, secure
in their private knowledge that their "marriage" is founded on a murder.
Criminality's presence, at first suggested behind the facade of the Newton
family home then concealed in the construction of the paper house, remains
undisclosed in this apotheosis of the couple which concludes the film.
Criminality, Hitchcock insists, hides within domesticity; or, to put it another
way, domesticity is merely the most hidden criminality.

And it is no accident, given the fears shaping the film, that Charlie finds
herself married to a detective, a cop, a representative of Law and Order.
Graham affirms that "the world needs a lot of watching." What needs watching, in other words, are those women who yearn to exceed their juridical
limits—consignment to husband and family—as Charlie once did and perhaps
will do again. (It is remarkable how obsessed Hitchcock is with this theme of
watching and investigating women and how he develops it further in the films
that follow *Shadow of a Doubt*.) Part of the "nasty taste" (Robin Wood's
phrase) which lingers after seeing this film consists of the fear that these illicit
desires of women are not easily eradicated, that the family Charlie and Graham
are going to form will produce offspring who will inevitably have the same
unruly desires that their mother once did.[12] In the novel *Dracula*, Jonathan
Harker, a man whose wife has been bitten by the Count, writes about vampires
in his journal: "Just as their hideous bodies could only rest in sacred earth, so
the holiest love [marriage] was the recruiting sergeant for their ghastly ranks."[13]
Similarly, the "recruiting sergeant" for the vampires torturing this very martial
film is the holy locus of the family. The family itself, by its mere existence,
produces those phallic/feminine desires it hopes to keep under wraps. But
those desires have a way of breaking through and throwing everything into
question—like the startling image of the waltzing merry widows erupting like
an hysterical symptom at four distinct points during the course of the film—a

disturbance of the narrative flow that is very unusual in a film of the forties. It is this cycle—the perpetual repetition of banal existence of the family, which generates the wish to escape and destroy it, which instills guilt for having the wish, which distorts the effect of the wish, which brings near death and a return to the family—that elicits Hitchcock's most profound disgust and transforms the family into the great Unsolved Crime. The fact that woman triggers this process makes her into a criminal, but she is a crime that can be "solved"—by means of marriage and a husband, or a brutal death.

One significant feature of the Law and Order that Charlie's phallicness threatens is the order of Time. What time is it? This insistent, if mute, question haunts the world of *Shadow of a Doubt* and indeed of many other Hitchcock films. When Uncle Charlie presents the Newton family with gifts, he gives Joe a watch. When Herb first appears in the film, he asks Joe the time. When Charlie rushes off to the library, there is a shot of the town clock. And the name of the sordid nightclub to which Uncle Charlie takes his niece is the 'Til Two Club. One implicit answer provided by the film to that nagging question is, it's bedtime, i.e., the time of sleep, the time of the dream, the time of wish fulfillment. (Remember that the two characters, Charlie and her uncle, begin the film lying in bed.) Sleep puts to sleep the time machine; sleep also brings an end to uprightness. Indeed one could view the film as Charlie's progress from lying down, dreaming, and leaving the bed to standing upright (with her husband), as erect as the columns of the church in front of which she stands at the end of the film. The world of the bed attempts to subvert the world of the upright—horizontal versus vertical. And the world of the bed is also the world of sick sexuality, the world of female sexuality, whose fiendish energy (so perceived by Hitchcock) breaks the bounds, breaks apart and levels the order of the Father, the order of Law and Time. Small wonder that his film is populated by cops, priests, and soldiers.

For Alfred Hitchcock, family relationships are a source of endless provocation. The family, in the course of its normal and natural existence, produces the most oppressive of tensions and the calm matter-of-factness with which it does so is what makes it so frightening. "It's not the horrible which shocks," writes Adorno, "but its self-evidence."[14] In *Shadow of a Doubt*, the family with its glow (its halo) may seem like a warm bath, but it all too readily becomes a swamp of frustrated yearnings, breeding demons of female emancipation whose ferocity it is barely able to contain. The representative American family, in short, is the true horror of the film.

> I had a family. They can be a nuisance in identity but there is no doubt no shadow of a doubt that that identity the family identity we can do without.
>
> —GERTRUDE STEIN[15]

Notes

1. Elizabeth Hardwick, *Sleepless Nights* (New York: Random House, 1979), 107.
2. Freud and Breuer, *Studies on Hysteria*, trans. James Strachey (New York: Avon Books, 1966).
3. Hands have a special authority in Hitchcock's films, and the vampirism pervading those films is given its paradigmatic expression in the form of the grip. Cf. the shot of Bruno's hand retrieving the cigarette lighter from the sewer in *Strangers on a Train;* Bruno stomping on Guy's hands in the same film as Guy desperately holds on to the merry-go-round as it swings out of control; Uncle Charlie squeezing the napkin in *Shadow of a Doubt;* Babs, dead, clutching Rusk's stickpin so tightly in *Frenzy* that he has to break her fingers in order to retrieve it; and the striking opening shot of *Vertigo* of the criminal's hand grasping the ladder.
      Characters embracing, as many people have noticed, often lovingly resemble a strangling: Henrietta's initial appearance in *Under Capricorn* in which she places her hands on the neck of her lover/husband, Sam Flusky; Kendall and Thornhill on the train in *North by Northwest;* also Vandamm's hand on Eve's neck at the auction in the same film.
      Think also of the results of so many of the murders or near murders—a stunning shot of the victim's hand with the fingers resolutely outstretched and far apart, a hand that, in its shock, no longer grasps: Marion's hand during the stabbing in the shower in *Psycho;* Melanie's and Mitch's hands, pecked in *The Birds;* Brenda's hands during the strangling in *Frenzy;* and Bruno's fist opening at the end of *Strangers on a Train* to reveal the cigarette lighter. Hitchcock's characters often seem spellbound—like Uncle Charlie and his automatism mentioned above—in the grip of something or other; and it seems as if the aim of murder is to break the grip of whatever or whomever the murderer thinks, consciously or not, is feeding on him.
4. A phrase from Michel Foucault, *Madness and Civilization*, trans. Richard Howard (New York: Vintage Books, 1973), 110.
5. Donald Barthelme, *The Dead Father* (New York: Farrar, Straus, and Giroux, 1975), 3.
6. Philip Rieff, "Fellow Teachers," *Salmagundi*, no. 20 (1972): 34.
7. Quoted in Hardwick, 62.
8. A phrase I borrow from Roland Barthes, *A Lover's Discourse*, trans. Richard Howard (New York: Hill and Wang, 1978), 119. In this connection we might ask why Hitchcock's characters are always eating. The appetitive mode predominates, and after the bedroom, the dining room is probably Hitchcock's most favorite setting. References to food and eating are innumerable. Some outstanding examples: "You never did eat your lunch today, did you?" are the first words spoken in *Psycho;* there are the disgusting meals prepared by the inspector's wife in *Frenzy;* Rusk, again from *Frenzy*, is the owner of a produce distributing company who is often seen biting into a piece of fruit (Is there a sly homosexual reference here? Rusk as the big Fruit?); Bruno and Guy meet in the dining car of the train in *Strangers on a Train;* the townspeople of Bodega Bay stand in a diner and watch the birds attack in *The Birds;* very erotic exchanges take place around the dinner table in *Notorious* and *North by Northwest* (Eve Kendall: "I never discuss love on an empty stomach."); and in *Shadow of a Doubt* when Uncle Charlie overhears Joe and Herb mention that the other suspected "merry widow" murderer walked into the propeller of a plane, he declares: "I could sure eat a good dinner today."
      That eating is connected to vampirism (feeding on someone) seems obvious, but exactly how it's connected, I'm uncertain. There are, I am sure, other meanings attached to this hunger that rages throughout Hitchcock's work. This endnote, along with the others, states in a very speculative way, as something to think about, various themes entwined in Hitchcock's films which should be explored more thoroughly than they have been.
9. Freud and Breuer, 202.
10. Hitchcock's world is populated by glowing objects, of which the ring is one, objects possessed by light as if radioactive (like the wine bottles in *Notorious*), acquiring a life as eerily vivid as that of the protagonists. In *The American Cinema* (New York: E. P. Dutton, 1968) Andrew Sarris has written: "Hitchcock's objects are never mere props of a basically theatrical mise en scène, but rather the very substance of his cinema. These objects embody the feelings and fears of characters as object and character interact with each other in dramas within dramas" (p. 59).
      But why? Why do objects figure so luminously and become the "very substance of his

cinema?" One possible answer lies in Hitchcock's connection to Expressionism. Everyone seems to agree on Hitchcock's debts to that artistic movement, a movement that, to speak very simplemindedly, emphasized the subjective over the objective, that attempted "to 'express' emotional states through a distortion of objective reality" (see Robin Wood, "Retrospective").

Yet Expressionist inwardness, it seems to me, necessarily makes objects seem like characters and characters seem like objects. Theodor Adorno has written: "The more the I of expressionism is thrown back upon itself, the more like the excluded world of things it becomes. . . . Pure subjectivity, being of necessity estranged from itself as well as having become a thing, assumes the dimensions of objectivity which expresses itself through its own estrangement. The boundary between what is human and the world of things becomes blurred" (*Prisms* [cited below], 262).

11. To modify a phrase of Hannah Arendt's in *Men in Dark Times* (New York: Harcourt Brace Jovanovich, 1968), 98.
12. Robin Wood, *Hitchcock's Films*, 2nd ed. (London: A. Zwemmer, 1969), 69.
13. Bram Stoker, *Dracula* (1897; reprint New York: Dell Books, 1977), 330.
14. Theodor Adorno, *Prisms*, trans. Samuel and Shierry Weber (London: Neville and Spearman, 1967), 248.
15. See Judith Therman, "A Rose is a Rose is a Rose is a Rose Gertrude Stein," *Ms.*, vol. 2, no. 8 (1974): 54.

SHADOW OF A DOUBT (Universal, 1943). *Producer:* Jack H. Skirball, *Script:* Thornton Wilder, Alma Reville, Sally Benson, from a story by Gordon McDonnell, *Photography:* Joseph Valentine, *Editor:* Milton Carruth, *Sets:* John B. Goodman, Robert Boyle, A. Gausman, L. R. Robinson, *Music:* Dimitri Tiomkin, *Costumes:* Adrian, Vera West, *Players:* Joseph Cotton (Charles Oakley), Teresa Wright (Charlie Newton), Patricia Collinge (Emma Newton), MacDonald Carey (Jack Graham), Henry Travers (Joe Newton), Hume Cronyn (Herb Hawkins). 108 minutes.

The Moral Universe of Hitchcock's *Spellbound*

Thomas Hyde

One would hardly want to rank *Spellbound* (1945) as one of Hitchcock's richest or most perfectly conceived films. Even the Master himself (he can be puckishly agreeable when offered negative opinions of his work) told Truffaut in his interview book that it was "just another manhunt story wrapped up in pseudo-psychoanalysis."[1] Truffaut, concurring, dismisses the film as "somewhat of a disappointment" after a few brief exchanges. Robin Wood in his *Hitchcock's Films* devotes but a short paragraph to *Spellbound*, citing the incongruous Dali dream sequences and a troublesome "split in the thematic material" between the growth of the relationship of Ingrid Bergman and Gregory Peck and the progress of the murder plot.[2] The film has its share of other weaknesses; Truffaut (assisted by Hitchcock) catalogues most of them: the Hollywood treatment of psychoanalysis in parts of Ben Hecht's script; Miklos Rozsa's grotesquely overdramatic score; Gregory Peck's insufficiently convincing portrayal of a potential madman-murderer. Yet the presence of flaws hardly justifies a lack of critical press, especially when a virtue can be produced for every flaw (not the least of which is Ingrid Bergman's exquisite, dimensional performance), and particularly when the so-called flaws are often as interesting as the virtues. It is worth looking at *Spellbound* to discover what it is that makes it so pleasurably and uniquely a Hitchcock film.

As the precursor of *Vertigo*, *Psycho*, and *Marnie*, *Spellbound* is Hitchcock's first film to deal with pathological mental cases and, even more prominently than in these or in any others, with psychoanalysis. Here John Ballantine, who suffers from amnesia, assumes for a time the identity of a Dr. Edwardes, who is scheduled to replace the head of an insane asylum, a Dr. Murchison. The possibility is raised later that Ballantine murdered Dr. Edwardes and took over his identity out of guilt. Ballantine undergoes a journey through a series of mental as well as physical landscapes in order to trace down the clues to his real identity and to uncover the roots of his debilitating guilt complex. In all this he is aided by a psychiatrist, Dr. Constance Peterson, and by her mentor, Dr. Alex Brulov. In the end Dr. Murchison is exposed as the real murderer.

Now it is significant that in a film about psychoanalysis the cure for John's amnesia is not found on the analyst's couch but rather emerges from a series of experiential trials culminating in John's physically reenacting the episode which originally triggered his disturbance — the murder of Dr. Edwardes on the ski slope at Cumberland. Here, as elsewhere, Hitchcock seems to be responding to the common belief that the psychiatric patient can be cured of his deep problems by just talking them out. But this does not necessarily mean that Hitchcock is attacking psychoanalysis itself. Rather, as treated in the film, psychoanalysis becomes a figure which Hitchcock employs to express his disapproval of certain kinds of attitudes and assumptions associated with its application, so as to bring out the real issues with which he is concerned. Psychoanalytic practice is a vehicle for making an artistic statement; it is both MacGuffin and metaphor. It is not really even John Ballantine's film, for while the sensational psychoanalytic murder-mystery plot holds our immediate surface attention, Hitchcock's sustained, essential focus here is on the emotional and moral development of Constance Peterson in her relation with Ballantine. The film depicts a learning process, not only that of Ballantine's recovery of his lost identity by following his guilt feelings to their unconsciously repressed source but that of Constance forging a new identity by tapping a suppressed capacity within herself for feeling and committed action. What is being emphasized and approved here by Hitchcock is Constance's trusting involvement with John.

Ultimately more absorbing than the determination of John's innocence is their personal transformation — becoming integrated within themselves and so redeemed for each other. Our interest in this is mediated less by the suspense elements through which Murchison's ostensible guilt is revealed than by the undercurrent of implication whereby a more basic, universal culpability is exposed in each of the characters. *Spellbound* shows the unwarranted guilt complex to be a much rarer phenomenon than we might be inclined to suppose. In exploring the question of the appropriateness of one's feelings of guilt and self-doubt, *Spellbound* suggests a relation between moral and mental health that receives its most comprehensive exposition later in the character of *Psycho*'s Norman Bates. Hitchcock seems to be saying that guilt may be damaging when it remains beyond one's ability to act on it, but also when it is absent or unheeded. Guilt can be a healthy signal to direct one's awareness to what is, in Hitchcock's moral universe, a potential for moral error native to the human condition.

One of the major themes pointed up consistently in the film is the inadequacy of intellectual analysis when it is divorced from compassionate, understanding involvement. This is introduced in the initial sequences as the classic opposition of book knowledge versus experiential knowledge, connected with the education of Constance Peterson. The film begins with Mary Carmichael, an inmate of the hospital, whom we see display a rather thinly concealed hostility toward men (she nuzzles up to Harry the aide, then scratches his arm). In the subsequent session with Constance she then tells of another would-be seducer who got his moustache bitten off for his trouble. Taking the bait Hitchcock dangles for the amateur psychiatrist here, we can infer that Mary encourages men to accept this role in order to punish them and that it indicates some deeply rooted sexual conflicts in Mary, possibly Oedipal in nature, possibly having to do with forbidden childhood feelings toward a father figure that she has not yet been able to overcome. Although she may desire a mature relationship with a man, she can't accomplish it under the contradictory terms she has established. Constance seems the cool, rational opposite of Mary. Starched and stiff in her white hospital coat, Constance's backed-off, cerebral, patronizing stance contrasts sharply with Mary's cultivated attractiveness and her passionate, lascivious behavior ("Psychoanalysis bores the pants off me!"). Mary reacts to Constance's unfeeling attempts at analysis by throwing a book at her and calling her "Miss Frozen-Puss."

If we haven't already guessed it, when Constance next spurns Dr. Fleurot's advances we become aware that her detached, clinical attitude is not reserved solely for her professional relationships, but extends to the private ones as well. Fleurot lectures her on her "lack of human and emotional experience." "It's rather like embracing a textbook," he says. "You're exactly like Miss Carmichael. I'd like to throw a book at you — but I won't." Despite Fleurot's vicious, juvenile sniping at her later and his subsequent jealousy, we can appreciate his frustration and see that he is basically correct in his estimation of her. She has evidently been dependent on books as the source of her knowledge of human behavior at the expense of direct, intimate experience. (In this respect, Constance is related to the know-it-all, bookish little sister figures such as Ann in *Shadow of a Doubt* and Barbara in *Strangers on a Train*.) And she *is* like Mary Carmichael in exhibiting a milder form of Mary's hysteria. We are, after all, given no indication that Fleurot does not genuinely care for her, even though in his approach he resembles more than slightly the masher from Philadelphia and the house detective in the Empire Hotel. Constance may understandably be repulsed by his aggressive moves, but the fact is, her aggressive rejection of him is symptomatic of her ignorance of certain legitimate human needs and obligations, not only those of others, but her own as well.

Moreover, Constance is to be seen as accountable for this in a way in which Mary is not; Constance has no excuse for not regarding the responsibility to be aware of her own and others' emotional requirements. She is not prevented from investigating and evaluating her own responses, as Mary is by her mental condition. Constance's detachment and frigid demeanor, the complacent, presumptuous distancing of herself from human contact, is tantamount to the sin of pride. It is a willed and willing choice on her part, and this neglect of worldly knowledge is especially debilitating in a person of her profession, dedicated to helping people with serious problems of their own. The starting point for the evolution of Constance's trust in instinct and passion is her "love at first sight" introduction to Dr. Edwardes in the dining room at the asylum. The turning point, however, comes with her choosing to disregard reason and accompany Edwardes rather than revealing him to the police when he leaves the asylum. It is appropriate that the awakening in Constance of a person of open feeling should proceed from a spontaneous decision which logical calculation would have counselled her to avoid. For Constance, Dr. Edwardes's book on the guilt complex, which she thinks she ought to read, is superseded by an immersion in first-hand experience.

Having witnessed her obliviousness to the needs and motives of others, we now observe Constance's blindness to her own emerging feelings, her self-deception with regard to her reasons for staying with John in his hotel room in New York. She tells him she has come to help him, but only as a doctor, and as they embrace she murmurs, "It has nothing to do with love, nothing at all, nothing at all." Our interpretation of this transparency has been prepared for in previous scenes depicting her romantic distraction with John. What is at stake here is her ingrained definition of herself, her confidence in her intellectual and professional competency, her maintenance of a customary, secure decorum. Her precarious illusion of aloofness from and control over her world is being threatened by the passionate feelings involuntarily called forth from her. Her basic assumptions having been called into doubt, her circumvention here follows the same pattern as John's amnesia: the blocking-off (more consciously impelled in Constance than in John) of the recognition of fallibility for fear of disturbing one's stable orientation to an imposed, faulty conception of reality. Constance's turning away from the haven of established authority is the right move to make, but with it comes the shocking awareness of the illusion of her own autonomy, to be replaced slowly by a more true, more sober vision of the limitations of personal freedom and independence.

As Constance progresses in discovering her capacity for the expression of feeling, we are made very conscious of her vulnerability in extending herself to John. Our responses to this are mixed. On the one hand, there is the matter of John's innocence or guilt in respect to killing Edwardes. We are warned by Dr. Murchison that John is a "paranoid imposter" and that he is certainly guilty of dispatching Edwardes. Dr. Alex's condemnation of Dr. Edwardes for harboring John ("What kind of doctor is it that wants to bring a dangerous patient into a bowling alley?") also accents Constance's impulsiveness and seems to cast doubt on her ability to judge wisely. She does underestimate Alex in his ability to "put two and two together." He has seen through their husband-and-wife story, and in the apparently menacing scene with John and the razor, where we are made the victims of our own expectations, Dr. Alex accordingly turns the tables on John. Constance subsequently tells Alex, "I couldn't feel this way about a man who was bad, who had committed a murder," an indication of her gain in self-perception in acknowledging the demands of her emotions. Yet it also seems at this point that she has swung too far in the direction of relying exclusively on instinct and emotional prejudice in evaluating John's character. Alex *is* wrong, however, in censuring her emotional fidelity to John, and Constance must abandon the paternal possessiveness and protection of Alex, and the kind of reserved authority he stands for, in favor of a more mature and responsible relationship with John. Constance's problem here still is her lack of self-doubt, her lack of an accurate perspective on the scope of her actions and abilities with respect to the scope of circumstance, the way things operate in the world. She is correct in remaining with John and helping him to handle what her psychological probing has released. She must come to feel the full impact of what it means to be responsible for penetrating to the deepest center of one's selfhood and to realize the problem of coping with what one finds there. Just as the turning point of John's rejuvenation occurs on the ski slope in the revelatory return to the childhood source of his guilt complex, so Constance begins her real transformation immediately after this, with the numbing shock that the happy ending to their romance and the vindication of her plans and efforts have been overturned by the emergence of the fact that Edwardes was murdered. Her reaction, looking up at John but not meeting his eyes, reflects her realization that despite having uncovered the origin of John's complex, despite the voice of her intuition, she could still be wrong about his capacity for evil. The vision of doors swinging open at her first kiss with John is replaced by the vision of cell doors swinging closed, the end to which her presumption has led her. Her following distress at Alex's house marks the critical point of her diminishment at the perception of her own certain guilt: in being responsible because of pride, self-interest, and complacency for bringing about the reversal of her own intentions and for assigning the man she loves to a fate her efforts were designed to avoid. Having now been humbled by the vision of her own culpability and the complexities of character and situation of which she had not been aware, the way has been prepared for her to form a more realistic, adjusted idea of herself and the life she has been leading. Her traumatic downfall has also been her salvation. She is now able to return to life and to act in accordance with a greater awareness of the moral weight of involvement, the implications and consequences of her action, and the limitations of her abilities.

Particularly enigmatic here is the problem of John's behavior, his response to certain stimuli, the matter of his guilt. John's amnesia, we are told, is the result of the repression of memory by the subconscious mind in order to evade damaging self-incrimination arising out of a past childhood event. We find that John did indeed kill his brother in a boyhood accident, and the similarity of Edwardes's death at Cumberland provoked the amnesia as a defense. But along with the repression or guilt, a simultaneous desire for and fear of punishment manifests itself obliquely in John's actions, a tension of anxiety that is linked to aggressive and sexual energy. John's taking on of Dr. Edwardes's identity can be interpreted as an unconscious desire to be exposed and to confess. There is an implied parallel here with Garmes, whose example lends weight to the suspense at Constance's involvement with John. Like John, Garmes suffers from a guilt complex; he believes himself to have killed his father. Constance's counsel to Garmes is a rather unhelpful assurance: "People often feel guilty about things that happened in their childhood." Prevented from confronting and confessing the source of his very real guilt, Garmes eventually finds a punishing, destructive outlet for his anxiety, a possibility we later feel is imminent in John. Constance's dismissal here is a further symptom of her overall naiveté. She is ignorant of the meaning and importance of guilt related to crimes, real or imagined, since she has not faced the possibility of sin in herself. She is mistaken about the nature of one's experience of guilt. What she has to learn is that guilt is not explained away or suppressed, for it will surely break out again and, while it may be mistaken and damaging to blame oneself for unconscious intentions or acts for which a person cannot be held responsible, to be without a sense of guilt or doubt may be equally invidious.

Unlike Garmes's, John's guilt seems to have sexual dimensions that are manifested more clearly on the surface. John's repressed feelings on occasion erupt past his normal exterior in displaced, hostile outbursts of aggression when triggered by the reminders of the guilty incident of his brother's death — dark lines and the color white. These signs almost always appear when he is in the company of Constance. The first time this occurs, John's "spell" is brought on as a result of what is supposed to be a swimming pool that Constance has drawn on the white tablecloth. However, the drawing is also clearly vaginal in shape. In other instances, she discourages his forceful advances in order to interrogate him about his guilty past. John subsequently falls into his trance, and apparently influenced by the earlier denial of his gratification, his subconscious aggressions emerge in resentment: "If there's anything I hate it's a smug woman!" John's outbursts here resemble those of Fleurot. John, a medical student, is connected with Fleurot by Dr. Murchison's comment too, that Fleurot exhibits "the manners of a medical student" in regard to his bitter remarks directed at Constance. John's treatment of Constance suggests that he too harbors an immature attitude toward women and sex, one which links him to Fleurot, the house dick, and the masher. John's relationship with Constance, to be healthy and lasting, must be free of the taints of exploitation and self-indulgence. John must come to dissociate aggression from sex and to expend those aggressive energies in useful labor — as Alex points out to Constance: "There's lots of happiness in working hard — maybe the most." Perhaps we are to see that John is not to be considered responsible for this behavior, in the same way as Constance's other admirers in the film, because of its origin in his unconscious guilt problems. If this is so, then the solving of John's guilt complex by the divulging of its origin in childhood fears (punishment grossly out of proportion to offense = undue guilt) implies that John's aggression-sex problems are also on the way to being healed. The last scene of the film, showing John taking a more suitable, responsible stance toward marriage, can be interpreted as indicating the growth of John's edification that has coincided with Constance's development in the film.

The thematic and moral issues raised by the interaction of characters and situations in *Spellbound* are summarized in two major pairs of scenes incorporating subjective camera shots occurring near the beginning and end of the film and serving as reference marks against which may be measured the progress of the characters and the advancement of the film's statement. The first pair of incidents, in retrospect, calls our attention to the progress of Constance as, from her point of view, the camera tracks up the stairs of the asylum to bring into central notice the door of Dr. Murchison's room. In both cases, it is Constance's willing choice to climb the stairs and confront what is beyond the door that is the major issue. Throughout the film John has been associated with guilt, aggression, emotion, and with downward movements, descending inside himself, into his dreams, uncovering his subconscious and repressed memories, and discovering his relation to this inner life. Constance has been associated with self-certainty, reserve and reason, and with ascending movements, moving outward to experience in the world, to encounters with others, expanding her consciousness of the potential for both love and destruction in human character and human relationships. Here in the initial instance it is the false Dr. Edwardes who waits on the other side of the door. She is unaware of the dangers and complications her involvement with him may entail: she is only vaguely conscious of the nature and force of her newfound feelings to which she will accede. She crosses to the library first to get Dr. Edwardes's book, a symbol of her diluted life of intellectual retreat. She chooses to cross the threshold, and as she faces John across another doorway, her real motives begin to become clear: "I thought I wanted to discuss your book with you—I'm amazed at the subterfuge." This is the beginning of self-revelation. The second tracking shot, reminding us of the first and its associated implications, calls our attention to the progress that has been made, the difference in Constance. In this case, it is the duplicitous Dr. Murchison who inhabits the room, and Constance, having suffered through the experiencing of guilt in herself and in John, is now fully armed with the knowledge of what she is doing and its possible consequences. Where in the first scene the essential rightness of following her instinctual desires was emphasized, her choice to enter the room this time is a measure of her realization of the depth of complexity and responsibility that such a commitment necessitates.

The final set of scenes recapitulates cinematically the major themes developed within the film: the deception of appearances, the untrustworthiness of authority, the nature of guilt and sin, and the moral responsibility of human involvement. They occur from the point of view, first, of John Ballantine and, second, of Dr. Murchison. In the context of the first shot, Ballantine has descended the stairs at Dr. Alex's home to confront Alex at his desk, again across a doorframe. John is in one of his trances, his hand clutching a razor, which we are made to think he will use on Alex, since he has just spared the sleeping Constance. The situation is symbolic of the primal scene, with John competing with a father-figure for the possession of Constance. As John raises to his lips the glass of white milk, which we know will serve to fuel the fire of his aggressions, the camera is John's eyes. Alex is seen through the bottom of the glass as the milk gradually rises up and the screen fades to white. What we learn, of course, is that the threat, while real enough by itself, was not to be carried out so inevitably as we thought. With the drugged glass of milk, the distinctions between victim and victimizer begin to break down, but with the advantage here on the side of the one most consciously aware of the deep motives and vulnerability of others.

Likewise, in the final confrontation between Constance and Dr. Murchison, it is Constance who must put what she has learned about herself on the line by trusting in her intuition of its applicability to Murchison. The situation here is advanced a rational and moral notch from the previous one. Like John, Constance must face down the figure of fatherly authority in order to win her lover, but here the similarity ends. She knows that Murchison is the murderer of Edwardes and is aware of what may be the ultimate consequences to herself of this act of emotional fidelity to John. Murchison proves his skill at analysis by correctly interpreting the dream that damns him as guilty, parallel to Alex's deciphering of John's illness and unconscious intent in the former scene. The gun, seen from the subjective point of view of Murchison, corresponds to the glass of milk as the externalization of apparent danger. As the gun and camera follow Constance across the room, she appeals to Murchison on the basis of logic not to commit a second murder for, she says, considering his mental condition at the time, he would not be accounted guilty or responsible for the first. As with Garmes and later with John, the resort to reason proves inadequate. Murchison, having failed to admit his own moral condition to himself, is done in by his own complacency. The light of truth bursts in through the hole in Constance's reasoning, inflaming his sense of guilt rather than absolving it. The destructive pointer of blame, associated now with self-righteous authority, comes round to confront itself, and ourselves.[3]

The simplistic question, then, of the efficacy of reason over emotion has been transcended in the course of the film through its demonstration of the imperatives of self-awareness, love, and responsible involvement with others. More humbly conscious of their own capacity for error and the nature of the world's demands, Constance and John deserve to be reunited, saved for a better life. Rather than kiss and part, like the other couples in the train station, their approved example is to kiss and remain, in faith and trust, together.

Notes

1. François Truffaut, *Hitchcock* (New York: Simon & Schuster, 1967), 118.
2. Robin Wood, *Hitchcock's Films* (New York: A. S. Barnes, 1977), 44.
3. Robin Wood says of this shot that "it is one of the rare instances I can think of in Hitchcock of a *pointless* use of identification technique, since none of us want to shoot Ingrid Bergman and we feel no connection of any kind with the murderer" (p. 44). I disagree that there is a lack of connection. It's just that the connection is of an odd sort. The shot involves a *disparity* between our feelings and Murchison's action that is very much to the point. True, we don't want to kill Ingrid Bergman: neither, really, does Murchison. The gun suddenly turned on *us,* though, brings home, if just for an instant, the enormity and reality of suicide. This puzzling personal threat, brief and implausible as it may be, gives us a shock, disturbs our security, and mobilizes a self-preservation response so different from the one of the head we are supposed to be in that it forces us to query Murchison's reasons with a sense of urgency that no other treatment of the scene could provoke.

SPELLBOUND (Selznick, United Artists, 1945). *Producer:* David O. Selznick, *Script:* Ben Hecht, Angus McPhail, from the novel *The House of Dr. Edwardes* by Frances Beeding (pseud. of Hilary St. George Saunders and John Palmer), *Photography:* George Barnes, *Editors:* William Ziegler, Hal C. Kern, *Music:* Miklos Rozsa, *Costumes:* Howard Greer, *Dream Sequence:* Salvador Dali, *Players:* Ingrid Bergman (Dr. Constance Peterson), Gregory Peck (John Ballantine), Leo G. Carroll (Dr. Murchison), Norman Lloyd (Garmes), Michael Chekhov (Dr. Alex Brulov), Rhonda Fleming (Mary Carmichael), John Emery (Dr. Fleurot). 111 minutes.

CHAPTER THIRTEEN

Notorious:
Perversion par Excellence

Richard Abel

Notorious is the proper name for such a grim fairy tale, not only because of its "tainted" heroine and its outrageous plotting but principally because of a perversion of the conventional fairy tale narrative, perversions in the ritual of sexual coupling, and a consequent rupture in audience identification or spectator placement. Perversions make *Notorious* (1946) one of Hitchcock's most deceptive and disturbing films.

To begin with, let us accept Peter Wollen and John Fell's simplified schema of the Proppian fairy tale structure.[1] A task is set for the hero by a dispatcher (father or family). If he performs it successfully, the hero will be rewarded — the gift of the heroine. The task is to liquidate a lack, to find and return an object of desire or possession (sometimes the heroine herself) which usually has been separated from the dispatcher by a deceitful villain. In his quest, the hero sometimes receives the aid of a helper or magical agent. After setbacks and delays the hero vanquishes the villain, retrieves the object, and claims his reward.

In *Notorious* this basic structure undergoes striking transformations. The task or quest can be divided into three parts. Initially, Prescott (the dispatcher) sends Devlin (the hero) to retrieve Alicia Huberman (the object/heroine) from her traitorous father and drunken playmates — led by a gentle old sugar daddy yachtsman. The task is quickly performed — with a midnight punch, a morning glass of orange juice, and the "right words" from a surreptitious recording. There is no reward here. Or, more precisely, Devlin and Alicia are on the point of rewarding one another, with one another, when Prescott separates them (the interrupting phone call). The separation apparently results from the appearance of Alexander Sebastian (the villain), but actually he is introduced by Prescott and his men (becoming known through their words). A specific task now is set for the heroine, and the hero is reduced to functioning as her helper (at the riding club their dress codes even imply a sex role reversal — Alicia in hat

162

and tie, Devlin hatless and tieless). She is to discover a secret/object the villain possesses. Through trickery, Prescott, with Devlin's tacit consent, turns Alicia (disguised in her former state) over to Sebastian. A "perversion" of the conventional structure is already apparent: the reduction/submission of the hero, the transformation of the heroine from object to subject/agent (but through deliberate "tainting"), the deception played on the villain. The dispatcher Prescott manipulates all for his own ends and seems about to reward no one.

Alicia performs her task and passes on the key to the secret (hand to hand, bottle for bottle) through Devlin to Prescott. Undeceived at last, Sebastian, aided by a devilish mother, traps the heroine in his "castle" and turns her into a "sleeping beauty." The final task is assumed by Devlin alone. No longer directed by the now ignorant Prescott, he drops his guise and enters the "castle" as the "knight in shining armor" to awaken and rescue the "damsel in distress."[2] Alicia helps him now with even more secrets and, at the last moment, Sebastian abets their escape only to be sacrificed for their "happiness." The conventional structure reasserts itself, with an important difference. The dispatcher is replaced by the villain — as manipulator and, more importantly, as the one who rewards: it is Sebastian who now authorizes (reluctantly) the reunion of hero and heroine. Despite this change in function, Devlin and Alicia abandon him to death ("That's your headache").

Read in this fairy tale form, *Notorious* can be said to distribute its main characters along the axis of parents versus children.[3] Special prominence is given the "father" figures who function through sets of oppositions and substitutions.[4] There are three crucial "father" figures. The first serves immediately to define Alicia — the daughter of a traitorous father, she is "guilty" politically, a "marked woman" by association. The syntagmatic repetition in sequence 1 (shots 1–3, 4–6) clearly substitutes her for the expected father as court adjourns. Several sequences later, however, the association is presented as false (the recorded voices), and Alicia is allied ("a job") with Devlin and, through him, with a second "father," his boss, Prescott. The job can "make up for her father's peculiarities," and the death of her father (also made known through Prescott) transforms/"frees" her ("it's as if something had happened to me, not him"). Her new identity emerges in love for Devlin. The absent, denied father is replaced momentarily by the hero (marked as early as sequence 5 when, over the recorded voices of daughter denying father, Devlin approaches Alicia and positions himself beside her).[5] In the midst of external dangers, a couple is formed — a standard Hitchcock theme.

In accepting Alicia, however warily, Devlin acts for himself against a second "father" figure, the dispatcher, Prescott. In effect, he violates "the law of the father."[6] The retribution is swift and humiliating. The dispatcher-father ignores the changed identity of the heroine, sets up the villain as the (semic) antithesis of the hero (short/tall, fair/dark, elderly/young, warm/cold, charming/sarcastic), and gives the heroine to him instead of to the hero (Alicia matching Alex).[7] Submissive, impotent, castrated (the celebratory bottle of wine left behind with Prescott), Devlin joins Prescott in perversely using Alicia, turning her back into what she is not.[8] To restore Alicia and reestablish their sexual union, Devlin must again violate the "law of the father" and act on his own.[9] When he does, in the end, the "castle" opens miraculously for him, and even Sebastian accedes to his demands. Through the act of defying both "father" figures, the couple reforms—in guilt.

The villain introduces a further acting out of parental defiance. In accepting the disguised Alicia, Sebastian, too, acts for himself and against the wishes of a dominant mother. Because mother and son already form a "complete" couple in the "castle," Alicia intrudes as a powerful rival ("You are jealous of her just as you've been jealous of every other woman who's shown an interest in me").[10] Her presence betrays the double function of the villain—he is both son and "husband" to the mother. He, too, acts the "father." The function is marked by his age ("tired . . . this business makes me feel old and look old"), his friendship with Alicia's father, his oppositeness to Prescott. As the antithetical "father" who is actually son, Sebastian makes the "castle" the site of a perversion that is as much sexual as political.[11] By unlocking the door to the cellar, Devlin and Alicia expose the secret, the "other" bottle of wine, which marks the false love between her and Sebastian and the explosive love (incest) which unites mother and son. Once Sebastian realizes the secret is out (in a reverse transfer of knowledge), authority shifts from the motherless, mateless Prescott to this "unwholesome" couple of mother and son. Consequently, it becomes "right" that these false "parents" are defied and abandoned, that this "tainted" couple (politically, morally, and sexually) is replaced by a "purified" one.

This ritual of couple formation at the expense of the family (father/ mother) also operates within a more specific system of the film: the stance and gesture of characters within the space of the frame and the syntagmatic placement of that positioning.[12] Devlin's submission to Prescott and, consequently, to his rival, Sebastian, is articulated paradigmatically across a series of related sequences. In sequence 5, Alicia had come out of her room to join Devlin and take the job he offered; in sequence 15, she again comes out of her room to face Devlin and now Prescott behind him. It is Prescott she asks to help clasp her necklace (cf. Devlin's earlier "gift" of the scarf round her waist); and when Devlin moves to the left behind his boss, Prescott is positioned between them and warns them to "keep shy of one another." When Alicia comes to the office with Sebastian's marriage proposal in sequence 19, again Prescott is positioned beween the two, syntagmatically (looking screen left towards Alicia and screen right towards Devlin). Once more he separates them, doubly, crucially, when his off-screen agreement to her marriage speaks through Devlin's silence. Suppressed, deprived of power and desire, Devlin yields his position beside Alicia to Sebastian, beginning with the staged incident at the riding club. In sequence 14, a shot of Devlin sitting alone screen left at a bar table is separated by a fade from the next shot of Alicia sitting alone screen right at a restaurant table. Sebastian enters and assumes the screen-left position opposite Alicia which Devlin had previously filled (cf. sequence 7 at the outdoor cafe). Again at the racetrack Devlin yields the position screen left opposite Alicia to Sebastian. Finally, in the cellar confrontation, Devlin and Alicia are positioned spatially and syntagmatically opposite Sebastian until a three-shot centers Devlin between wife and husband. His departure leaves Alicia and Sebastian together but separated through intercutting.

Hero and villain now take exactly opposite actions in the face of "parental" authority. Betrayed by Alicia, Sebastian returns to Mother. From Sebastian's point of view, a shot of Alicia in bed is replaced by one of his mother in bed (sequence 29 to sequence 31). As she listens to the tale of her son's "foolishness," a mid-shot of Mother dissolves into and out of a full shot of Alicia sleeping unaware, confirming the displacement and marking her threat to Alicia through enclosure. After circling Sebastian (in a movement peculiarly similar to Devlin's circling Alicia after she consents to the job—sequence 5), Mother positions herself screen right opposite her son and resumes control over him, speaking her murderous plan through his silence. Later, in a *mise en scène* (sequence 38) that explicitly contrasts the actions of hero and villain, Devlin faces his "father" for the last time. Devlin's screen-left position repeats Sebastian's, while Prescott's screen-right position in bed matches the mother's. Only here Devlin is standing and Prescott, in contrast to the mother's "gangster-style" smoking, is contentedly munching on cheese and crackers (an image at odds with the continual comments on his handsomeness). "Father" and "mother" functions seem iconically reversed. The decision to check on Alicia (to rescue her) is Devlin's, not Prescott's ("Go ahead *if you want*" — my emphasis). Although Prescott consents, Devlin's action is independent and threatens the operation to the point where only Alicia's information saves it from irreparable bungling. Thus, these paradigmatic sequences of "child" confronting "parent" have pointedly opposite conclusions. Submitting to mother (playing "father") leads the villain to his death, while defying the "father" (playing "mother") leads the hero to the heroine and their union/happiness.

The "figure" of the hero and heroine's sexual union is established in the famous long-take "nuzzling" shot on the balcony in sequence 10. There the codes and signifiers made pertinent are character position (Devlin screen left facing Alicia screen right), gesture (kissing, gazing into one another's face and eyes), voice (low, soft whispering), camera position (medium close-up to close-up), camera movement (dolly-in from medium close-up to close-up and follow-dolly to sustain the close-up), and cutting (uninterrupted long take).[13] The disappearance of that moment, the distintegration of their union, is articulated in their very next sequence together through reversals in the signifiers of each of the pertinent codes. After learning what her job entails, Devlin returns to Alicia on the apartment balcony. Now their positions are reversed; there is no dolly-in from the mid-shot; the look and kiss are denied; the voices are raised; and, when Devlin refers coldly to her promiscuous past, the shot is broken by a cut to Alicia alone in close-up. The signifiers conspire their separation. The purpose of the film will be to reconstitute that first moment by reinventing the specific instances of the pertinent codes.

The ritual of the hero and heroine's progress from separation to reunion thus can be traced through the pertinent codes of their remaining sequences together. At the racetrack, for instance, a mid-shot places them side by side, Devlin screen left and Alicia screen right (matching Sebastian and his mother in the off-screen private box behind them). This time, however, they do not face one another; again there is no dolly-in from mid-shot; and when Alicia reports the addition of Sebastian "to her list of playmates," the shot now is broken by a cut to Devlin alone in close-up. A new variation in the codes of character position and cutting emerges. The next shot shows Alicia in close-up as she suddenly turns (in profile facing screen left) to snap at Devlin's sarcastic response. The return cut to Devlin shows him from Alicia's point of view, also in profile facing screen left. The intercut profiles and disorienting change in camera position mark the force of her desire and his refusal. After another mid-shot of the two, the same profiles are repeated in an alternating series until Alicia in close-up turns forward and hides her look behind a pair of binoculars.[14] The alternation continues through another shift in camera position (to an extreme close-up of Alicia) that accompanies her gesture of lowering the binoculars and her gaze. When she suddenly turns to the left in profile again ("Is that all you have to say?"), the point-of-view shot of Devlin's profile returns, but he now turns forward as if finally to look at her. The expectant reciprocity of looks is denied, however, by his words ("Dry your eyes, Baby, it's out of character") and a cut to Sebastian coming forward through the crowd. When the mid-shot returns, Devlin has turned his back to the camera while Alicia remains facing forward, and Sebastian enters to stand between and separate them.

Later in the "castle" wine cellar, suddenly the moment nearly erupts in the form of a ruse after the two are discovered by Sebastian. The series of alternating shots between Devlin and Alicia kissing and Sebastian looking on gives way momentarily to several privileged close-ups of their embrace. All but two of the pertinent codes return (camera movement and lack of cutting). Devlin's look (still quizzical but affected) and Alicia's breathy cry ("Oh, Dev!") briefly mark the rediscovery of desire. But the cutting allows Sebastian once more to intervene and the alternating series to resume its dominance. The final meeting on the park bench reconfirms their separation, but the last shot of the sequence announces a shift. An unexpected change in camera position suddenly puts Devlin in close-up profile looking right—the paradigmatic opposite of his position in the racetrack sequence and the perfect complement to Alicia's profile looking left. As much as his anxious glance after her, it marks his change of mind and the possibility of reunion.

Finally, in the rescue sequence, as Devlin enters the "castle" bedroom where Alicia has been held captive, all the signifiers of the pertinent codes are reinvented. The sequence begins as a variation on sequence 5, when Devlin entered Alicia's bedroom in Miami. Once again he approaches her bed to save her from the "intoxications" of drinking (the liquor of her "playmates"/the drugged coffee of the "castle"). Almost immediately the intercutting between them gives way to a re-creation of the moment on the balcony—in mid-shot Devlin (screen left) leans over Alicia (screen right); the camera dollies in to close-up; Devlin looks intently at her and places his head on the pillow to touch her lips; he whispers to her gently; the shot is unbroken as the camera dollies out slightly and tilts up for Devlin to sit her up in bed. What had taken a half-dozen sequences to accomplish earlier (rescue, job acceptance, love) is telescoped into six shots, Devlin's continuous movement right towards Alicia and the single long-take shot of their reunion. The only variation in the pertinent codes is a cut to an extreme close-up of the two embracing (as in the cellar sequence) and a cut back to the close-up as they cross the room (the follow-dolly returns, sustaining their close-up embrace) to the door. The extreme close-up is marked by an 180-degree track-pan that reverses their position within the frame, effectively transposing the earlier signifiers of separation into signifiers of union (Alicia screen left now ends the shot murmuring, "you love me"). The "figure" of union reemerges from a synthesis of previous variations and inversions of the pertinent codes. Instead of moving right towards the dispatcher-father and separation, as in sequence 12, the reunited couple moves left to face the villain in the final confrontation.

The villain's position with regard to the hero and heroine creates a perversion of the conventional audience identification that operates in the "classical" American cinema.[15] The balcony sequence of "nuzzling" already pushes audience identification to the point of excess, arresting us in fascination of "the perfect image." Hitchcock himself has described it as a "ménage à trois"—of hero, heroine, and spectator.[16] The erotic pleasure of the moment is ours as much as theirs for our being absorbed so closely and at such length in the embrace (that it is Cary Grant and Ingrid Bergman we are joining is no small matter). The desire to see the couple reunited is no less than our desire to repeat that "ménage à trois" moment of pleasure. And is it not intensified by the "tainting" of the heroine—masked by our desire to "save" her, "purify" her, have her for ourselves? Thus do we (males, at least) become rapt voyeurs and the narrative, the quest, is propelled by our desire. "Performance as a remembering, the production of a memory."[17]

In the racetrack sequence we suddenly discover that the villain is not only the antithesis/complement to the hero and dispatcher-father but our opposite/second as well. As we watch Devlin and Alicia for signs of reawakening love, Sebastian watches too—behind them and for exactly the opposite reason. A voyeur like ourselves, he watches, not out of desire, but out of fear. Interrupting the hero and heroine, he becomes our enemy as well — the source of hindrances, delays, and threats to the couple's reunion and our pleasure. At the party our expectant watching is paralleled, even taken over (in point-of-view shots) by Sebastian's scrutiny; and in the cellar again he intervenes — from the other side — to separate Devlin and Alicia and repress our renewed pleasure.

The villain's position is troubling for us in another way as well. Though politically and morally contemptible, his gentlemanly attitude towards Alicia at first contrasts with that of Devlin's caddishness. His love perhaps is even stronger than Devlin's, i.e., his defiance of Mother versus the hero's submission to "father." Furthermore, the film suddenly allows him the status of subject during the sequence when he discovers Alicia's betrayal of his love. As spectators we are made to share that feeling of betrayal. He is victimized nearly as much as Alicia, and doubly victimized when he submits to the power of Mother again.

The final sequence brings our conflicting responses to a head. Although he has nearly murdered the heroine and still is motivated by his own desire to survive, the villain now fulfills our desire by helping Devlin and Alicia escape the "castle." He speaks the words we want to hear (even Mother wants to hear), words that will open the door for them. When Devlin locks the car door on him (shot from his point of view) and speeds off with Alicia smiling, Sebastian is abandoned and deceived once more. And the film keeps us behind with him. As Sebastian turns to walk back to the "castle," moving from close-up (looking off left after the departed car) to long shot, the camera begins to dolly slowly after him. The movement inexorably closes off the space around him, seems to "push" him towards the fatal door, as if operating out of *our* desire to get rid of him. The contradiction rubs; we have become the agents of death for the character whose action has fulfilled what we so desired — the reunion of hero and heroine, the re-creation of "the perfect image." The rub worsens when we realize that the close-up (privileging his feeling of doom) and the dollying camera that follows him (echoing the dollies associated with Devlin and Alicia) equally make us share his approaching death. The closure we had sought, indeed are responsible for, rips us asunder.[18] Where earlier defiance of the "father" split hero and heroine, this act of defiance splits us, the spectators. The guilt the hero and heroine have incurred by their defiance is displaced through the villain onto us.

Notorious — the pleasure that turns perverse.

Notes

1. Peter Wollen, "*North by Northwest:* a morphological analysis," *Film Form,* vol. 1, no. 1 (1976): 32, 34. John Fell, "Vladimir Propp in Hollywood," *Film Quarterly,* vol. 30, no. 3 (1977): 20. For analyses based on A. J. Greimas and Tzvetan Todorov (which also support this reading of *Notorious*), see Alan Williams, "Structures of Narrativity in Fritz Lang's *Metropolis,*" *Film Quarterly,* vol. 27, no. 4 (1974): 17–24, and Charles F. Altman, "Classical Narrative

Revisited: *Grand Illusion," Film Studies Annual,* (West Lafayette: Purdue University, 1976): 87-98.

2. Bruno Bettelheim, *The Uses of Enchantment* (New York: Knopf, 1976), 111-16, 225-36. Bettelheim analyzes this kind of fairy tale in terms of Oedipal conflicts and resolutions.

3. Roland Barthes, *S/Z* (New York: Hill and Wang, 1974), 35-36.

4. Cf. Raymond Bellour, "Le blocage symbolique," *Communications,* no. 23 (1975): 242-50.

5. In one shot the camera dollies back in front of Devlin as he moves away from the phonograph; in the next the camera dollies in (from Devlin's point of view) towards Alicia's bedroom door as she comes forward brushing her hair. Just before it stops in a mid-shot of her in the doorway, however, Devlin enters from the left foreground to stand beside her and turn back towards the camera — the shot shifts internally from subjective to omniscient point of view, from the level of the diegesis to the level of the discourse.

6. Charles Altman explains the Lacanian basis of this concept in "Psychoanalysis and Cinema," *Quarterly Review of Film Studies,* vol. 2, no. 3 (1977): 250-60.

7. Barthes, 67-68.

8. More than any other Hitchcock film (except perhaps *Vertigo*), the text repeatedly makes the heroine the victim of men's actions.

9. From another perspective, the text works according to our expectations of how a certain "star" behaves: it presents Cary Grant initially as "not-Cary Grant" and narrates his becoming "Cary Grant."

10. This form of the Hitchcock couple reaches its apotheosis in *Psycho.*

11. Cf. *North by Northwest* where the villain Vandamm is brother, "husband," and "father" to his sister; "father" and "lover" to Leonard; "father" and brother-in-law to Valerian.

12. In a slightly different form, William Rothman postulates a similar ritual pattern in "Alfred Hitchcock's *Notorious," Georgia Review,* vol. 39, no. 4 (1975): 885. It should be remarked that the initial version of my own essay was presented as a paper on "Hitchcock's *Notorious:* Myth and Ritual" at the 1977 convention of the Midwest Modern Language Association. As I was reworking the paper to submit to *Wide Angle,* Dudley Andrew suggested that I take a look at Rothman's essay. Doing so helped me to differentiate more clearly my own "structuralist" analysis of the film from his "phenomenological" analysis. Accordingly, the version that I submitted to *Wide Angle* included some half-dozen endnote references to Rothman's essay, most of which highlighted the distinctions between my analysis and his. Following an editor's request for fewer citations, I deleted all but one of the Rothman notes. Given an opportunity to reconsider the matter further before publication, I would have reinserted at least one of those deleted notes and called attention to the very different analytical methods of our two essays.

13. At least four of the six (character position, camera position, voice, camera movement) are established even earlier in the second sequence at Alicia's party in Miami.

14. A fine irony here. The object of Alicia's gaze, the horse race, is reflected on her lenses and literally denies her look (to Devlin and to us). Similarly, Sebastian uses his binoculars to hide from his mother his attempt to watch Alicia and Devlin.

15. "Narrativisation is the complex operation of the film as narrative and the setting of the spectator as subject *in the operation.* . . ." Stephen Heath, "Film Performance," *Cine-tracts,* no. 2 (1977): 12.

16. François Truffaut, *Hitchcock* (New York: Simon & Schuster, 1967), 327-28.

17. Heath, "Film Performance," 13.

18. The locus of the difference between the subject of the enounced and the subject of the enunciation shifts onto us. Cf. the outrageous "ménage à trois" that ends *Psycho.*

NOTORIOUS (RKO, 1946). *Producers:* Alfred Hitchcock, Barbara Keon, *Assistant Director:* William Dorfman, *Script:* Ben Hecht, *Photography:* Ted Tetzlaff, *Editor:* Theron Warth, *Sets:* Albert S. D'Agostino, Carrol Clark, Darrell Silvera, Claude Carpenter, *Music:* Roy Webb, *Costumes:* Edith Head, *Players:* Ingrid Bergman (Alicia Huberman), Cary Grant (Devlin), Claude Rains (Alexander Sebastian), Leopoldine Konstantin (Mrs. Sebastian), Louis Calhern (Paul Prescott). 101 minutes.

CHAPTER FOURTEEN

Strangers on a Train

Robin Wood

The first shots introduce us to two pairs of men's feet as their owners arrive at a station. The two are characterized by means of their shoes: first, showy, vulgar, brown-and-white brogues; second, plain unadorned walking shoes. A parallel is at once established in visual terms: or, more precisely, a parallel is imposed by the editing on what would otherwise be pure contrast. Each shot of the first pair of feet is promptly balanced by a similar shot of the second. On the train, we are shown the feet again, moving to the same table. It is always Bruno's feet that we see first—he arrives at the station first, he sits down first; it is Guy's foot that knocks his accidentally, under the table, leading directly to their getting into conversation. Thus Hitchcock makes it clear that Bruno has not engineered the meeting, despite the fact that he knows all about Guy ("Ask me anything, I know the answers") and has the plan for exchanging murders ready to hand: it is rather as if he is waiting for a chance meeting he knew would come. This gives us, from the outset, the sense of some not quite natural, not quite explicable link between the two men.

The contrast between them is developed explicitly in the dialogue. Guy is planning a career in politics: in Hitchcock's films, politics, government, democratic symbolism (the Statue of Liberty in *Saboteur,* the U. S. Capitol in this film, Mount Rushmore in *North by Northwest*), are always associated with the idea of an ordered life, set against potential chaos. Bruno, on the other hand, has been expelled from three colleges for drinking and gambling and lives mostly for kicks. Guy wants to marry Ann Morton, a senator's daughter; Bruno is associated with his mother (by means of the ornate tiepin, a gift from her, which bears his name). Bruno, despite the fact that he has flown in a jet and driven a car blindfolded at 150 mph and has a theory that "you should do everything before you die," envies Guy: "I certainly admire people who do things"; and, "It must be pretty exciting being so important—me, I never do anything important." We register this sense of impotence as probably, at bottom, sexual: it links up with Bruno's voyeuristic prying into Guy's love life.

Yet behind the contrast, the parallel established by the editing of the opening shots becomes manifest. Both men, like so many of Hitchcock's protagonists, are insecure and uncertain of their identity. Guy is suspended between tennis and politics, between his tramp wife and his senator's daughter, and Bruno is seeking desperately to establish an identity through violent, *outré* actions and flamboyance (shoes, lobster-patterned tie, name proclaimed to the world on his tiepin). His professed admiration for Guy is balanced by Guy's increasing, if reluctant and in part ironically amused, admiration for him. Certainly, Guy responds to Bruno—we see it in his face, at once amused and tense. To the man committed to a career in politics, Bruno represents a tempting overthrow of all responsibility. Guy fails to repudiate Bruno's suggestive statement about Miriam ("What is a life or two, Guy? Some people are better off dead") with any force or conviction. When Bruno openly suggests that he would like to kill his wife, he merely grins and says, "That's a morbid thought"; but we sense the tension that underlies it. When he leaves the train he is still laughing at Bruno, but he leaves his lighter behind. This lighter, on which our attention has already been focussed by a close-up and some commentary in the dialogue, is to be of crucial importance in the plot. It was given to Guy by Ann Morton, and bears the inscription "A to G" with two crossed tennis rackets: it is through his tennis that Guy's entry into politics has become possible. Guy's forgetfulness at this moment belies his dismissive joking air when Bruno asks if he agrees to the exchange of murders ("Of course I agree—I agree with *all* your theories"). He is leaving in Bruno's keeping his link with Ann, his possibility of climbing into the ordered existence to which he aspires. The leaving of the lighter is one of the visual equivalents Hitchcock finds for the interior, psychological analysis of the Patricia Highsmith novel that was his source.

Guy, then, in a sense connives at the murder of his wife, and the enigmatic link between him and Bruno becomes clear. Bruno is certainly a character in his own right, realized in detail with marvellous precision; but he also represents the destructive, subversive urges that exist, though suppressed, in everybody: he is an extension, an embodiment, of desires already existing in Guy. In their first conversation, as they face each other, the cross-cutting between them gives us Guy's face unshadowed, Bruno's crossed with lines of shade like the shadow of bars. He is continually, in these early stages of the film, associated with shadows and with darkness; the development of the film can partly be seen in terms of his forcing himself into the light for recognition. He understands Guy's darker motives better than Guy does himself: "Marrying the boss's daughter—the shortcut to a career." Nothing later in the film, and especially not the uneasy, formal relationship between the lovers, contradicts this assessment.

The next sequence introduces us to Miriam and defines Guy's position more clearly. Miriam—hard, mean, slovenly, at once contemptible and pathetic in her limitations—is one of those Hitchcock characters created in the round with the utmost economy in a few seconds: a gesture of the hands, a drooping of the mouth, a slovenly way of turning the body, dull yet calculating eyes peering shortsightedly through her glasses. She is more than a character. We are introduced to her in the record shop where she works, and the association of her with revolving objects (taken up later in the fairground sequence) suggests the futile vicious circle of her existence, the circle from which Guy wishes to break free. We have already seen Guy's lack of insight into other people in his inability to deal firmly with Bruno, and seen too that this lack is basically one of self-awareness; so we have no difficulty in accepting the premise of his involvement with Miriam.

After the row in the record shop, during which Guy "warns" Miriam and shakes her violently, the phone call to Ann: "You sound so savage, Guy"—"I'd like to break her foul, useless little neck . . . I said I could strangle her"—shouted over the roar of an approaching train. Cut to Bruno's hands—his mother has just manicured them, and he is admiring them, flexing the fingers. The cut finally clinches the relationship between the two men, making Bruno an agent for the execution of Guy's desires.

The fairground and amusement park is a symbolic projection of Miriam's world: a world of disorder, of the pursuit of fun and cheap glamour as the aim of life, of futility represented by the circular motion of merry-go-round and ferris wheel that receive such strong visual emphasis in almost every shot. The whole sequence is realized with a marvellous particularity and complexity. Through Miriam, Hitchcock evokes a whole social milieu, small-town life in all its unimaginativeness and restriction. The sequence is introduced by the long-shot of Miriam's home, from Bruno's viewpoint as he waits for her to emerge: respectable-looking, white-fronted house, mother sitting outside on porch, calling, "Now don't be out late" to Miriam as she runs down the steps with her two boyfriends, holding hands, giggling childishly. We think back to the sullen girl in the record shop. At the fairground, she makes the boys buy her an ice-cream cone, talking at the same time about hot dogs, and they tease her about eating so much. We remember that she is pregnant. She talks about her craving—the boys laugh: "Craving for what?" She turns, gazing around the fairground through her glasses, licking at her ice cream like a spoiled schoolgirl, looking at once childish and sensual, and her eyes fix on Bruno, watching her from a distance. Not only is the character rendered with precision: an attitude to her is precisely defined, an attitude totally devoid of sentimentality, astringent yet not without pity. She is not pathetic in herself (she is never aware of needing anyone's compassion), but her situation—the narrow, circumscribed outlook, the total lack of awareness—is both pathetic and horrible. And what is being defined, ultimately, is the world from which Guy is struggling to escape: contaminated by that world (remember the impurity, exposed by Bruno, of his motives for wanting to marry Ann), he cannot free himself cleanly as he wants.

The sequence of events leading up to the murder throws further light on both Miriam and Bruno: the strangling is invested with a clear sexual significance. Miriam, at her first glimpse of Bruno, sees something more intriguing — more *dangerous* — than she can find in her two very unmysterious boys. She gives him the come-on, unmistakably, demanding to go to the Tunnel of Love loudly, so that he will hear. As her boys fail to ring the bell at the "Test Your Strength" machine, she looks around for him, and when he materializes mysteriously on her other side, she smiles at him. He shows off his strength to her ("He's broken it!"), first proudly flexing his hands, which are emphasized by the low camera angle, afterwards waggling his eyebrows at her. Then the merry-go-round: circling motion, raucous music, painted, prancing horses, more flirtation from Miriam. She calls — loudly again, like an announcement — for a boat ride. More revolving in the backgrounds as they get the boats: the ferris wheel behind Bruno, huge waterwheel beside the Tunnel of Love ahead of Miriam. From here, the sexual symbolism accumulates strikingly. They pass through an archway to the boats, above which is written "Magic Isle" — where Miriam will shortly be murdered; the boats cross the lake, enter the tunnel (where Bruno's shadow ominously overtakes Miriam's), out again onto the lake. Miriam runs away on the isle, purposely losing the boys. Then a lighter is thrust before her face and struck, "A to G": "Is your name Miriam?" "Why, yes," she smiles seductively, and Bruno drops the lighter and strangles her.

Her glasses fall off, one lens shatters, and the murder is shown to us reflected in the other lens, inverted and distorted. The lens itself recalls lake and tunnel and is a further sexual symbol. The shot is one of the cinema's most powerful images of perverted sexuality, the murder a sexual culmination for both killer and victim. It ends with Bruno's hands enormous in the lens as he moves back from the body. We see the lighter, "A to G," on the grass, and remember Guy's words on the phone: "I could strangle her." Having retrieved it, Bruno returns to his boat through a chaos of promiscuity — pairs of lovers on the grass all around: the chaos world has been finally defined, the "Magic Isle" becomes an island of lost souls. The association of sexual perversion with the sense of damnation will be taken up again more forcefully in *Psycho*. Bruno, with his close relationship with a crazy mother, is an obvious forerunner of Norman Bates.

As he leaves the fairground, Bruno helps a blind man across the road. At the time, it seems merely a cleverly ironic touch, a trifle glib; but in retrospect it takes on a deeper meaning. Henceforth Bruno will be haunted by the memory of Miriam's eyes looking at him through her glasses in which the lighter flame is reflected; his helping of a blind man with dark glasses is an act of unconscious atonement. The sequence ends with Bruno looking at his watch: cut to Guy, on a train, looking at *his:* the visual link again used to enforce the connection between them.

Later, we see Guy reaching his rooms in Washington. On one side of the street, stately, respectable houses; towering in the background, on the right of the screen, the floodlit dome of the U. S. Capitol, the life to which Guy aspires, the world of light and order. On the other side of the street, deep shadow and tall iron-barred gates from behind which Bruno calls. The light-and-darkness symbolism—Guy turning from the lighted doorway of the house towards the shadow, away from the Capitol dome—is simple, but not naive or ridiculous, and handled naturally and unobtrusively. Bruno beckons, a shadow among shadows. Again we see him with bars across his face: at the start of the ensuing dialogue he is behind the bars, Guy in the open. He gives Guy the glasses, reminds him about the lighter—"I went back for it, Guy." Guy is horrified. Then: "But, Guy, you *wanted* it. . . . We planned it together. . . . You're just as much in it as I am. . . . You're a free man now." The phone rings in Guy's rooms, a police car approaches, stops outside, and Guy promptly joins Bruno behind the bars, in shadow: a free man. He says, "You've got me acting like I'm a criminal," and we have a subjective shot of the police from Guy's position behind the bars. The scene gives a beautifully exact symbolic expression to Guy's relationship to Bruno and what he stands for.

More light and darkness in the next sequence: Guy answers his phone, Ann tells him to come around. Right of screen: a large, lighted lamp, Guy holding the receiver to his ear, Ann's voice coming through. Left of screen: heavy shadow, Miriam's glasses dangling downwards in Guy's other hand. The hands remind us of a pair of scales. We then see Guy and Ann together for the first time, and Hitchcock shows us their rather remote, uneasy relationship. Ann strikes us as the older, certainly the maturer, the more completed: the dominant partner. Their kiss lacks real intimacy or tenderness. She tells him she loves him and he replies, "Brazen woman, I'm the one to say that": an odd, endistancing, defensive kind of joke. As Ann, her father, and her sister Barbara break the news, and Guy makes a feeble attempt at surprise, our view of the lovers' relationship is confirmed by Ann's obvious suspicions that Guy has killed Miriam: she tells him, with heavy significance, "She was strangled"; and she is visibly relieved when he explains his alibi. If the world from which Guy wishes to escape is defined for us by Miriam, then Ann—formal, rather hard, rather cold, in Ruth Roman's unsympathetic performance—defines the life to which he aspires: a life of imposed, slightly artificial orderliness. As for his guilt, Hitchcock makes it very clear that what he can't bear is, not the idea that he has been indirectly involved, at any rate by desire, in the death of a human being, but the fear of being found out: it is the only feeling he reveals in his conversation with Bruno and all that he and Ann reveal in this scene.

The moral point is made clearly when Senator Morton rebukes Barbara for saying of Miriam, "She was a tramp," with the remark, "She was a human being." The rebuke, for the audience, has relevance to the lovers as well.

Yet despite the critical attitude adopted towards the lovers' relationship, we are made aware of its importance for Guy. Ann is more than a way to a career, she represents in herself something of the ordered world he aspires to. Thus the kiss that closes the sequence, which Guy, eyes looking straight into the camera, scarcely returns, is in contrast to the kiss that opened it: the *potentialities* of the relationship are threatened by the concealment of his involvement in Miriam's murder.

In the ensuing sequences Bruno increases the pressure on Guy to murder his father. First, the phone call to Ann's house: Guy hangs up. Second, the scene where Guy and Hennessy (the detective detailed to watch him) walk together past the Capitol building. In the setting of spacious, ordered architecture, Guy says, "When I'm through with tennis I'm going into politics," and looks across to see Bruno watching from the steps, tiny in long-shot. Third, the letter from Bruno pushed under Guy's door. Fourth, the scene where Ann sees Bruno for the first time. She and Guy are in the Capitol building when Bruno calls Guy from among the pillars: "You're spoiling everything. . . . You're making me come out into the open." Fifth, Guy receives the plan of and key to Mr. Anthony's house. Then, at last, the famous shot of Bruno watching Guy at the tennis court, all other heads turning to follow the ball, Bruno's conspicuous because motionless, his eyes fixed on Guy: a moment at once funny and unnerving. He now manages to meet Ann while Guy practices.

These scenes work beautifully in terms of suspense, but here as elsewhere it is necessary to ask, Of what exactly does this suspense consist? We feel uneasy, not just because pressure is being brought to bear on Guy to make him commit a murder, but rather because what he wants to hide is indeed "coming out into the open." Think back to a character I have hitherto neglected: Ann's sister Barbara. In the first scene at Senator Morton's house, Barbara's function is clearly to express, directly and unhypocritically, what everybody — including the spectator — is slightly ashamed to find themselves thinking: that it is really an admirable thing from all points of view that Miriam is dead. Her frank and shocking remarks recall Bruno's justification of killing — "Some people are better off dead" — and therefore involve the spectator with Bruno; they also prompt the senator's rebuke — "She was a human being." In other words, conflicting, apparently mutually exclusive responses are set up in the spectator, with disturbing results. We respond strongly to Barbara's no-nonsense honesty, but we are made ashamed of that response. This conflict within the spectator is the essence of the ensuing suspense: we, as well as Guy, are implicated in Miriam's murder. Bruno's symbolic progress, each step bringing him closer and clearer — telephone, distant figure, close figure lurking among shadowy pillars, figure sitting in full sunlight, young man in conversation with Ann, intruder from the chaos-world into the world of order—represents the emergence of all we want concealed: our own suppressed, evil desires.

Bruno's appearance at the party marks his final eruption into the world of order: the demand for recognition of the universality of guilt by a world that rejects such an assumption. The centerpiece of the scene—in some respects of the whole film—is Bruno's near strangling of Mrs. Cunningham. It derives its disturbing power again from a subtly aroused conflict, the attractiveness and the danger of that connivance at common guilt which Bruno represents. First, we are disarmed by Bruno's casually irreverent deflation of a dignified, self-righteous judge: how is he able to sit down to dinner after sentencing someone to death? The way the judge responds to the insolent question plainly makes the point that his way of life depends on such questions never being asked. The lightly humorous treatment releases us from some of the uneasiness we feel at responding to Bruno and prepares us for the next step—Bruno's conversation about murder with Mrs. Cunningham.

Here the underlying assumption of the film (subversive, destructive desires exist in all of us, waiting for a momentary relaxing of our vigilance) becomes explicit. Mrs. Cunningham's denial that *everyone* is interested in murder breaks down abruptly when Bruno asks if there haven't been times when she has wanted to kill someone—*Mr.* Cunningham, perhaps? There follows the richly comic exchange of murder methods, culminating in Bruno's demonstration of silent strangling—the method he used on Miriam—with Mrs. Cunningham as guinea pig. As his hands close on the old woman's throat, Barbara comes up behind her, Bruno sees her and, for the second time, is reminded by her (dark hair, round face, glasses) of Miriam. He goes into a "sort of trance," Mrs. Cunningham is nearly killed, and the sequence ends with Barbara, who has realized that Bruno was really strangling *her*, in tears. The scene is a superb example of the Hitchcock spectator trap. First, belief in established order has been undermined in the deflation of the judge; then the dialogue with Mrs. Cunningham and her friend, because of its light tone, gives us license to accept the notion of common guilt as something of a joke, to connive at it, allowing ourselves to be implicated in the "game" of murdering Mrs. Cunningham, who is anyway a rich, trivial, stupid old woman. Then abruptly the joke rebounds on us—we have nearly been implicated in another murder: swift modulation of tone has seldom been used to such disturbing effect. We are horrified to find that we have momentarily identified ourselves with Bruno (the sequence contains a number of subjective shots where we are placed in his position). We have the feeling, even, that we, through a lack of vigilance, have released these destructive forces by conniving at them. But the final emphasis is on Barbara, and we recall that earlier it was she who was used to make explicit our conventionally suppressed feeling that Miriam's murder was all for the best. She seemed before to give validity to the release of the anarchic forces of desire; now she is punished by the very forces she helped release, and we with her. The scene leads us straight to the essence of Hitchcock, the view that ordered life depends on the rigorous and *unnatural* suppression of a powerfully seductive underworld of desire, and we see the reason for the stiff formality of the world of order in the film.

The scene is rich in other ways too. The three minor characters, the judge, Mrs. Cunningham, and her friend, are realized with marvellous economy and precision, the realization being, as always, as much a crystallization of an attitude towards them as the objective description of character; there is nothing indulgent about the humor with which these representatives of the world of order are presented. The incident also further illuminates Bruno, whose symbolic function in the film is by no means undermined by the fact that he is also a character created in the round. Mrs. Cunningham, like Bruno's mother, is rich, spoiled, foolish, and indulgent; he is able to handle her so adroitly because he is used to managing his mother, manipulating her reactions. This is the kind of relationship he can manage, a relationship based entirely on power, wielded through a combination of cunning and insidious, self-insinuating charm — his ability to involve others in his sickness. Finally, the sequence shows the toll his life and actions are taking of him, his thoroughgoing cynicism and complete lack of remorse belied by his obsession with Barbara's (i.e., Miriam's) glasses and neck, the ineradicable memory of that other relationship expressed in the shot of his anguished face as he tries to strangle Mrs. Cunningham. As his hands are pulled away from her throat, he falls back in a swoon.

It is the near strangling of Mrs. Cunningham that forces the spectator to come to terms with his attitude toward subversive desire and prompts Guy, under pressure from Ann, to divulge the truth to her — without, however, acknowledging any personal guilt, of which he obviously remains quite unaware. He tells Ann, "I'd do his murder, he'd do mine"; to which she responds, suggestively, "What do you mean — *your* murder, Guy?" Her first reaction was, "How did you get him to do it?" The removal of doubts between the lovers marks a necessary stage in the action. Their relationship is now on a surer footing, giving Guy the strength to take steps to extricate himself. The next sequence, in which he visits Mr. Anthony's house at night, is a turning point and a critical crux.

The emphasis is, again, on suspense: in successive shots we see Guy take the gun Bruno has sent him, elude his "tail" by using the fire escape, and cross the moonlit lawn of the Anthony grounds in long-shot, like a shadow. We don't know at all clearly what he intends to do or what will happen to him. Suspense is built up as he enters the house (using the key Bruno has sent), consults Bruno's map to find the father's room, encounters a snarling mastiff on the stairs, subdues it, finds the room, transfers the gun (hesitating for a moment with it in his hand) from his breast pocket to his side pocket, creeps into the bedroom, approaches the bed, calls in a whisper, "Mr. Anthony . . . I want to speak to you about your son . . . about Bruno." Then the dark figure on the bed switches on a lamp and reveals himself as Bruno.

At first glance this seems, indeed, to be that "mere" suspense that is all Hitchcock's detractors see in his films: externally applied, rather cheap. And if we assume that Guy knows precisely what he is going to do in Mr. Anthony's house, the criticism is unanswerable. Hitchcock is cheating, basing the suspense on a deliberate misleading of the spectator. There are, however, points which suggest that this is too superficial a reading: that Guy has indeed made up his mind to visit Mr. Anthony, but there remains a possibility, right up to the moment of hesitation outside the bedroom door, that he will change his mind and shoot him. With this in mind, the sequence assumes quite a different aspect.

The first hint comes in fact several scenes earlier when Guy is talking to Hennessy in his rooms before the party. The camera looks down as Guy opens the top drawer in which Bruno's gun is lying, and we see the two men, with the gun strongly emphasized in the foreground of the screen. Guy has just been telling Hennessy he will have an early night: he is in fact planning to visit the Anthony house. But they are now discussing Hennessy's suspicious colleague, Hammond, and, as we see the gun in the drawer, Hennessy says, "He doesn't trust anybody — not even himself." The whole shot is framed and directed in such a way as to give a particular significance to the remark, linking it with the gun. Then, in the house, we have the moment of hesitation itself. This is either the decisive moment of the scene or a very cheap trick indeed: cheap, because it falsifies a character's behavior for the sake of producing a shiver — if the gesture doesn't imply uncertainty as to what to do with the gun, then it has no meaning at all. Finally, shortly after the discovery that it is Bruno on the bed, Guy tells him, "You're sick," adding, "I don't know much about those things. . . ." It is the nearest to an explicit statement in the film of that lack of self-awareness so plentifully illustrated elsewhere. The "suspense" of the sequence, then, has a point: the spectator's uncertainty as to what Guy is going to do corresponds to the character's own inner uncertainty. And the moment of final decision is the turning point of the film: henceforward, Bruno is openly *against* Guy, no longer wanting anything but revenge. The conflict has changed levels, and the struggle for self-preservation is the price Guy must pay for his involvement; an involvement partly expiated by the decision taken outside Mr. Anthony's bedroom.

But, this said, it must then be admitted that to raise such doubts is to acknowledge a dissatisfaction with the sequence. Guy's uncertainty is not sufficiently realized, a fault due perhaps to the limitations of Farley Granger as an actor, which led Hitchcock to put more weight on that one gesture with the gun than it can stand. But the criticism is of a misjudgment, a local failure of realization, not a major lapse in artistic integrity. [—Now I'm not so sure. The compromise over the hero figure that fatally flaws *Torn Curtain* offers a close parallel, and one cannot but feel that Hitchcock's uncertainty of handling in the scene of Guy's visit to Bruno's house has its roots in his fears of the effect of so morally dubious a "hero" on box-office response. "Major lapse in artistic integrity" is perhaps not too strong a description. —R.W. 1968.]

*   *   *   *   *   *

Ann's interview with Bruno's mother is the next step in the working out of the situation on its new level, the protagonists now ranged openly against one another. In Mrs. Anthony's insanity we see (as we are to see it later, more extremely, in the amalgam of Norman Bates and his mother at the end of *Psycho*) the ultimate extension of the chaos-world. The woman's very existence depends on the complete rejection of all value judgments, the final denial of responsibility. In fact, "irresponsibility" is the word she uses to excuse Bruno: with a smile of maternal indulgence, a little knowing shake of the head, she says, "Sometimes he's terribly irresponsible." To which Ann returns a moment later, "He's *responsible* for a woman's death."

The famous cross-cutting between the tennis match and Bruno's journey with the lighter gives us a very different sort of suspense—simpler, less disturbing than before, as befits this phase of the action. The tension we feel now is not uncomplicated by conflicting responses (who hasn't *wanted* Bruno to reach the lighter?), but the struggle has become clear and simple, the forces of good and evil are now separate and clearly aligned. Despite this, some very interesting points arise.

First, the development of that elementary yet elemental light-darkness symbolism: Guy fights for victory on the brilliantly sunny tennis court as Bruno struggles to reach the lighter which has slipped through a grating down a drain. One doesn't want to reduce the film to simple, pat allegory (Hitchcock resolutely defies any such treatment), but the cutting between sunny open court and shadowy enclosed drain carries powerfully evocative overtones: underlying the whole action of the film, we can see as its basis the struggle for dominance between superego and id. Secondly, we remember that tennis has been established from the start as Guy's means of access to the ordered world, his ladder from the previous life with Miriam to his projected political career; it is therefore appropriate that his fate should depend now on his ability at tennis. Furthermore, this test is made explicitly one of character, even of character development. Guy, in his desperation to finish the match in time, has to change his whole manner of playing (as the commentator points out)— he abandons his usual cautious long-term strategy in favor of a "grim and determined" open battling style. His whole career—even the desire to marry

Ann—has been a matter of careful strategy: now he is forced to fight openly for what he wants. Thirdly, it is significant that the outcome of the entire film should be made to depend upon the retrieving of the lighter, symbol of Guy's involvement with Bruno, of his placing himself in Bruno's hands. Great emphasis is laid on it—and on the "A to G" inscription—every time it appears. It is Guy's strongest *concrete* link with the ordered world; now he must reenter the chaos-world in order to retrieve it, thereby risking final submersion.

The fairground climax gives us the ultimate development of that world in its magnificent symbol of the merry-go-round that gets out of control. Guy struggles for his life—for more than his life—on the insanely whirling machine beneath the metallic hoofs of hideously grinning and prancing dummy horses: the horses on which Bruno, with Guy's implicit consent (the lighter), set about "seducing" Miriam. Guy is denied the satisfaction—we are denied the release—of a straightforward victory: the merry-go-round terrifyingly breaks down, Guy is thrown clear, Bruno is crushed under the wreckage. He dies obstinately refusing repentance, and Guy seems involved forever. Then, as he dies, Bruno's hand opens: the lighter is in his palm.

The very last scene of the film (where Guy and Ann move away pointedly from a friendly clergyman on a train) shows us, with light humor, Guy, united with his senator's daughter, resolutely—even somewhat extremely and rigidly!—resisting the possibility of further temptation. The stiff unnaturalness of the couple's behavior is perfectly logical: Guy's involvement with Bruno has been worked out in action—he has never faced its implications, and his personality remains to the end unintegrated, his identity still potentially unstable, the threat of disorder to be held back only by rigid control.

Strangers on a Train draws together many themes already adumbrated in earlier films, which will be taken further in later ones: the theme of what Conrad calls the "sickening assumption of common guilt" (developed especially in *Psycho*); the theme of the search for identity (*Vertigo*); the theme of the struggle of a personality torn between order and chaos (perhaps the most constant Hitchcock theme); and, in close conjunction with this, the notion of experience therapy—the hero purged of his weaknesses by indulging them and having to live out the consequences (*Rear Window*). We find here, too, the characteristic Hitchcock moral tone: the utterly unsentimental and ruthless condemnation of the forces that make for disorder, coupled with a full awareness of their dangerously tempting fascination, a sense of the impurity of motives. Does Guy love Ann, or is she merely the way to success? Clearly both: good and evil are inseparably mixed. And, running through the film, there is that Hitchcockian humor which itself represents a moral position: it is the manifestation of his artistic impersonality, of his detached and impersonal attitude to themes which clearly obsess him. Yet the film leaves one unsatisfied (not merely disturbed). The fault may lie partly with the players: Farley

Granger, a perfect foil to John Dall in *Rope,* is too slight a personality to carry much moral weight, so we feel that Guy's propensity for good or evil is too trivial: Ann (Ruth Roman) is a cold, formal woman, so there is little sense, at the end, that Guy has won through to a worthwhile relationship. There is not enough at stake: his triumph over too slight an evil (in himself) has won him too equivocal a good. Consequently, the effect seems at times two-dimensional, or like watching the working out of a theorem rather than a human drama; and the film, if not exactly a failure, strikes me as something less than a masterpiece.

One has no qualifications about Robert Walker's Bruno or about any of the scenes built around him. The film's two classic sequences, in fact, seem to me the first fairground sequence and the scene of the Morton's party. Here the characteristic Hitchcockian moral tone is felt in all its disturbing complexity.

STRANGERS ON A TRAIN (Warner Bros., 1951). *Producer:* Alfred Hitchcock, *Script:* Raymond Chandler, Czenzi Ormonde, Whitfield Cook, from the novel by Patricia Highsmith, *Photography:* Robert Burks, *Editor:* William H. Ziegler, *Sets:* Ted Haworth, George James Hopkins, *Music:* Dimitri Tiomkin, *Costumes:* Leah Rhodes, *Players:* Robert Walker (Bruno Anthony), Farley Granger (Guy Haines), Ruth Roman (Ann Morton), Leo G. Carroll (Senator Morton), Patricia Hitchcock (Barbara Morton), Laura Elliot (Miriam Haines), Marion Lorne (Mrs. Anthony). 101 minutes.

PART FOUR

The
Later
Films

In *The Strange Case of Alfred Hitchcock* Raymond Durgnat divides
Hitchcock's career into thirteen periods or "lives," the divisions corresponding
roughly to successive changes in Hitchcock's studio affiliations—from
Gainsborough to British International to Gaumont British to Gainsborough to
Selznick to Warner Brothers, etc. Clearly Durgnat's polemical purpose in so
doing—as his subsequent realignment of Hitchcock's career by theme and
genre indicates—was to counter the then prevailing wisdom which preferred
British Hitchcock to Hollywood Hitchcock and identified the former almost
exclusively by reference to the comedy thrillers made for Gaumont British and
Gainsborough, i.e., the films from *The Man Who Knew Too Much* (1934) to
The Lady Vanishes (1938).

In *Hitchcock—The Murderous Gaze* William Rothman also undertakes a
revision of the Hitchcock canon. He discusses five films in depth—*The Lodger,
Murder!, The 39 Steps, Shadow of a Doubt, Psycho*—in support of his claim
that "*Psycho*'s position is already declared, indeed already worked out, in *The
Lodger*" (p. 2), as if period distinctions among Hitchcock's films finally ought
not to matter much. Thus Rothman's running commentary on Hitchcock's
development does not divide up the British filmography as neatly as Durgnat,
discussing the period in generic and thematic rather than chronological terms.
But in his culminating discussion of *Psycho* Rothman still sketches an account
of Hitchcock's American period which suggests four phases akin to Durgnat's
chronological scheme: the forties films, from *Rebecca* (1940) through *Stage
Fright* (1950), which Rothman describes by and large as "a time of searching"
during which Hitchcock worked out the terms of his relationship to Hollywood
and to America; the early fifties films, from *Strangers on a Train* (1951)
through *Dial "M" for Murder* (1954), wherein we see "the full flowering of
[Hitchcock's] mature art"; the "mature period" proper, beginning with *Rear*

Window (1954) and identifiable largely with Hitchcock's Paramount films through *Psycho* (1960), though both *The Wrong Man* (Warner Brothers) and *North by Northwest* (MGM) are usually included in the category; and the final films, beginning with *The Birds* (1963), where the rapport of audience and auteur which characterized Hitchcock's previous period broke down, in part at least because Hitchcock slowly lost the services of his closest collaborators— Cary Grant, Grace Kelly, Robert Burks, Bernard Herrmann.

Readers of *A Hitchcock Reader* will have noticed that our own division of Hitchcock's career into three periods—the British, the Hollywood, the "later films"—is at best a rough approximation of such organizational schemes as those of Durgnat and Rothman, far plainer than Durgnat's "Plain Man's Hitchcock." But we really had a second history in mind beyond or behind that of the films themselves—the history of Hitchcock criticism, especially that which developed in the English-speaking world in response to the radical rethinking of Hitchcock initiated in the middle and late 1950s by the young Parisian turks at *Cahiers du Cinéma*.

Five names are crucial here, though each in odd ways (for references see the introduction and bibliography of Part I). The *Cahiers* ringleaders were clearly Eric Rohmer and Claude Chabrol, as evidenced by the publication in 1957 of their *Hitchcock*. The oddities here are two: the book concluded with a relatively lengthy discussion of *The Wrong Man,* at that time Hitchcock's latest film, though not one highly regarded by the English-language press; and the book itself was not available in English until 1979. François Truffaut, under the sometimes discomfited tutelage of André Bazin, was also a Hitchcock partisan, though his book on Hitchcock did not appear until 1966 (1967 in English). But Truffaut's general influence on English-language film scholarship, in particular his championing of auteur criticism, gained crucial currency through his filmmaking (*The 400 Blows* was released in 1959) and through the work of Andrew Sarris (whose auteurist pantheon of the American cinema first appeared in *Film Culture* in 1963). Jean Douchet played the crucial role of extending the "catholic/mystical" reading of Rohmer and Chabrol to the post–*Wrong Man* films. His "La Troisième Clé d'Hitchcock," published in three installments in *Cahiers* in 1959 and 1960, while ranging widely in its references to Hitchcock's oeuvre (partly in homage to Rohmer and Chabrol), devotes its most concerted attention to three films—*Rear Window, North by Northwest,* and *Psycho*—all from Hitchcock's mature period. Lastly, there is Robin Wood whose "Psychoanalyse de *Psycho*" (which eventually became the crucial chapter in his 1965 *Hitchcock's Films*) appeared in the same number of *Cahiers* (no. 113, pp. 1–7) as the last of Douchet's three pieces.

Facts of language and timing are crucial here. English language Hitchcock criticism through the middle 1970s is largely a debate between those, like Wood, who found the *Cahiers* approach to Hitchcock to be a great advance, and those like Penelope Houston, the editor of *Sight and Sound,* who found the *Cahiers* line irredeemably silly and inflated for proclaiming Hitchcock as profound and profoundly a film artist as Bergman or Antonioni. It is highly ironic—highly Hitchcockian—that many parties to the debate over Hitchcock's authorship and stature, especially its more journalistic American participants, had never read its central documents; hence the importance of Robin Wood who literally stood, for a time, as the only "original" bridge between Hitchcock's French-speaking partisans and his typically more skeptical English-speaking reviewers.

Moreover, the crucial period during which the debate took place was 1960 through 1963, i.e., between *Psycho* and *The Birds*. Under the influence of Douchet and Wood a central canon of Hitchcock texts was forming: *Vertigo*, *North by Northwest*, and *Psycho* were all vivid in memory, though *Vertigo*, like *Rope*, *Rear Window*, the remake of *The Man Who Knew Too Much*, and *The Trouble with Harry*, would soon be withdrawn from circulation—due in part to various legal problems but also as the result of Hitchcock's disappointment at the public reception of *Vertigo* and, later, of *The Birds* and *Marnie*. The question of Hitchcock's artistic stature was thus ripe for the asking, the lines were well drawn, and with the release of *The Birds* in 1963 and *Marnie* the following year the battle was joined in earnest.

In retrospect the lines were far too narrowly drawn. In its original edition Wood's book covered only seven films in detail: *Strangers on a Train*, *Rear Window*, *Vertigo*, *North by Northwest*, *Psycho*, *The Birds*, and *Marnie*. The dissenting essays—such as those by William Pechter and O. B. Hardison cited in the introduction to Part I—focused on more or less the same films. But to say that the lines were drawn too narrowly is not to imply that the films included within the canonical circle were unworthy of the attention they received, however historically contingent that attention may initially have been. They are *still* the films most frequently attended to; witness the work of Raymond Bellour whose close readings of *North by Northwest*, *Psycho*, *The Birds*, and *Marnie* have far exceeded in rigor and complexity the original ambitions of the *Cahiers* crew: Bellour's *North by Northwest* essay is probably longer than the whole of the Rohmer/Chabrol book.

A consequence of allowing this historical focus on the canonical "later films" to determine our choice of essays is the necessity of slighting some films from the same period—most regrettably *To Catch a Thief* and *The Trouble with Harry*—which have not figured prominently in the tradition of Hitchcock criticism. But the alternative was to misrepresent, or underrepresent, that tradition. Thus we found the prospect of providing multiple perspectives on the canonical later films especially compelling for providing readers an opportunity to see the tradition in action. Changes in the traditional canon will undoubtedly come, but they will gain interest and validity for being grounded in a thorough understanding of how the current canon came into being.

One measure of the underlying validity or productivity of the current canon is the fact that the terms of argument established by reference to such films as *Vertigo* and *Psycho* have proven appropriate across the whole range of Hitchcock's works, as a glance at nearly any essay in this anthology will confirm. On this latter account it is worth remarking how little the Ian Cameron/ Richard Jeffery piece on "The Universal Hitchcock" has become dated since its original publication in *Movie.* Thus almost any issue germaine to Hitchcock criticism can be discussed by reference to his "later films." For brevity's sake, however, we have chosen to introduce the essays in this section by following a single thread: we might call it, in a backhanded reference to Penelope Houston, "the figure in the carpet."

In his discussion of *Strangers on a Train* Robin Wood dwells on the "ironic" quality of the film, what Wood calls its "characteristic Hitchcock moral tone: the utterly unsentimental and ruthless condemnation of the forces that make for disorder, coupled with full awareness of their dangerously tempting fascination." Some difficult questions are involved here. In what sense can a film be "aware"? By what property of act or action can a film utter a "condemnation"? Or is Wood treating the film itself as a "speech act," as communicating its author's state of mind? Or, to take a second example, consider the following passage from David Kehr's 1984 *Film Comment* article on Hitchcock's "lost films": "In these films, Hitchcock can be seen doing what he refused to do in life: acknowledging his status as a creator and struggling to come to terms with that status. Though art isn't always the primary theme, it is always closely related to the perennial thematic center of Hitchcock's work: the problem of guilt. If Hitchcock always refused to confess his artistry—and went to maniacal lengths to protect himself from the accusation—it's because art was Alfred Hitchcock's dirty secret, his original sin" (p. 10). But how does a film "acknowledge" or "confess"? And how does a director get a film to do such things or get film critics to attribute them? That is, by what logic do critics like Wood and Kehr propose to discern the "figure" of the director within the complex thematic/formal weave of the cinematic "carpet" bearing his signature?

At heart such discernment or attribution depends on or interprets a commonsense analogy implicit in the terminology of screen credits: "Directed by Alfred Hitchcock." Pictures do not take themselves—cameras must be pointed, "directed"—so it is easy to think of the camera as an embodiment of its director's gaze or intention. A photograph necessarily implies or "connotes" a photographer. But it is a curious property of photographs, or at least of the responses they typically evoke, to connote "photographer" by exclusion. What we typically see within the frame is the "subject" of the photograph—a room, a scene, a street, a face—the photographer is out of frame, "off screen." Hence the somewhat paradoxical fact that film authorship is perceived simultaneously as both an active and a passive undertaking—active for taking photographs, passive for taking no visible part in them.

This basic paradox of authorship is often repeated in reference to the spectator and to what critics have understood as conventional habits of viewing. Hollywood films have long been subject to charges of escapism; of promoting vicarious experience, chiefly through the mechanism of viewer/ character "identification"; of manufacturing an ersatz world which viewers respond to passively, as if the film world were as real and as intractable as the world of their daily lives, though the film world is also experienced as having been cut to the measure of desire—so that film viewers are encouraged in this sense to desire their own passivity, as if the world "as it is" were always already "desirable."

In recent years such charges have been renewed and rewritten in light of advances in the realms of semiotics, psychoanalysis, and feminism, as the Robin Wood and Marian Keane essays on *Vertigo,* the Margaret Horwitz piece on *The Birds,* and Michele Piso's analysis of *Marnie* well attest (see the introduction to Part V for further elaboration of the psychological background to these views). But the basic equation (and puzzlement) here has been relatively constant: authorial self-effacement, the director's retreat behind the image, is taken to encourage viewer "passivity" before the image. By the same token, authorial self-assertion, the director's calling attention to the fact of his or her direction, to the fact that what we are watching is not a real world but a film world, is taken to encourage in viewers an "active" and "self-aware" form of spectatorship. This formulation of the relation of author, film, and viewer explains the central importance attached by most latter day critics to textual "reflexivity": only by showing an active form of directorial or spectator self-consciousness at work (or so goes the argument) can critics justify their desire to criticize and to make positive claims about the likely cultural effects of the films on which they have chosen to focus. Several of the following essays are exemplary instances of this approach to film criticism.

The locus classicus here—as the Robert Stam/Roberta Pearson essay and the first part of Robin Wood's contribution to this section confirm—is *Rear Window,* the very title of which, as Stam and Pearson elaborate it, "evokes the diverse 'windows' of the cinema: the cinema/lens of camera and projector, the window of the projection booth, the eye as window, and film as 'window on the world'." But two such analogies are crucial, each of which bears on the activity/passivity dilemma.

One of these (first elaborated by Jean Douchet in "Hitch and His Public") is the viewer/character analogy: Jefferies (James Stewart) in his wheelchair is similar to the viewer in his or her theater seat, isolated, motionless, passive, yet intensely, "voyeuristically" interested in the events which transpire on the apartment window "movie screens" opposite his own rear window. But as Stam and Pearson read the film, this habit of voyeuristic looking is then called into question by means of a second analogy, that of Jefferies and Hitchcock. Each is a photographer; each depends for a living on his ability to capture the bizarre and exciting on film. By thus splitting the directorial function Hitchcock evidences a kind of self-consciousness which eludes Jefferies until late in the film when he watches his own surrogate, Lisa (Grace Kelly), searching the apartment where Jefferies believes a murder has taken place. When Thorwald returns and catches Lisa in the act, however, Jefferies is forced to confront the very fear his voyeurism had sought to mask or ignore — his fear of sexual intimacy with Lisa. For once he wishes he were close to her, and he can't be. Moreover, this implicit critique of the Jefferies character effects a realignment of the operative analogy. No longer is it viewer/character or character/director; now it is a viewer/director analogy. By thus allying himself with his audience, Hitchcock encourages a species of viewer self-consciousness akin to the actively reflexive self-consciousness embodied in *Rear Window* itself.

A similar logic runs through the essays by Keane and Stanley Cavell, though modified on at least two accounts. *North by Northwest*, as Cavell reads it, presents us with three director surrogates, as opposed to *Rear Window*'s one — the Professor (Leo G. Carroll), who invents a fictitious government agent to divert attention from the real agent played by Eva Marie Saint; Philip Vandamm (James Mason), the master spy who falls for the Professor's ruse and whose henchmen effectively "cast" Roger Thornhill (Cary Grant) in the "George Kaplan" role; and Roger Thornhill/Cary Grant, himself a director and victimizer, especially of women, but the only one of the three director surrogates who earns the right to direct himself, for having been so thoroughly the victim of the others. (Is this why, of the three, Grant is most closely allied with Hitchcock, as if Hitchcock too were a victim?) A similar doubling of director surrogates is also evident in *Vertigo*, as both Wood and Keane observe; Scottie's efforts to remake Judy as Madeleine are disturbingly akin to Elster's original casting of Judy in the very same role; in each case a species of murderousness is at work.

The primary difference between Cavell and Keane on the one hand and the kind of reasoning represented by Pearson and Stam on the other involves essentially different understandings of the "ontology" of the cinematic image. Pearson and Stam clearly assume, as do many of the writers they cite, that "activity" of a certain type ought to be valorized or encouraged — an activity of aesthetic, political, and sexual self-criticism by contrast with the viewer "passivity" or "complicity" allegedly encouraged by most instances of the "classical narrative cinema." Paradoxically, one component of this passive acceptance of mainstream cinematic conventions is the conviction (explicated chiefly by Laura Mulvey, contested here by Marian Keane) that "looking" in the Hollywood film is split along conventional sexual lines: males (Hitchcock, the typical viewer) are the active and controlling lookers, females merely the passive objects of the male gaze. It is hardly the case that Keane and Cavell are unmindful of the authority and activity of Hitchcock's authorship. Each proposes to speak of Hitchcock's authorship on his behalf, as if Hitchcock were using them to lodge his claims to artistic authority. But each also goes on to declare that on one crucial account Hitchcock's authorship is passive, and positively so.

That is, Cavell and Keane introduce another level to discussions of activity and passivity by dwelling on the identities of the beings who inhabit the worlds of the films under scrutiny. In his essay on *North by Northwest*, for example, Cavell declares "Cary Grant" to be a primary subject of the film, one of its primary sources (as much a source as *Hamlet*). Similarly, in her reading of *Vertigo* Keane declares the "flesh and bloodness" of Kim Novak and James Stewart (qualities brought out in them by the photographic power of the camera's gaze) to be as much the subject of Hitchcock's meditations as the more overtly dramatic events their characters enact. Partly what Cavell and Keane have in mind here involves an artistic persona, a set of connotations built up around an actor or actress through the course of a career. Cavell is explicit on this account in tracing the history of Grant's earlier work with Hitchcock and also with Howard Hawks.

But equally important is what Keane (citing Cavell) calls "photogenesis," by which she refers to the fact that *Vertigo*, like most Hitchcock films, is especially dependent for its meaning upon particular faces, particular physiognomies (even if the particular face in question, as Cavell has it in discussing *North by Northwest*, is the face of the world itself). One of the chief differences between theater and cinema for both Keane and Cavell is the fact that, in Cavell's words, "film actors and their characters get stuck to one another" and are thus inseparable. *Hamlet* will always be *Hamlet*, whoever plays the title role. But there is no *Vertigo* apart from Novak and Stewart. This argument underlies Keane's view that Hitchcock's remarkable and sustained attention to faces and expressions in *Vertigo* (especially in those moments when Judy or Scottie stares directly into the camera) amounts to a declaration of authorial passivity before the world, a realization and recognition of the contingency of the cinematic medium. As Keane phrases it, "Hitchcock can place his subjects in worlds tailor-made for the emergence of their inner selves, but he does not have the power to invent these beings." It is precisely for denying the flesh and bloodness of Judy Barnes that Scottie stands condemned at the end of *Vertigo;* it is precisely in acknowledging the flesh and bloodness of Kim Novak, James Stewart, and Cary Grant that Hitchcock evinces his most profound and moving understandings of the medium of cinema, of its paradoxical capacity to be actively passive, or passively active, as if to challenge those very categories of being or perception. Hitchcock shows us a way of looking at the world in these later films that is far more reflective and confessional than many are willing to grant. We might say, echoing Keane's characterization of Scottie in *Vertigo*, that in his later films Hitchcock is exploring the feminine regions of himself, his own sensitivity and passivity and bitterness before the world, as if he too were a vengeful "bird," poised and hovering above an incomprehending community.

Three closing cautions are in order here, especially given the temptation to credit Hitchcock (as above) with a particular state of mind like bitterness or a desire for revenge. Two of these are urged by Robin Wood in his essay on *Vertigo:* (1) In discussing Hitchcock's authorship we are not primarily concerned with the artist's private life; the films he made are "public" in the sense that we are all free to ponder their meaning. We may finally want to attribute that meaning to Hitchcock, to believe in our heart of hearts that Hitchcock would confirm our interpretations; but no better confirmation exists (or is likely to) than actively attentive re-viewings of the films themselves. (2) We need also to be cautious in presuming that Hitchcock's films are typical—each of the others or any of the "classical Hollywood cinema." As Wood points out, to follow Bellour in describing all Hollywood films as "machines for producing a couple" is to deny many essential differences and to restrict severely the opportunities available to viewers and critics.

The third critical caution emerges from Marshall Deutelbaum's historical study of the circumstances surrounding the production of *The Wrong Man.* On one crucial account Hitchcock's artistic practice refused the self-effacement typical of Hollywood; in the vast majority of his films Hitchcock puts in a cameo appearance at one point or another (see Maurice Yacowar's appendix to *Hitchcock's British Films* for elaboration). Quite often such appearances explicitly identify Hitchcock as an artist—helping the musician with his timing in *Rear Window*, for example, or climbing aboard a train with a string bass in *Strangers on a Train.* But Hitchcock ostensibly eschews the role of artist in his introductory comments to *The Wrong Man*, where he promises that *this* story, unlike his "thrillers," is "a true story, every word of it." In so doing, however, Hitchcock only further reinforces his status as a fabulist, as a practitioner of the craft of fiction, because most of what makes *The Wrong Man* a Hitchcock film, as Deutelbaum demonstrates, had nothing to do with the facts of the case on which it is based. Latter-day audiences might well be excused for missing that, for treating *The Wrong Man* as they would any other Hitchcock film. It remains a striking footnote to the history of Hitchcock's relation to his public that no one among the film's original audience (to judge by contemporary reviews) seems to have noticed what is arguably Hitchcock's most overt challenge to his audience, his most explicit claim to the acknowledgment of his authorship: he tells a familiar story *his way*, playing havoc with the well-publicized facts of Emmanuel Balestrero's case for the sake of his artistic vision. But as another of Hitchcock's fabulist/surrogates once put it in bringing to life another case history: "Here I was born, here I died; you took no notice." The caution here: trust not the teller but the tale.

References and Suggested Readings

Allen, Jeanne Thomas. "The Representation of Violence to Women: Hitchcock's *Frenzy*." *Film Quarterly*, vol. 38, no. 3 (1985): 30–38.

Appel, Alfred, Jr. "The Eyehole of Knowledge: Voyeuristic Games in Film and Literature." *Film Comment*, vol. 9, no. 3 (1973): 20–26. On *Rear Window, Vertigo*, and *Frenzy*.

Bailin, Rebecca. "Feminist Readership, Violence, and *Marnie*." *Film Reader*, no. 5 (1982): 24–36.

Bazin, André. "Hitchcock versus Hitchcock." *Cahiers du Cinema in English*, no. 2 (1966): 51–59.

Bellour, Raymond. "*Les Oiseaux:* analyse d'une séquence." *Cahiers du Cinéma*, no. 216 (1969): 24–38.

_____. "Le blocage symbolique." *Communications*, no. 23 (1975): 235–350. *North by Northwest* as Oedipal fable.

_____. "Hitchcock, The Enunciator." *Camera Obscura*, no. 2 (1977): 69–94. Mostly on *Marnie*.

Bergstrom, Janet. "Enunciation and Sexual Difference (Part I)." *Camera Obscura*, no. 3-4 (1979): 32–69. On *The Birds, Marnie*, and Raymond Bellour.

Bernstein, Z. Samuel. "Lovely . . . Lovely . . . Lovely. . . ." *Focus!*, no. 8 (1972): 40–44. On *Frenzy*.

Brill, Lesley. "*North by Northwest* and Hitchcockian Romance." *Film Criticism*, vol. 6, no. 3 (1982): 1–17.

Brown, Royal S. "Herrmann, Hitchcock, and the Music of the Irrational." *Cinema Journal*, vol. 21, no. 2 (1982): 14–19.

Cameron, Ian. "Hitchcock and the Mechanics of Suspense." In Ian Cameron, ed. *The Movie Reader*. New York: Praeger, 1972, 26–29.

_____. "Hitchcock 2: Suspense and Meaning." In Cameron (cited above), 30–34. A two-part essay on the second version of *The Man Who Knew Too Much*.

Corliss, Richard. "*Topaz*." *Film Quarterly*, vol. 23, no. 3 (1970): 41–44.

_____. "*North by Northwest*." In *Talking Pictures*. Woodstock: Overlook Press, 1974, 191–95.

Cumbow, Robert C. "Caliban in Bodega Bay." *Movietone News*, no. 41 (1975): 3–8. On *The Birds*.

Ebert, J. "*Vertigo:* The Secret of the Tower." *Framework*, no. 13 (1980): 17–18.

Flitterman, Sandy. "Woman, desire, and the look: feminism and the enunciative apparatus in cinema." In John Caughie, ed. *Theories of Authorship*. London: Routledge & Kegan Paul, 1981, 242–50. On *Marnie*.

Foley, Jack. "Doubleness in Hitchcock: Seeing the Family Plot." *Bright Lights*, no. 7 (1978): 15–28, 31.

Gow, Gordon. "*North by Northwest*." *Films and Filming*, vol. 21, no. 1 (1974): 50–54.

Greenspun, Roger. "Plots and Patterns." *Film Comment*, vol. 12, no. 3 (1976): 20–22. On *Family Plot*.

Hartman, Geoffrey H. "Plenty of Nothing: Hitchcock's *North by Northwest*." *Yale Review*, vol. 71, no. 1 (1981): 13–27.

Houston, Penelope. "A Hitchcock Double." *Sight and Sound*, vol. 26, no. 1 (1956): 30–32. Brief reviews of *The Trouble with Harry* and the 1956 version of *The Man Who Knew Too Much*.

Johnson, William. "*Marnie*." *Film Quarterly*, vol. 18, no. 1 (1964): 38–42.

_____. "A Fine Frenzy." *Film Comment*, vol. 8, no. 4 (1972): 55–57.

Keane, Marian. "The Designs of Authorship: An Essay on *North by Northwest*." *Wide Angle*, vol. 4, no. 1 (1980): 44–52.

Kehr, David. "Hitch's Riddle." *Film Comment*, vol. 20, no. 3 (1984): 9–18. On the "lost" Hitchcock films.

Kindem, Gorham Anders. *Toward a Semiotic Theory of Visual Communication in the Cinema*. New York: Arno, 1980. On Hitchcock's use of color.

McBride, Joseph. "*Topaz*." *Film Heritage*, vol. 5, no. 2 (1970): 17–23.

Miller, Gabriel. "Hitchcock's Wasteland Vision: An Examination of *Frenzy*." *Film Heritage*, vol. 11, no. 3 (1976): 1–10.

Mulvey, Laura. "Visual Pleasure and Narrative Cinema." *Screen*, vol. 16, no. 3 (1975): 6–18. Remarks on *Vertigo*.

Nichols, Bill. "For the Birds." In *Ideology and the Image*. Bloomington: Indiana Univ. Press, 1981, 133–69.

Perkins, V. F. *Film as Film: Understanding and Judging Movies*. Baltimore: Penguin Books, 1972. Discussion of *Rope, The Man Who Knew Too Much, Psycho*, and *Marnie*.

Poague, Leland A. "The Detective in Hitchcock's *Frenzy:* His Ancestors and Significance." *The Journal of Popular Film*, vol. 2, no. 1 (1973): 47–59.

Rosenbaum, Jonathan. "*Family Plot.*" *Sight and Sound,* vol. 45, no. 3 (1976): 188–89.

Rignall, John. "Alfred Hitchcock's *Frenzy.*" *Monogram,* no. 5 (n.d.): 17–18.

Rose, Jacqueline. "Paranoia and the Film System." *Screen,* vol. 17, no. 4 (1977). On *The Birds.*

Rothman, William. "Against 'The System of the Suture'." *Film Quarterly,* vol. 29, no. 1 (1975): 45–50. Discusses *The Birds* in replying to Daniel Dayan's "The Tutor Code of Classical Cinema," *Film Quarterly,* vol. 28, no. 2 (1975): 39–47.

―――. "*North by Northwest:* Hitchcock's Monument to the Hitchcock Film." *North Dakota Quarterly,* vol. 51, no. 3 (1983): 11–23.

Sgammato, Joseph. "The Discreet Qualms of the Bourgeoisie: Hitchcock's *Frenzy.*" *Sight and Sound,* vol. 42, no. 3 (1973): 134–37.

Skoller, Donald. "Aspects of Cinematic Consciousness." *Film Comment,* vol. 8, no. 3 (1972): 41–51. An early and extended discussion of *Vertigo* as an "illusionist" narrative by comparison with *Last Year at Marienbad* and *Wavelength.*

Turner, Dennis. "Hitchcock's Moral Frenzy in the Declining Years." *film/psychology review,* vol. 4, no. 1 (1980): 35–58. On *Frenzy.*

Walker, Michael. "The Old Age of Alfred Hitchcock." *Movie,* no. 18 (1971): 10–13. On *Topaz.*

Weis, Elisabeth. "The Sound of One Wing Flapping." *Film Comment,* vol. 14, no. 5 (1978): 42–48. On *The Birds.*

Wilson, George M. "The Maddest McGuffin: Some Notes on *North by Northwest.*" *Modern Language Notes,* vol. 94, no. 5 (1979): 1158–1172.

Wollen, Peter. "*North by Northwest:* A Morphological Analysis." In *Readings and Writings: Semiotic Counter-Strategies.* London: Verso, 1982, 18–33.

CHAPTER FIFTEEN

Hitchcock's *Rear Window:* Reflexivity and the Critique of Voyeurism

Robert Stam and Roberta Pearson

I chose this picture of all the films I have made, this to me is the most cinematic.[1]
— ALFRED HITCHCOCK

"We've become a race of Peeping Toms."
— Stella in *Rear Window*

Hitchcock's characterization of *Rear Window* as the "most cinematic" of his films points to its most striking feature: its status as a brilliant essay on the cinema and on the nature of the cinematic experience. A paradigmatic instance of reflexivity, the film performs the metalinguistic dismantling of the structures of scopophilia and identification operative in dominant cinema generally and in Hitchcock's own films particularly, even while exploiting those very structures. The film focuses attention on what Geoffrey Nowell-Smith calls the "intersubjective textual relation," the relationship between the film and the spectator.[2]

Jean Douchet, writing in *Cahiers du Cinéma* in 1960, was among the first to point out the reflexive dimension of *Rear Window*. Douchet compared the protagonist, played by Jimmy Stewart, to a projector, the building across from his window to the screen, and added that the Stewart character is a spectator who "makes himself his own cinema."[3] Most critics have accepted Douchet's equation of the protagonist with director/spectator but have not gone on to detail the technical means and theoretical implications of that equation. Our purpose here will be to examine *Rear Window* not only as a reflexive film-about-film but also as a multitrack inquiry concerning the cinematic apparatus, the positioning of the spectator within that apparatus, and the sexual, moral, and even political implications of that positioning.

The film's action is circumscribed within a single set, an elaborately constructed block of Greenwich Village apartments surrounding a courtyard. All the events take place either in the apartment of the protagonist, a free-lance photographer named L. B. Jefferies (James Stewart), or in the courtyard and neighboring apartments. The rear window of Jefferies's apartment overlooks an architectural triptych of three buildings. The right-hand building houses a struggling composer and a couple, while the left-hand building houses a pair of newlyweds and a woman with a pet bird. But the film concentrates especially on the characters living opposite Jefferies: the sculptress on the first floor, her neighbor "Miss Lonelyhearts," the dancer "Miss Torso," and the salesman Lars Thorwald and his invalid wife. An unhappy couple with a dog and two "party girls" fill the other apartments.

The film's diegesis spans four days in the life of Jefferies, emphasizing his interactions with the visiting nurse Stella (Thelma Ritter), his girlfriend (Grace Kelly), and his detective friend Doyle (Wendell Corey), along with various neighbors, particularly Lars Thorwald (Raymond Burr). Temporarily immobilized by an accident, Jefferies spends his time spying on his neighbors. Stella arrives to feed and massage him and lectures him for preferring to watch the titillating acrobatics of Miss Torso rather than marry the mature and beautiful Lisa. That same night, Lisa arrives, argues with Jeff about marriage, and leaves in anger. After her exit, we hear a crash and a scream which we later learn to have signalled the demise of Mrs. Thorwald. Jeff alternately dozes and watches Thorwald, who repeatedly ventures out into the rain with a large suitcase. The last of his departures, this time accompanied by a woman, finds Jeff asleep.

On Thursday, Jeff begins spying on Thorwald in earnest, first with binoculars and then with a telephoto lens. Thorwald's actions—washing a knife and a saw, tying up a trunk—strike him as suspect. On sketchy evidence, he decides that Thorwald has murdered his wife. Lisa initially mocks his suspicions, but Jeff finally convinces her and recruits her as partner in the investigation. The next day, he attempts to convince Detective Doyle, but Doyle, after a minor investigation, concludes that Thorwald is innocent. Jeff and Lisa momentarily abandon their investigation, but the murder of a dog rekindles their suspicions. Thorwald must have killed the dog, they reason, because it had been digging around Mrs. Thorwald's corpse.

On Saturday, Jeff and Lisa begin to pressure Thorwald. Jeff lures him away from the apartment complex to allow Lisa and Stella to forage for clues. Lisa surreptitiously enters Thorwald's apartment where she finds the most vital clue—Mrs. Thorwald's wedding ring. Since no "normal" woman would travel without her wedding ring, she can only have been murdered. Thorwald returns before Lisa can effect her escape, however, and she is saved only when the police arrest her for breaking and entering. Stella departs to post bail, leaving Jeff exposed to Thorwald, who has now spotted Jeff as his antagonist. A confrontation ends with Jeff's falling out of the rear window and Thorwald's arrest. An epilogue intimates that Jeff and Lisa have reached tentative accommodation concerning their relationship.

The title *Rear Window,* apart from the literalness of its denotation, evokes the diverse "windows" of the cinema: the cinema/lens of camera and projector, the window in the projection booth, the eye as window, and film as "window on the world." The apartment complex, for its part, forms an artistic as well as a social microcosm. Its Greenwich Village setting metonymically evokes "artistic milieu," and its residents take pictures, sculpt statues, compose music, and perform roles. Like the cinema, the complex "englobes" the signifiers of other arts. The architectonic stylization and painterly artifice of the set betray what is transparently a studio product. Its inhabitants, furthermore, together reproduce the division of labor typical of Hollywood studio production. Virtually all the members of this *cinemato-graphicum mundi* are artists, or actors, or are engaged in an entertainment-related profession. The composer and Miss Torso are involved in the performing arts, the sculptress in a plastic art. Thorwald sells costume jewelry, with its connotations of glamor and artifice. While we never learn the occupations of Miss Lonelyhearts or the newlyweds, they participate in the theatricality of everyday life, acting out charades for Jeff's benefit and ours, the groom carrying his bride over the threshold and Miss Lonelyhearts staging a dinner for an imaginary male companion. Within this interplay of art and experience, every human gesture becomes potentially transmutable into a kind of entertainment.

The very language of *Rear Window* resonates with the terminology of entertainment. Lisa speaks of the "opening night" of Jeff's final week "in a cast." Pulling the drapes, she tells Jeff that the "show is over" and promises "coming attractions." The film highlights the intertext of this entertainment through self-referential allusion. The sequence of slides that Jeff projects calls attention to the static photograph as the primordial point of departure for cinematic illusion. Lisa's speculation that the dog might have been killed because he "knew too much" alludes to a title Hitchcock liked so much he used it on two occasions. More importantly, the film foregrounds the generic intertext in which fiction films operate. The world across the courtyard is presented as a series of framed genre pantomimes in which accompanying music largely substitutes for a dialogue track. Jefferies begins, prior to picking up the telephoto lens, by watching what amounts to an early silent "tableau" film, stylistically characterized by long-shot and static camera. The performing inhabitants of the various apartment/frames, meanwhile, seem to have strayed directly from the various genres of the classic Hollywood film.[4] Miss Lonelyhearts is borrowed from an earnest fifties social realist film like *Marty;* Thorwald comes from a murder mystery; the dog couple comes from a domestic comedy. The songwriter belongs in a musical bio-picture such as *Till the Clouds Roll By.* Laboring away at his compositions, he provides commentative music for Jeff's "film" as well as our own. (Surrogate artist, he clearly stands in for Franz

Waxman, whose work he literally performs, much as Jefferies stands in for Hitchcock, and his final version of "Lisa" exactly coincides with the conclusion of the film.) Miss Torso, finally, belongs in an MGM musical, when not in fifties soft-core porn. A vulgar utopian, she transforms the quotidian—brushing her teeth, checking the refrigerator—into musical-comedy-style song and dance.

As *magister ludi* of these cinematic games, Jefferies clearly functions as substitute director/auteur. Hitchcock presents us with a protagonist whose activities partially analogize and at times literally mimic those of the director. Jefferies the photojournalist, like Hitchcock, is both artist and technician, professional and visionary. Lisa's succinct resume of his activities—"going from one place to another taking pictures"—applies equally to Hitchcock. Within the fiction, moreover, Jefferies enjoys partial directorial control over his "film," since binoculars and telephoto lens facilitate a multiplicity of setups and perspectives. His narrative and actantial function, finally, consists in persuading a number of characters, let us call them "spectators," to look where he has looked before. He channels and guides their glance, framing their vision and imposing his interpretation.

Surrogate for the director, Jefferies functions on a deeper level as a relay for the spectator. Indeed, Jefferies and the apartment complex taken together may be taken to prefigure what has come to be called, after Jean-Louis Baudry, the "cinematic apparatus," that is, the instrumental base of camera, projector, and screen as well as the spectator as the desiring subject on which the cinematic institution depends for its object and accomplice. That institution, Metz tells us, demands an immobile secret viewer who absorbs everything through his eyes. The wheelchair-ridden Jefferies exemplifies this situation of retinal activity and enforced immobility; he is indeed, as Lisa remarks in another context, "travelling but going nowhere." The cinematic apparatus, "prosthesis for our primally dislocated limbs," combines visual hyperperception with minimal physical mobility. Binoculars and a long lens grant Jefferies the illusory god-like power of the "all-perceiving spectator." Hitchcock thus suggests a congruency between the situation of the protagonist, who experiences his reality within the fiction as though he were watching a film, and our own situation as spectators watching the protagonist watch his film.

The identity of Jefferies's situation and our own accounts for a frequent verbal ambiguity in *Rear Window;* the shifter "they" can often refer either to the characters in the fiction or to ourselves in the audience. When Lisa speaks to Jefferies about "rear-window ethics," he remarks: "Of course, they can do the same thing to me—watch me like a bug under glass if they want to." His comment, like virtually everything in this complexly overdetermined film, has more than one meaning. Ostensibly referring to his neighbors, it applies equally to the cinema audience watching Jimmy Stewart "like a bug under glass" as he delivers the line in close-up.

In his state of inhibited motoricity and exacerbated perception, Jefferies embodies the living death of the dream-like spectatorial experience. The simulation apparatus called the cinema, for Baudry, not only represents the real but also stimulates intense subject-effects. The shadowy figures on the screen, the darkness of the theater, the sealing off of everyday pressures, all foster an artificial state of regression not unlike that engendered by dreams. The cinema, in this sense, constitutes the approximate material realization of the unconscious goal of returning to an earlier state of psychic development, a state of relative narcissism in which desire is "satisfied" through a simulated reality. The first time we see Jefferies, significantly, he is asleep, as if everything we are about to see were in some sense his dream. Indeed, the vacillations in his attentiveness almost seem designed to evoke the diverse points on the continuum of sleep and wakefulness anatomized by Christian Metz in "The Fiction Film and Its Spectator" (Part III of *The Imaginary Signifier*). At times, he is sound asleep and presumably dreaming; at others, he dozes intermittently; and at still others, finds himself in a state of animated attention, dreamlike in its intensity, reminiscent of that provoked in the spectator by Hitchcock's own films, of which *Rear Window* is a particularly spellbinding example.

The mechanism of gratification in the cinema, according to Metz, "rests on our knowing that the object being looked at does not know it is being looked at."[5] *Rear Window* constantly underscores the voyeuristic abuse to which the cinema, as the privileged medium of the eye, is so often susceptible. The film proliferates in explicit references to voyeurism, to "Peeping Toms" and "window shoppers," and it is hardly accidental that Stella refers to Jefferies's telephoto lens as a "portable keyhole."[6]

Jefferies, for his part, is a quintessential exemplum of "a race of Peeping Toms." His profession of photojournalism assumes and exploits a kind of voyeurism. (Hitchcock underlines this voyeuristic undercurrent by having his glamor pinups neighbor with his disaster photos.) His leisure mirrors his labor. At work, he observes the world's catastrophes from what is usually a safe distance. At home, he indulges, from his rear-window post, in what Metz calls "unauthorized voyeurism." Overseeing the world from a sheltered position, he indulges his scopic drive, the desire to "take other people as objects, subjecting them to a controlling and curious gaze."[7] His neighbors, with the possible exception of Miss Torso, are nonconsenting exhibitionists, pure objects for his superior gaze. He bears the look that confers power. He is the warden, as it were, in a private panopticon. Seated in his central tower, he observes the wards ("small captive shadows in the cells of the periphery") in an imaginary prison. Michel Foucault's description of the cells of the panopticon — "so many cages, so many small theaters, in which each actor is alone, perfectly individualized and constantly visible" — in some ways aptly describes the scene exposed to Jefferies's glance.[8]

The cinematic spectator is caught in a play between regression and progression. The images received come from without, and in this sense the movement is progressive and directed toward external reality; yet due to inhibited mobility and the process of identification with both camera and character, the psychic energy normally devoted to activity is channeled into other routes of discharge. It is no surprise, therefore, that the "complement" of Jefferies's voyeurism is a certain passivity. At the beginning of the film, he consistently opts for inactivity and for the inertia of what he himself calls the "status quo." But although he avoids relationships with friends and lovers and neighbors, he is passionately absorbed in the *spectacle* of his neighbors' lives. Busily spying into the apartments opposite, he can barely pay attention to his interlocutors in the same room. His involvement with people exists in inverse proportion to their distance from him; such is his code of perspective. "Pay attention to me," Lisa demands. "You're not on the other side of the room," Jeff answers, and his response reveals more than he knows. Jefferies prefers his thrills to be vicarious. He would rather watch Miss Torso than touch the flesh-and-blood woman next to him, which is why Lisa contemplates turning herself into a distant and exotic appearance — by "moving into the apartment across the way and doing the dance of the seven veils." The tension between the regressive and progressive paths even takes the form of a physical tussle concerning the direction in which Jeff's wheelchair will face: will it face out the window toward Miss Torso, and metaphorically the cinema, or will it face toward the apartment, Lisa, and "reality."

Jefferies is our specular reflection, our double. We do not merely watch him performing actions; we perform the identical action — looking. But at the same time that Hitchcock leads us to participate vicariously in Jefferies's voyeurism, he also frustrates and refuses to satisfy it. An early shot epitomizes this refusal. Two women on a rooftop, presumably Greenwich Village "bohemians," discard their clothes to sunbathe. A helicopter approaches and hovers overhead. The implication: those aboard the helicopter are spying on the women. The helicopter provides a perfect "vehicle" for the spectatorial desire to enjoy a fantasy omniscience, to go everywhere and see everything, and especially for the socially constructed (and largely male) desire to see women in states of undress. The helicopter evokes the technological resources available to the cinema and enlistable in the service of the scopic drive. Yet Hitchcock withholds the "payoff" of these resources by denying us the point-of-view shot from the helicopter. We never see the women; we become aware, rather, only of our desire to see them. The desire is not fulfilled but only designated and exposed.

Jefferies's voyeurism goes hand in hand with an absorbing fear of mature sexuality. Indeed, the film begins by hinting at a serious case of psychosexual pathology. The first image of Jefferies, asleep with hand on thigh, is quietly masturbatory, as if he were an invalid who had just abused himself in the dark. A radio commercial allusion to that "run-down listless feeling" is followed by a series of comments by both Stella and Lisa that might be taken to refer to sexual impotence: "You're not too active. . . ." "How's your leg?" . . . "Is anything else bothering you?" Lisa is clearly the sexual initiator—"How far does a girl have to go before you notice her?" she asks—and Jeff the reluctant object of her desire. Stella calls him "reasonably healthy" but wonders about a "hormone deficiency." She berates him for speaking in euphemistic abstractions ("Our relationship is maturing") rather than acting like a sexed human being. Her notion of the normal operations of Eros consists in lust ("You get excited") sanctified by an institution ("You get married"). She defends a kind of *amour fou*—"like two taxicabs crashing"—sublimated and blessed by the State.

As object lesson for Stella's domesticated version of surrealism, Hitchcock has the newlywed couple enter their apartment on their wedding night. The commentative music of "That's Amore!" underscores the paradigmatic nature of their appearance. The couple, eager to consummate their relationship, demonstrate in pantomime the model relationship of which Jefferies has so far shown himself to be incapable. They play out the typical final episode of a classical Hollywood film, generally oriented, as Bellour points out, toward the "constitution of the couple." (That the couple so constituted begins to exhaust the sexual charms of marriage in a matter of days suggests both the limits of Stella's philosophy and Hitchcock's fear of the "desire that speaks in the woman's look.") Jefferies, symptomatically, is bored by this spectacle of consummation, preferring either exhibitionism (Miss Torso) or the morbid concatenation of marriage and violence (the murder of Mrs. Thorwald). Jefferies resists Lisa's sexual demands much as the groom fatigues of the bride's, but in Jefferies's case voyeurism plays a primordial role in sexual apathy. Lisa is more than willing to go to bed, but Jeff prefers to fall asleep with his binoculars. Voyeurism, passivity, and implied impotence are shown to form a melancholy constellation of mutually reinforcing neuroses.

The voyeur, according to Metz, is careful to maintain a gulf between the object and the eye: "His look fastens the object at the right distance, as with those cinema spectators who take care to avoid being too close or too far from the screen."[9] Voyeurism renders desire as a purely visual activity. As long as the voyeur remains hidden, the contradictions of his own perspective can be ignored. His invisibility produces the visibility of the objects of his gaze. But the frame, the rear window, which guarantees the innocuous integrity of the visible for the voyeur and thus his pleasure, remains intact only so long as the viewing remains surreptitious.

The central trajectory of *Rear Window,* in this sense, consists in the progressive shattering of Jefferies's illusion of voyeuristic separation from life and the concomitant rendering possible of mature sexuality with Lisa. This shattering progresses by several stages. At the beginning of the film, Jefferies retains the privileged position of the moviegoer; he observes without being observed. This sheltered position gives Jefferies a factitious sense of superiority; he feels superior, for example, to his double in solitude, Miss Lonelyhearts. But this illusion of distance and superiority soon comes under attack. Lisa tries to keep Jeff from being a mere spectator by turning on the lights and wheeling his chair around away from the window. The danger looms, meanwhile, that Thorwald will discover he is being watched. On Thursday morning, as Jeff tries to persuade Stella that something is amiss in the Thorwald apartment, Thorwald himself comes to the window and looks around the courtyard. Jeff instinctively wheels backward in a kind of panic, and warns Stella to move away from the window.

The next stage in this shattering of illusory distance occurs when Lisa enters Thorwald's apartment. She leaves her seat in the theater, as it were, and enters the screen, the space of the spectacle. When Lisa is threatened by Thorwald's imminent return, Jeff reacts like the naive spectator lurking within even the most sophisticated: he addresses advice to the unhearing screen: "Lisa, what are you doing?" . . . "Come on, get out of there!" His reactions mirror our own; he articulates our responses as feeling spectators. But this moment is highly overdetermined and polyvalent. Is this the typical Hitchcockian fusion of danger and desire? Can Jeff love Lisa only when she is threatened with death? Or can he only identify with a Lisa transmogrified into spectacle, framed within the rectangular windows of Thorwald's apartment? What *is* clear is only his own powerlessness. The "blessing" of passive distance has become a curse. The apartment, formerly his sanctuary, and the apartment complex, his panopticon, have now become his trap.

The progressive breakdown of Jeff's voyeuristic passivity is further marked by two particularly chilling moments. In the first he is touched indirectly, by Thorwald's look, and in the second he is violated directly, by Thorwald's hands. The first moment, in which Thorwald looks at Jeff and thus at us, violates the dominant convention stipulating that the film remain radically ignorant of its spectator and that the actor never acknowledge the camera and thus the audience. This moment of the returned glance, of the *voyeur vu,* is often imbued with anxiety in Hitchcock's work. (One thinks, for example, of Melanie caught in Mitch's binoculars as she espies him from Bodega Bay.) It is the moment of a kind of power shift. Thorwald, because of his guilty act, had something to conceal; now Jeff, because of his guilty look, is forced to conceal. Jeff had said of Thorwald at one point that he had a "guilty look," as if he were afraid of being seen. Now that phrase is made to rebound, ironically and retroactively, against Jeff himself. His first reaction, typically, is to turn off the lights, i.e., to try to return himself to a privileged cinema-like situation. Like the spectator, he is afraid of the reciprocal glance. Both we and he feel "discovered."

Thorwald's invasion of Jefferies's apartment brings the scopic inversions of the film to their paroxysm. In a narrative chiasmus—the rhetorical figure which operates by the repetition and, simultaneously, the inversion of the relationship between two words in the course of a sentence—Jefferies and

Thorwald come to exchange places. Jefferies, delegate for the cinema's all-perceiving observer, has visually "broken into" and "entered" Thorwald's apartment; now Thorwald returns the favor. The spectacle, formerly kept at a safe distance by the no-man's land of the courtyard—figuratively the space between spectator and screen—comes to invade the spectator. Thorwald becomes the ambulatory embodiment of filmic displeasure. King Kong is unchained and attacking the audience. Jeff defends himself by setting off flashbulbs, hiding his eyes with each flash. He treats Thorwald as if he were part of a film to be watched in the dark. If the film becomes too frightening, turning on the lights makes it disappear. Failing that, the childlike spectator can hide his eyes; what is no longer seen is no longer there. From another perspective, Jeff tries to blind Thorwald; his only defense is to deprive the aggressor of the look that confers power. But Thorwald remains menacingly real, demanding reaction as a human being rather than a character in a film. Thorwald breaks down the very condition of Jefferies's voyeurism as the Peeping Tom spectator receives the equivalent of the hot pokers of which Stella had spoken, but with the punishment displaced from the eyes to the second broken leg which Jeff suffers in his (redemptive) fall.

The critique of voyeurism in *Rear Window* is not elaborated only through narrative structure and thematic motifs; it is realized through the manipulation of the precise code most relevant to that critique—the code of point of view. And this manipulation is far more rigorous and subtle than most critics have acknowledged. For many critics, *Rear Window* is largely restricted to Jefferies's point of view. "With the exception of one slow pan across the apartments," writes Donald Spoto, "we see [the neighbors] only as Jeffries [*sic*] sees them."[10] For Robin Wood, only once does Hitchcock grant the viewer information that Jefferies lacks. In all other cases, according to Wood, "we are allowed to see only what he sees, know only what he knows."[11] But if it is arguably true that we know only what Jefferies knows, it is manifestly not true that we see only what he sees. To begin with the obvious, Jefferies does not see himself as voyeur. "If you could see yourself, . . ." Lisa tells him, "with binoculars! . . . It's a disease!" In the sequences that take place *within* the apartment, moreover, Lisa, Stella, and Doyle are all granted some point-of-view shots. Jefferies's perspective does predominate in the masked, relatively close shots correlated with the binoculars and telephoto lens, but many of the other shots might be more accurately described as from the point of view of the rear window rather than from that of Jefferies himself. Many shots, as we shall see, embody the point of view of *no* character. Some of the most striking subjective shots, finally, are associated not with Jefferies but with Thorwald. Repeated shots render Thorwald's blanched-out vision of Jefferies armed with flashbulbs and trying to blind him. These dazzling shots mark Thorwald's "takeover" of the point of view, and in this sense form an integral part of the film's structure of inversions and reversals.

The credit sequence already "announces" the rift between Jefferies's point of view and that of the authorial instance. This sequence, in which titles are superimposed on a shot of the rear windows of Jefferies's apartment, shows three bamboo matchstick blinds successively rolling up, with no sign of human intervention. The rolling up of the final blind coincides with the title "Directed by Alfred Hitchcock." The apparently self-generating movement of the blinds, combined with the self-designation of the author, anticipates and "triggers" the subsequent slow pan around the courtyard, a shot pointedly unauthorized by any character within the fiction. Hitchcock further under-scores its unauthorized nature by revealing Jefferies only at the conclusion of the shot, sound asleep and turned *away* from the window. The camera then leaves the sleeping Jefferies and makes another self-flaunting tour of the court-yard, this time pausing to inspect specific apartment windows.

The twice-asserted autonomy of this initial pair of counterclockwise pans around the courtyard anticipates a structuring series of similar pans around the courtyard, none of which are from Jefferies's point of view. Each moves coun-terclockwise around the courtyard and ends with Jefferies in his apartment. In the first two of these pans, he is asleep; in the third, he is being massaged by Stella; and in the fourth, he is being kissed by Lisa. A final pan, during the epilogue, again finds him asleep. Thus Hitchcock repeatedly calls attention to the enunciation, conventionally suppressed in many classical films, by empha-sizing the gestural autonomy of the camera and its independence from any particular vision.

These counterclockwise tours of the courtyard also serve to situate Jefferies within the social space of the apartment complex; they tell us that he forms part of this space and cannot therefore be merely its observer or spectator. The film repeatedly contrasts Jefferies's fragmented view of this space with the spatial unity implied by the continuous pans. Jefferies's view of the complex is rendered through the fragmentation of montage: the ping-pong–like play of shots of Jefferies and subjective shots of the apartments. His vision of the courtyard is disconnected; he does not see it as a continuous space. The neighbors do not form part of a community; they are isolated prey for his "controlling and curious gaze." Only gradually does Jefferies realize that he too forms part of the larger social space. His final fall into the courtyard, in this sense, signals his incorporation into that space. His illusion of separation, from Thorwald and the community, has been literally annihilated.

Through Jefferies, Hitchcock indicts not only voyeurism — or more accu-rately, he reminds us that he himself, his characters, and the spectators share this penchant — but also the social isolation that makes voyeurism the normal condition. Stated differently, the indictment of voyeurism is intimately linked to the film's valorization of neighborliness. At one point the woman grief-stricken over the murder of her dog excoriates all the neighbors for their selfishness: "You don't know the meaning of the word 'neighbors'." As they stand on their fire escapes or at their windows, she screams: "Neighbors like each other, speak to each other, care if anybody lives or dies. But none of you do!" In short, she accuses all of the neighbors of resembling Jefferies, disengaged onlookers incapable of commitment or solidarity. Her question, "Which of you did it?" is "answered" by an extreme long-shot which includes all the buildings and observers around the courtyard. Thus the film implies a certain collective responsibility and the critique of a social world constituted by isolated monads.

At times *Rear Window* touches on what might be called the political dimension of voyeurism. If the narrative ultimately confirms Jefferies's suspicions of Thorwald, it also sensitizes us to the danger of political abuse of the power conferred by the look. Like Coppola's *The Conversation* two decades later, *Rear Window* is, among other things, an essay on the nature of surveillance.[12] And if *The Conversation* clairvoyantly predicted the abuses of Watergate and Abscam, *Rear Window* in some ways echoes the historical ambiance of McCarthyite anticommunism. McCarthyism, after all, is the antithesis of neighborliness; it treats every neighbor as a potential other, alien, spy. It fractures the social community for purposes of control. Jefferies is an anonymous accuser whose suspicions happen to be correct, but the object of his hostile gaze might easily have been as innocent as Father Logan in *I Confess* or Christopher Emmanuel Balestrero in *The Wrong Man,* to cite two other fifties films with anti-McCarthyite resonances.

Rear Window also explores the sexual politics of looking. Voyeurism in the film is largely defined as a masculine activity, even though the object of that voyeurism, through a kind of displacement, is rendered as male. The cinema, by analogy, is defined as the product of the male auteur/spectator/voyeur who at best enlists some women as accomplices in his voyeuristic activities. (Only Jeff, significantly, is allowed to look through the phallic telephoto lens.) But while Lisa and Stella, at least in the beginning, look directly at Jefferies, he looks away toward women and men transmuted into spectacle. And when the women turn their eyes toward the spectacle, they see differently, showing enhanced capacities for empathy and comprehension, especially in relation to other women. Lisa understands instantly that Miss Torso is not in love with the man she kisses on the balcony and knows, without ever having met her, what Mrs. Thorwald would or would not have done. The female spectator in the text, in sum, demonstrates a sensibility quite distinct from that of the male.

A simplistic reading of *Rear Window* would monolithically condemn the protagonist's behavior as totally reprehensible. But in fact the Jefferies of the end of the film is quite different from the Jefferies of the beginning. His ordeal is also a cure, both social and sexual. Although at first impelled by morbid curiosity, Jefferies proceeds, over the course of the film, from scopophilia to epistemophilia, from indifference to concern. The aloof observer is finally compelled to take sides, to intervene, arguably to the benefit of the larger society. While Jefferies's pursuit of Thorwald begins as a voyeuristic game played by a hermeneutic detective, it becomes in the end a response to the dog owner's indictment; Jefferies *does* care "if anyone lives or dies."

Hitchcock, who quite typically superimposes murder and marriage, the hermeneutic and the erotic, has Jefferies's social rehabilitation coincide with a sexual cure whereby the problematic protagonist is divested of his psychosexual impedimenta and rendered ready for marriage. The solution of the murder mystery is made to parallel the evolution of Jefferies's personal relationships. His relationship to Lisa is, at the outset, not unlike his relation to his neighbors. She is acceptable to him only in the form of distant spectacle. The change in Jefferies can be gauged by comparing her first and final appearances. Her initial appearance is as an expressionist shadow crossing Jefferies's sleeping face. She looms above him in outsized close-up, her bright red lips large and somewhat menacing. The *mise en scène* renders Jefferies's fear of her closeness as a threat to voyeuristic distance. When she kisses him, he awakens and asks, "Who are you?" She then retreats, reestablishing the necessary gulf, and turns on the lights, leaving him in the shadows, returning him to his spectatorial position. The gap is steadily narrowed throughout the film, however, and by the final shots it is virtually eliminated. Lisa comforts Jefferies after his fall. The shot, with typical Hitchcockian circularity, echoes their initial encounter, yet this time her appearance is not threatening but nurturing, as she holds his head in her lap, bending protectively with the folds of her skirt enveloping him. Jefferies, the paradigmatic spectator, has realized the corollary psychic costs of both voyeurism and solitude. While Lisa may be no expert on "rear window ethics," the film shows Hitchcock to be their brilliant exponent.

Rear Window provides an object lesson in the processes of spectatorship. "Tell me what you see and what you think it means," Lisa tells Jefferies, and her words evoke the constant process of vision and interpretation, inference and intellection, inherent in the "reading" of any fiction film. "I just want to find out what's the matter with the salesman's wife," says Jefferies, thus articulating our wish concerning the film. Jefferies, Lisa, Stella, and Doyle collaborate in producing the meaning of the spectacle before them, much as we collaborate in producing the signification of the film. They pressure the film, as well, with their desire for a story. In fact, some of them would prefer a murder story; they, like us, would be disappointed to discover that Mrs. Thorwald was actually alive and well.

With its insistent inscription of scenarios of voyeurism, *Rear Window* poses the question that so preoccupies contemporary film theory and analysis: the question of the place of the desiring subject within the cinematic apparatus. This theory and analysis shifts interest from the question, "What does the text mean?" to, "What do we want from the text?" "What is it you want from me? . . . Tell me what you want!," Thorwald says to Jefferies, and his question, ostensibly addressed to the protagonist, might as well have been addressed to us. What indeed do we want from this film or from film in general? To this question—which filmmakers, critics, and spectators must ask themselves—*Rear Window* offers a complex and multilevelled response. The spectators in the film—Jefferies, certainly, but also Lisa, Stella, and even Doyle—want first of all to *see,* to peek into the private corners of the lives of others. The technical instruments at Jefferies's disposal come in answer, as it were, to this primordial desire. Beyond that, these spectators want to identify with the human figures within the spectacle. When Lisa enters into what had been defined as the space of the spectacle—Thorwald's apartment—Jefferies's "investment" becomes clear. Most of all, these spectators want to experience certain "subject effects." They want to find themselves in a heightened state of pleasurable absorption and identification. Jefferies the spectator begins as listless and apathetic, but he gradually comes alive through what he sees. He savors the experience of "coming alive," even though at times it entails pain and anxiety. Furthermore, he shares the experience with others within a kind of ephemeral *communitas* of spectators. His metamorphosis from distant observer into excited vicarious participant "allegorizes" the transformation engendered in us by the narrative procedures and identificatory mechanisms of Hitchcock's cinema, and even that engendered by *Rear Window* itself.

While it is true that *Rear Window* short-circuits voyeuristic involvement by making the audience aware of itself as audience and of the film as artifice, it is also true that our relation to the spectacle remains voyeuristic in the sense that we identify strongly with characters in a fiction and identify even more to the extent that we, like the protagonist, are voyeurs. The distancing of *Rear Window* is not, finally, Brechtian. For Brechtian theater, there is no suspense, no pathos, no catharsis, while *Rear Window* builds to a catharsis which purges the tensions generated by the diegesis. We, like the protagonist, are presumably "cured." *Rear Window* is both indictment and defense of the cinema. Just as scopophilia can incline toward normality (a healthy curiosity) as well as abnormality (a morbid voyeurism), so the cinema can be life-enhancing or destructive. *Rear Window,* at once a cautionary tale for voyeurs and an ode to the cinema, presents both alternatives with extraordinary lucidity.

Notes

1. Alfred Hitchcock, "*Rear Window,*" quoted in Albert J. LaValley, ed., *Focus on Hitchcock* (Englewood Cliffs: Prentice-Hall, 1972), 40.
2. Some of the key essays in the discussion of the apparatus are Jean-Louis Baudry, "Cinema: The Ideological Effects of the Basic Apparatus," *Film Quarterly,* vol. 27, no. 2 (1974–75) and "The Apparatus," *Camera Obscura,* no. 1 (1976). Also of interest are Christian Metz, *The Imaginary Signifier* (Bloomington: Indiana Univ. Press, 1982) and Jean-Louis Comolli, "Machines of the Visible," anthologized in Stephen Heath and Teresa de Lauretis, eds., *The Cinematic Apparatus* (New York: St. Martin's Press, 1980).
3. Jean Douchet, "Hitch et son Public," *Cahiers du Cinéma,* vol. 19, no. 3 (1960): 10.

4. We are indebted to Noël Carrol for this insight.

5. Christian Metz, "History/Discourse: A Note on Two Voyeurisms," *Edinburgh Magazine* (1976): 23.

6. Although the cinema is founded on the pleasure of hearing (Lacan's *pulsion invocante*) as well as on the pleasure of looking (scopophilia), Hitchcock throughout emphasizes the visual rather than the aural dimension of voyeurism. Jefferies is granted access to music and noise but not to distant conversations staged as pantomimes. It should also be pointed out, however, that the sound track itself makes frequent allusion to voyeurism. The lyrics of Bing Crosby's "To see you is to love you/and I see you everywhere" (ironically superimposed on Jefferies's observation of Miss Lonelyhearts) is in this sense exemplary: "To see you is to want you/ and I see you all the time/ On the sidewalk/in the doorway/ I see you everywhere/ To see you is to love you/ and you're never out of sight/ and I'll love you/ and I'll see you/ in the same old dreams tonight." A veritable ode to scopophilia, the song fuses sight in desire in its evocation of the distant dream-like loving common to voyeur and spectator.

7. Christian Metz, "The Imaginary Signifier," *Screen,* vol. 16, no. 2 (1975): 60.

8. Michel Foucault, *Discipline and Punish: The Birth of the Prison* (New York: Vintage, 1979), 200.

9. Christian Metz, "The Imaginary Signifier," 60.

10. Donald Spoto, *The Art of Alfred Hitchcock* (New York: Hopkinson and Blake, 1976), 241.

11. Robin Wood, *Hitchcock's Films* (New York: Castle Books, 1969), 65.

12. Although *The Conversation* is often compared to *Blow-Up,* it actually has more in common with *Rear Window.* Both the Hitchcock film and the Coppola film are structured around the comeuppance of the voyeur, or, in the case of Harry Caul, of the auditeur. Just as Jefferies represents an analogue to the director/spectator/voyeurs, so Harry Caul is sound director, editing different takes into a final text, as well as voyeur/auditeur, eavesdropping on the private lives of others. The "cure," however, is in his case somewhat less effective.

We would like to thank Karen Backstein and Louise Spence for their helpful comments.

REAR WINDOW (Paramount, 1954). *Producer:* Alfred Hitchcock, *Assistant Director:* Herbert Coleman, *Script:* John Michael Hayes, from the novel by William Irish (pseud. of Cornell Woolrich), *Photography:* Robert Burks (Technicolor), *Editor:* George Tomasini, *Sets:* Hal Pereira, Joseph McMillan Johnson, Sam Comer, Ray Mayer, *Music:* Franz Waxman, *Costumes:* Edith Head, *Players:* James Stewart (L. B. Jefferies), Grace Kelly (Lisa Freemont), Wendell Corey (Tom Doyle), Thelma Ritter (Stella), Raymond Burr (Lars Thorwald), Judith Evelyn (Miss Lonelyhearts). 112 minutes.

Finding the Right Man in *The Wrong Man*

Marshall Deutelbaum

Because it embodies so many of its director's recurrent themes within its true story, *The Wrong Man* occupies a special place among Hitchcock's films. In it, for once, reality seems to validate the motifs that run through his fictional tales. Now, however, these familiar motifs of the normal world thrown into chaos, the innocent man wrongly accused of a crime, the transference of guilt as an innocent character assumes responsibilities for another's crime, and the uncertainty of appearance are rooted in the true sufferings of Christopher Emmanuel Balestrero, a musician in the Stork Club band. Here, then, it is a real man who is mistakenly arrested for a crime he did not commit and his real wife who irrationally blames herself for his arrest and suffers a nervous breakdown as a result of the unwarranted guilt she heaps upon herself. Here, too, it is only by chance that the real thief is finally apprehended. Thus in contrast to his other films, no one might object that *The Wrong Man* is woven from artificial coincidence or complain that its sudden turns strain anyone's sense of plausibility. Indeed, Eric Rohmer and Claude Chabrol celebrate the place of *The Wrong Man* in Hitchcock's oeuvre for its triumph of fact over fiction which "brings together the themes scattered throughout his work," while demonstrating their existence in the world.[1]

Hitchcock further underlined the essential truthfulness of *The Wrong Man* by his decision to film the story entirely on location in a semidocumentary style, using many of the actual participants to play themselves in minor roles. *The New York Times* ran two articles describing the location shooting, noting that Hitchcock was "a stickler for fidelity to detail."[2] This same emphasis on the narrative's authenticity marks Hitchcock's long cameo appearance in a precredit sequence as he speaks directly to the audience. Presenting himself in extreme long-shot as a miniscule figure lost in the emptiness of a vacant soundstage — vacant perhaps because this film was shot on location — Hitchcock visually signals the astringent, semidocumentary style of the film to come as he declares its basis in fact:

> This is Alfred Hitchcock speaking. In the past, I have given you many kinds of suspense pictures. But this time I would like you to see a different one. The difference lies in the fact that this is a true story, every word of it. And yet, it contains elements that are stranger than all the fiction that has gone into many of the thrillers that I've made before.[3]

It should not be surprising in light of such emphasis on the truthfulness of both its story and photographic style that *The Wrong Man* should seem to many to be one of Hitchcock's visually barest and least manipulative films. François Truffaut expresses this attitude best when he describes the feel of the film's story in relation to its stark visual style as "the roast without the gravy, a news event served raw. . . ."[4] Yet despite *The Wrong Man*'s apparent fidelity to truth and its relatively plain visual style, a careful consideration of the film will reveal that Hitchcock manipulates both the facts of the story and the film's images in order to test his viewer's perceptions. A survey of earlier accounts of Balestrero's ordeal will illuminate the ways in which both Hitchcock and the film's images lie when they claim to be transparently true.

Balestrero's misfortune had first been presented to the readers of *Life* magazine in "A Case of Identity," by Herbert Brean.[5] Not only had Balestrero been arrested for twice robbing an insurance office some two blocks from his home but by a bizarre coincidence he had duplicated a curious spelling error in the original holdup note when the police dictated it to him. In the face of this apparently damning piece of evidence and the testimonies of the office clerks who identified him as the thief who had robbed their office on 9 July and 18 December 1952, Balestrero began to assemble the evidence that would prove he could not have been that robber. He hired former New York State Senator Frank D. O'Connor as his attorney and began to reconstruct his activities for those dates. He remembered that on the July date he and his wife, Rose, were guests at the Edelweiss Farm near Cornwall, New York. That particular day had been the birthday of the owner's wife, though a party for her had been cancelled because she was ill. Instead, Balestrero remembered, he had spent the time playing pinochle with other guests. O'Conner took depositions from those players attesting to that fact.

Though it took him a little longer to remember, Balestrero finally recalled that at the time of the December robbery he had been troubled with abscessed teeth. Indeed, a check of his dental records revealed that the right side of his jaw had been so swollen on December 14 that the teeth could not be extracted. Moreover, because the swelling had not lessened by the 22nd (four days after the second robbery), his dentist had sent him to see his family doctor for treatment. Because none of those who identified him as the holdup man had mentioned this swelling, it was unlikely that he was actually the man who had robbed them. The prosecution's case was additionally weakened by the inability of the police to locate either of two items among Balestrero's effects: the lined notebook from which the robber had torn the paper on which he wrote the holdup notes or the blue overcoat worn by the robber during the second robbery. As Rose insisted to the police, her husband owned only a gray topcoat.

At the same time that Balestrero was working to prove his innocence, however, Rose developed the illogical belief that she was responsible for her husband's misfortune because he had gone to the insurance office for her sake. If he had not gone there to borrow money against their insurance policies to pay for her emergency dental work, she reasoned, he never would have been mistaken by the clerks for the robber. Tormented by this thought, Rose suffered a nervous breakdown within a short time and entered a sanitarium in the country. Balestrero was himself such a timid man that O'Conner feared that he, too, might suffer a breakdown during the trial. Indeed, the trial proved to be an unexpected ordeal when, despite the strength of his alibis, it ended in a mistrial when a juror who had already made up his mind interrupted the State's case to ask aloud: "Judge, do we have to listen to all this?" It was only by chance that, before the second trial could start, the actual robber, Charles James Daniell, was caught and confessed to 40 robberies, including the two for which he knew Balestrero had been arrested. At the time this story appeared in *Life,* Rose had recovered enough to spend weekends with her family.

These details of the case are worth repeating, for they form the basis for the first dramatization of Balestrero's story, also entitled "A Case of Identity," broadcast on "Robert Montgomery Presents," on 11 January 1954.[6] Adapted for television by Adrian Spies, the three-act drama managed to fit Balestrero's ordeal within the program's hour length by employing voice-over narration to stitch together its key moments. Despite its hurried pace, it is entirely faithful to Brean's original article and holds up remarkably well in comparison with *The Wrong Man*. Also staged in a semidocumentary style, with filmed footage of Balestrero's neighborhood cut in from time to time, the similarity of some scenes in the two dramatizations is quite striking. The staging of Balestrero's arrest on his doorstep, for example, is quite similar in both the television and film versions. *Life* celebrated the broadcast with a brief story illustrated by a photograph of Balestrero watching the re-creation of his experiences.[7]

In addition to illustrating the widespread publicity which Balestrero's story received, the original *Life* article and the television dramatization help us realize how much of the true story was eliminated in *The Wrong Man*, despite Hitchcock's declaration to the contrary. While *The Wrong Man* retains the general details of Balestrero's arrest and trial, as well as the details of Rose's breakdown, the weak points of the police investigation, the ease with which Balestrero was able to establish his alibis, and the effectiveness of his attorney have been eliminated from the screenplay. To a certain extent, these excisions make the story more dramatic. Without any mention of the missing topcoat and notebook, the evidence against Balestrero seems more conclusive. The alleged death of all the witnesses who played pinochle with Manny on the July date makes Fate in the film seem all that much more against him. Similarly, O'Connor's claim in the film that he had had little experience with criminal cases makes Balestrero's trial seem all the more chancy. Even the dissolve from Balestrero's face to Daniel's is a dramatic contrivance. Though Balestrero was a religious man and prayed at his trial, Hitchcock embellishes the truth when he dissolves from the accused man's face to the face of the thief, as though to suggest that Manny's prayer is the cause of Daniel's arrest. In fact, as in the television drama, Balestrero was not praying, but playing in the Stork Club band at the time of Daniel's arrest.

Apart from their increased dramatic effect, one might usefully consider these deviations from the truth of the *Life* and televised accounts within the context of the self-conscious conflict between fact and fiction that had become well established in postwar Hollywood films. To be sure, the mixture of fact and fiction in earlier films is hardly remarkable. Much of the output of Warner Brothers since the 1930s had consisted of fictional films based on factual events. Conversely, "The March of Time" series produced by Twentieth Century-Fox between 1934 and 1953 regularly embellished its factually based material with liberal doses of fiction. In the postwar years, however, in a number of the films now associated with *film noir,* fact and fiction were often presented as antagonists within the same film. In semidocumentary police procedurals, for example, the protocols of fiction came to be associated with duplicitous criminality, while in the fiction film the truth of reality was self-defeating. Two films in particular, *The Naked City* (Universal-International, 1948, directed by Jules Dassin) and *The Glass Web* (Universal-International, 1954, directed by Jack Arnold) epitomize the dynamics of this antagonism and offer a background against which to consider the play of fact and fiction in *The Wrong Man*.

The Naked City grew out of Malvin Wald's experiences making documentaries in the Army Air Corps during World War II. When he later proposed to Mark Hellinger that these same techniques might be employed in shooting a feature film entirely on location, Hellinger bankrolled him to a monthlong research trip to New York City to develop a story suited to such a semidocumentary format. Wald spent the time learning the details of police procedures and studying the department's files of unsolved homicides for an adaptable subject. As Wald explains, the police were suspicious about his declared interest in authenticity:

> They started to give me an informal third-degree. No rubber hoses or bright lights. Just the names of a few current murder movies they had seen—and hated. I hadn't written any of the films, but still I started to sweat—a kind of guilt-by-association feeling for the writers who did.

> Finally I confessed: Many Hollywood writers had gotten trapped in the excitement of their stories and had been careless with the truth. I promised to try to avoid that pitfall—and write an honest film about police detectives, if it ever got produced.[8]

Finally, Wald wrote a story based upon the unsolved murder of a model named Dot King, fashioning a hypothetical solution to the case for the sake of a traditional script.

This mixture of fact and fiction is reflected formally in the finished film as well, for in place of the traditional written credits, *The Naked City* begins with a combination of voice-over credits and introductory commentary spoken by Hellinger himself and presented against aerial shots of Manhattan:

> Ladies and gentlemen, the motion picture you are about to see is called *The Naked City*. My name is Mark Hellinger. I was in charge of its production. And I may as well tell you frankly that it's a bit different from most films you've ever seen. It was written by Albert Maltz and Malvin Wald, photographed by William Daniels, and directed by Jules Dassin. As you see, we're flying over an island, a city, a particular city. And this is a story of a number of people. And a story, also, of the city itself. It was *not* photographed in a studio, quite the contrary. Barry Fitzgerald, our star, Howard Duff, Dorothy Hart, Don Taylor, Ted De Corsia, and the other actors played out their roles on the streets, in the apartment houses, in the skyscrapers of New York itself. And along with them, a great many New Yorkers played out their roles also. This is the city as it is—hot summer pavements, the children at play, the buildings in their naked stone, the people without makeup.[9]

Thus *The Naked City* signals its superior truthfulness by replacing the standard printed credits with the conversational voice of Mark Hellinger, the well-known New York newpaperman whose familiarity with the city authenticates his pose as a truthful narrator. Yet in the same way that Wald's story mixes fact and fiction, this opening sequence intercuts authentic shots of New York with staged shots involving the story's fictional characters.

As a police procedural, *The Naked City* follows the homicide squad's investigation of a young model's murder. The search also serves to initiate a young detective, Jimmy Halloran, into the approved, step-by-step procedures under the watchful eye of experienced Lt. Muldoon. While the detectives' work is rational and methodical, the criminals they hunt and the false leads they encounter are based upon fanciful fictions. Indeed, Muldoon identifies their unknown suspect as a fictional character named "J. P. McGillicuddy," his generic term for all as yet unidentified suspects. A sweetly demented woman who tells Muldoon that the killer will confess if a hound dog's tooth is buried at the dead woman's grave, along with a fantasy confession by the dead woman's grocery boy claiming he stabbed her to rid the world of her immorality, point toward the ways that make-believe is associated with the crime throughout the film.

Eventually, the investigation ties the woman's death to a ring of jewel thieves specializing in thefts from wealthy families. Its mastermind, Frank Niles, is an inveterate liar who fabricates all sorts of stories about himself, even when none are necessary to establish an alibi. Niles is a compulsive fabulator, creating a wartime persona for himself and fictionalizing his successes as a businessman before finally admitting that he is a compulsive storyteller. Niles's various stories are so fanciful that Muldoon finally declares, "In a lifetime of interrogating and investigating, you are probably the biggest and most willing liar I have ever met." Niles's admission that he is a liar ties lying to fictional performance as he replies: "All right, I'm a liar. I'm a circus character altogether." The curious phrase, "circus character," points in turn to Willie Garzah, the member of the gang who did kill the model. As it turns out, Garzah was once an acrobat. Significantly, his identity is finally established at a gym. The sequence begins before the investigating detective arrives as a trainer coaches a pair of intertwined professional wrestlers how to grimace and groan as though they were in terrible pain. When the detective introduces himself to the trainer, the wrestlers suddenly pause—clearly in no pain at all—to listen to his questions. Garzah had been a wrestler too, committed like them to performing in the most fictional of sports.

If various sorts of fiction are associated with the criminals in the semidocumentary *The Naked City*, fiction extracts its revenge from fact in *The Glass Web*. Following its credit sequence, the film begins with the apparent murder of a woman at an abandoned desert mine. After the killer dumps her body down the mine shaft, however, the camera pulls back to reveal that the action has taken place in a television studio during the weekly Wednesday night broadcast of "Crime of the Week," a program which prides itself on presenting "the true story as it exactly happened." Within the narrative, the conflict between fiction and fact is embodied in the antagonism between Don Newell, the show's writer, and Harry Hayes, the man who researches the details of the murders and casts each week's show.

Doggedly committed to factual accuracy, Hayes continually faults Newell for valuing dramatic effect more highly than literal truth. One argument between them is worth quoting because it illustrates the conflict inherent in their opposing points of view. Hayes complains that Newell's latest script is flat because he has ignored factual detail:

Newell: But who the devil cares about that if the scene plays?

Hayes: Well what we're selling is realism. The people who watch our show every Wednesday night want to eavesdrop on murder. They want to smell the stink of murder. They love it! And they watch our show instead of the others because they know I give them the truth. . . . I was a police reporter long enough to know that the people buy the little details, the quirks, the idiosyncrasies, the poor slobs in the news.

Over the course of the narrative, the conflict between the two men—

concretely, the conflict between fact and fiction—is played out through the murder of an actress with whom they have both been involved, the same actress who is "murdered" in the film's opening sequence. Hayes murders her, then writes a script about her murder for the show, which suggests through circumstantial evidence that Newell was her killer. As one might expect in this fictional work, however, Hayes's passion for accuracy leads him to include details in the script which only the actual killer could know. A fictional work, *The Glass Web* allows the writer of fiction to triumph as the devotee of fact outwits himself by his slavish regard for it.

Despite their opposite attitudes toward fact and fiction, both *The Naked City* and *The Glass Web* visually signal the antagonism between them through formal devices which strain classical norms—the lack of traditional opening credits in the former and the initial uncertainty of whether the desert murder in the latter is to be read as fact or fiction within its diegesis. In part, some foregrounding of narration in this way is common at the beginning of Hollywood films. As David Bordwell observes:

> Classical narration emerges quite overtly in the film's opening moments, during the credits and the early scenes, and then becomes more covert, letting character causality caught in *medias res* carry the narrational burden. . . . Once the action gets going, the narration slips into the background . . . but the narration may become overt again by an anticipatory cut or a stressed sound-image juxtaposition.[10]

These two films differ from the norm, however, because voice-over narration in the one and the constant diegetic conflict between fact and fiction in the other keep narration from ever slipping entirely into the motivated illusion that constitutes classical narration. Narration in these films never quite becomes invisible.

Unlike *The Naked City* and *The Glass Web*, *The Wrong Man* does not present the antagonism of fact and fiction directly within its diegesis. Rather, the film employs a series of markers which question whether its semidocumentary format, as a style, is any more truthful a form of representation, better suited to factual material, than the well-established Hollywood studio style. In their introductory remarks to viewers, both Hellinger and Hitchcock emphasize how different the photographic styles of their films are from studio norms and leave us to infer from the references to "buildings in their naked stone" and "people without makeup," as well as from Hitchcock's stance on a vacant soundstage, that there is some special connection between their comparatively plain visual style and the factualness of the stories photographed in this manner. How different the semidocumentary style was thought to be from studio standards can be gauged from a piece about the location shooting of *The Wrong Man* which appeared in *American Cinematographer*. Frederick Foster quotes Hitchcock's expression of concern that the film's visually bare semidocumentary style might damage the professional reputation of Robert Burks, his longtime cinematographer:

> Perhaps remembering Bob Burks's fine color photography on other pictures and the new prestige he acquired last year as result of winning an Oscar for the photography of *To Catch a Thief,* Hitchcock said to him: "Perhaps you may not want to do this picture, Bob. I wouldn't want the stark, colorless documentary treatment I expect to reflect on your reputation as a photographer." Burks reassured Hitchcock that if he was willing to risk his reputation on the picture, he'd gladly go along with him.[11]

Burks willingly filmed *The Wrong Man* in this way because he understood that such a plain style authenticated its subject by making it appear unmanipulated, as though it were caught in an actuality. For as Burks says about filming in a precinct house: "Here, as in all the other interiors, the lighting maintained a stark, natural aspect—free of all the frilly touches that might otherwise be given such a set on a studio sound stage. Hitchcock had emphasized he wanted it to look like a newsreel shot" (p. 114). But how true, in fact, are newsreel shots? Some of the changes that Hitchcock made in Balestrero's case, along with some formal features in the film, call the apparent truthfulness of the semidocumentary style into question, encouraging attentive viewers to see it as no more transparent than the classical studio style it seems to refuse. The perceptual problems posed by the film demonstrate that the semidocumentary style offers no more honest or direct a rendering of what transpires before the camera's lens.

The Wrong Man's credit sequence introduces the first of a pair of lap dissolves which embody the problem of perception as a matter of legibility. The initial series of lap dissolves presents an evening at the Stork Club in a temporally condensed manner as dissolves connect separate moments from early evening when the club is filled with patrons to closing time, as the last lingering couple finishes the final dance. The shots are filmed from a fixed setup with the camera aimed across the dance floor toward Balestrero and the band. In condensing the evening in this way, the lap dissolves function in a purely conventional manner, as does the music from the band which helps to hide the eliminated moments by remaining continuous. David Bordwell's comments about the conventional use of diegetic music to mask lap dissolves are worth quoting here because they can help us to understand how unremarkable these are in some ways—particularly because the example he cites is very like the opening of Hitchcock's film:

> In the sound film, diegetic music could cover certain gaps at the level of the image while still projecting a sense of continuous time. For example, in *Flying Fortress* (1942) a couple sit down to dinner in a restaurant while a band is playing. The meal is abbreviated by means of dissolves, creating ellipses on the visual track; but the band's music continues uninterrupted. The bleeding of music over large ellipses suggests how easily the

temporal vagueness of music can make sound fulfill narrative functions.
(p. 46)

However, because the appearance of new credits coincides with the dissolves, the passage of the evening is far less legible than it might be in a series of conventional lap dissolves. Reading the new words makes it doubly difficult to read the new image and vice versa. Thus the sequence formally initiates the question of perception which haunts the text for both characters and viewers until it is resolved in the second lap dissolve, from Balestrero's face to Daniel's.

In contrast to the first, the second lap dissolve could hardly be more legible. Not only is the dissolve so slow that both men's faces merge for a while, but even the sound track changes at the point that Daniel's face becomes distinct from Balestrero's. Where there is nondescript music on the sound track while Balestrero's face dominates the image, street noises replace the music once Daniel's face is distinct. The fact that the dissolve also conveys simultaneity—Balestrero prays at the same time Daniel begins the robbery which results in his arrest—further underlines the opposite purposes of this pair of dissolves. The first dissolves confound perception, while the later one insists upon it.

Between these lap dissolves, the same concerns with legibility and perception are manifested in the narrative in a variety of ways. Not only does Balestrero's arrest depend upon the mistaken perception of the office workers who misidentify him, but a curious incident involving his sons just before he leaves for the insurance office points to the same matter in more explicitly dramatic terms. Robert, the elder son, has been practicing Mozart on the piano. He complains that his brother, Greg, has purposely been annoying him by hiding in a closet and playing a different melody on his harmonica at the same time. While Rose struggles to settle their dispute, it finally takes Manny to quiet the boys:

Robert: Will you tell Greg to quit playing the mouth organ while I practice!
Rose: Greg. Greg!
Robert: Will you tell him!
Rose: Gregory!
Gregory: Yes, mother?
Rose: Don't play the harmonica while Robert is playing the piano.
Gregory: But I was playing the same thing!
Rose: [to Robert] Was he?
Robert: He thinks he was, but . . .
Gregory: I was!
Robert: I don't want you playing, even if it is the same. [to Rose] He hides in the closet and makes noise.
Rose: Robert!

Manny: What's all this?

Rose: Oh, Robert was playing the piano and Greg was spoiling the music.

Gregory: I didn't.

Robert: You did!

Gregory: I was playing the same!

Robert: You were not!

Manny: You know, Bob, sounded to me—that last part when Greg was playing along—sounded to me like he caught the melody.[12]

Manny finally calms them with the promise of fifteen-minute lessons that night for each boy on his respective instrument. Manny is arrested when he arrives home that evening, however, and never has the chance to give them their lessons.

In a displaced manner, the boys' disagreement concisely encompasses what will become the narrative's main dramatic issues, announcing them as a summary agenda for the remainder of the film to consider in detail. Whether the boys are playing the same or different melodies prefigures the confusion that will develop over whether Balestrero is the same man who twice robbed the insurance company's office or is a different man. More directly related to our purposes, however, Greg's hiding in the closet hints at the phantom presence of Daniel, the real robber, throughout the film.

As a careful examination of *The Wrong Man* reveals, the real thief is often visible in the film as he and Balestrero cross paths. Balestrero actually bumps into Daniel outside the Victor Moore Arcade while on his way to the insurance office inside, where the employees will mistakenly identify him as the man who twice robbed them. After his arrest, the police take Balestrero to a liquor store that had also been robbed in order to give the employees a chance to identify him. As Manny leaves in a squad car afterwards, Daniel walks past the liquor store on the sidewalk. Similarly, after Balestrero is led from a paddy wagon into Felony Court for his arraignment, the camera holds on the scene long enough to show Daniel strolling through the frame after Manny has disappeared from sight. Thus while Daniel's overt appearance late in the film, in the long lap dissolve which superimposes his face upon Balestrero's, is generally regarded as the film's most striking device, the dissolve simply makes his presence manifest.

As the dissolve and subsequent face-to-face meeting between Balestrero and Daniel in the precinct house reveal, the men share only a slight facial resemblance, much too superficial to register in the long-shots in which they cross paths. Hitchcock takes great pains, therefore, to augment their physical resemblance through the more prominent details of clothing which consistently differentiate them from the appearance of the other men in the film. Both, for example, wear essentially the same hat. In addition, unlike others in the film, they consistently keep the collars of their (different!) coats turned up in a similar fashion. And while these may seem like negligible details—if there is anything negligible in a drama so closely focused on the misperception of details—the film's dissolves and explicit dramatic concerns about the discrimination of similarities and differences establish a context which urges one to be more attentive to such slight comparisons. Thus Balestrero's promise of music lessons to his sons suggests the film's larger offer of lessons about the apparent legibility of the semidocumentary image. Through these transformations of melodies into men, of a hidden child into a hidden thief, and of promised music lessons into a demonstration of how one must learn to read images too, *The Wrong Man* encourages thoughtful viewers to be more attentive to their own perceptions. Seeing is always problematic, and not even the supposedly objective eye of the semidocumentary camera can relieve the human eye of its responsibility to see clearly by always calling its perception into question. As much as the thematic concerns embodied within Balestrero's case are typical of Hitchcock's narratives, this general truth about perception is one of his abiding concerns, frequently presented, as here, in formal terms.

Notes

1. Eric Rohmer and Claude Chabrol, *Hitchcock: The First Forty-Four Films,* trans. Stanley Hochman (New York: Frederick Ungar, 1979), 145.
2. See "Court Is Turned into a Movie Set," *New York Times,* 9 April 1956, and "All Around the Town with *The Wrong Man:* Hitchcock Troupe Shoots New Thriller at Surface and Underground Sites," *New York Times,* 29 April 1956; reprinted in *The New York Times Encyclopedia of Film* (New York: Times Books, 1984).
3. Here, as elsewhere, all dialogue quoted from *The Wrong Man* has been transcribed from the viewing print.
4. François Truffaut, *The Films in My Life,* trans. Leonard Mayhew (New York: Simon & Schuster, 1978), 84.
5. Herbert Brean, "A Case of Identity," *Life,* 29 June 1953, 97–100, 102, 104, 107.
6. I am indebted to Dan Einstein, Curator of the ATAS-UCLA Television Archives, for arranging for me to view a copy of this dramatization.
7. See "Balestrero's Nightmare: *Life* Story of Musician Falsely Accused of Theft Is Hit on TV," *Life,* 1 February 1954, 45–46. The role of Balestrero was played in this dramatization by Robert Ellenstein. His Balestrero is much more timid than Henry Fonda's portrayal in *The Wrong Man.* Is it merely a coincidence or an example of jokey casting that Ellenstein plays the henchman in *North by Northwest* who mistakenly identifies Roger Thornhill as George Kaplan in the Plaza Hotel's Oak Bar?
8. Malvin Wald, "Afterword," in *The Naked City: A Screenplay* (Carbondale: Southern Illinois Univ. Press, 1979), 138. Wald's claims for the aesthetic reasons for shooting on location ought to be balanced by an awareness of the numerous economic reasons which made location filming attractive in the 1940s. See William Lafferty, "A Reappraisal of the Semi-Documentary in Hollywood, 1945-1948," *The Velvet Light Trap,* no. 20 (1983): 22-26.
9. This speech does not appear in the published screenplay.
10. David Bordwell, Janet Staiger, and Kristin Thompson, *The Classical Hollywood Cinema: Film Style and Mode of Production to 1960* (New York: Columbia Univ. Press, 1985), 69.
11. Frederick Foster, " 'Hitch' Didn't Want It Arty," *American Cinematographer,* vol. 38, no. 2 (1957): 85.
12. In Spies's dramatization, Robert becomes angry when his younger brother continues to mimic his every word, including his question about what they are having for dinner. The argument over music, Gregory's hiding in the closet, and the promise of music lessons are newly created for the film.

THE WRONG MAN (Warner Bros., 1956). *Producers:* Alfred Hitchcock, Herbert Coleman, *Assistant Director:* Daniel J. McCauley, *Script:* Maxwell Anderson, Angus McPhail, from Anderson's "The True Story of Christopher Emmanuel Balestrero," *Photography:* Robert Burks, *Editor:* George Tomasini, *Sets:* Paul Sylbert, William L Kuehl, *Music:* Bernard Herrmann, *Players:* Henry Fonda (Christopher Emmanuel "Manny" Balestrero), Vera Miles (Rose Balestrero), Anthony Quayle (Frank O'Connor), Esther Minciotti (Mrs. Balestrero, Manny's mother), Richard Robbins (Daniel). 105 minutes.

Male Desire, Male Anxiety: The Essential Hitchcock

Robin Wood

It would be difficult to overestimate the importance—both for Hitchcock scholarship and for anyone who loves the cinema—of the long overdue rerelease of the five "missing" films from Hitchcock's Hollywood period. *Rope* is unique in his career—and indeed in the history of commercial cinema—for its uncompromising use of the ten-minute take; *The Trouble with Harry*—though few will accord it major status—is unique for its tone (not, it is true, the only Hitchcock comedy, but the only truly *Hitchcockian* comedy); *The Man Who Knew Too Much* is self-evidently superior to the British original, though a few diehard British critics still refuse to see this. The real irreplaceable loss all these years, however, has been that of *Rear Window* and *Vertigo:* Hitchcock's reputation does not, of course, stand on them alone, but they are central and indispensable to any valid assessment of his achievement. It is fitting and timely that *Vertigo* is at last inscribed in the final "ten best" list of *Sight and Sound*'s 1982 International Critics' Poll.

Twenty years ago, I was writing *Hitchcock's Films,* a book that opens with the question, "Why should we take Hitchcock seriously?" The meaning, at that time, would scarcely have been altered if I had written simply, "*Should* we take Hitchcock seriously?" It would have been unthinkable at the time to refer to "Hitchcock scholarship," whether as something that existed or as something that *ought* to exist (at least in the English-speaking world—a body of such scholarship was already developing in France). Today, the "should" seems to have been answered almost unanimously in the affirmative, but the "why" still remains very much an open question. We have, at any rate, passed far beyond the point where formulas like "skillful entertainer" and "master of suspense" were felt to be adequate. One hopes also for general agreement that the question of the artist's private life—was he lovable, hateful, admirable, despicable, pitiable, and so on?—is one with which serious criticism has no concern, though our society's cult of the individual makes it a recurring danger.

What has happened in the past twenty years is not, of course, a mere shift in the critical consensus on a single director: the entire perspective and objective of film criticism have been transformed. The introduction of semiotics and structuralism, the politicization of film theory during the late sixties and seventies, the new emphasis on concepts of ideology, the vital and radical input of feminist theory, the growing importance of psychoanalytic theory (especially as a political weapon)—all these interrelated phenomena have ensured that we can no longer look at the films as we used to, as "works of art" on "universal" human themes. As our culture moves into increasingly fundamental schisms and increasingly polarized confrontations, other, more pressing issues supervene, and *must* do so if the practice of criticism is not to be doomed to triviality: especially, the question of the films' place in culture—their relationship to the "dominant ideology" of patriarchal bourgeois capitalism on the one hand and, on the other, to the progressive and radical movements that seek its overthrow. Instead of "Why should we take Hitchcock seriously?" the opening question of my book, were I writing it today, would be the central question that haunts contemporary Hitchcock criticism in article after article: "Can Hitchcock be saved for feminism?"

At the center of the recent advances in Hitchcock criticism is unquestionably the work of French critic Raymond Bellour, responsible for the development, in North America as well as Europe, of a veritable "Bellour school." (See, among dozens of examples, Deborah Linderman on *Blackmail* and Michael Renov on *Notorious* as well as Bill Nichols on *The Birds*.) It is extremely frustrating that Bellour's work remains, for most of us, so inaccessible, scattered among various periodicals, some of it available in English only in mimeographed seminar papers distributed within obviously limited circles. Now that his essays—in the original French—have been gathered together into a book (*L'Analyse du film*), one hopes that it will be published in translation as soon as possible.

I cannot, in the space available, do even rough justice to Bellour's work for those readers unfamiliar with it (the best introduction is the interview by Janet Bergstrom in *Camera Obscura* [no. 3-4], which also contains Bellour's essay on *Psycho*). When my own book appeared in 1965, it was praised for its "close reading" of the films. Bellour's work, at the very least, makes such a conception of "close reading" obsolete. His shot-by-shot analyses, his meticulous examination of the functioning of the cinematic codes operative within a given segment, his ability to relate minute specifics to the operation of the film as a whole (and, beyond that, to the operations of the "Hollywood machine")—all this has me lost in admiration.

Which does not prevent doubts from setting in. I am worried by a sense that the overall tendency of Bellour and the "Bellour school" is ultimately reductive. (The same kind of objection applies to Peter Wollen's famous Proppian analysis of *North by Northwest* in *Readings and Writings:* see Seymour

Chatman's review of Wollen's book in *American Film,* vol. 8, no. 9.) For me, the most important and profitable development in film criticism in the last twenty years has been the concept of "ideological contradiction." The tendency of Bellourian criticism has been to iron out contradiction in favor of demonstrating the workings of "classical narrative," the "classical realist text," the "classical Hollywood film": always the same narrative, always the same film.

At a particularly alarming moment during a film conference in Australia in December 1982, Bellour informed us that there is no essential difference between *Bringing Up Baby* and *North by Northwest.* After all, both end with the hero rescuing the heroine by pulling her up by her arm. The implication seemed to be that there is also no *essential* difference between these and other Hollywood films: they are all "machines for producing the couple" (a formula I find at once marvelously suggestive and profoundly unsatisfying). What semiological criticism crucially, and in some respects disablingly, lacks is a concept of "tone," a factor that may in many cases directly undermine and contradict the conventions of narrative movement. *Rear Window* and *Vertigo* can both, I suppose, be read as "machines for producing the couple" (*Vertigo,* as it were, by default, since the failure of the specific couple confirms the couple's general ideological desirability). That is not at all how *I* see the films, and the readings I shall offer are completely at odds with it.

The charge of misogyny constantly recurs, and at all levels of critical writing: from personal gossip (Hitchcock treated his female stars—or some of them—callously) to the most meticulously detailed analyses of the filmic texts (for example, Nichols on *The Birds*). I certainly do not intend to claim that there exists in Hitchcock's work an uncontaminated feminist discourse, a view of women that feminism could unproblematically appropriate; nor shall I deny that there erupts periodically in his work an animus against women and, specifically, against the female body. This can be seen at its grossest in *Frenzy* (the rape and murder of Barbara Leigh-Hunt and the notorious potato-sack scene— the latter the more disturbing in that Hitchcock clearly supposed it to be funny). Yet, even there, it is profoundly troubled by contradiction (the two women in question are, after all, by far the most sympathetic characters in the film), and it is precisely this sense of disturbance within the films that opens them up to a feminist analysis. The contradictions have the effect of calling into question, and in some cases disrupting beyond all possible recuperation, the male drives and fantasies that provide the films' initial impulse. At their best, the films dramatize and foreground not merely tensions personal to Hitchcock, but tensions central to our culture and to its construction and organization of sexual difference.

My prime concern here is a rethinking of *Vertigo.* Rereading the original attempt to interpret the film in my book, I find many of the perceptions valid but am greatly dissatisfied with their formulation. That particular chapter, especially, is shot through with a subtle and insidious sexism (at that time I had no awareness whatever of the oppression of women within our culture), and, closely related to this, it strikingly lacks any psychoanalytic account of the nature of "romantic love," accepting it as some eternal and unchangeable given of "the human condition." I want, however, to preface this with a few sketchy remarks about *Rear Window*, "notes toward a reading" that, complete, would require at least an entire issue of *American Film*. I shall consider two interconnected themes of the film that now appear crucial to an understanding of it.

Castration. In *Rear Window* a photographer, wheelchair-bound with a broken leg, whiles away the hours spying on his neighbors with a telephoto lens — until he discovers a murder and becomes determined to catch the murderer. Most critical accounts have centered on its status as "artistic testament." It is a film about the experience of film viewing, with Jefferies (James Stewart) as the spectator, the apartments he watches as the screen. This reading is certainly supported by much of the film's detail and, more generally, by its central tension: the events in the apartments reflect the spectator's fantasies, yet the spectator has no control over them, so that dream can turn to nightmare at any moment. However, such an account requires careful definition. First, it seems quite misguided to see the film as an allegory about "the cinema." Insofar as this works, the film is an allegory about *Hitchcock's* cinema, which is highly idiosyncratic. Second, the spectatorship inscribed in the film is by no means neutral: it is unambiguously male. Far more important, it seems to me, than the "artistic testament" dimension of the film is its dramatization of fundamental male sexual anxieties. Clearly, those anxieties are rooted in the fear of castration, and, equally clearly (from a psychoanalytic viewpoint), castration is represented by Jefferies's broken leg.

The term "castration" has caused certain problems and confusions. Is it meant literally or symbolically? The confusions disappear if one recognizes it as both. Within patriarchal culture, the phallus is the supreme symbol of power; conversely, power is "phallic." Loss of power on any level (money, prestige, social status, authority over women, domination of children, and so forth) is therefore symbolic castration. At the same time, this is seen as reactivating the *literal* castration fears of childhood. Language acknowledges such a connection quite clearly: the word "impotence" (often used to mean "powerlessness") invariably carries sexual overtones.

Castration, then, at the beginning of *Rear Window*, is signified not only by the broken leg but also by the smashed camera. Jefferies's potency as a male expresses itself as much in his role as a free-lance photographer as in anything directly sexual, his recklessness and initiative taken as the guarantee of "masculinity." It is the fear of castration and the drive to reaffirm "potency" that the male spectator is invited to identify with. As the film develops, Jefferies attempts to assert his "possession of the phallus" through the power of "the look," a substitute for both the smashed camera and the broken leg (the latter explicitly associated with the deprivation of sexual activity). Hence the significance (and the comedy) of the *growth* of the look as the film progresses: first the eyes, then binoculars, finally a huge erect telescope. But Jefferies's pursuit of power through the look only confirms, repeatedly, his impotence, a point brought home to him (and to us) in the two major climactic scenes: Lisa's search of Thorwald's apartment and the culminating Jefferies-Thorwald confrontation, where the "potency" of Jefferies's flashbulbs proves insufficient to save him.

Marriage. Rear Window is crucially about marriage, and its radicalism lies in the connection it makes between that and the castration theme. Marriage is seen as the castration of the male. Stated like that, the film appears brazenly misogynist, and in many ways it is capable of sustaining such a reading. But only if one ignores other elements. What it is really about is the impossibility of successful human relations within an ideological system that constructs men and women in hopelessly incompatible roles: it relates quite fascinatingly to the "wandering versus settling" antinomy that Peter Wollen sees as central to John Ford and to the Western. At its center are Jefferies, the ideal American male (the "wanderer-adventurer," even if at second hand: he photographs the adventures of others), and Lisa, the ideal American female (settled, eminently civilized, constantly pressuring Jefferies to "settle down" with her, the perfected "object for the gaze"). They are macabrely reflected in the Thorwalds (the wanderer-adventurer reduced to traveling salesman, his wife "settled" to the extreme of being bedridden). All the other apartment dwellers relate to this theme (with marvelous precision and economy—there is neither redundancy nor irrelevance). They variously embody the twin hells of marriage and singleness, in a civilization that demands the former while rendering its success impossible. What the emphasis on castration and impotence ultimately achieves is the calling into question of our culture's concept of "potency" (masculinity), with the insupportable demands it makes on men and women alike.

With *Vertigo,* I want to examine the first four sequences (culminating in the introduction of Madeleine) in some detail as the basis for a psychoanalytic (and political) reading of the film that I shall subsequently develop. In *Vertigo,* James Stewart plays a detective who falls in love with the object of his surveillance, Madeleine, who eventually commits suicide, or so it appears. Stewart meets Judy, who resembles the dead woman (Kim Novak in both roles), tries to remake her in the suicide's image, and eventually discovers that Judy, in fact, *was* the woman he loved, a part she was playing in a greedy husband's plot to murder his wife.

The opening sequence (the chase, the fall) is among the most succinct and abstract Hitchcock gave us; it is also characteristically fragmented in editing, requiring twenty-five shots. The abstractness is established in the first image: a metal bar against an out-of-focus background that a hand suddenly clutches. Then the camera pulls back, the background becomes a San Francisco city-scape, and three men clamber over the top rung in a rooftop pursuit. We are given only the most minimal narrative information. The second man is a policeman, so the first must be a criminal; the third is Scottie (James Stewart), clearly the male protagonist. He is connected to the cop by being a pursuer, but connected to the criminal by being in plain clothes (nothing tells us at this point that he is a police detective; he might be a reporter or merely a conscientious citizen). The first three shots strongly emphasize the three-character structure: (1) Each man in turn climbs over the bar. (2) An extreme long shot contains all three men within the frame simultaneously. (3) Each man in turn leaps to another roof (Hitchcock cuts before we see Stewart fall and clutch the gutter, an action given us in shots 4 and 5).

At this point begins an alternating pattern — a favorite structural method of the mature Hitchcock, the first of many in the film — that continues almost uninterrupted to the end of the sequence: a series of nine shots, all medium close-up, taken from an identical camera position, of Scottie hanging (nos. 6, 8, 10, 12, 14, 16; then 21, 23, 25); an alternating series, slightly less consistent, of six shots showing Stewart's point of view (nos. 9, 13, 15, 17; then 22, 24; though 15 — the uniformed policeman reaching down — is ambiguous, the position of the camera being inexact). This second series includes, of course, the famous "vertigo" shot (no. 9) with the simultaneous track-out/zoom-in, an effect repeated later in the two tower sequences, at the middle and end of the film. The interruption of the alternating pattern, on which the sequence pivots, gives us the policeman's attempt to save Scottie (with the scene's only dialogue — "Give me your hand") and the start of the policeman's fall (nos. 18, 19, 20), at which point the alternation, thrown temporarily out of rhythm, is resumed.

The sequence represents perhaps the most extreme and abrupt instance of enforced audience identification in all of Hitchcock — an effect to which the technical means (point of view, alternation, vertigo shot, even the jarring rhythmic lurch at the policeman's fall) all contribute. Usually, however, he is far more circumspect, building identification gradually through a complicated process of curiosity, sympathy, emotional involvement (see, for instance, the opening of *Psycho,* where the first clear-cut point-of-view shot — the street crossing seen through Marion's windshield — does not occur until about fifteen minutes into the film). What makes possible this drastic and brutal assault on the spectator? Most obviously, the extreme physical danger, which is the simplest and most basic of the conditions that encourage spectator identification.

It is the most obvious factor but perhaps not the most important. The sequence carries very strong and potent psychoanalytic resonances with as much claim to "universality" as the fear of heights. One such resonance arises from "the fall" itself. One common explanation of dreams of falling (and the sequence's abstraction makes it very dreamlike) is that they reproduce, or at least *refer to,* the birth trauma (from which viewpoint it is interesting that we never see Scottie "let go"). Another, more substantiated by the text, arises from the insistence on *three* characters and their interconnection. They can be taken to represent the fundamental Freudian triumvirate id-ego-superego. The id is associated with unrestrained libido, pursuit of pleasure, which is—in our surplus-repressive culture—commonly associated with criminality. The superego is conscience, the law, the internalized authority of the father—our psychic police officer in fact. The ego is the self, within which the struggle for dominance between the id and the superego is played out. At the opening of *Vertigo,* then, the symbolic father is killed and the "son," if not the actual agent of his death, is responsible for it. The id escapes to wander freely in the darkness, reflected—at the end of the film—in the fact that the murderer, Gavin Elster, is never caught. Scottie is left hanging (we never see, or are told, how he gets down). Metaphorically, he is suspended for the remainder of the film.

The second sequence (in the apartment of Midge, Scottie's ex-fiancée) offers an even more extreme example of the Hitchcockian principles of fragmentation and alternation: more extreme, because the "action"—mainly an extended conversation—could easily have been filmed in a single take, with the exception of a single "subjective insert." Hitchcock breaks it down into sixty-two shots, only five of which contain the two characters in the frame together. The entire scene is constructed in alternating series broken only at certain privileged moments—Midge/Scottie; female space/male space, each defined by the framing and by its own significant object (Scottie's cane, the model brassiere being sketched by Midge, a commercial artist) prominent throughout each series.

Apart from the opening establishing shot (whose function, although both characters are in frame, is to stress the distance that separates them), Midge and Scottie are shown together at three points in the action:

1. Shot 31 (the exact midpoint and pivot shot of the scene, privileged as its only long take): It includes the conversation about the new brassiere with its "revolutionary uplift." Midge remarks to Scottie, "You know about such things—you're a big boy now," as she initiates him into its secrets.

2. Shots 47 and 48: Scottie suggests a method of overcoming his acrophobia, and Midge promptly takes over as organizer, fetching the stepladder. In the ensuing shots (in which the alternation is resumed), she will "push" Scottie—verbally—to the point where he collapses with an attack of vertigo.

3. Shot 62 (the final shot of the sequence): Midge comforts the distraught Scottie in her arms, holding his head to her bosom.

All of these moments have a common theme: the presentation of Midge as mother figure, as made explicit in the dialogue—"Don't be so motherly" (later, in the scene in the nursing home, Midge will say, "Mother's here"). The two come together only in the mother-child relationship; otherwise (and crucially in their discussion of their brief engagement and the possibility that it might be renewed) they are kept rigorously separated.

Of the two, only Midge is permitted close-ups (shots 36 and 38), and they are used to comment on Scottie, to call him into question. They occur during the discussion of the engagement ("Good old college days" — Midge), which lasted "three whole weeks" and was called off by Midge herself (despite the fact that "you know there's only one man in the world for me"). The close-ups emphasize the troubled and enigmatic nature of her glances at Scottie; they suggest an inadequacy in him — an impossibility of a mature relationship — whose nature is left unformulated.

Other components of *Vertigo*'s thematic are introduced during the scene, centered on certain key words or concepts: "free," "available," "wander." Scottie is about to become "free" of the corset he has worn since his fall (if it is valid to relate the fall to birth trauma, the corset logically becomes swaddling clothes). The word "freedom" will recur throughout the film, connected to the word "power" and consistently associated with male prerogative, the freedom and power of domination. Gavin Elster, in the next sequence, refers nostalgically to the "power" and "freedom" of the old San Francisco. The bookstore owner, describing the casting aside of Carlotta Valdes, the historical figure whose portrait fascinates Madeleine, remarks, "Men could do that in those days — they had the freedom, they had the power." And Scottie, unmasking Judy/Madeleine at the end of the film, asks her contemptuously if, "with all that freedom and all that power," Elster just "ditched" her.

"Freedom," then, is freedom to dominate women or to throw them over — even murder them — when they become inconvenient. It is associated with the past, when "men could do that" — the past to which Madeleine belongs and Midge emphatically does not. Scottie is still "available" for marriage ("That's me — Available Ferguson"); but the film, in a brilliant ellipse, instantly connects this sexual "availability" to Gavin Elster (as the old adage has it, "The devil finds work for idle hands"). Inherent in Scottie's situation is the notion of "wandering" — though the word itself will not occur until the next scene. With the "father" dead and the "id" at large, Scottie's immediate step has been to leave the police force (the "law"); Midge asks what he intends to do now. He will "do nothing for a while." He is free to follow desire wherever it leads, to wander.

The freedom, the availability, the wandering, however, also associate logically with the metaphoric suspension, with the abyss into which Scottie may fall, vividly evoked in what is, remarkably, the sequence's only point-of-view shot, Scottie's hallucinatory vision from the top of Midge's stepladder. Also relevant here is the question of identity: the fluidity, the lack of definition suggested by the range of names Stewart's character accumulates in the course of the film. He will tell Madeleine, "Acquaintances call me Scottie, friends call me John"; he presents himself as "Available Ferguson"; Elster calls him "Scottie"; Midge uses the boylike "Johnny-O" (at one point "John-O"); Madeleine says, "I prefer John," but Judy calls him "Scottie."

The third sequence (divided from the second by Hitchcock's personal appearance and two dissolves, as if to mark it as a decisive new beginning) is also built on alternation patterns, but the series are interrupted much more frequently by two-shots. The main purpose of these is to underline — with the additional emphasis of a low angle — Elster's growing domination of Scottie as he imposes his story on him. Scottie sits, Elster stands; when Scottie rises, Elster moves to the room's higher level, dominating even in long-shot. Though Elster was Scottie's schoolmate, we register Elster as significantly older (partly because we habitually think of James Stewart as young, even in middle age, "boyishness" being one of the basic components of his star persona). Elster becomes, in fact, a new father figure, but a father "outside the law" (the dialogue stresses Scottie's withdrawal from the police force). In terms of the traces of Catholic mythology that linger on in Hitchcock's work, Elster is the devil, his function being essentially that of tempter. He knows Scottie's weaknesses, and in effect offers him his own "wife," Madeleine (the film never invites us to take any interest in his plot to murder his *real* wife).

Madeleine's fascination for Scottie is set up before she appears. Elster presents her as a feminine mirror image. She "wanders" (from this point on the word will weave through the film, repeatedly linking Scottie and Madeleine), and there is also the question of *her* identity (Madeleine Elster, Carlotta Valdes? — though the latter name itself is not introduced until later). Above all, Elster tempts Scottie with "power" and "freedom," marked by a striking cut on dialogue: (1) Back view, Scottie looks at the print of old San Francisco; Elster speaks of "color, excitement, power. . . ." (2) Cut to medium shot of Elster against a window through which we can see the cranes of his shipyard; he completes the sentence: ". . . freedom." The image associates the term with wealth, industry, and the possibility of escape (abroad or into the past), after which the conversation shifts to Scottie's task, the surveillance of Madeleine.

The fourth sequence, at Ernie's restaurant, offers us (and Scottie) Madeleine. Indeed, it is important that she appears to *offer herself*, at least to the gaze. The fascination is conveyed in the sequence's first shot. Starting from Scottie at the bar, and as if taking its impetus from his look, the camera draws back over the restaurant, turns, cranes, then moves slowly in toward Madeleine's back, her shoulders exposed above an emerald-green stole, the green with which, both as Madeleine and as Judy, she will be associated throughout the film and which links her ironically to the *sequoia sempervirens*, "always green, ever living." It is not — cannot possibly be — a point-of-view shot, yet it has the effect of linking us intimately to the movement of Scottie's consciousness. The camera movement is utterly unlike anything in the film up to that point, introducing a completely new tone, the grace and tenderness underlined by Bernard Herrmann's music. Madeleine is presented in terms of the "work of art," which is precisely what she is. Her movement through the doorway suggests a portrait coming to life, or a gliding statue; when she pauses and turns her head into profile, the suggestion is of a cameo or silhouette, an image that will recur throughout the film. As work of art Madeleine is at once totally accessible (a painting is completely passive, offering itself to the gaze) and totally *in*accessible (you can't make love to a picture).

At this point it becomes possible to draw all the threads together; but to do so it is necessary to digress again briefly into psychoanalytic theory, to consider the nature of desire and how it is constituted within patriarchal culture. The first love object, prototype of all subsequent love objects, is the mother's breast, to which the infant traditionally is put immediately after birth. The infant is born totally under the sway of the pleasure principle (which Freud associates with the id): she or he has no sense of "otherness," no sense of the mother as an autonomous person; the expectation is of instant, total, always available gratification. This innate "original desire" (I mean the term at once to evoke and oppose the familiar Catholic interpretation of Hitchcock in relation to "original sin") immediately comes into conflict with the reality principle and has to learn to modify itself to accommodate the facts of existence, but it remains the basis on which adult desire is built. It is also, of course, what adult desire must *transcend* if any equality in relationships is to be achieved, though adult desire will still be ultimately dependent on original desire for its energy.

It is essential to the logic of patriarchy that original desire be repressed in women (it would promote bisexuality and sexual activeness, what Freud termed the woman's "masculinity") and encouraged in men. The heterosexual male—our ideological lord of the universe—is taught from infancy to believe in his superiority, his inherited rights, essentially, to "power and freedom." The possibility of regression to the infantile state, the unconditional demand for the "lost breast," is therefore much stronger in men than in women. The most obvious manifestation of this regression is the phenomenon called "romantic love," with its demand for perfect union and its tendency to construct the loved person as an idealized fantasy figure, the necessary condition for "perfect union" being the denial of otherness and autonomy. It is this regression that *Vertigo* so incomparably dramatizes. I know of no other film that so ruthlessly analyzes the basis of male desire and exposes its mechanisms.

Around this, everything falls into place: the reactivation of the birth trauma actually accompanied by the death of the father, the urge for freedom and wandering, the rejection of Midge, the appearance of Gavin Elster as tempter, the gift of Madeleine. One may ask why Midge, who so clearly offers herself as a mother, is impossible for Scottie; there are a number of answers. For one thing, she is too *explicitly* the mother. As such, she is a reminder to Scottie of his dependence. More important, the lost breast is not to be identified with an actual mother. On the contrary, the crucial characteristic of the object of original desire is that it be capable of being totally dominated, with no autonomous existence or desire of its own. As mother, Midge is dominating and active, a defined ego, with her own drives and demands, the chief of which is that Scottie learn to grow up. What she wants is a relationship of equals. Further, she demystifies sexuality (specifically in relation to the breast, explaining the mechanics of the brassiere), and for the romantic lover, sex must always remain mystified. She is finally disqualified by her accessibility.

It is obvious that original desire can never be fulfilled. The lost breast cannot be refound, because it never existed. The fantasy of fulfillment depends, paradoxically, on the inaccessibility of the object. Madeleine dies (both times) at the moments when she threatens to become a real person. It will be clear that, as a construct, a work of art, she perfectly satisfies every condition for the lover's fantasy. When she dies, she has to be re-created; when she is Judy, Scottie can't bear to touch her. One of the cinema's most perverse (and most "romantic") love scenes—so perverse it couldn't possibly be filmed—is the scene implied after Scottie brings Madeleine back from her plunge into San Francisco Bay: that he undresses the woman he loves, believing her to be unconscious, while in reality she is *pretending* to be unconscious. It is the nearest the romantic lover can come to physical union without sacrificing something of his fantasy. Judy's unforgivable crime is not accessory to murder or even duplicity; it is that she isn't *really* Madeleine.

Madeleine's ultimate fascination lies in her association with death (as Carlotta she is already dead). As original desire can never be fulfilled in life, to surrender to it is to give oneself over to the death drive: hence the Romantic obsession with unions in death, of which Wagner's *Tristan und Isolde* is the supreme expression in Western culture (the "Liebestod" is repeatedly evoked, though never actually quoted, in Bernard Herrmann's score).

Whatever the conscious motivation, the importance of Hitchcock's decision to divulge the solution of the mystery two-thirds of the way through the film cannot be underestimated. Until that point the spectator is locked almost exclusively into Scottie's consciousness (the only exceptions are three brief moments involving Midge, which hint at the possibility of critical distance but are not strong enough to offset the dominant identification pattern): the fascination Scottie feels for Madeleine is also his. (I use the masculine deliberately— the spectator constructed by the film is clearly male.) The shock we experience at the revelation goes far beyond anything that can be accounted for merely in terms of premature disclosure, testifying to the power and "universality" within our culture of the desire drive the film dramatizes. *We* also, at first, can't forgive Judy for not being Madeleine, in whose reality we have been seduced into investing so much.

The revelation immediately exposes the entire "romantic love" project of the first two-thirds of the film as a fantasy and a fraud; thus it turns us back, quite ruthlessly, onto Scottie and ourselves. It also gives us access to Judy, who is not a work of art but a human being, thus exposing the monstrousness of a project built on the infantile demands of the regressed male ego and its denial

of woman's human reality. Judy never becomes the film's central consciousness. She is permitted only six point-of-view shots during the entire film (as
against the number given to Scottie, which must run into three figures). Four
of these (two pairs, precisely symmetrical) are simply shots of trees through the
car windshield during the two drives to San Juan Bautista. A fifth is ambiguous: the shot of the broken petals on the water just before Madeleine's false
attempted suicide, a shot enclosed within an elaborate structure of Scottie's
point of view and equally readable as *his* empathic image of what Madeleine
sees. Only one shot from Judy's point of view actually excludes Scottie and
comments on him: the shot of lovers on the grass as they walk by the lake and
the Portals of the Past (it stands out the more for being an example of that
privileged Hitchcock fingerprint the subjective forward tracking shot).

Scottie's remains the central consciousness; what changes is our relationship to him. Identification is not so much annihilated as severely disturbed,
made problematic. We now know far more than he does, and what we know
reflects critically on him, on our own prior identification with him, and on the
whole concept of romantic love on which our culture has placed such high
ideological value. Throughout the scenes with Judy as Judy, the film's dominant system of alternating series based on Scottie's point of view partly breaks
down. Point-of-view shots are not absent (Judy seen in the upper window of
the Empire Hotel—as Madeleine was in the McKittrick Hotel—and, notably,
the "cameo" shot of Judy in silhouette-profile when Scottie brings her home
from Ernie's after their first date), but their number greatly decreases, to be
built up again strongly as Scottie reconstructs Judy as Madeleine. That the
film's efforts to reinvolve us in Scottie's consciousness and the project of reconstructing what we know to be a fantasy are *partly* successful testifies again to
the immense power of original desire and its derivative—romantic love—
within our culture. (Like the film, I am assuming that the spectator is male;
one looks forward eagerly, now that *Vertigo* is once again accessible, to articles
on it by women.)

It takes the final agonizing scenes—and Madeleine's second death—to
exorcise this decisively, but, of course, the total and unquestioning identification invited by the first part of the film is no longer possible. We are too aware
at that point that the fantasy *is* fantasy, and too aware of it as imposition on the
woman. The last third of *Vertigo* is among the most disturbing and painful
experiences the cinema has to offer.

VERTIGO (Paramount, 1958). *Producers:* Alfred Hitchcock, Herbert Coleman, *Assistant Director:*
Daniel McCauley, *Script:* Alec Coppel, Samuel Tayler, from the novel *D'entre les morts* by Pierre
Boileau and Thomas Narcejac, *Photography:* Robert Burks (VistaVision, Technicolor), *Editor:*
George Tomasini, *Sets:* Hal Pereira, Henry Bumstead, Sam Comer, Frank McKelvey, *Music:*
Bernard Herrmann, *Costumes:* Edith Head, *Titles:* Saul Bass, *Nightmare Sequence:* John Ferren,
Players: James Stewart (John "Scottie" Ferguson), Kim Novak (Madeleine Elster/Judy Barton),
Barbara Bel Geddes (Midge Wood), Tom Helmore (Gavin Elster). 128 minutes.

CHAPTER EIGHTEEN

A Closer Look at Scopophilia:
Mulvey, Hitchcock, and *Vertigo*
Marian E. Keane

I.

During the past fifteen years, feminist criticism has secured a place of central importance not only within film criticism but within the arena of critical thinking generally. Among the achievements of feminist criticism has been its dedication to employing psychoanalysis and political philosophy in the work of uncovering the meanings of films as they bear directly on and illuminate a cultural consciousness of women. The last decade in particular has seen feminist film critics calling for a revolution, for radical breaks with the established film criticism as well as with the conventional narrative structures of film, which they view as participating in strategies of domination and repression of women.

One of the issues in feminist film criticism has involved the erotic nature of viewing human beings, specifically women, on film. In "Visual Pleasure and Narrative Cinema," Laura Mulvey takes as her "starting point the way film reflects, reveals and even plays on the straight, socially established interpretation of sexual difference that controls images, erotic ways of looking and spectacle."[1] She asserts that "mainstream film encoded the erotic into the language of the dominant patriarchal order" and supports this assertion with a psychoanalytic interpretation of film's presentation of (viewed) human beings to viewers. Formally, Mulvey claims, film relies on a division or "split" between looking, which she calls the active role, and being looked at, which she claims is its passive opposite. On a narrative level, one of the ways in which this division is reproduced is by shots representing the view of one figure by another. In Hollywood films, she maintains, women occupy the passive position of being looked at, whereas men possess the active power of looking.

What draws me to address recent feminist criticism, and Mulvey's essay in particular, is certainly not an argument about the importance and the necessity of feminist criticism. The roles women play in films and the ways films understand and present women are of central importance. I share the aspirations of recent feminist criticism, but I am in disagreement with much of it.

In the case of Mulvey's essay, my disagreement rests with her understanding of the films she calls upon as evidence. It also rests with her reading of texts by Freud that she understands as providing a basis for her psychoanalytic critique of Hollywood films. Finally, and perhaps most importantly, I find inadequate Mulvey's concept of the camera, its powers, and the nature of its gaze. A corollary or consequence of this inadequacy is my dissatisfaction with her understanding of the nature of (human) photogenesis or, as Stanley Cavell has characterized this subject, of what becomes of human beings on film.[2] I understand the problems in Mulvey's critical approach to represent a willingness to repress, or at least an unwillingness to take seriously, the meanings of films that enter or are entered into discussions about the history and the nature of the medium of film. That Mulvey's views have impressed themselves on so many film critics and theoreticians surely means that something is right about them. Film can be used as she says; some films do work in these ways. But it is not the nature of the medium to require this. In particular, it is not true of the films I admire most, for example, *Vertigo,* from which I take and direct my commitments to film.

My dissatisfaction with Mulvey's assertions can begin to be set out in relation to her remarks on Hitchcock's *Vertigo,* her understanding of which is presented in a number of remarks summarizing the film's events and meanings. A problematic consequence of this method is that the film's specific framings, lines of dialogue, and authorship are neglected and lost.

Mulvey finds *Vertigo* "far from simply an aside on the perversion of the police," because the film takes as its subject "the active/looking, passive/looked at split in terms of sexual difference and the power of the male . . . encapsulated in the hero" (p. 16). Stating that the story is told primarily in terms of "subjective camera," from the point of view of the ex-detective played by James Stewart, she claims that Hitchcock and the camera are unequivocally allied with him throughout the film. She asserts that *Vertigo* goes a step further than most Hollywood films because it turns the "processes" the viewer employs back on himself and thereby demonstrates *how* visual and narrative pleasure are purchased at a woman's expense, but in the final analysis *Vertigo* is still a film in which the man's "curiosity wins through" and the woman "is punished" (p. 16).

In *The World Viewed,* Stanley Cavell observes that "the screen performer is essentially not an actor at all: he *is* the subject of a study, and a study not his own."[3] Since our thoughts in this essay are attuned to qualities of activity and passivity, it would be difficult to overlook Cavell's characterization or definition of all screen performers as more passive than active in relation to the camera and the film's director. Cavell's understanding of the (ontological) passivity of the camera's (human) subjects challenges Mulvey's general assertion that "the image of woman [is the] (passive) raw material for the (active) gaze of man" (p. 17).

Cavell complicates his analytical remark on film acting by inflecting it with a parenthetical remark that qualifies our understanding of the nature of human beings' "passivity" on film. "That is what the content of a photograph is," he declares, "—its subject" (p. 28). Cavell's claim that the content or meaning of a film is absorbed in the camera's attentive recording and the director's thoughtful understanding of the identities, physiognomies, emotions, mannerisms, and thoughtfulnesses of their human subjects is radical. Acknowledging film's photographic basis, Cavell calls upon us to acknowledge that film presents us with projections, hence displaced views, of real human beings who are simultaneously active and passive. Human figures on film reveal or display themselves, participating in the fixing of their presences on film. They are also revealed by the camera's (penetrating) gaze and the director's understanding of the significances inherent to specific human beings' presences on film.

This thesis underlies one of Cavell's central meditations in *Pursuits of Happiness*, where he reflects on the photogeneses of the stars who appear in the remarriage comedies he discusses. These sustained reflections offer concrete evidence for his claim that "the photographic power of the camera [gives] a natural ascendancy to the flesh and blood actor over the character he or she plays on film." The camera's power to displace character and meditate the flesh and blood performer underwrites a profound distinction between the mediums of film and theater, Cavell argues, because it "reverses the relation between actor and character in theater."[4]

For reasons indebted to Cavell's understanding of photogenesis, I will refer to James Stewart and Kim Novak by name in this essay. Insisting upon their flesh and blood identities (or on the flesh and bloodness of a man known as James Stewart and a woman known as Kim Novak) registers the fact of the camera's assertion of the flesh and blood performer over his or her character in a film. It asserts that *Vertigo* is a study of the significances of its leading figures' identities, that who Hitchcock and the camera reveal them to be and what they individually project on film lie at the heart of *Vertigo*'s meaning. Calling them by name is a way of making the claim that their presences on film are subjects for criticism in all of the ways their presences on film are subjects for the film itself.

Chief among the features of Stewart's photogenesis is his capacity for suffering, the most important quality of Stewart's presence on film that Mulvey can be said to ignore in her summary analysis of *Vertigo*. In a series of reflections on Stewart's photogenesis, Stanley Cavell suggests that he "projects a willingness for suffering" and declares further that this quality of Stewart's photogenesis "is [what] would admit him to the company of women [for example, Charlotte Vale/Bette Davis in *Now, Voyager*] whose search for their identities seems to have traced the contours of the subject of film [that I would characterize as] . . . the identifying or the inhabitation of a feminine region of the self, whether the person whose self it is be male or female."[5] Cavell's placement of Stewart in "the company of women" directly challenges Mulvey's view of Stewart/Scottie as an exemplar of active male power. Mulvey's view privileges selected features of Stewart/Scottie's identity as a character and reveals that she views him as an actor playing a role (as though *Vertigo* were a play) rather than as the camera's subject. In its denial of the camera's photogenic power and the film performer's precedence over his role, Mulvey's view of Scottie constitutes a profound denial of the medium of film and of the conditions of film acting.

II.

Mulvey's denial of Hitchcock and the meaning of the camera throughout *Vertigo* partly gives rise to, and is partly a consequence of, her view that the film (i.e., Stewart/Scottie and Hitchcock) subjects the Novak figure to punishment, a punishment partly derived from being looked at, "follow[ed], watch[ed], and fall[en] in love with" (p. 16) by Stewart/Scottie. But Mulvey seems to me to neglect, even to punish, the Novak figure in ways that are similar to, and can be revealed by studying, the Stewart figure's relation to Novak/Judy within the film. Mulvey's blindness to the woman and her central role in the film necessarily entails blindness to Hitchcock as well. In my view, the deepest criticism of Mulvey's reading of *Vertigo* emerges from *Vertigo* itself, from the woman in the film and the film's author.

Mulvey claims that "apart from one flashback from Judy's point of view, the narrative is woven around what Scottie sees and fails to see" (p. 16). But the "one flashback from Judy's point of view" that Mulvey glosses over, as though it were without importance, constitutes nothing less than the decisive turning point in *Vertigo*. Mulvey's unwillingness or failure to understand this crucial juncture and its significance is a critical error with serious implications.

The flashback sequence is inaugurated by a striking turn of Novak's head toward the camera that culminates in her look into the camera.[6] Her look into the camera registers what she knows, and the flashback that follows represents but a piece of that knowledge. She knows not only all that actually took place on the bell tower but that Stewart/Scottie is right to believe he has found Madeleine Elster again. When she looks into Hitchcock's camera, she is acknowledging her identity as Madeleine, and we cannot assume that we yet know all that this acknowledgment means.

Novak/Judy's look into the camera also declares her awareness of the camera's presence; her look acknowledges Hitchcock and us. During the first part of this scene, when she and Scottie converse in her hotel room, her head is conspicuously turned away from the camera, a precise choreography characteristic of Hitchcock's direction. Novak/Judy turns to face the camera on the heels of Scottie's departure, revealing that she knows she is not alone. The sustained look she gives the camera initiates the camera's possession of her story, represented by the flashback, and establishes a deep bond between her and the camera that is not broken for the remainder of the film. (I am, of course, aware that any specification of what the events—such as a camera movement or placement or a human being's look—in a film "declare" is controversial. Such specifications are acts of criticism, and my own readings of *Vertigo*'s events and declarations are open to further acts of criticism. It is my point that Mulvey's specifications preempt such acts of criticism in favor of a theory of film that does not allow criticism to test it. In this sense, it is unempirical.)

When Novak/Judy looks into the camera, her look is fearful. But what is she afraid of? William Rothman argues in *Hitchcock—The Murderous Gaze* that the handful of beings, such as Uncle Charles, Diana Baring, Norman Bates, and, we should add, Judy Barton, allowed the privilege of gazing directly into Hitchcock's camera, all share a singular and profound consciousness of their fates. Their mysteries are the mysteries of Hitchcock's camera. We cannot say all that Novak/Judy is afraid of at this moment. Her fears can only be understood fully when we look at the final moments of the film, when they materialize mysteriously in the shadows of the bell tower. We should expect, however, that what she views there will be, in part, a figure for Hitchcock's camera, an embodiment of its gaze.

After the flashback, we return to Novak/Judy in her room and view her alone, a scene to which Scottie is not privy. She starts to pack but breaks off to write Scottie a letter. Wishing to free him of his guilt and his memory of Madeleine, her letter tells him about Elster's plan to murder Madeleine, that Elster chose him specifically because of his acrophobia, and that the Carlotta Valdes story was part fiction, part truth. "Everything went as planned," she writes, "except I fell in love with you. That wasn't part of the plan." She loves him still, she continues, and if she had the courage she would remain, she would lie about the past and start over again with him. When she tears up the letter, rises, and begins to unpack her bags, her resolve is clear. She has found that courage to start again, to step out of what in *Psycho* is called "a private trap." The remainder of the film is a study of her love for Stewart/Scottie and of his attachment to her.

At no point in *Vertigo* does Stewart/Scottie possess a knowledge of the camera commensurate with Novak/Judy's. In Rothman's terms, we can say that Novak/Judy exhibits *hubris* when she decides to step out of her private trap and to deny the past. But Stewart/Scottie's *hubris* is both graver and more complete. His obsessive re-creation of Madeleine is only one level of his *hubris*. It is equal *hubris* in the world of a Hitchcock film for him to deny his own participation in his suffering and to deny Hitchcock's camera. It is *hubris,* too, to deny his passions and sexuality so profoundly, his fears of which are manifest symbolically or symptomatically in his dizziness (such as that sustained during his and Novak's second kiss) and in his fallings (such as happens in his dream).

Mulvey describes the Stewart figure as possessing, brandishing, and relishing a position of active power in relation to the woman, but the truth is that he suffers throughout *Vertigo.* He suffers from the moment he painfully discovers his acrophobia on the rooftop, through his involvement with Madeleine, under the condescending and barbed censure of the court officer at the hearing, and up to his dream, the final nightmare of his life until the end of the film. His dream renders him a catatonic in a sanatarium, immobilized by depression, past the loving reach of Midge (Barbara Bel Geddes), the therapeutic reach of doctors, and even the cobweb-chasing spirit of Mozart.

When Stewart/Scottie emerges from the hospital, his suffering continues. A series of short sequences shows him retracing the steps of his relationship with Madeleine. Each blonde woman in the distance causes his heart to leap as he believes, for an instant, that she has returned. But he is looking for a woman who has died, a ghost.

When he finds Judy, his suffering is not over. He will not be satisfied until the ghost is made flesh, until he has created a living woman out of the dead one. Mulvey claims that Scottie "reconstructs Judy as Madeleine, forces her to conform in every detail to the actual physical appearance of his fetish" (p. 16). "Fetish" and "fetishism" are important terms in Mulvey's understanding of how sexuality functions and is contained in classical films. Mulvey's concept of "fetishism," however, is too extended or metaphorical to bear the weight she puts upon it, as for example when she claims that Scottie is "reconstructing a fetish" when he insists that Judy's clothes and hair style and color match Madeleine's. Stewart/Scottie is not reconstructing a fetish; he is creating a woman in fulfillment of his *vision.* This construction of Judy as Madeleine is, with terrible irony, destructive; it may be even more brutal than Mulvey's idea of "fetish." What is shown to be brutal in *Vertigo* is the nature of human desire and need, not some function of a particular phase of male development whose correction it is fairly simple to imagine.

III.

Mulvey's failure to recognize the Novak figure's centrality and Hitchcock's allegiance with her is partly the consequence of her prejudicial understanding of Stewart/Scottie. Mulvey reflects on but half of the man's nature when she isolates his power from his suffering in relation to the woman he loves. Mulvey's understanding of Novak/Judy denies the active aspect of her decision to stay with Stewart/Scottie and it denies his passivity as well—that he is played for a sucker, first by Elster and Judy and then by Judy alone when she withholds from him a fact about her identity: that she is, as Barbara Stanwyck/ Jean/Eve is in Sturges's *The Lady Eve,* positively the same woman. Mulvey's partial (or prejudicial) understanding of Scottie is an expression of her theoretical view that sexuality in Hollywood films is founded in a division between looking and being-looked-at, between activity and passivity, between masculinity and femininity.

Mulvey posits that "the image of woman as (passive) raw material for the (active) gaze of man" (p. 17) is at the heart of Hollywood conventions. She claims further that film offers two pleasures to its viewers. She identifies the first as scopophilia, which she takes to be "using another person as an object of sexual stimulation through sight" (p. 10). The second pleasure, "developed through narcissism and the constitution of the ego," derives from the viewer's "identification with the image seen" (p. 10). In male stars and only in males, Mulvey asserts, can the viewer find an ego ideal.

Mulvey claims Freud as the authority on scopophilia:

> Originally, in his *Three Essays on Sexuality* [1905], Freud isolated scopophilia as one of the component instincts of sexuality that exist quite independently of the erotogenic zones. At this point he associated scopophilia with taking other people as objects, subjecting them to a controlling and curious gaze. . . . In this analysis, scopophilia is primarily active. (Later, in *Instincts and Their Vicissitudes,* Freud developed his theory of scopophilia further, attaching it initially to pregenital autoeroticism, after which the pleasure of the look is transferred to others by analogy. . . .) Although the instinct is modified by other factors, in particular the constitution of the ego, it continues to exist as the erotic basis for pleasure in looking at another person as object. At the extreme, it can become fixated into a perversion, producing obsessive voyeurs and peeping toms, whose only sexual satisfaction can come from watching, in an active controlling sense, an objectified other. (pp. 8–9)

Mulvey's account presents itself as simply a transcription of Freud, but it is not. At no point does Freud claim to have a "theory of scopophilia" or that scopophilia subjects others to a "controlling and curious gaze." (This claim makes little sense in any case. If a look is curious—say a child's look at his or her mother's body—it does not know what it will find. How can such a look also be controlling? What can it control?)

Neither does Freud claim that scopophilia is "essentially active." To this last idea he directs a number of remarks in "Instincts and Their Vicissitudes," where he declares that "the only correct statement to make about the scoptophilic instinct would be that all the phases of its development, the autoerotic, preliminary phase as well as its final active or passive form, co-exist alongside one another; and the truth of this becomes obvious if we base our opinion, not on the actions to which the instinct leads, but on the mechanism of its satisfaction." Freud provides another sketch of the development of instincts as "a series of separate successive waves, each of which is homogeneous during whatever period of time it may last, and whose relation to one another is comparable to that of successive eruptions of lava." He concludes: "at [a] later period of development of an instinctual impulse, [the fact that] its (passive) opposite may be observed alongside of it deserves to be marked by the very apt term . . . ambivalence."

In both "Three Essays" and "Instincts and Their Vicissitudes," Freud singles out scopophilia-exhibitionism and sadism-masochism precisely because "these are the best-known sexual instincts that appear in an ambivalent manner."[7] His crucial discovery is that these instincts always appear in pairs or, as he puts it specifically, "[a] sadist is always at the same time a masochist" and "exhibitionists . . . exhibit their own genitals in order to obtain a reciprocal view of the genitals of the other person."[8] Freud's discovery that scopophilia-exhibitionism and sadism-masochism are sexual instincts that occur in ambivalent form constitutes a deep insight into the nature of human sexuality. But of even greater importance is Freud's placement of his study of these instincts at the service of his thoughts about loving, the subject that guides his entire study of human sexuality. Freud's discovery of the ambivalence of these sexual instincts played a crucial role in his deepening understanding of his central subject in both "Three Essays" and "Instincts and Their Vicissitudes": the antithetical relation of love and hate.

Mulvey identifies active controlling looks with men and passive looked-atness with women, alignments Freud explicitly rejects when he discovers that the active and passive forms of the instincts are always found together in the same human being. She pairs active-male and passive-female in pointed disregard of Freud's statement that "the coupling of masculinity with activity and of passivity with femininity meets us, indeed, as a biological fact; but it is by no means so invariably complete and exclusive as we are inclined to assume" (14, p. 134).

Acknowledging the confusion surrounding the concepts of "masculine" and "feminine," Freud distinguishes three uses of these concepts in a footnote in "Three Essays." His precisely drawn definitions are valuable to our discussion of Mulvey's views:

> "Masculine" and "feminine" are sometimes used in the sense of activity and passivity, sometimes in a biological, and sometimes, again, in a sociological sense. The first of these meanings is the essential one [for psychoanalysis]. When, for example, "libido" was described [in the text] as being "masculine," the word was being used in this sense, for an instinct is always active even when it has a passive aim in view. The second, or biological, meaning of "masculine" and "feminine" . . . can be determined most easily [because each is] characterized by the presence of [sexual organs and functions]. . . . The third, or sociological, meaning re-

ceives its connotation from the observation of actually existing masculine and feminine individuals. Such observation shows that in human beings pure masculinity or femininity is not to be found either in a psychological or a biological sense. (7, pp. 219–20)

It is hard to imagine how Freud could be clearer on this subject. He explicitly declares that in psychoanalytic usage the term "masculine" does not indicate a quality that is possessed by men only and that "feminine" does not describe an instinct or quality that can be understood as the special province of women. Freud is also clear on the subject of activity and passivity, in particular in his view that instincts are *always* active, "even if they have a passive aim in view." To arrive at Mulvey's view, one would have to set out an understanding of human sexuality that competes with Freud's on a number of levels, that divides instincts into categories of activity and passivity, and that aligns them according to biological distinctions between the sexes rather than according to the psychoanalytic meanings of the terms "active," "passive," "masculine," and "feminine" that Freud specifies.

IV.

Mulvey's view that the camera is an active, controlling male gaze shares the partiality or incompleteness of her understanding of the Stewart figure in *Vertigo* because the camera also possesses both active and passive possibilities or ontological qualities. In his reflections on the camera's nature in *The World Viewed* Stanley Cavell cites drawing the camera back, panning, and close-ups as gestures that exemplify the camera's active possibility. He calls these gestures "images of perfect attention." Cavell continues to reflect on the camera's dual nature and writes, "Early in its history the cinema discovered the possibility of *calling* attention to persons and parts of persons and objects; but it is equally a possibility of the medium not to call attention to them but, rather, to let the world happen, to let its parts draw attention to themselves according to their natural weight" (p. 25).

Every shot in which the camera does not perform a gesture declaring its active attention to persons or parts of persons and objects within the frame realizes and displays the camera's ontological passivity in relation to the world it views. Cavell mentions that certain directors, such as Vigo, Dreyer, and Renoir, explore this possibility in their work. In their films, the conditions of the camera's passivity are meditated and give rise to the conditions, at once moral and aesthetic, that hold in the worlds of their films.

In *Hitchcock — The Murderous Gaze,* William Rothman argues that Hitchcock's films are meditations on the camera's nature, perspicuous critiques of the camera's active and passive aspects. Hitchcock's understanding of the medium of film culminates with *Psycho,* Rothman declares, and with the creation of Norman Bates, a figure at once active (a murderer) and passive (witness to the fact of his "mother's" acts of murder), guilty and innocent, utterly subjugated to his "mother's" will and all powerful. Norman is also the last in a line of Hitchcockian figures, among whom Handell Fane in *Murder!* can be counted, who are sexually ambiguous and ambivalent. These figures, Rothman shows, are surrogates of Hitchcock's camera. Their sexual ambiguity or ambivalence expresses Hitchcock's understanding of the camera as both active and passive.

Their thoughts focused on different features of the medium, Cavell and Rothman both argue that the camera's nature is fundamentally active *and* passive. As Freud argues against separating the active and passive forms of an instinct, so Cavell and Rothman argue against separating the camera's active and passive possibilities. They argue that these two possibilities continuously inform one another and moreover that the ways they inform one another lie at the heart of the medium itself. To separate its active and passive qualities, or to assume that the camera's gaze is only one and not the other, is to deny the camera's nature. To divide the camera's possibilities in relation to Hitchcock's work is to fail to acknowledge his deepest meditations, the deepest meaning of his art.

In *Vertigo,* Hitchcock's camera takes in the world under its gaze; it "lets the world happen." It also performs a number of gestures that constitute declarations about the camera's nature and its powers. These are declarations of Hitchcock's authorship, representative both of what he understands the camera to be and what he understands his act of filmmaking to be. *Vertigo's* central meditations, which must be understood as preoccupations of Hitchcock's authorship and as conditioned by the photogenic qualities of the film's two leading figures, involve a pair of the camera's possible relations to human beings under its gaze. Both of these relations are violent. One is the camera's power to penetrate its subjects to their deepest cores, and both Novak/Judy and Stewart/Scottie are subject to this power. The other is the camera's capacity to display on the screen its (human) subject's inner desires or fears. This complicated power is represented in Stewart/Scottie's view of the world opening up as an abyss beneath him when he grips the rain gutter during his first attack of acrophobia, for instance. Hitchcock also meditates on this power through the Stewart character's obsessive transformation of Novak/Judy into Madeleine. Let me give an example of each of these powers of the camera in relation to Stewart/Scottie.

When Stewart/Scottie sits bolt upright in bed and lunges toward the camera at the end of his dream, his eyes are fixed open and his face is filled with terror. He projects himself directly toward the camera, but his eyes, immersed in his dream, do not take in the camera. (His look at this moment opposes Novak/Judy's look that acknowledges the camera.) His absorption in his inner world blinds him to beings in the world of the film (chiefly to the Novak figure) and to Hitchcock (represented by the camera) who require his acknowledgment. Glassy with horror, his eyes are blinded by the vision of his fate projected in his dream. Therein, with his endless falling into an open grave, he is identified with Madeleine's death. The dream further identifies his desire for her as inseparable from his desire for Carlotta Valdes, the ghost who had possessed Madeleine. Figured in his dream, this man's dread is that he is nothingness, that he can be penetrated completely. We might characterize this as his fear that he too is a ghost.

Just as Stewart/Scottie's dream sketches his deepest fear of being nothingness, the camera, maintaining its fixed position in the face of his lunge toward it, threatens to penetrate him completely, to pierce through him and reveal his insubstantiality. This profound condition of James Stewart on film was discovered first by Frank Capra in *It's a Wonderful Life* (1947). The same look, and the same possibility that the camera might plunge through him, occurs in that film at the moment Stewart, dwelling in the world of his wish turned nightmare, registers his mother's refusal to acknowledge that he is her son. He walks down the porch steps of her house until he fills the frame and stands on the verge of having the camera go through him. Though Hitchcock contemplates the implications of Stewart's photogenesis more completely, both he and Capra reveal that Stewart's curse, at once embedded within him as his deepest private fear and exposed by the camera's power to penetrate its subjects, is that he is insubstantial, incorporeal, nothingness itself.

This is the fear that motivates Stewart's deep attachment to Madeleine, because she too suffers the unrest of a ghost dwelling on earth. It is because he finds a soul with which to identify his own — a lover's aspiration — that he falls in love with Madeleine and re-creates her.[9] And it is because his attachment to Madeleine never acknowledged the real woman, divorced from her relation to Carlotta Valdes, that he can repeat to Novak/Judy on the bell tower that she was always "a counterfeit." Any flesh-and-blood woman is a counterfeit of the ghost he loves.

The second central meditation of Hitchcock's camera is figured in Stewart/Scottie's sustained violations of Novak/Judy. At every escalation of his demands upon her, the film — Hitchcock — indicts his project further. Stewart/Scottie's vision requires violations of Judy on all different levels, but none looms so large and monstrously as his necessary denial of her actual, real being.

When Novak/Judy emerges from the bathroom fully realized as Madeleine, the shot presents Stewart/Scottie's point of view. She is surrounded by glowing, diffused light, and the shot is overlaid with gauze. Suffused with special effects, this shot registers Stewart/Scottie's final violent achievement. This woman is a figment of a dream, an apparition.

A deep issue raised by this shot is that it is not clear whether the vision of Novak/Judy as Madeleine is projected out of the deepest regions of Stewart's being, or if the camera — Hitchcock — subjects him to a view that satisfies his inner desires. This same question applies to all of the vertiginous shots in the film. Are they presented by Stewart/Scottie, or are they the work of a God-like figure, Hitchcock, who has singled Stewart out and undertaken a special meditation of him? Another way of thinking about this issue would be to ask, is Stewart/Scottie active in his relation to specific views he has, views of the world opening up into an abyss, for example, or the view of Novak/Judy as Madeleine once again? Are these views his projections, hence his work? Or are they Hitchcock's doing, hence views that force Stewart to suffer passively the sight of his deepest fears and wishes?

These shots realize the fears and wishes that dwell in the deepest regions of Stewart/Scottie's being. They are also displays of Hitchcock's authority, declarations of his commanding presence as *Vertigo*'s author. Rothman's readings of Hitchcock's films reveal that Hitchcock consistently uses shots such as those that register Stewart/Scottie's vertigo in order to announce his authorial power and to raise issues about a leading figure's relation to the world of the film. Rothman identifies the cause of a Hitchcock character's vertigo as "the realization that he has been singled out by the agency that presides over the world, that his world has been created in the image of his innermost fears."[10] These shots declare, not Stewart/Scottie's, but Hitchcock's authority over the views that compose the film and the fates of the human beings that dwell in its world.

V.

Hitchcock's work, especially in the fifties, is absorbed in studying specific photogenic features and significances of major stars, and *Vertigo,* in its study of James Stewart's presence on film, is no exception. Like his highly enigmatic surrogate Elster, Hitchcock selects Stewart. Scottie's acrophobia makes him the right man for Elster's job (or should we say, makes it possible for him to be Elster's victim?). Acrophobia is a metaphor for the qualities of Stewart's presence on film that Hitchcock studies and relentlessly exposes throughout *Vertigo.* Within the world of the film, his acrophobia is called a weakness and his selection by Elster cursed as a setup. But what makes Stewart the right man for Hitchcock's job?

In "Visual Pleasure and Narrative Cinema," Laura Mulvey implies that the relationship between *Vertigo* and *films noirs* is central to its meaning when she takes Stewart/Scottie's occupation as a detective to motivate the film's narrative. Earlier I cited Cavell's emphasis on Stewart's projecting "a capacity for suffering" and his consequent placing of him "in the company of women." Mulvey, on the contrary, situates Stewart/Scottie among the heroes of *films noirs* when she claims that *Vertigo*'s narrative is told primarily in "subjective camera." But by allying himself with and privileging the woman's story in *Vertigo* in a way no *film noir* has ever done, Hitchcock breaks with the genre's characteristic absorption in the man's dilemma (falling in love with a villainous woman). While *Vertigo* undeniably invokes *film noir*, it does so, like *Stage Fright*, in order to undermine the genre's central assumption about the camera—that it and the hero's subjectivity are a single "I."

Cavell instructs us to look more deeply at *Vertigo*'s story and figures by revealing their proximity to what are typically called women's films which Cavell identifies as preoccupied with the search for one's identity and "the identifying and the inhabitation of a feminine region of the self." *Vertigo*'s attentiveness to these subjects in relation to both the man and the woman in the film results in its deep affinity with, not *film noir*, but film melodrama.

The conditions or meaning of Stewart's presence on film, his quest for confirmation of his existence, and his related fear that he is a haunted being are exposed in *Vertigo*. Hitchcock selects and places Stewart in a world where he suffers as both his private dreams of romantic happiness and sexual satisfaction and his deepest fears are presented to him. We might say that *Vertigo* places Stewart in a world designed to gratify him, if we add that we cannot take it for granted that gratification will not expose horrifying truths about one's desires. If Stewart stands to achieve happiness in this film, once Judy's re-creation as Madeleine is complete, he also stands to learn about his desire for happiness, and so to come face to face with his ruthlessness, his violence, and the extent to which his fantasies control him and limit his ability to accept reality and, in particular, Novak/Judy's real existence.

In the world of *Vertigo,* Stewart is not in the happy—if at times difficult—circumstance that Cary Grant enjoys in the world of *North by Northwest*. He is not even offered the reprieve that Henry Fonda is offered in *The Wrong Man*. In each of these films, Hitchcock authors a fate for his leading man that is partly contingent upon the meaning of his individual photogenesis. What this means is that I understand the first occurrence of Stewart's acrophobia, presented in a point-of-view shot that tortures him, to declare Stewart's status as *condemned*. Let me demonstrate what I mean by this by reading the film's closing sequences.

From the start of the closing sequence, during their drive to the mission, Hitchcock presents shots of Stewart/Scottie from Novak/Judy's point of view that were absent in the parallel sequence of their first drive to San Juan Bautista. The most striking and disturbing of these shots is of Stewart/Scottie framed in profile. This shot resembles the stunning profile shot of Uncle Charles (Joseph Cotten) in *Shadow of a Doubt*. Uncle Charles's subsequent gesture of turning his head to meet the camera's gaze distinguishes that moment from this in *Vertigo* and him from Stewart/Scottie.[11] But the shots are deeply related in their announcements of their subjects' villainy. At this moment, we know that Stewart/Scottie is capable of murder.

With each shot in this sequence of their drive, Hitchcock declares his sympathy with Novak/Judy and exposes Stewart's violence and madness. Once they reach the bell tower, things happen very quickly: Stewart/Scottie conquers his acrophobia, learns that Judy was Elster's lover, and pieces together Madeleine's murder. For agonizing moments, we cannot tell whether Stewart will act on the horror of his disillusionment and anger, and so will kill Judy, or whether he will risk the fall that has terrified him figuratively throughout the film, and so will concede to his desire and fall in love. Leaning out of a corner of the tower, Judy tells him all those things are past; all that matters is that she loves him. As she steps forward to kiss him, he murmurs — as she had unforgettably murmured to him during the first scene at the mission — that it's too late. But they kiss nonetheless, and his words are proven false. This time their embrace does not envelop Stewart in a dizzying, exhilarating, and agonizing world of fantasy. For the first time, the woman he loves is not an apparition in his arms.

But turning her head, Novak/Judy again directs a look to the camera. As in the crucial "flashback" sequence, this look declares her knowledge. What she views fills her with terror and she breaks away from Scottie. We cut to a shot of what she sees, a view of an obscured and shrouded figure standing in the recesses of the tower. The figure speaks in a high-pitched voice not unlike Mother Bates's. "I heard voices." We cut back to the shot of Novak, framed by the arch window, with Stewart to the right of the frame. She stares at the figure, turns, and leaps from the bell tower. (It is also possible to think that she falls from the tower, an understanding that implicates Hitchcock further in her death. This is an implication which my understanding of this moment — that she leaps — does not deny but allows.)

What does Novak/Judy see when she looks to the camera? What so fills her with terror? As with Stewart/Scottie, we cannot draw an absolute boundary between what Novak/Judy projects from within herself and what Hitchcock presents for her view. In one reading, then, the shrouded, obscured figure represents to her the being of Stewart/Scottie's vision, and so it is a representation of herself as a spectre. This spectre is what she became in Stewart/Scottie's romantic vision. Judy grasps in an instant the actual figure he desires and grasps at the same moment that this spectre is a consummate denial of her existence. My other reading of this moment (part of whose obscurity is its very fleetingness) is that Novak/Judy, at the moment they kiss, feels herself already a ghost. The figure in the shadows is then a projection of her inner being, the part of her denied and excluded by Stewart/Scottie's vision.

What Novak/Judy reveals that she knows in these charged moments is that their relationship cannot ever fully break Stewart/Scottie's preoccupation with and attachment to nothingness. She knows that his love will never grant her existence the full acknowledgment real love requires. In their kiss, her alternatives have become clear: that she either becomes a ghost, a disquiet and possessed apparition, or she forever agrees to violate her own desires, and her own being, by accepting the conditions of Scottie's love. In either reading, the figure in the shadows emerges as the spectre of a life endured without acknowledgment, her fate if she lives on with this man.

Her leap from the bell tower is both her declaration that she refuses the violations of Stewart/Scottie's vision, and it is her final and decisive proof to him that she is not a ghost but a living being. Her act forces him to recognize that all along he has been wrong, deeply and profoundly wrong, to deny her his acknowledgment, to desire instead a ghost. Her words in the forest assume the power of prophecy: "Somewhere in here I was born; here I died. . . . You took no notice." The partiality, the incompleteness of Stewart/Scottie's capacity to acknowledge another's real existence and love stands forever exposed. Harboring the fear that he is himself nothingness, Stewart/Scottie conjured a vision of nothingness and breathed life into it throughout his re-creation of the ghost Madeleine.

A reading of the final sequence is incomplete without understanding that, at another level, what Novak/Judy sees rising up in the shadows of the bell tower is an embodiment of Hitchcock's camera. Once again, Hitchcock acknowledges Novak/Judy's singular capacity to understand the conditions that hold in the world of the film by singling her out as the audience for his theatrical presentation. Reading the shadow-figure as an embodiment of Hitchcock's camera, which itself suffers the conditions of being a spectre, an unacknowledged and sexless existence, does not alter our previous readings. But in this gesture of presenting himself as an exemplar of the horrifying fate which Judy stands to suffer in relation to Scottie, Hitchcock seals his bond with the Novak figure. Hitchcock endorses Novak/Judy's leap because it certifies, as no other act can, her actual existence. The other possibilities—life as a spectre or Stewart/Scottie's life—stand condemned.

VI.

If a question lingers, we might formulate it along these lines. Do the similarities between Stewart/Scottie's re-creation of Judy as Madeleine and Hitchcock's work as director naturally align Hitchcock and his leading man more profoundly than each of Hitchcock's announcements of his allegiance with the woman?

I am prepared, in ways Mulvey appears not to be, to claim that Hitchcock reflects upon the act of directing a film through Stewart/Scottie's re-creation of Madeleine. But Hitchcock distinguishes his powers as a filmmaker from Stewart/Scottie's act of "casting" Novak/Judy as Madeleine. In *Vertigo*, as in others of his films, Hitchcock declares that his powers are contingent upon the human beings under his camera's gaze. In his precise meditation of Stewart's and Novak's presences on film he reflects on the fact that he did not, and cannot, create (these) human beings. Hitchcock can place his subjects in worlds tailor-made for the emergence of their inner selves, but he does not have the power to invent these beings. *Vertigo,* like each of Hitchcock's films, acknowledges its medium's ontological condition of tragedy. It calls upon us to acknowledge that its figures possess the causes of their bereavement within themselves.

When Stewart/Scottie "casts" Novak/Judy as Madeleine, he undertakes to re-create a human being who exists in his private fantasies, as though he were casting a part in a play. Novak's photogenic importance to *Vertigo* derives partly from her projection of and the camera's insistence upon her corporeality. This feature of Novak's presence on film measurably contributes to the film's exposure of the ruthlessness of Stewart/Scottie's changes in her appearance, changes which demonstrate, like a proof, Novak/Judy's possession of an inner being that remains constant and in need of acknowledgment. Our and Hitchcock's certainty in and identification with Novak/Judy's inner being are declared in the outrage we feel toward Stewart/Scottie's desires and demands. We and Hitchcock hold against him his failure to acknowledge *her* in each of her theatrical incarnations. The effect of *Vertigo's* attention to Novak's physicality is as a testament to her metaphysical integrity.

Casting Judy/Novak in the part of Madeleine, Stewart/Scottie denies or opposes the condition of film that Hitchcock meditates. He masks, or violates, her real existence in a way no camera can but, rather, in the precise manner of theater. While it is true (and typical of Hitchcock's work) that Hitchcock presents a version, or an understanding, of directorial powers through a surrogate within the film, it is also true (and equally typical of Hitchcock) that he systematically distinguishes himself from that surrogate and what he represents.

In my reading of *Vertigo,* the Novak figure occupies the center of the film. *Vertigo* offers a lesson to its viewers in which the Novak figure represents the film and Hitchcock, and the Stewart figure stands in for those viewers whose attachments elsewhere make them incapable of acknowledging the film or its maker. *Vertigo* addresses and answers the claim that women can suffer unacknowledgment in a film. The precise ways in which the man's visions deny the woman's own existence are opposed and his inability to acknowledge her is condemned.

Mulvey's account of *Vertigo,* which she grasps as illuminating her ideas, is blind to the woman's role within the film and to Hitchcock's allegiance with her. Mulvey's relation to *Vertigo* is the equivalent of Stewart's relation to Novak within the film. Mulvey is not engaged in changing a woman's hair color or clothing but in fundamentally altering Freud's thoughts and the meanings of films. Where Scottie re-creates Madeleine on the basis of his vision of a ghost, Mulvey re-creates Hollywood films on the basis of her own visions of men, women, and the medium of film. Mulvey's vision denies elements *as fundamental* to the history of Hollywood film and to Freud's thought as Judy's real existence is to the meaning of *Vertigo.* As I hear it, their replies to Mulvey echo

Novak's tragic words to Stewart: "Here I was born, here I died; you took no notice." Perhaps because at some level Mulvey's own vision is unacceptable to her, she presents it as though it were an acceptable transcription of Freud and as though she were speaking for all women about things we already know to be true about Hollywood films.

While I demonstrate in my reading of *Vertigo* that the sexual politics and meaning of Hollywood films cannot be presumed in the way Mulvey presumes them, an equally important purpose of the arguments in this essay is to register a claim. If feminist criticism is to understand itself to be deeply informed by Freud's thinking (as Mulvey declares her thinking to be) and by film history (which Mulvey also declares to be the case, though she understands that as a sad rather than wonderful fact), then it must recognize that, as in Freud's work and in films of major importance, its central subject is loving. In my view, feminist thinking cannot contribute as importantly as it should to the fields from which it derives its intellectual power in the absence or the avoidance of reflections on the nature and the meaning of loving that are as serious as those contained in the works feminists refer to and the films they study.

Notes

1. Laura Mulvey, "Visual Pleasure and Narrative Cinema," *Screen,* vol. 16, no. 3 (1975): 6-18.
2. Cavell's understanding of photogenesis constitutes one of his central arguments about the nature, meaning, and importance of the medium of film. Here I am referring to "What Becomes of Things on Film?," *Themes Out of School* (San Francisco: Northpoint Press, 1984), 173-83, the essay of his that most explicitly reflects on the subject of photogenesis.
3. Stanley Cavell, *The World Viewed: Reflections on the Ontology of Film* (Cambridge: Harvard Univ. Press, 1979), 28.
4. Stanley Cavell, *Pursuits of Happiness: The Hollywood Comedy of Remarriage* (Cambridge: Harvard Univ. Press, 1981), 157.
5. Stanley Cavell, "What Becomes of Things on Film?," 179-80. Cavell elaborated his understanding of the woman's film, or film melodrama, in a series of lectures at Harvard University during the spring of 1984 and in his paper, "Two Cheers for Romance," delivered at a symposium called "Passionate Attachments: The Essential but Fragile Nature of Love" held in New York on 10 November 1984 and sponsored by the Columbia University Center for Psychoanalytic Training and Research.
6. Disagreements about whether Judy looks directly into the camera, slightly off to the right of the camera, or more than slightly off to the right of the camera can last long into the night. Our inability to determine whether she, or any figure whose gaze is directed at the camera, looks directly into the camera is not due to a failure of our attentiveness to film. It is the consequence of—hence exposes as an issue—the mysteriousness of the camera's presence within the world of a film. There is no such thing as a direct look into the camera because there is no equivalent to gazing into the camera's eye; it has no eye even though, paradoxically, it is only a gaze. Our fascination with determining whether a look is directed at the camera or slightly off masks the deeper issue at hand; that is, what does it mean for that figure to direct his or her gaze to the camera? What does the figure's gesture reveal about the camera?
7. All references to Freud are to *The Standard Edition of the Complete Psychological Works of Sigmund Freud,* trans. and gen. ed. James Strachey (London: Hogarth Press, 1957). All references thus far are to "Instincts and Their Vicissitudes," vol. 14, 130-32, hereafter cited in the text by volume and page numbers.

 8. Freud, "Three Essays on Sexuality," *The Standard Edition*, vol. 7, 159 and 157, hereafter cited in the text by volume and page numbers.
 9. This phrase, "a soul with which . . .," was written by Bronson Alcott in his diary upon his recognition of his deep love for Abby May, whom he married. For this access to the Alcotts, I am grateful to Madelon Bedell's biography of the family, *The Alcotts* (New York: Clarkson N. Potter, 1980).
10. William Rothman, *Hitchcock — The Murderous Gaze* (Cambridge: Harvard Univ. Press, 1982), 362.
11. Rothman's description of this gesture as one of "meeting the camera's gaze" is perspicuously apt (see p. 216 of *The Murderous Gaze*). The look that Judy gave the camera, discussed earlier in this essay, is another instance of this gesture. My weighting of her look, whether one agrees that she looks directly at the camera or not, and my claim about its importance within the film are derived from Rothman's recognition that this gesture is repeated and crucial to Hitchcock's cinema, a point of criticism that demonstrates Rothman's philosophical, theoretical, and practical view, which I share, that Hitchcock's allegiances and thoughts are ascertainable only through investigations of the camera's relation to its human subjects throughout a given film.

My thanks are due to William Rothman and Stanley Cavell for their suggestions and editorial remarks on this essay.

CHAPTER NINETEEN

North by Northwest

Stanley Cavell

Philosophy's all but unappeasable yearning for itself is bound to seem comic to those who have not felt it. To those who have felt it, it may next seem frightening, and they may well hate and fear it, for the step after that is to yield to the yearning, and then you are lost. From such a view of philosophy I have written about something called modernism in the arts as the condition of their each yearning for themselves; naming a time at which to survive, they took themselves, their own possibilities, as their aspiration — they assumed the condition of philosophy. What I found in turning to think consecutively about film a dozen or so years ago was a medium which seemed simultaneously to be free of the imperative to philosophy and at the same time inevitably to reflect upon itself — as though the condition of philosophy were its natural condition. And then I was lost.

But this is said after the fact. Over and over I have had to find again my conviction in these matters, to take my experience over the same path, finding the idea of film's philosophical seriousness first to be comic, then frightening, then inescapable. To achieve this conviction in the films of Alfred Hitchcock is not something I can imagine apart from a continuing conversation about film and about philosophy with William Rothman, whose conviction in the precision of Hitchcock's self-consciousness and passionate exploration of that self-consciousness in his films has convinced me to find this for myself. My remarks on *North by Northwest* are guided, more specifically, by two ideas from Rothman's forthcoming book on Hitchcock, *Hitchcock — The Murderous Gaze:* first, that Hitchcock's interpretation of the power of the movie camera — for example, its power of interrogation of its human subjects — is something Rothman calls its murderousness; and second, that the Hitchcock film, hence Hitchcock, is first fully formed in *The 39 Steps,* in its weaving of Hitchcock's interest in his themes of the murder thriller together with the themes of romance.[1]

In *Pursuits of Happiness* I put together seven Hollywood romances of the thirties and forties and claim that they define a particular genre, something I

call the comedy of remarriage. It happens that Cary Grant is in four of the
seven; Katharine Hepburn is the only other principal to appear in more than
one. In my account of Howard Hawks's *Bringing Up Baby* (one of the seven
films in question) I claim that Grant's saving Hepburn from falling, at the
close of the film, by hoisting her hand in hand onto the ledge of a scaffold, a
place that also looks like a crib or treehouse, upon which they embrace, is
alluded to by the conclusive hoisting in *North by Northwest* from a ledge onto
an upper berth. If I will not ask you out of the blue to believe this connection,
still less will I ask you to believe an allusion from *North by Northwest* to *The
Philadelphia Story,* another of the seven films with Cary Grant, when Grant
(or rather Roger Thornhill) early in *North by Northwest* tries to make the
police and his mother believe what happened to him at the mansion in Glen
Cove, and the place of liquor bottles is shown to be occupied by books.
Thornhill's drinking is the subject of much attention in the opening sequences
of *North by Northwest,* that is, as long as his mother is present; and C. K.
Dexter Haven (Grant's role in *The Philadelphia Story*) cured himself of alco-
holism by reading books, a process apparently from which he acquired the
authority to affect the destiny of his love. I will wind up saying that *North by
Northwest* derives from the genre of remarriage, or rather from whatever it is
that that genre is derived, which means to me that its subject is the legitimizing of marriage, as if the pair's adventures are trials of their suitability for that
condition. Perhaps this only signifies that *North by Northwest* is a romance. It
is in any case the only one of Hitchcock's romantic thrillers in which the
adventurous pair are actually shown to have married. It is also the only one in
which the man of that pair is shown to have a mother—a mother, needless to
say, whom he is shown to leave, and to leave running (out of the Plaza Hotel,
away from his abductors, but at the same time away from his mother, who
shouts after him to ask whether he will be home for dinner). The fate of the
mother in *The Birds* will complicate this story. And naturally certain of Hitchcock's villains, and certain of his heroines, are allowed to have mothers.

But let us begin as uncontroversially as we can. *North by Northwest*
contains as one of its stars Cary Grant. It underscores this uncontroversial fact
in two principal ways: first, by remark after remark about his nice-looking,
vaguely familiar face and about his being irresistible and making women who
don't know him fall in love with him, together with several double takes when
strangers look at his face (a man going into a phone booth Grant is leaving, a
woman who, after as it were seeing who he is, wants him to stop in her hospital
room); and second, by allusions to each of the other films Hitchcock made
with Grant. *To Catch a Thief* also has him at the end holding a woman by the
hand over a precipice, and in that film he is comically shown to be irresistible;
Suspicion climaxes with a wild ride down a coast road in a convertible driven by
Grant, from which he seems to shove someone out and from which someone

who might be poisoned almost falls over a cliff into the sea; and the basic situation of *Notorious* is gone over again (a loose woman's liaison with something like a foreign agent is exploited by an American intelligence agency; the assignment thwarts Grant's desire; it leads to the woman's mortal danger from which Grant rescues her).

There seem to be two immediate reasons in *North by Northwest* for insisting upon the presence of Cary Grant: first to redeem him from certain guilts acquired in those earlier environments, especially in allowing him to overcome the situation of *Notorious,* as if film actors and their characters get stuck to one another, and as if he is being readied for something purer in this context; and second, to inscribe the subject of film acting, and acting generally, as a main topic of this film, which is to say, a main branch of its investigation of the nature of film. The topic is invoked over and over in *North by Northwest:* Philip Vandamm (James Mason) hardly says a word to Grant that does not comment on his acting; the Professor (Leo G. Carroll) requests him to act a part; and Eve (Eva Marie Saint) compliments him on his performance in the scene they have just acted out for Vandamm's benefit. The theme of theatricality is generalized by the fact that the part Thornhill is asked and forced to play is that of someone named George Kaplan, who doesn't exist; but to play the part of a fictional character is just what actors normally do. It happens that in the fiction of this film this new fictional identity is imposed by reality, thus generalizing the theme further into the nature of identity and the theatricality of everyday life.

It is, I think, part of Hitchcock's lingo to be referring to these facts, and more, in the exchange on the train between Thornhill and Eve about the monogram on his matchbook. "Rot," he says, "it's my trademark." She asks what the "O" stands for. "Nothing," he replies. In a Hitchcockian context this means both that this man knows that the advertising game (and the modern city generally which it epitomizes) makes up words that are rot but also that it would be rot to think this is all he means. Thornhill and Eve have already questioned his identity and spoken about his familiar face. So in part what or who is "nothing" is the film character (here, Roger Thornhill) in comparison to the film actor playing him. Cary Grant would be more or less who he is if Roger Thornhill had never existed, whereas Roger Thornhill would be nothing apart from Cary Grant (a form of consideration broached as long ago as Erwin Panofsky's "Style and Medium in the Motion Pictures"). "Nothing" equally means that the film *actor* is nothing in comparison to the power of the camera over *him*. This is not so much in need of argument as of interpretation. *North by Northwest* interprets the actor as a victim, as if of foreign views of himself. This thought puts two figures in the film in the role of directors, the Professor and Vandamm, who create scenarios and make up parts for people.[2] On Vandamm's first encounter with Thornhill he draws some theatrical curtains across proscenium-sized windows, shutting the world out, and arranges for Thornhill to be killed, as if punishing him for acting; the Professor lets this go on until forced for the sake of his own script to intervene.

The "nothing," or naught, in the ROT monogram equally appropriately stands for origin, so its simultaneous meaning is that the actor is the origin of the character and also the origin of what becomes of himself or herself on film. The further thought that the human self as such is both an origin and a nothing is a bit of Cartesianism that is conceivably not called for in the context of this film. (To say that Hitchcock is up to it if he wants it is to say that Hitchcock is as intelligent as, say, Samuel Beckett and that he is as good at what he does as Beckett is at what he does.)

But I was trying to begin uncontroversially. The film is called *North by Northwest.* I assume that nobody will swear from that fact alone that we have here an allusion to Hamlet's line that he is but mad north-northwest; even considering that Hamlet's line occurs as the players are about to enter and that *North by Northwest* is notable, even within the oeuvre of a director pervaded by images and thoughts of the theater and of theatricality, for its obsession with the idea of acting; and considering that both the play and the film contain plays-within-the-play in both of which someone is killed, both being constructed to catch the conscience of the one for whose benefit they are put on. But there are plenty of further facts. The film opens with an ageless male identifying himself first of all as a son. He speaks of his efforts to keep the smell of liquor on his breath (that is, evidence of his grown-up pleasures) from the watchful nose of his mother, and he comes to the attention of his enemies because of an unresolved anxiety about getting a message to his mother, whereupon he is taken to a mansion in which his abductor has usurped another man's house and name and has, it turns out, cast his own sister as his wife. (The name, posted at the front of the house, is Townsend, and a town is a thing smaller than a city but larger than a village, or a hamlet.) The abductor orders the son killed by forcing liquid into him. It is perhaps part of the picture that the usurper is eager to get to his dinner guests and that there is too much competitive or forced drinking of liquor. Nor, again, will anyone swear that it is significant that the abductor-usurper's henchmen are a pair of men with funny, if any, names and a single man who stands in a special relationship with the usurper and has a kind of sibling rivalry with the young woman that this son, our hero, will become attracted to and repelled by. These are shadowy matters, and it is too soon to speak of "allusions" or of any other very definite relation to a so-called source. But it seems clear to me that *if* one were convinced of *Hamlet* in the background of *North by Northwest,* say to the extent that one is convinced that Saxo Grammaticus's *Danish History* is in the background of *Hamlet,* then one would without a qualm take the name Leonard as a successor to the name Laertes.

We have further to go. In Saxo Grammaticus's telling of the story the son's enemies send a beautiful woman to seduce him; he is to believe that he and the woman meet by chance. When questioned about what happened between them he says he raped her; she has agreed to back his story since they had known one another in the past. This figure is, as editors have noted, a peculiar prototype for Ophelia, but we can take her as near perfect for Eve Kendall. Thornhill does not, it is true, say that he raped her, but he describes something happening between them, in the name of love, that they both call murdering her. Hitchcock here is following one of his favorite identifications, that of killing with intercourse, the other side of a metaphysical wit's identification of dying with orgasm. It is also to the point, thinking of Thornhill's attention to his clothes, that Hamlet's prototype in Saxo Grammaticus is pictured as covering himself with dirt. That Hitchcock has gone back to the source or origin of the story of Hamlet, as well as to the play, is a reason not to have the title *exactly* from *Hamlet.*[3]

I note two or three further echoes of the play. Thornhill's problem begins when he is confused with, so to speak, someone who doesn't exist, let us say it is a nothing, or let us say a ghost; and when the woman betrays him he finds her out by following the itinerary dictated by the ghost. And then the son protects himself, saves his life, by what I would like to describe as feigning madness — in the auction scene in which he pretends not to know how you join in bidding for things. The auctioneer at one stage says, "Would the gentleman please get into the spirit of the proceedings?" that is, be decorous, be socialized; but society has been forcing an identity and a guilt upon him that he does not recognize as his own, so the natural hope for a way out is to abdicate from that society. Thornhill's identifying "rot" as his trademark by now irresistibly suggests to me Hamlet's sense of something rotten.

Allow for the sake of argument that *Hamlet* is present in the film in some fashion. Of what interest is this, I mean of what interest to Hitchcock? I have various speculations about this based on my claim that *North by Northwest* invokes *Hamlet* in conjunction with the source of the story of Hamlet and on my sense that *North by Northwest* plays a special role in Hitchcock's oeuvre, a summary role. I take Hitchcock, as it were, to be saying something like the following. Granted that it is not necessary for anyone, let alone a filmmaker, to disclaim the intention of trying to compete with the quality and the importance of *Hamlet*, it is nevertheless my intention, as the filmmaker I am, to compete with Shakespeare in his handling of sources and in this way, or to this extent, to show myself to do whatever it is I do as well as Shakespeare does whatever it is he does. It is with sources as Coleridge famously remarked about Shakespeare's stories: "My belief is that he always regarded his story, before he began to write, much in the same light as a painter regards his canvas, before he begins to paint — as a mere vehicle for his thoughts — as the ground upon which he was to work." But then of course (still speaking for Hitchcock) the question is what one means by "sources." The story is one source, lifted often from indifferent places that would not constitute sources unless I had been inspired to make them such. So is the past body of my work a source, as *North by Northwest* makes explicit. So are what some people call "locations," which for me are places whose genius I wish to announce or to become. So are what other people call "actors," whereas for me what is called "Cary Grant" is considerably more than what that may be taken to mean. So is what you might call the camera a source. . . . You see the point.

But why is it *Hamlet* about which this is all, according to my speaking for Hitchcock, being said? I think there are two reasons. First, *Hamlet* is perhaps the most popular, or famous, of the greatest works of world literature; the man who on the basis of his kind of thriller became perhaps the most famous director of films in the world, and for a longer period than any other, and whom just about any critic recognizes as in some sense brilliant, may well be fascinated by and wish to comprehend this fact. Surely the play's fame cannot be the result of its actually being *understood*. Second, *Hamlet* is the subject of what is still probably the most famous Freudian interpretation of a work of art, Ernest Jones's *Hamlet and Oedipus*. Given the blatant presence of Freudian preoccupation and analysis in Hitchcock's work I see in his allusion to *Hamlet* a kind of warning to Freudians, even a dare, as if to say: of course my work, like any art, is subject to your interpretations, but why are these interpretations so often so obvious, unable to grasp the autonomy, the uniqueness, of the object? (Hitchcock would not be the first artist of this century to feel he has to pit his knowledge of human nature against the thought of the man who is said to have invented its science.)[4]

The origin of Eve Kendall in Hitchcock's own past work is explicit enough. She succeeds the prim, good-looking, blonde stranger in *The 39 Steps* whom an earlier Hitchcock hero had met on a train as he was trying to elude the police and get to a person who could clear him of the suspicion of having put a knife in someone's back; and at the end of that train ride there was also a professor. But this time, over twenty years later and in another country, the woman *offers* rather than refuses him help. This proves, initially, to be treachery rather than salvation, but it affords a picture of a relationship to women that this man, now and in the past, had not known. This woman's apparent faith in him succeeds both Madeleine Carroll's early skepticism about his predecessor (Robert Donat), who spends much of *The 39 Steps* trying to overcome it; and her faith succeeds more immediately the skepticism of his mother, to whom he had said goodbye just before encountering Eve on the train. The effect of these substitutions is elaborate and paradoxical, and all in favor of Eve.

Aligning, in retrospect, the Madeleine Carroll figure with the present mother, doubt is cast on the picture of marriage in the final shot of *The 39 Steps;* the man puts his arm around the woman with the handcuffs still dangling from his wrist, a picture suggesting that marriage is a kind of voluntary handcuffing (a portable version of the ball and chain). On the other hand Eve is made to incorporate both the good woman and the adventuress of *The 39 Steps*, that is, both the marriageable and the unmarriageable woman. The most delicious linking of them is made openly by Eve when she explains her interest in Thornhill to him by saying, "It's going to be a long night and I don't particularly like the book I've started. Know what I mean?" The Madeleine Carroll figure had been reading a book when Donat burst in on her. Thornhill knows what she means, as if seeing a dream coming true. And in that dream, and its responsibilities, the man's task will not be just to save himself and save his country's secrets from leaving it and thus win himself a suitable mate. He has first of all to save the bad woman, to rewrite the earlier plot which in effect began by killing her off, to rescue or redeem or resurrect her, that is to say, to put the good and the bad together. This is rather more like *creating* a suitable mate for himself.

Why is she his to rescue? Both the Professor and Eve tell him he is responsible for her condition, the one because he has cast suspicion on her, the other because men like him don't believe in marriage. But I think the film shows two further causes. First, in addition to her incorporating at least two of the women from *The 39 Steps* she also incorporates the mother, perhaps the mother he never had, protecting him from the police by hiding him in a bellying container that shows she holds the key to his berth. (This wasn't necessary: the fact that she subsequently hides him from the porter sufficiently well in the washroom proves that.) It is every bit this birth he is reciprocating in his closing gesture of the film. Second, he has passed some kind of ordeal at her hands in the crop-dusting sequence, and his survival here somehow entitles them to one another—as if his survival, or revival from a Frazerian cornfield, had given them the key piece of knowledge with which to overcome their unlucky erotic pasts, which accordingly would be the knowledge that ecstasy such as she invites is not necessarily death dealing. I am taking it that she is not purely reluctant to send him to meet Kaplan. She is not worried that he is a murderer but that she is. They are both about to undergo an education in these matters. Redemption for them both is under way. But it is not a simple matter to put such knowledge into the world—say, in the form of marriage—and there is danger ahead.

How is it that he is equipped to meet the danger; I mean how does he know that the attempt is the most important thing in the world? I must now put the uncontroversial aside and put forward a bunch of assertions.

I begin by reinterpreting, or interpreting further, Thornhill's survival of the attack by the plane. The attack is the central image of his victimization. I said earlier that this is the form in which his being an actor is to be declared; and just now I said that his sexual redemption depended on what you might call his survival of a kind of victimization by, or a willing subjection to, an assault of feeling. Something cataclysmic happened to Thornhill and Eve the night before, and I understand the attack the next day to be simultaneously a punishment for the night and a gaudy visual equivalent of it. Then I understand the crop-dusting plane, instrument of victimization, as a figure for a movie camera: it shoots at its victims and it coats them with a film of something that both kills and preserves, say that it causes metamorphosis. I claim evidence for the association of the prairie with the, let us say, inner landscape of the train compartment in the way a close-up of Eve's face at the Chicago train station dissolves into the establishing aerial shot of the road and fields of the plane attack. That conjunction of color and mood I claim asks for an allegorical identification of the woman and this stretch of land, but this is just something further each viewer must try out on his or her own. It is on this ground that the man undergoes his Shakespearean encounter of nothings — the nothing of Thornhill meeting the nothing of Kaplan — the attack on his identity, as it were, by itself. The recognition of the plane sent by Vandamm as a figure for the camera accounts satisfactorily for his gathering his stolen secrets on microfilm. This, in turn, would be a way Hitchcock has of saying that film — anyway in his camera — is the recorder of state secrets.

Put this together with the other overt declaration of the movie camera, this time by synechdoche rather than metaphor: I mean the telescope on the terrace of the Mount Rushmore memorial focussed on the faces of the presidents. A lot is being woven together here. We have cut to the presidents' faces from a close-up of Grant's face, turned toward us and suddenly illuminated as for examination by a harsh light from what we understand fictively to be a plane turning in his direction, hence what we understand literally and figuratively as a piece of photographic apparatus. We are being told that this face belongs to just one person on earth and that we are going to have to think about what that means. The cut from that image to the image of the presidents evidently poses some matching of Grant's face with the faces of stone, a matching generally prepared of course by the insistent references to the familiarity of his face but prepared more specifically by his having shaved with the miniscule razor and brush. Letting the phallic symbolism alone for a while, the question is certainly being posed about the sizes things are. Thornhill and Eve have had an exchange about whether he is a little boy or a big boy, and now the issue is about what size the human face of flesh and blood is in comparison with faces on the face of a granite mountain and the size of both in comparison with the photographic projection of the human face. A question is thus raised about what Grant is (made of), about what it means that he has become a national monument, and hence about what a monument is. So at the same time a question is raised about what presidents are and about what it means to know and remember them. These comparisons are underscored when it turns out, directly, that our initial view of the presidents' faces is an image of them as seen through a telescope set up for the pleasure and instruction of tourists. The image is possessed for us by, let us say, Thornhill, but there is no reason to think that anyone present wouldn't see the same image, the one we have now. Its being Grant who looks through the telescope at the famous stone faces identifies the conditions of his existence as a screen actor and thus identifies the mode in which we see him and think we know him. And I would be willing to swear from the fact alone of the way Grant is standing behind that telescope that he is also meant as a surrogate for the one who is capturing these images for our pleasure and instruction. But the Professor is there with Thornhill as we cut to him standing before the telescope, so the matter of directorial surrogates must be complicated.

Let us run through the evidence for Grant/Thornhill as surrogate for Hitchcock. There is, first of all, the hint laid down by Hitchcock's having autographed himself in this film as someone who misses a bus: Thornhill is the only (other) character in the film before whom a bus shuts its doors and drives off. Again, however we are to understand Thornhill's participation in the killing of the real Lester Townsend in the United Nations building, we must understand him as what this moment visually declares him to be, someone who betrays by showing a picture, that is, a picture which is, or which causes, a knife in the back—a reasonable, or anyway Hitchcockian, description of Hitchcock's narrative procedure. Now take the telescope and the two men on the terrace. Thornhill's initial reaction to the view through the telescope is to say "I don't like the way Teddy Roosevelt is looking at me." And he will say, "I think he's telling me not to go on with this harebrained scheme." This could be a line Hitchcock is allowing Grant to use about himself, perhaps about his role in this strenuous film, perhaps about his career as an actor. (I wouldn't put it past Hitchcock to be alluding to the fact that Grant shares a name with a president of the United States, one famous for drinking, and one in particular that only Teddy Roosevelt among the four presidents figured at Mount Rushmore would have known was a president.) But the Professor's response suggests something else first: "He's telling you to walk softly and carry a big stick." This makes a certain amount of sense said either to Grant or to Thornhill. It makes much better sense said to Hitchcock, hence said as it were to himself, that is, by one directorial surrogate to another. The exchange about a harebrained scheme and walking softly, as behind a big camera, would express a moment of self-doubt on Hitchcock's part to be overcome by the course of this film; and since this film is a kind of summary or anthology of his mature career as a whole, the doubt must be about the course of his mature career as a whole. If one were prepared to believe this, one would be encouraged to take the title *North by Northwest* not as naming some odd direction but as titling a search for directedness, a claim to have found it, as of the course of a career. (We will come to a more general reason for taking the title this way.) Hitchcock's identifying himself with the actor figure permits him a certain opposition to the two more explicit director figures, that is, permits him to claim opposition to the way other directors operate; his testimony is to show himself the victim as well as the inquisitor of his trade, the pursued as well as the pursuer, permitting himself to be looked back at.

This prompts me to collect one of the last of Hitchcock's inclusions in his anthology: his reference to *Rear Window,* whose hero (James Stewart) also looks through a telescope, now explicitly a telescopic camera lens and thus more explicitly conferring an identification as a film director, and whom someone or something eventually also looks back at through his telescope in a way he does not like. The Stewart figure has a kind of comic Hamlet derivation in that he sees everything and is debarred from taking action (by a broken leg in a cast). The thing that looks back at him, locking gazes with him, is the man whose murdering of his wife and dismemberment and disposition of the pieces of the body Stewart's camera has divined; and this too feels like an act of identification, between viewer and viewed, between director and subjects. Hitchcock's confession is a terrible one. (It may just be worth remembering that the Hamlet figure in Saxo Grammaticus dismembered the body of the figure that became Polonius and disposed of the parts in a sewer; and just worth putting this together with Thornhill's early dictation to his secretary of a note to accompany a gift of gold-wrapped candy: "This is for your sweet tooth, and all your other sweet parts.") The brighter side of Hitchcock's sensing an identification of himself with Hamlet claims his position as that of an intellectual, as possessed of a metaphysical imagination, and as unknown (partly because of the antic disposition he puts on).

What I just called Hitchcock's terrible confession — it is something I understand by Rothman's detection of Hitchcock's murderous camera — was going to be the guiding subject of these remarks, the thought that filming inevitably proceeds by severing things, both in cutting and, originally, in framing, and that Hitchcock is fully sensible of this fact and responsible to it. While it is buried in *North by Northwest* in the rarified reference to the original Hamlet story it is, if you allow the subject, blatantly posed by the gigantic heads of the monument and by the matching of Grant's head with them. The suggestion is that these memorializations have required acts of severing. This would be something else Grant does not like when he sees something looking back at him through the telescope. And it is this fate that Thornhill is saved from in earning the rescue from the faces of the monument. So when I say that Grant's looking through the telescope represents our perception of film, of something I mean by viewing, I am proposing that a theory of this mode of perception will be given in a theory of the perception of part-objects, as this is broached in the work of Melanie Klein. Such a theory should be able to help account for a pair of familiar facts in looking at film: that there may apparently be the most fantastic disproportion between what is actually shown on the screen and the emotion this elicits; *and* that this disproportion can be resisted, the emotion fail to appear. After all, many people think, or think they think, that *North by Northwest* is a light comedy. But while I have left the theme of severed objects as an undercurrent of these remarks I decided against making it explicit (then I partly changed my mind).

What is it that looks back through the telescope at Thornhill, who presumably has no special relation to those heads (anyway not Grant's relation)? It is puzzling that he should say it is Teddy Roosevelt since that head is, from the angle taken, quite retracted in comparison to those of Washington, Jefferson, and Lincoln and is not facing in the right direction. We are in any case being asked to let ourselves be puzzled by what it is we see when we are looking at the results of a movie camera and also by what the Mount Rushmore Memorial betokens. I figure what looks back through the lens not to require eyes, not even images of eyes, but to be whatever it is that a movie camera looks at, which is to say, whatever power it is that is solicited from us in perceiving things on film. I once said that the images of photography are of the world as a whole, and now thinking of what looks back at a director — an image's original audience as emblematized by these mountainous heads of the presidents, cliffs turned into faces — I would like to say that what looks back, what reveals itself to the viewer's gaze, is the physiognomy of the world, say the face of the earth. To animate, or reanimate, or humanize the world and so achieve a reciprocity with it is a recognizable aspiration of some poetry and some philosophy, as for example when Thoreau writes in the chapter "The Ponds" in *Walden:* "A lake is the landscape's most beautiful and expressive feature. It is earth's eye; looking into which the beholder measures the depth of his own nature." Thornhill's capacity for beholding nature in this way — as unsevered — would be a sign that he is to be saved.

The Mount Rushmore Memorial is a crazy American literalization of this ambition of reciprocity with the world. More specifically it literalizes such an idea as Walt Whitman's that America's mountains and prairies are the greatest of its poems. It is as if the monument proposes a solution to an American ambivalence as old as the pilgrims about the land of America: that it is human, in particular female, a virgin and yet a nourishing mother, but at the same time that we have raped her, blotted nature out by wanting our mark upon her.[5] (I have suggested that the film *North by Northwest,* in the crop-dusting sequence, invokes that ambivalence and calls for a solution to it.) The proposed solution of the monument is that if the mark is big enough and art enough and male enough, the doom of progress may be redeemed. Hardly a saving message to be drawn from the observation and memory of Washington, Jefferson, and Lincoln.

The *Encyclopedia Americana* notes that the faces of the monument measure some sixty feet from chin to forehead and adds, rather proudly I thought, that this is twice as high as the head of the Giza Sphinx. But what else is there to think about but their monumentality, and what more to conclude on their basis than that America has become twice the land of Egypt, twice as enslaving and twice as mysterious? Hitchcock shows that for a projected screen image to encompass the size of these faces is the work of an instant, and thus he at once declares his work in competition with Mount Rushmore as a monument to America, about America, and asks for a meditation on what can now constitute monumentality, on what can be made so as to show the value in commemorating. This is a reason that this film is at pains to anthologize the whole body of Hitchcock's mature, mostly American, work, to throw it all into the balance as a kind of rededication. Rededication is an appropriate mood before a monument, particularly in a moment of self-doubt. And even if this monument exemplifies competition and domination as much as it does commemoration, still it is about founding fathers, a wish, however awkwardly expressed, to get back to origins. Hitchcock has been careful to dissociate his attitude toward the monument from Vandamm's contemptuous dismissal of it with his opening question to Kaplan/Thornhill at the cafeteria: something like, "Now what little drama have you invited me to witness in these gay surroundings?" (*This* Englishman does not belong to the place but owns a structure mythically close to it, pitched out from the land, less a dwelling than a space station.) And what better rededication than to compete with this monument's way of remembering by showing your fellow inhabitants a better way—a way that does not attempt to petrify and sever the past but to revise the inheritance of it, to reinherit it?

Before giving the answer I have, I pause to note that we could look back and recount the main topics of *North by Northwest* as topics of seduction—our seduction by one another, by beautiful women and beautiful men and beautiful things, by mothers, strangers, liquor, fame, monuments, politics, America, art, film. The present film asks us to consider our attachments to things less in the light of what things they are than in the light of what mode of attachment we take toward them—for example, fetishistic, scoptophilic, masochistic, narcissistic, or in general, to use a key word of Emerson's, partial. One result of such consideration might be the thought that a healthy suspicion and testing of our attachment to film should extend to our attachment to, say, literature as well and that film and literature are each capable of helping us in this extension.

The mountain-monument seems to have become just another landscape of a cold war, the scene of an escape, as though we had lost the capacity for attachment altogether; but then it is the site of the playing out of one of drama's oldest subjects, the rights of love against the rights, anyway the requirements, of politics. We might come to think that the escape of this pair is seen by Hitchcock to be of national importance. Who are they, and what are they doing on this monument?

I will, as said, assert that they derive from, or from the same source as, the American comedy of remarriage, which I said means to me that their goal is the thing I call the legitimizing of marriage, the declaration that happiness is still to be won there, there or nowhere, and that America is a place, fictional

no doubt, in which that happiness can be found. The structure of these comedies, making the goal achievable, takes responsibility over a longish, extenda-
ble list of features, two of the principal ones being the achieving of a new
innocence and the establishing or reestablishing of an identity. These are pieces
of an ancient Hitchcockian problematic. So are the two further features of
remarriage comedies that I call the capacities for adventure and for improvisa-
tion. I mean by these capacities the virtues that allow you to become at home
in the world, to establish the world as a home. The capacities permit, if
necessary, living together on the road, as if loving were the finding of a direction, that is, or a directedness, just, as I mentioned, as Hitchcock's title *North
by Northwest* names otherwise than just a given direction. So important is it to
get this capacity for adventurousness straight that in the middle of their escape
down the monument the pair pause, comically, surrealistically, to discuss it (as
silent comics used to pause, in the middle of chasing one another, to catch
their breath). After his proposal to her she asks what happened to his two
earlier marriages. He says his wives left him because they found he led too dull
a life. For Hitchcock so daringly to mock the suspense he has been building up
over this escape, virtually declaring that the two are now standing on a platform in a studio, must mean that he wants to illustrate the significance of this
exchange, to enforce the assertion that dullness, taken as the opposite of adventurousness, where these are characteristics of human relationship, spiritual
matters, is not something that running around the face of the earth proves or
disproves, except allegorically. With those wives even this monumental situation of life and death would have been, spiritually speaking, dull; whereas
with Eve the "importance" of the time and place is unimportant for the opposite reason, that anything and everything can be an adventure, however untell-
able as such from outside. (This is roughly the sentiment of *Bringing Up
Baby*.)

The candidates for remarriage must, further, not be virgins, they must
have a past together, and they must talk well and wittily about marriage,
especially about whether they believe in marriage. The past the pair share in
North by Northwest is just one night, but it proves ample enough. And one or
both of the pair must maintain an openness to childhood, so it turns out to be
to Thornhill's spiritual credit that although in the course of the film he becomes big he remains a boy. (The childlike capacity of Grant's temperament on
film is stressed, I suppose discovered, in the comedies he made with Howard
Hawks.) The man in remarriage comedies is responsible for the education of
the woman as part of a process of rescuing or redeeming her from a state in
which she keeps herself; this may be characterized as a coldness or an inability
to feel, and the education typically takes the form of the man's lecturing or
haranguing the woman. In *North by Northwest* Thornhill identifies Eve as a
statue and accuses her of having no feelings to hurt, but we are shown by her
tears at this moment (at the auction) that what I earlier called the education in

his surviving her onslaught has taken effect; to begin her physical rescue, he will later write on his monogrammed matchbook a note that contains information no one else in the world is in a position to impart to her. We may also see in this successful delivery his finally getting a message through to a woman, the difficulty in doing which began this plot.

This is enough to let me outline what I take as the essential difference in structure between the romantic comedies of remarriage and Hitchcock's romantic thriller. The goal of the comedies requires what I call the creation of the woman, a new creation of a new woman. This takes the form in the comedies of something like the woman's death and revival, and it goes with the camera's insistence on the flesh-and-blood reality of the female actor. When this happens in Hitchcock, as it did in *Vertigo*, the Hitchcock film preceding *North by Northwest*, it is shown to produce catastrophe: the woman's falling to her death, precisely the fate *averted* in *North by Northwest*. Here, accordingly, it is the man who undergoes death and revival (at least twice, both times at the hands of the woman) *and* whose physical identity is insisted upon by the camera.[6] Hitchcock is thus investigating the point that the comedies of remarriage are least certain about, namely, what it is about the man that fits him to educate and hence rescue the woman, that is, to be chosen by the woman to educate her and thereby to achieve happiness for them both.

But again, why is the rescue to be achieved from the face of this monument? I have called it the face of the earth, the earth itself become visible, as pure surface. These tiny creatures are crawling between heaven and earth, a metaphysical accomplishment, as if becoming children again. Hamlet, feeling like a child, claims this accomplishment for himself as he decrees that there shall be no more marriages. Thornhill proposes marriage as he and the woman hang from a precipice; a gallant concept, as if marriage were a presence of mind, requiring no assurance of a future. Close-ups of the pair on the surface of the monument faces show them as if on an alien planet. There is no longer nature on the earth; earth is no longer an artifact by analogy, intimating God; it is literally and totally artifact, petrified under the hands of mankind. To place your film in competition with such an achievement is to place it in competition with film's own peculiar power of preserving the world by petrifying it, or anyway fixing it in celluloid. The couple in remarriage comedies are isolated at the end, expected to legitimize marriage without the world, which has no help for pain. The surface of Hitchcock's Mount Rushmore strikes me as a place of absolute spiritual isolation, civilization engulfing even empty space. In one of his first American films, *Saboteur* (to name a final excerpt in this anthology), a man holds a villain from a ledge at the top of the Statue of Liberty, but the villain's sleeve comes loose and he falls to earth. To fall from Mount Rushmore, as I am imagining it, would be to fall off the earth, down the vast edges drear of the world.

Thornhill lifts Eve up directly from the isolation of the monument's ledge to the isolation of the marriage bed, as if identifying both places as the scene of cliff-hangers and declaring that they are at home in both. At the lift Leonard is overcome and drops the statue Eve has been identified with, which breaks against the granite monument, opening to produce some film, I take it the present film. I in effect describe *The Philadelphia Story* as a film produced by a rescue which takes the form of the breaking of a statue in favor of a woman. I also claim that the remarriage is, using a repeated phrase of that film, of national importance. My ground is the thought that while America, or any discovered world, can no longer ratify marriage, the achievement of true marriage might ratify something called America as a place in which to seek it. This is a state secret.

Notes

1. Rothman's book was published by Harvard University Press in 1982. I am also indebted to Marian Keane's "The Designs of Authorship: An Essay on *North by Northwest*," *Wide Angle*, vol. 4, no. 1 (1980): 44–52. I should like to mention here Robin Wood's *Hitchcock's Films* (South Brunswick and New York: A. S. Barnes, 1969), an intelligent, literate statement about the films of Hitchcock, which, while comparatively early as these things go in English-speaking circles, continues to repay reading. For an account of *North by Northwest* at once more suspicious than mine (about the value of the film) and more gullible (about Hitchcock's remarks about it and about the film's apparently casual evaluation of itself, so to speak), see George M. Wilson's "The Maddest McGuffin: Some Notes on *North by Northwest*," *Modern Language Notes*, vol. 94, no. 5 (1979): 1159–72.
2. A consequent moral equation between these figures is being drawn, another point I took away from a conversation with Rothman and Keane.
3. Subsequent to the original publication of this essay I looked up another document familiar in *Hamlet* scholarship that Professor Geoffrey Bullough, in volume 7 of his *Narrative and Dramatic Sources of Shakespeare*, describes as "the German prose play *Der Bestrafte Brudermord oder Prinz Hamlet aus Dännemark*, the degenerate version of an English play probably taken over to the Continent by English actors before 1626" (p. 20). Professor Bullough prints the play (among the Sources, Possible Sources, Probable Sources, Probable Historical Allusions, and Analogues; specifically as an Analogue) in an English translation entitled *Fratricide Punished* revised from one made for H. H. Furness's *The New Variorum Edition* of *Hamlet* of 1877. In this play the Laertes character is named Leonhardus.
   I mention this not exactly to clinch my suggestion that the name Laertes may be seen to survive in the name Leonard; and not just to indicate a perfectly obvious place in which Hitchcock might have learned this change of name (Furness's famous editions and compilations), a source he may very well have meant to leave a clue for in his own change; but primarily to make explicit the question of when and how a matter of interpretation gets clinched in one's own mind. It *might*, I think, have happened to me on discovering Leonhardus; but in fact it came with the emphasis on "rot," as read in the paragraph following the one to which this note is appended.
4. Even Raymond Bellour's useful and sophisticated study of *North by Northwest* ("Le blocage symbolique," *Communications* no. 23 [1975]: 235–350), judging from one hurried reading, has not, it seems to me, cleared itself of this question. My remark is directed only to the first half of this monograph-length paper. The second half, devoted to a geometry of the crop-dusting sequence, I have not looked at sufficiently to have a judgment of.
5. Two valuable accounts of the history of American attitudes toward the American land are Edwin Fussell's *Frontier: American Literature and the American West* (Princeton, N.J.: Princeton Univ. Press, 1965), and Annette Kolodny's *The Lay of the Land: Metaphor as Experience and History in American Life and Letters* (Chapel Hill, N.C.: Univ. of North Carolina Press, 1975).
6. That a given genre yields an adjacent genre by having one of its features "negated" in this way is

something I give a little theoretical attention to in the introduction to *Pursuits of Happiness* (Cambridge: Harvard Univ. Press, 1982).

NORTH BY NORTHWEST (Metro-Goldwyn-Mayer, 1959). *Producers:* Alfred Hitchcock, Herbert Coleman, *Assistant Director:* Robert Saunders, *Script:* Ernest Lehman, *Photography:* Robert Burks (VistaVision, Technicolor), *Editor:* George Tomasini, *Sets:* Robert Boyle, William A. Horning, Merrill Pyle, Henry Grace, Frank McKelvey, *Music:* Bernard Herrmann, *Titles:* Saul Bass, *Players:* Cary Grant (Roger O. Thornhill), Eva Marie Saint (Eve Kendall), James Mason (Philip Vandamm), Jessie Royce Landis (Clara Thornhill), Leo G. Carroll (the Professor), Martin Landau (Leonard). 136 minutes.

CHAPTER TWENTY

The Universal Hitchcock

Ian Cameron and Richard Jeffery

In his interviews, Hitchcock, feeling himself suspected of being secretly an intellectual, rarely admits to anything incriminating. At question time he displays footwork of a nimble grace rivalled only by the steelier performances of Otto Preminger: unshaken by the near-certifiable imbecility of his interrogators, he raises the press conference to the level of art. Hitchcock is not the man to be trapped into saying anything that would detract from his chosen image: he is the Master of Suspense, not a mere intellectual. While he skilfully adjusts his performance to suit his listeners, even to encourage them, he disavows any intellectual intent in his films—"I'm more interested in the technique of storytelling by means of film rather than in what the film contains."

All this seems like fine ammunition to the critics who can still see Hitch only in terms of the genteel trivia he served up in the thirties. Penelope Houston, in her right-minded worm's-eye view of Hitchcock, derived much comfort from his answer to the critics of a certain French magazine when they asked: "What is the deepest logic of your films?"

"To put the audience through it," said Hitch, and for once in an interview, he was telling the truth, the whole truth, and nothing but the truth. Realizing that initial reactions to the cinema are essentially emotional rather than intellectual, he thinks and is willing to talk about his films in terms of inducing emotions in the spectators: "You should not be permitted to reason. Because the film should be stronger than reason." In Hitchcock movies, where nothing appears just because it happens to be in the shot, everything is calculated for the single purpose of inducing emotions. Naturalistic details are not included to show us the real world for its own sake. There is an ulterior motive: to make us feel (whether or not we think) that we are watching things relevant to our own experience. Hitchcock is fond of scenes in ordinary places like shops, offices, or restaurants, and in this he is capitalizing on the complacency he attacks with *The Birds*. In familiar, safe places, where we spend large parts of our lives, nothing ghastly is likely to happen.

At least as crucial to the Hitchcock method as setting and camera technique is his concern with character, his selection of words, movements, and tones of voice. He means his characters to stand up to a good deal of examination. That they should be convincing is only another means to the Hitchcockian end. However complex they may be, they are not there to be studied but to generate emotions in the spectator. In *Marnie,* which shows Hitchcock at his most extreme, and most powerful, we are continually prevented from examining the heroine's emotional disturbances with detachment because of the related emotional disturbances that are being produced in us.

Many critics refuse to admit that *Marnie* produces any reaction in them beyond disappointment or irritation. Perhaps, in the way of film critics, they are reacting only to the film level of its script, in which Hitchcock's *Marnie* is nowhere to be found. The predictable common ground among the film's detractors is their refusal to admit that it affected them emotionally.

Penelope Houston pointed out gleefully that almost any interpretation would fit *The Birds.* The lady has an unfortunate knack of using such true and interesting statements as if they were damaging criticisms. The ambiguity of the film's meaning is a prime virtue. If it had a specific allegorical meaning, it would have a particular relevance to each spectator, who could then deal with it on its own level. But its very ambiguity makes the threat operate irresistibly at every level of audience consciousness.

The events in *The Birds* could represent the end of the world: Judgment Day. After all, in the words of the Book of Common Prayer: "The day of the Lord cometh as a thief in the night: and when men shall say, Peace, and all things are safe, then shall sudden destruction come upon them . . . and they shall not escape." In another way, too, it is Judgment Day. For all its major characters it is the all-time moment of truth, when they are revealed for what they are. Its *modus operandi* is the biblically traditional one, the plague, with the birds as a temperate zone-equivalent for the locust trouble that hit ancient Egypt. As a vision of Judgment Day, it is singularly astute: a miniature version, cut off from the world at large, which is only in evidence through a couple of radio broadcasts that minimize the peril. In fact Hitchcock eliminated shots of the Golden Gate Bridge covered in birds. Any attempt to show world-wide destruction would have transformed the whole effort into a piece of science fiction fantasy, an *On the Beach.*

But *The Birds,* while it contains references to Judgment Day, is not completely an allegory. It shows only a tentative sorting out of the characters, and the essence of the ending is that life still has to be attempted even in a world completely dominated by birds—at the end there is no doubt that the birds have won: the people are leaving, the birds remain. *The Fall of the Roman Empire* is much more nearly about the end of the world, at least about the end of *a* world. The essence of *The Birds,* as of all late Hitchcock movies, is that it applies not just to people in a specific situation (like the end of the world) but to everyone, and most immediately to the audience in the cinema.

Why do the birds come? Perhaps as a punishment—the Judgment Day references carry with them hints of Divine retribution. The two evident sins for which humanity (as represented by Melanie Daniels and the inhabitants of Bodega Bay) is to be punished are complacency and mendacity. Melanie's main behavior pattern in the first part of the film is lying, and Mitch Brenner and the townspeople are complacent, for example, in assuming that Melanie is *merely* as she appears: a rich socialite. Characteristically, Hitchcock ensnares us into finding ourselves taking exactly the same attitude toward Melanie: after she has delivered the lovebirds to the Brenner farm, she gets back into the boat and pushes off with an oar while the boat is still tied by its stern to the landing stage. Aha, we think smugly, stupid bird! But not a bit of it. Melanie is demonstrating her capability in boats by using the stern line to swing the boat around for her return to the town.

The two sins are linked in Melanie's complacent lying and in everyone's lying complacency about nature. *The Birds* is a film about man and nature: not a *Man of Aran* or a *Where the River Bends* about isolated or pioneering man surviving in the face of environmental rigors—that would be too particular, too distant and therefore alien to Hitchcock's purposes. He treats this traditional theme in a novel manner, picking on the one angle that could interest him in a generally un-Hitchcockian subject. He looks at the attitude of comfortably civilized people towards nature. The people of Bodega Bay do what the rugged pioneers could not, they represent *us*.

Their attitudes are very typical and, furthermore, we are made to find ourselves sharing them. They could mostly be summed up by one complacent answer to the question, what is nature there for? It is there for us. We know that nature is red in tooth and claw, but we choose to ignore this in favor of enjoying it as decor. "Birds are not aggressive creatures," says Mrs. Bundy whose avocation is bird-watching. "They bring beauty into the world."

Hitchcock expounds his theme of man and nature largely in terms of man and man. To the inhabitants of Bodega Bay, Melanie is just a rare migrant: a rich socialite on the wing. All through the film, we see and are involved in reactions to people and situations which assume that everything is as it appears and can be judged and sorted away according to past experience—reactions of just the sort that Hitchcock films discourage. The key to all the complacency is the desire to pigeonhole experience into known categories that make life seem more secure and comprehensible. When Mrs. Brenner's hens stop eating, she assumes that she has been sold bad feed. She is very upset indeed when Fred Brinkmeyer, the storekeeper, tells her that Dan Fawcett's hens have also stopped eating and that Dan Fawcett bought a different brand of feed. Categorization is even essential to the workings of society: Annie Hayworth complains that because Fred Brinkmeyer can't remember names, the mail never gets to the right place.

Hitchcock's position, which is not *stated* but *felt,* in *The Birds* extends the view of the world, which found a multiplicity of individual expressions in his earlier films, to the level of a universal generalization. The red herrings that swam in shoals through his earlier films were evidence of Hitchcock's mistrust of appearances: nothing is as it seems. The desire of the characters for security leads them to assumptions that are contradicted by the very nature of the world in which they live.

Against a view of the bird attacks as retribution could be set the disproportion between the punishment and the sins which at least to the audience seem small. The travelling salesman could perhaps have deserved his fiery doom, indirectly caused by the birds, for suggesting that they were messy creatures and should be wiped out. But the unfortunate Dan Fawcett, found in the wreckage of his bedroom with his eyes pecked out, had apparently done nothing worse than keeping chickens. Above all, what had Annie Hayworth done? As played by Suzanne Pleshette, she is the most sympathetic of the leading characters. She may be lying to Melanie and herself about her reasons for staying in Bodega Bay (she is obviously still in love with Mitch), and there are at least two good dramatic reasons why she should perish. But at least individual retribution is not behind the action of the birds. As the inhabitants of Bodega Bay are meant to typify all of us, they could be the subjects of that old Hitchcock device, transference of guilt, this time on a suitably universal scale, from the whole world to them—a Christ population!

In fact, the disparity between sin and retribution provides no case against the Judgment Day interpretation. The idea that retribution ought to operate quantitatively has a most unHitchcockian complacency about it. A long line of unfortunates in Hitchcock movies have apparent peccadilloes. The logic inherent in making the punishment fit the crime is anyway anathema to Hitchcock. *The Birds* turns the logic of appearances inside out with quite unprecedented thoroughness.

The reason that the birds come is because Hitchcock sent them, and if anyone is being punished, it is us. In the movies, the director can have the role of God. Hitchcock is the only director to take the part wholeheartedly. He is the Manipulator of Coincidence, who involves the McKenna family in a political assassination in London by making a bus from Casablanca to Marrakesh swerve on the road at the beginning of *The Man Who Knew Too Much*. And he alone is in control of the feelings of the audience in the cinema; where in *The Birds* he loses that control, it is because the divine apparatus of special effects lets him down. The attacks are sometimes a relief in their unconvincingness after the suspense of the build-up. In view of Hitchcock's awareness of the sexual nature of suspense, even this defect has a certain suitability.

If Hitch is aiming his birds at us, the attacks are calculated for maximum disturbance. They attack out of a clear sky in the most reassuringly domesticated of landscapes: once more our complacency is being used against us. We do deserve all we get, because like the McKennas, by seeking excitement, we have wished the trouble upon ourselves. We must have wanted the birds to come, otherwise we would not have spent our money at the box office.

The use of birds as the assault vehicles is also calculated as a particular affront to our feelings about birds: known carnivores like eagles are even avoided in favor of commoner and apparently friendlier species. In our hubristically man-centered view of the world we even like to see birds as little people. This anthropomorphism makes us want to put them in little houses; the first sequence of *The Birds* even has a miniature tenement for birds. It is illustrated by the lovebirds which lean out as Melanie's car rounds a corner on the road to Bodega Bay.

If we tend to view birds as people, the film encourages us to view people as birds. Melanie has bright eyes and a tendency to cock her head on one side inquiringly or seductively. Her car emits bird-like screeches as it swoops down the zigzag road into Bodega Bay. The children's voices in the school are unnaturally shrill. The first assault on Melanie by a single gull comes when she is at her most bird-like. The crows mass for the attack on the school while the children are singing inside. Shock at birds attacking people is coupled with shock that they attack each other in a most inhuman fashion.

The attacks have their effect on the audience because they are arbitrary in their operation (it is very disturbing that the birds suddenly stop when they have almost broken into the Brenner house) and really unexplained in their origin. Hitchcock inserts a sequence in the restaurant in which he systematically destroys possible explanations put into the mouths of the customers, who together form a microcosm of America and whose mutually exclusive complacencies demonstrate the impossibility of resistance. "It's the end of the world," says the drunk, with some glee and much biblical quotation. If he represents religion, Mrs. Bundy's complacency is that of science which has a totally anti-Hitchcockian method, making theories based on observation with the aim of increasing the predictability of things. She refuses to believe the facts because they don't square with her scientific knowledge. The salesman who wants to wipe out the birds is the representative of militarism (the birds could of course represent Communists, who are always Among Us and waiting for the time when they can take over). The militarist's happy assumption that the birds *could* be wiped out is destroyed by Mrs. Bundy's science which demonstrates their overwhelming numbers. Having discounted the answers provided by religion, science, and militarism, Hitchcock shows us public opinion as a fourth major force. It is personified by the woman who sits with her children, eating southern fried chicken and not wanting to hear about the danger. She tries to silence the ominous reports by saying that her children are afraid—which they are not, until they sense her fear. She tries to escape, and when a bird attack stops her, she turns on Melanie and accuses her of being the cause of the attacks, which she says (wrongly) didn't happen until Melanie came there. Public opinion turns to witch-hunt—nothing more than a desperately compla-

cent search for an explanation of the attacks. But while the woman is address-
ing Melanie, the camera takes up Melanie's subjective viewpoint, so that the
words are addressed straight to us: "I think you're evil." Although the woman
is hysterical and there is no firm connection between Melanie's arrival and the
bird attack, we feel guilty. The guilt is emotionally aroused and totally irrational.

If the apparently unprovoked assault of *The Birds* is an allegory of anything, it is an allegory of Hitchcock's films. He is a specialist in attacks on the
audience. He has attacked us with kidnapping, with attempted and (in *Psycho*) actual murder of our identification figure, with unjust accusation of murder, and with the guilt of actually having murdered. The latter is not logically
comparable with the others but emotionally is just as much an attack on us as
spectators. We haven't committed a murder, but Hitchcock uses all his resources to make sure that we feel guilty about it. This irrational guilt is not
intended as a moral lesson (though it may have that effect) but as a device to
break down our defenses.

In the films where the attack is logically an external coincidence (like *I
Confess*), the guilt is brought in separately. Very often it's sexual: some kind of
love affair among the principals, morally or psychologically dubious enough to
make us uneasy and excusable enough to keep us involved.

In *Marnie,* guilt and insecurity are inextricably joined. The guilt is evoked
by Marnie's pathological stealing, lying, and frigidity, the insecurity by her
equally pathological fears, her nightmares, and her climactic near derangement. It is as if parts of Marion Crane and Norman Bates from *Psycho* had
been combined in one person. On the other hand, Marnie is also an extension
of Melanie, making her lying into a way of life. She also takes Melanie's sexual
traits to an extreme. In fact, she could well be the quintessence of Hitchcock's
hostile view of American womanhood. In an interview, which we hope to
publish some day in *Movie,* he says of Melanie in *The Birds* that the "the whole
performance, the whole shape deals with the smug American girl who talks
sex, lives sex, but won't go to bed. We have a vulgar phrase for that: they are
what are called cock-teasers." This characteristic is for Marnie both an unconscious necessity and a calculated manner of behavior. Her attractiveness is part
of her technique as a thief. There are other linkages between Melanie and
Marnie apart from the incarnation of both in the admirable Miss Hedren. They
have the same reaction to extreme stress — in one case the bird attack and in the
other the threat of sexual intercourse on the first night of the honeymoon. In
both films Miss Hedren cowers back on a sofa and draws her legs up under her.

Marnie is likeable, and we're encouraged to identify with her. She's happy
the first time we hear her speak, and even the furious Strutt, short of $9,967,
sums her up by saying, "She seemed so *nice*." We identify with her even more
closely by taking her contemptuous attitude toward the man whose lust has
made him an easy target for theft, as Strutt remembers her attractions for the

benefit of the detectives: "Size 8 dress, blue eyes, black . . . wavy hair." Hitchcock undermines our sense of security by making us identify with a woman who turns out to be a frigid kleptomaniac. The disturbances of her life involve us irresistibly. Meanwhile (apart from the exceptional dislocations from sanity), the sense of everyday life is maintained. If we stopped feeling the value of everyday life, the threat would lose its effectiveness.

Marnie's world, which we accept completely during the first part of the film, is represented in the structure of the images. *The Birds* was mostly built around level rectangles, ordinary and safe-seeming, echoing the shape of the screen. They are made up of buildings, cars, birdcages, and such places of comparative security. When, on a number of anxious fades, the rectangle is formed by two people, it looks much more vulnerable. At certain moments, particularly of stress (Mrs. Brenner's admission that she has never felt safe since her husband died and the attack on the house), Hitchcock slants the rectangle and destroys the stability of the image—a technique he has often used subliminally to undermine our own stability.

Marnie is built almost continuously out of slanted rectangles, from the very first shot of Marnie's conspicuously yellow handbag full of money forming a lozenge shape on the screen. The following sequence of her covering her tracks is shown in a series of close-ups of rectangular objects tilted with respect to the plane of the image: suitcases, social security cards, left-luggage locker and grating (down which she drops the key of the locker). So many shots can be seen as slanted rectangles that, while these are definitely unstable, any other shape comes to seem even more so, particularly the sensible level rectangles of Bodega Bay stability. Hitchcock uses the triangular compositions of *Rope* similarly, reserving the square, level two-shots for the most unnatural and discomforting moments, usually of psychological clash between the two young murderers.

After the decorous lettering of the credits in their comfortably rectangular border, backed by Bernard Herrmann's violently romantic music, the close-up of the handbag which starts the first shot establishes the slanted image. It is at first so close that we can see only the slant of her elbow with which she is holding the bag, and a slanted glimpse of what later turns out to be railway line. The camera slows down so that we can see her at full length: unattractive long black hair and a heavy suitcase. It follows her in this position then stops, while she continues walking away and then, at some distance from the camera, puts the suitcase down beside a seat and pauses there. Now we can see an empty station, shown in slanted, rectangular shapes arranged symmetrically on either side of the image.

It is a shot that is unusually arbitrary in appearance, even in the context of Hitchcock's essentially arbitrary *mise en scène*, which, although it may illustrate the action, is there for its own sake and just has to be accepted. If it weren't continuously fascinating, it would be intolerable. The first shot of

Marnie has the characteristic of Hitchcock tracking shots: it follows rather than leads by determining the movement of the character, so that we don't know where it's taking us. It is a shot of enormous complexity. From one point of view, it is a single-shot montage of bulging handbag, Marnie, and empty station, telling us quite clearly that she is travelling some distance at an unusual hour with this bag and its contents. The end of the shot has the chilly symmetry of a street or a corridor, seen down its length, an image Hitchcock uses in *The Birds* (for example where Mrs. Brenner starts down the corridor towards Dan Fawcett's bedroom) and more in *Marnie* where it fits more closely into the design. Its function is often to make us wonder what we may find at the other end. In this particular shot, the symmetry is broken slightly, obviously from choice, by the unassimilated cylindrical shape of a gasoline storage tower in the distance.

Again, the composition of the image — Marnie walking directly away from the camera down the straight line on the platform, which bisects the image, with the great slanting planes of the platform roof flying out at us on either side — is of the character having chosen a course and holding to it, threatened by the potential schizophrenia of the split, symmetrical picture.

Finally, the shot is a very direct image of Marnie's life, of getting away, with the camera in pursuit flagging and finally grinding to a halt, while Marnie doesn't stop until she is at a good distance and in her own world, suggested by the slanted perspectives of the platform roof above her. This interpretation of pursuer and pursued is encouraged by the next shot, which shows Strutt staring out of the screen as if the first shot had been a Hitchcock subjective shot from which he would cut to the person whose viewpoint he had been showing.

"Robbed!" says Strutt, and the sequence goes on to establish his furious determination on vengeance. He talks about it to the amused Mark Rutland, who's there on business. Rutland remembers noticing the dark-haired Marnie when she worked in Strutt's office. Only when the vengeful Strutt and the reflective Rutland have been established do we return to Marnie, and we aren't shown her face until she raises her blonde head from a handbasin in which is left the remains of the black dye. By presenting the situation in this way, Hitchcock makes sure that we don't feel the past has been erased and the guilt and threat can be forgotten. Guilt and threat have been too massively and immediately established. They will affect our reaction to everything.

What Hitchcock has established is the legal guilt and the apparent threat: theft and imprisonment. But in the Hitchcock world, where nothing is as it seems, one can expect the initial guilt-threat situation to reveal deeper guilt and more serious threat, in this case insanity. Although some spectators may derive a premature zoophilic *frisson* from Marnie's words to her horse, "Oh, Forio, if you want to bite anyone, bite me," we don't learn that there is anything psychologically wrong with Marnie until the sequence in which we meet Mother.

One of the points that emerged from *The Birds* was that the external threat has the function in the film of setting in motion an internal threat of at least equal gravity. The most distressing moment in *The Birds* comes after Melanie has been rescued from the attic, when she regains consciousness and starts fighting desperately with the Brenner family. It is no overstatement to say that the real threat is internal (the external one is, anyway, impartial and irresistible); just as in *The Man Who Knew Too Much*, the real threat to the family lay not in the kidnapping but in Ben's desire to dominate his wife.

The mother figures that are characteristic of Hitchcock movies usually serve to show up the absence of father figures. In *Marnie,* Mr. Rutland, Senior, is a nonentity, associated faintly with tastes for horses and pretty girls but really just with a taste for good cake at afternoon tea. The late Mr. Brenner in *The Birds* is remembered by Mitch's mother as a lost standard of protection: "If only your father were here," she screams at Mitch when she loses control. In his last three films, Hitchcock has gone even further in destroying the protection of the family by embodying the threat in Mother. Mrs. Bates destroyed Norman by indulging her lust and, when he killed her, took over his body. Mrs. Brenner is the one character to disintegrate in *The Birds* and represents the internal threat to a civilization under external strain; her function as a mother has often to be undertaken by Melanie, even by Annie.

In *Marnie,* Mother is the source of both guilt and threat. She has implanted in Marnie the frigidity which is not inherent in her character and which leads to the suicide attempt. It is not the guilt of stealing from which Marnie has to keep running away, although the legal guilt provides the *practical* reason for her flight. We know that Strutt, like the man Marion Crane robbed in *Psycho,* is unpleasant and probably deserved to lose his money. Whereas Marion's guilts are connected coincidentally with the threat of Mrs. Bates, in *Marnie* Mother's old *métier* as a whore is the direct source of both guilt and threat. Marnie commits her mother's murder and is pursued by the guilt of it. Mother remains marked by her guilt because she is crippled, and bodily affliction is the traditional mark of the sinner.

The first sequence at Mrs. Edgar's home starts with the corridor shape of the squalid street outside. We find that the house is clean and unexpectedly well furnished with Marnie's money. The sequence links together a number of factors, all introduced for the first time and linked together by their introduction in this setting. Marnie gives her mother lots of presents, but Mother doesn't show her appreciation as Marnie would like. Making connections after learning the denouement of the film, one realizes that this is not a sign, as Marnie thinks, that she doesn't love her, but that refusing to give love in return for gifts is part of her resolve to break away from her former life. Hitchcock emphasizes this in the physical nature of the attentions Marnie is demanding. The connection is further strengthened when Mother, Bernice, uses her bad leg, the relic of the murder, as the reason to stop Marnie snuggling against her.

We've already been shown that Marnie leads a double life, but this sequence provides the first example of her lying, and in the setting of her mother's home we hear the first clear statement of her frigidity in a conversation about Marnie's latest present, thus linking frigidity, Mother, and money:

Bernice: No man ever give me anything so good.

Marnie: Oh, we don't need men, Mama. We can do very well for ourselves, just you and me.

Bernice: A decent woman don't have need for any man.

In this sequence, too, the nightmare, in a mild and undefined form, is linked to Mother who interrupts it by coming up the stairs in the half-darkness. This shot, like Melanie's progress to the attic, is designed to capitalize on the audience's most irrational associations of upstairs and darkness with childish fears. But in *Marnie* darkness plays a much smaller part than in most Hitchcock films. The threat has come out into everyday life and there is no escape from it.

Marnie is desperately and irrationally jealous of the attentions her mother lavishes on the little girl Jessie, who evidently represents her as a child but whose treatment contrasts with the neglect Marnie must have experienced when Mother was with the clients. This neglect is shown in the climactic flashback as the start of the trouble—little Marnie, left alone during a storm, lying on a couch because her mother can't have her in the bedroom, disturbs Mother and lover with her cries. Jessie is not a specially nasty child. She just likes, in the self-centered way of children, to be the focus of attention. It is only because we are made to share Marnie's view that we see her as a particularly unpleasant child.

In Bernice's house we are subjected to red, a shock which is placed at the opposite end of the sequence from the nightmare: it comes right at the beginning. The two shocks are placed to undermine our defenses. Both coming palpably from within, they are set off by external stimuli (the gladioli and the near-quarrel in the kitchen), and have all the suddenness of attacks from outside. The sequence is framed by these two different pre-echoes of the end of the film, when the momentary dislocation threatens to become absolute.

The brief flooding of the screen with red is a parallel to the shot Hitchcock has imagined of a daisy in close-up suddenly stained with blood. Although many things in the world are red in color, only one meaning is attached emotionally to red in Hitchcock movies. Marnie's mental disturbance is an excuse for the sudden bloodstaining of the screen rather than its raison d'etre. The red on its various appearances foreshadows the shot at the end of blood spreading across the dead sailor's white T-shirt until it fills the screen. This image has further emotional extensions to the Victorian image of loss of virtue: blood on the sheet.

By the time Marnie goes into action at Rutland & Co., we have been shown her criminal past, her dream-like escapes with Forio, and her problems which are all linked to her mother. It has been demonstrated to us that these problems, as yet undefined, are more serious than the possibility of being caught by the police.

At Rutlands, Mark recognizes her but she doesn't recognize him—one respect in which her lack of interest in men is not ideal for her work. (And it is the gesture of pulling skirt over knees that gives Marnie away to him.) Mark has her taken on, invades her life, catches her when she commits the theft and tries to escape, forces her to marry him, and then patiently tries to cope with each further difficulty as it arises. We first see him at Rutlands introduced with some very emphatic Hitchcock montage of close-ups and shots from his point of view into an interview in which he takes a hardly apparent, but crucial, part. This pattern of close-ups and subjective shots is Hitchcock's normal way of dealing with identification figures, but at this stage our identification cannot suddenly transfer to him. The effect here is one of invasion, of having him thrust right into our faces.

The massive close-ups of Mark are the first of many compositions in which slanting lines are provided by his broad shoulders. Here he is leaning casually against a wall of the office. Mark's contribution to the slanting compositions comes about by necessity: he takes such a large part in the film that he has to be involved in its design. Yet his integration into the slanted compositions indicates that his invasion is an entrance and acceptance of Marnie's slanting world as it is.

Mark's most complete acceptance of the Marnie world comes after their marriage when, as a step in his attempt to break down her resistance to him, he fetches her horse, Forio. The horse evidently represents the life Marnie wants to lead. After the confinement of offices, hotel rooms, and railway stations, Marnie galloping out on Forio is an image of freedom—but even the image of freedom is illusory in its appearance, for she is riding in front of a studio back-projection machine.

The contrast between Mark's world and Marnie's is shown in his ownership of a car against hers of a horse. If Marnie's unrealistic world is represented by horse and obvious back-projection, Mark's real one is shown in the sleek modern car and apparently real backgrounds—in fact, back-projection but without the transparent artifice of Marnie's. But the car is more than a symbol of Mark's life. The physical fact of journeys in it—taking Marnie back to Rutlands, back to be confronted with her past in Baltimore—reverses her escapes by train and taxi. The car, Mark's life, is a cage around Marnie (just as the birds made a telephone box into a cage for Melanie). The main interrogation sequences take place in the car (or in bedrooms, which for Marnie are even worse). It is even in the car that Mark first makes her aware that he is pursuing her. After she has accepted his invitation to the races, she says, "Are you fond of horses?" "No," he replies, "not at all."

Mark is still a surprising figure to find in a Hitchcock film. Any kind of effective help or protection has usually been avoided: witness the absence of father figures. The Mark character in one form or another is still a comparatively new arrival in Hitchcock. In the films of the fifties, however, the central figures were more reliable and the situations less irresistibly overwhelming. In the last three films, the situations are extreme, the attacks are not temporary but relentless, and the figures we identify with are women and thus vulnerable in a way that we can hardly feel James Stewart or Cary Grant to be. Mitch in *The Birds* is a new figure (of whom possibly a trace is to be found in the John Gavin character in *Psycho*) of possible security, slightly aggressive but genuine.

Mark is a much more emphatic development of the essentially good-natured Mitch. Mark, however, is not just a nice guy. He keeps his only relics of his dead wife in a glass case and talks about training a jaguarundi to trust him. "You don't love me," says Marnie in the car on the way back from Garrods, "I'm just something you've caught! You think I'm some kind of animal you've trapped!" "That's right, you are," replies Mark in a determinedly calm voice, "and I've caught something really wild this time, haven't I? I tracked you and caught you and by God I'm going to keep you." While it is obvious that Mark does love Marnie, there are suggestions of Scottie's desire in *Vertigo* to have a woman completely in his power. Even Marnie perceives that there is something pretty bent in Mark's feelings towards her when he is hot to play Mental Health Week: "Talk about dream worlds! You've got a pathological fix on a woman who is not only an admitted criminal but who screams if you come near her. So what about your dreams, Daddy, dear?" After all, Mark does use Marnie's crime as a way of forcing her to marry him, hardly a normal expression of love.

Hitchcock encourages our identification with Mark during the honeymoon sequence. We wait expectantly with him as he nervously fixes drinks while he waits for Marnie to emerge from the bathroom. What is she going to be wearing when she emerges? Plenty, we discover. By identifying with Mark, we are made to feel how unreasonable is her treatment of him. There's some very smart work with the costumes around here. The nightgown which covers even her arms to the wrists poses the question of entry. When Mark cannot restrain himself any longer, he puts into effect the answer which will have occurred to most of the audience by ripping it off, then shamefacedly covers her with a bathrobe. Huge close-ups of him pressing her down on the bed quickly kill our identification with him by making us see the meaning of the experience for Marnie.

Our identification with Mark resumes when he wakes up to find Marnie gone, when he thinks she has actually killed herself. This is the only place in the film where there is a strong suggestion that any of Marnie's sufferings have transferred to Mark. The search is handled with great emphasis in the series of static corridor shapes, increasingly enclosed, as he runs towards us along empty decks, and particularly in the two terrifyingly subjective moving shots of gray, turbulent sea, which illustrate his fears for her.

The film, then, represents the clash of two dream worlds which are incompatible. Alternatively it is a Christian parable of two sinners helping each other. There is no doubt that, whatever his motives, Mark does help Marnie. Once Marnie is able to accept his attentions or, initially, his help, the focus of his mental abnormality will be destroyed and one presumes that he will then be able to love Marnie in a "normal" manner.

Mark's attempts to cure Marnie carry her no further than wanting to be cured. "Why can't you leave me alone?" is finally replaced by "Oh, why can't somebody help me?" Fade out.

Fade in to a high-angle shot along the main hall of the Rutland house as guests come in for the party at which Marnie is to be presented to them. Yet another statement of the corridor image, this shot is built to a high pitch of suspense as the camera moves in towards the door through which the guests are entering, and we realize, as the camera gets closer, someone is going to come in. The someone is Strutt. The whole link from one sequence to the next has, in spite of the totally different technique, the same feeling of causal relationship as the very protracted dissolve in *The Wrong Man* between Manny Balestrero praying in front of a crucifix after the mistrial and the right man walking towards the camera.

Strutt as the answer to anyone's prayers is a remarkable idea, but Marnie's trouble cannot be resolved as simply as Manny's. There has to be a cathartic experience in order to bring her to a normal life. The structure of the film suggests that only when she gets as far as wanting help can it come to her. As a result of Strutt's appearance, she is raised to a level of hysteria, from which there is no physical escape because of Mark. While he negotiates with Strutt, Marnie has to go out with the hunt. The combination of panic and hysteria caused by Strutt and another red crisis triggered by a brightly colored hunting jacket sends her galloping away, urging Forio on faster and faster. The cause of the accident is partly her own involuntary feelings, but her insistence that she should herself shoot the injured Forio is something more: it is the destruction of her dream world, of which her stealing is part. The reason why she cannot steal from the Rutland safe lies in the death of Forio rather than prevention by her feelings for Mark. The destruction of one part of her life has to be complemented by that of her sexual guilt, just as the revelation of the one was complemented by the revelation of the other at the start of the film. The relationship built up at the beginning between mother and daughter has to be broken down before the proper one can begin to appear, as it does at the end of the film. All Hitchcock provides is signs of hope. As at the end of *The Birds,* the internal threat has been ended, but the external threat, here danger of arrest, remains.

THE BIRDS (Universal, 1963). *Producer:* Alfred Hitchcock, *Assistant Director:* James H. Brown, *Script:* Evan Hunter, from the novella by Daphne Du Maurier, *Photography:* Robert Burks (Technicolor), *Special Photographic Effects:* Laurence A. Hampton, Ub Iwerks, *Editor:* George Tomasini, *Sets:* Robert Boyle, George Milo, *Electronic Sound Score:* Bernard Herrmann (consultant), Remi Gassman, Oska Sala, *Players:* Tippi Hedren (Melanie Daniels), Rod Taylor (Mitch Brenner), Jessica Tandy (Mrs. Brenner), Suzanne Pleshette (Annie Hayworth), Veronica Cartwright (Cathy Brenner), Ethel Griffies (Mrs. Bundy), Charles McGraw (Sebastian). 120 minutes.

MARNIE (Universal, 1964). *Producer:* Alfred Hitchcock, *Assistant Director:* James H. Brown, *Script:* Jay Presson Allen, from the Winston Graham novel, *Photography:* Robert Burks (Technicolor), *Editor:* George Tomasini, *Sets:* Robert Boyle, George Milo, *Music:* Bernard Herrmann, *Players:* Tippi Hedren (Marnie Edgar), Sean Connery (Mark Rutland), Diane Baker (Lil Mainwaring), Louise Latham (Bernice Edgar), Martin Gabel (Strutt), Bruce Dern (the sailor), Mariette Hartley (Susan Clabon), Alan Napier (Mr. Rutland). 130 minutes.

CHAPTER TWENTY-ONE

The Birds: A Mother's Love

Margaret M. Horwitz

Critics have argued that Alfred Hitchcock's *The Birds* (1963) is exemplary in depicting male aggression against a female protagonist.[1] *The Birds* lends itself to such a discussion, particularly the initial portion of the film which concentrates on the conflict between Mitch Brenner and Melanie Daniels.[2] However, conflict among the female characters is equally important in *The Birds*, especially in the relationship between Melanie and Lydia Brenner (Mitch's mother). Indeed the centrality of the mother's role in the film makes it possible to consider *The Birds* as the middle film of a trilogy including *Psycho* (1960) and *Marnie* (1964).

I believe that in *The Birds*, as in *Psycho*, the heroine is punished by the hero's mother because of the heroine's desirability to him. This process is a result of the male character's inability to successfully resolve an Oedipal relationship. In *Psycho* the mother and son are united in the character of Norman, whose psychotic behavior is revealed and explicated at the end of the film. *The Birds* is interesting precisely because it contains no such resolution.

In fact *The Birds* cannot be fully explained at a manifest level because of a process of distortion deriving from a latent level and appearing in the text as the supernatural—namely, the wild birds. For this reason a psychoanalytic model is most appropriate. My contention is that the birds' aggressive behavior is a displacement for maternal possessiveness (exemplified by Lydia Brenner) to which Melanie poses a threat. In this view, the bird attacks function primarily as extensions of Lydia's hysterical fear of losing her son, Mitch.

There is no suggestion that Mitch's relationship with his mother is actually incestuous, but they do operate as a "couple" throughout the film. With Melanie's arrival in Bodega Bay the narrative seems to pose the question, "Who will be Mitch's 'wife'?" Throughout *The Birds* the characters assume shifting roles within an Oedipal family configuration.

The film initially establishes a three-way female rivalry over Mitch between Annie Hayworth (the schoolteacher), Melanie, and Lydia. Annie's jealousy is quite apparent during her first meeting with Melanie, directly pre-

ceding the sequence where Melanie surreptitiously enters the Brenner home
and is then attacked by a sea gull. Annie correctly assumes that the lovebirds
Melanie wished to give Cathy (Mitch's adolescent sister) are some kind of
sexual exchange between Mitch and Melanie.[3] As Melanie drives away Annie's
intense gaze follows her. This dissolves to a shot of Melanie's hand writing a
note "To Cathy" (which she will place next to the birdcage in the Brenner
house).

As the film progresses, it becomes increasingly clear that the central conflict is between Lydia and Melanie. When Melanie meets Lydia for the first
time in a cafe, a few minutes after Melanie has been attacked by the gull,
similarities in their hairstyles and clothing are evident which heighten our
sense of their rivalry over Mitch. Lydia is obviously displaced when Mitch
invites Melanie to dinner during this sequence which ends on Lydia's reflective
gaze.

At this point it is possible to retroactively consider the first "bird attack" —
a gull deliberately swoops down on Melanie in her boat — as an expression of
Lydia's jealousy.[4] Better yet, we might see it as a kind of relay from Annie to
Lydia, since this same sort of transference initiates the bird assault during
Cathy's birthday party.

I suggest that the wild birds are the expression of a form of "surveillance"
built into the structure of the transitions between sequences in the film. The
dissolve from Annie's face to Melanie's hand at the end of their first meeting
links Annie's house to the Brenner house, Melanie's destination. And Lydia's
gaze, which ends her first meeting with Melanie, dissolves to a shot of Melanie
returning to Annie's house (opening a scene during which Melanie and Annie
notice wild birds flying overhead). It is as if Lydia "followed" Melanie back, the
birds functioning as an extension of her look.

In almost every case the transitions between sequences are initiated by the
glance of female characters and operate to connect these characters across time
and space in the narrative. Significantly, such transitions precede virtually all of
the fourteen instances where the wild birds appear to us in Bodega Bay prior to
the final sequence of the film. This provides further evidence for the link
between female characters and the birds.

Transitions:
1. Annie at mailbox. Dissolve to CU of Melanie's hands as she writes note,
   "To Cathy."
   —Gull attack on Melanie in boat.
2. CU of Lydia's face in restaurant. Dissolve to Melanie walking through
   Annie's gate.
   —Birds flying over Annie's porch.
3. Melanie and Annie looking up at birds. Dissolve to Melanie's car ap-
   proaching Brenner house.
   —Sound of birds as Melanie gets out of her car.

4. CU of Lydia's face in the kitchen. Dissolve to Mitch and Melanie walking to her car.
   —Birds on telephone wires.
5. Mitch walking to the house, his back to the camera. Dissolve to Melanie entering Annie's house.
   —Bird on the porch.
6. Melanie and Annie on either side of the door. Fade to Mitch and Melanie walking up the hill.
   —Attack on the birthday party.
7. Two little girls between Mitch and Melanie after the birthday party attack. Dissolve to Lydia looking out window.
   —Attack of birds through the fireplace.
8. Melanie at window watching Lydia leave in the truck. Dissolve to LS of Lydia's truck arriving at Fawcett farm.
   —Discovery of Dan Fawcett's body (and dead birds).
9. Lydia's face as she lies down. Dissolve to Melanie in her car driving up to the school.
   —Attack on school children.
10. Melanie at the steering wheel of a car after the attack on the school children. Dissolve to Melanie talking to her father on the phone at the cafe.
    —Attack on the gas station and telephone booth.
11. Birds filling the sky after the gas station attack. Fade to Mitch and Melanie walking up to the school.
    —Discovery of Annie's body (crows on the house and school grounds).
12. Melanie, Cathy, and Mitch in the car outside Annie's. Dissolve to Brenner house, track to Mitch boarding it up (with Melanie's assistance).
    —Flocks of birds fly in the distance.
13. CU of Melanie looking up at the birds. Dissolve to Lydia sitting to the right of the piano.
    —Attack on the Brenner house.
14. Mitch and Melanie in the foreground. Lydia and Cathy in the background. Dissolve to fire in the fireplace; cut to Lydia on piano bench.
    —Attack on Melanie.

The wild birds function as a kind of malevolent female superego, an indirect revelation of Lydia's character. She is a possessive mother, intent upon furthering a symbiotic, Oedipal relationship with her son. During the final bird attack on the Brenner home Lydia grasps at Mitch's arm in a manner identical to the way in which the gulls had just attacked him.

There is no suggestion, as there might be in a science fiction film, that she has *control* over the birds. But the wild birds call up associations which point to their suitability as a displacement of energy from Lydia. They are evocative of the mythological "Harpies," which were depicted as flying creatures, part bird and part woman, armed with hooked beaks and claws.[5] The birds also call to mind "Furies," which were represented as female "avenging spirits" who punished moral transgression.[6]

From the beginning of the film, when Melanie lets a canary loose in a pet shop, birds are associated with female hysteria and destructiveness.[7] But the appearance of the wild birds is more specifically linked to maternal anxiety which seeks to punish any form of sexual expression. Melanie's real "crime" has nothing to do with her pranks; rather it is her desirability to and desire for Mitch, since this threatens to upset the equilibrium Mitch and Lydia have as a "couple."

Mitch's relationship with his mother has the Oedipal double edge of child/husband. The postal clerk confuses Melanie by referring to Lydia "and the two children," meaning Mitch and Cathy. Mitch spends every weekend at home and calls his mother "dear" and "darling." Their scene alone together in the kitchen during Melanie's first evening at the Brenner house has strong domestic overtones (Mitch dries the dishes). During this scene, Lydia questions Mitch about the propriety of Melanie's conduct, bringing up a gossip column rumor that Melanie had jumped nude into a fountain in Rome the previous summer.

In the next scene Mitch acts as a relay for Lydia, using the statements she made to him to "cross-examine" Melanie who sits in her car like a defendant in a witness box. But there is also a sexual double entendre in their banter; Mitch is clearly interested in Melanie. We hear the ominous sounds of bird calls during this conversation, and at the end of the sequence Mitch suddenly notices birds lined up on the telephone wires behind him. Lydia's jealousy, politely understated to Mitch during the kitchen sequence, erupts at this point in the gathering of birds who survey the scene.

Interestingly, the film actually refers to the Oedipal formulation of the Brenner family, only to deny it. Annie tells Melanie in the next sequence, "Maybe there's never been anything between Mitch and any girl," but then asserts that Lydia is not a "jealous woman," nor a "possessive mother . . . with all due respect to Oedipus." However, her explanation of Lydia's behavior remains unconvincing and confusing.[8] Again we see how a psychoanalytic model is helpful, since the text denies (repressed) contradictions to which it cannot admit at a conscious level. Lydia's jealousy is expressed instead through the bird assaults which become increasingly vicious as Mitch and Melanie grow closer. Two of these scenes in particular bear close examination for the ways in which a connection between the birds and maternal possessiveness can be inferred: Cathy's birthday party and the final attack of the film which is against Melanie alone.

Just prior to the birthday party Mitch jokingly tells Melanie, "You need a mother's care, my child." This leads to a serious exchange between the two which is quite telling:

Melanie: You know what a mother's love is?
Mitch: Yes, I do.
Melanie: You mean it's better to be ditched?
Mitch: No, I think it's better to be loved.

We sense that Melanie's compulsive joke playing is a reaction to her mother's abandonment of her (cf. *Marnie,* where the mother is the cause of her daughter's antisocial behavior). Melanie's lines suggest how iniquitous "motherly love" is in this film.

The camera pans with Mitch and Melanie as they walk together down the hill to the birthday party; it stops on Annie who reacts with a grimace at the sight of them together. Annie turns to look at Lydia, then there is a closer shot of Lydia as she looks in the direction of Mitch and Melanie. As she leaves the frame, we cut back to Annie glancing at the sky as a child's voice cries, "Look, look!" We see a shot from Annie's point of view of a bird, followed by a shot of the bird striking Cathy against the head. Cathy, blindfolded while playing a children's game, says, "No touching allowed." This sequence of events leads to a particularly violent assault upon the children. Significantly, it is preceded by a relay of looks from Annie to Lydia (both of whom are obviously jealous).

Why is Cathy attacked in the party sequence? I believe she is being punished specifically for her insistence that Melanie come to the party and in general for encouraging Melanie's continued presence in Bodega Bay. Indeed, Cathy's function as a character is crucial in driving the narrative forward. Mitch goes into the pet shop where he first meets Melanie to purchase lovebirds for Cathy. Melanie goes to Bodega Bay to deliver the birds "To Mitchell Brenner," as she writes on an envelope, before deciding ultimately to give them "To Cathy." In order to find out Cathy's name Melanie makes her first trip to the schoolhouse and meets Annie. Because of this gift, Cathy immediately befriends Melanie when she comes to dinner and convinces her, through Mitch, to stay for the party.

In fact, a second question the narrative poses is "Who will be Cathy's 'mother'?"[9] Lydia and Melanie alternate during the film in assuming a mother's role toward Cathy. This conflict is of course connected to the first question of which woman, Lydia or Melanie, will be Mitch's "wife." Throughout the film there is a play between Mitch/Melanie and Cathy as a family (especially when Annie's body is found), and Mitch/Lydia and Cathy (with Melanie as a threat to that structure).

In addition to Cathy being punished for befriending Melanie, something along the lines of a malicious initiation rite is going on at the children's party. It is Cathy's eleventh birthday party and also her entry into puberty. For Lydia she is "a child" even though earlier Cathy asks Melanie, with respect to the lovebirds, "Is there a man and a woman?" That is, she is beginning to wonder about sexual identity. At the party there is a double meaning in Cathy's response when the bird strikes her, "No touching allowed." She believes another child has hit her. But at another level, it is an oblique reference to Melanie and Mitch who are at the same moment walking together as a pair.

More importantly, Cathy is blindfolded. There is a sense that the perverse mother's love portrayed in this film is responsible for a kind of castration of both men and women, boys and girls. And loss of sight is a customary figure for castration.[10] The bird attacks in the film often take place against objects associated with vision — windows, glasses, windshields, a telephone booth. During one attack Mitch says to Lydia, Melanie, and Cathy, "Cover your eyes." Later, a little girl's glasses are broken in an assault upon the schoolchildren. This notion of castration is certainly implied by the death of Dan Fawcett, whose plucked-out eyes are evocative of the original, mythological Oedipal figure. (Perhaps Lydia's discovery of Fawcett is a vision of her relationship with Mitch carried to its logical conclusion.) Furthermore, Melanie effectively loses her sight at the end of the film.

In the cafe scene which follows the attack on the schoolchildren Lydia is absent, but her role is appropriated by another woman — also a mother. Like Lydia she has two children, a boy and a girl, and no husband, and she holds her children under her arms (wings) like a mother hen. Female hysteria is again connected with the wild birds, since her anxious departure from the cafe precedes a bird attack on the gas station. It is this woman, again acting in place of Lydia, who afterwards literally *attacks* Melanie as the "cause of all this," and screams at her, "You're evil, *evil!*"[11]

In a sense Melanie *is* the cause since the entire narrative moves toward punishing her. The first and last bird assaults are against Melanie, the final one being a conclusion promised throughout the narrative. The attack on Melanie, which takes place upstairs in the Brenner house when she goes to investigate the sound of bird wings, takes on the nature of an obligatory scene.

When Melanie enters the room and points her flashlight at the bed off of which the birds arise, we see that there are crows and sea gulls. Both species attack her, underlining the importance of this scene, since hitherto the birds have attacked singly or in homogeneous groups. And unlike other attacks the birds shriek very little except at the beginning and the end of the sequence. Much more prominent is the sound of their wing beats.[12]

The transition into the "Melanie attack" sequence is significant. A shot of Melanie and Mitch (standing in the foreground) and Lydia and Cathy (in the background) dissolves to one of a fire burning in the fireplace. The fire is on the left-hand side of the frame, just where Melanie and Mitch were standing in the first shot. They appear to be consumed by the fire. This dissolve indicates that the configuration of Mitch and Melanie as a couple must be destroyed and that this action is somehow related to Lydia. The firelight reflected on Lydia's face in the first shot further strengthens this connection.

In this regard the attack on Melanie in the upstairs bedroom can be compared to the shower scene in *Psycho*. Norman is acting out the role of his mother, jealous of his desire for another woman, when he stabs Marion to death. Similarly, the birds can be seen as an expression of Lydia's jealousy.[13] Melanie does not die but is badly injured by the birds who swoop at her in a fashion very much like the thrusts of Norman's knife.

Melanie loses consciousness as a result of this final assault by the birds. This sequence, like many others in *The Birds*, is based on point-of-view cutting between Melanie's glance and the object of her glance. In a deep sense, then, the final assault against Melanie is an attack on her subjectivity.

We know that in this film loss of sight is a kind of castration, which is exactly its import here. When Melanie first regains consciousness she cannot see at all and strikes out blindly at Mitch. Later Mitch comes into the house to take her, Lydia, and Cathy out to the car. He sits down next to Melanie who does not respond but stares blankly ahead. Melanie's head is bandaged just above her eyes.[14] She has to be led from the house.[15] In a tone of voice suggesting insanity, she says, "No, no," reacting to a sight which jolts her out of her stupor—wild birds covering the porch and yard of the Brenner home.

This makes for an interesting comparison with *Marnie*. Marnie's cure is expected to be ultimately beneficial, but in the process she regresses, actually speaking in a child's voice. Melanie is also reduced to the state of a child—like another Cathy. In fact Melanie is attacked in Cathy's bedroom where the birds have broken in through the roof.[16] Moreover, Melanie is only discovered because Mitch and Lydia are looking for Cathy. Lydia calls, "Is Cathy there?" as Melanie finally succumbs to the attack and falls to the floor. In a sense the answer to that question is yes since Melanie has been "castrated," or in other words reduced to a state of helpless impotence analogous to that of a child.

All of the things which make her an adult woman—which make her desirable, capable of desire, hence powerful from Lydia's point of view—have been destroyed. The immediate result of each bird attack, from the very first one in the boat, is that Melanie's perfect coiffure is disarrayed. Her impeccable grooming, her poise, her beauty are systematically destroyed in the course of the film. Before the last attack on the Brenner house we see that her expensive dress is smudged, she wears no lipstick, her hair is no longer perfectly arranged. In the final assault against her this process is completed: her face, arms, and legs are badly cut, her hair is pulled awry, and her clothes are torn.

The film especially draws attention to her fingernails. From the opening scene in the pet shop in San Francisco to the point at which she opens the door to Cathy's room before the brutal assault, the redness of her nails is prominent. By contrast, when Melanie sits next to Lydia in the car at the end, a closeup of her hand on Lydia's reveals that Melanie's nails are chipped and without polish. Her fingernails are one indication of her power—her claws, to use bird imagery. By the close of the film, she has been declawed, rendered impotent, castrated.

Melanie's loss of power is also figured through her car. Initially it gave her the power to come to Bodega Bay, which in turn enabled her to form a couple with Mitch. When she and Mitch go to the schoolhouse for Cathy and find Annie dead, Mitch ends up driving Melanie's car. At the film's conclusion she is banished to the back seat, joined by Lydia.

What kind of a resolution is this? The lovebirds, Melanie's gift through which Lydia and Mitch's relationship was first threatened, are brought along at the last minute through Cathy's persuasion: this suggests that the element of conflict is still present. Furthermore, the wild birds have not been brought under control and we are uncertain whether they will attack again.

On the other hand it is clear that Lydia and Mitch are "reunited"; now they have two "children." It is as if Mother is in the back seat with the younger child who is sick, while Father, in the front seat, drives with the older child next to him. And Lydia certainly appears victorious when confronted with Melanie's traumatization. Only now does Lydia smile at her and hug her in response to Melanie's eyes searching Lydia's face like those of a grateful child. Significantly, Lydia is the only main character who has not been personally attacked, who emerges unscathed. The last shot of the car driving away can be considered a point-of-view shot from the perspective of the birds, underlining the impression that they have (Lydia has) achieved dominance.

Notes

1. Raymond Bellour, "The Birds: Analysis of a Sequence," British Film Institute, Education Advisory Board; and "Psychosis, Neurosis, Perversion," *Camera Obscura*, no. 3-4 (1979): 105–34; Janet Bergstrom, "Enunciation and Sexual Difference (Part I)," *Camera Obscura*, no. 3-4 (1979): 33–69.
2. Note that Bellour and Bergstrom have analyzed early sequences in Bodega Bay.
3. The same assumption is later made by Lydia; both women respond knowingly, "I see," when told that the birds are lovebirds.
4. Bellour, in "The Birds: Analysis of a Sequence," describes the first attack on Melanie by a sea gull as "the symbolic punishment which strikes her in Mitch's look in the metaphorical form of the killer birds" (p. 19). Bergstrom, referring to this Bellour article in her "Enunciation and Sexual Difference (Part I)," comments, "*Why* this should be the effect of Melanie's gift [of the lovebirds] is given only a veiled explanation" (p. 47). Bellour had referred to the "indiscretion" in Melanie's "look," but neither he nor Bergstrom offers a wholly sufficient account of why the gull represents Mitch.
5. Edith Hamilton, *Mythology* (New York: New American Library, 1969), 120.
6. Hamilton, 40.
7. Melanie's and (the pet shop saleswoman) Mrs. MacGruder's cries sound like bird cries. When Mitch returns the bird to its cage he says, "Back in your gilded cage, Melanie Daniels." This is significant since we learn in the same scene that Melanie is a practical joker who has had to appear before a judge, and Mitch, who is a criminal lawyer, tells her she should have been "put behind bars." Also, the prank for which Melanie had to appear in court resulted in the breaking of a window—a clear connection to the destructiveness of the birds later on and another link between Melanie and Lydia.
8. Annie says Lydia "is not afraid of losing Mitch," only of "being abandoned," and that Mitch "had just been through a lot with Lydia after his father died," and "didn't want to risk going through it all again."
9. In some sense Mitch functions from the beginning of the film as Cathy's "father." He wants to obtain lovebirds for her which are neither "too demonstrative" nor "too aloof," but "just friendly." Regardless of what age he is meant to be he appears old enough to be her father. Yet

one could argue that there is a "construction" of the father taking place through Mitch's dead father's portrait to which we are only slowly introduced. It is alluded to by Melanie and Mitch during Lydia's phone conversation with Brinkmeyer and visible merely in portions during Melanie's conversation with Cathy at the piano. It is seen fully and at an angle only after a bird attack in the Brenner living room. It assumes significance in a later attack on their home when Mitch rests on the piano bench under the portrait as Lydia sits in a chair next to him. Prior to this scene Lydia, very much the hysterical wife, screams, "If only your father were here." One could argue that Mitch is being pulled in the direction of becoming the "image" of his father, i.e., Lydia's "husband," at the same time he is developing a relationship with Melanie.

10. Stephen Heath, in his article "Difference," cites Freud, who notes the "substitutive relation between the eye and the male organ . . . in dreams and myths and phantasies," giving the Lady Godiva legend as an example of "blinding castration" punishment, *Screen,* vol. 19, no. 3 (1978): 87. If we reformulate this to another correlation, namely that between vision and *power,* we can understand using blindness as a figure of castration for both males and females.

11. Jacqueline Rose writes that one should "note that in this moment, all the men have been evicted from the image which shows the group of women crowded together as the support of 'the woman' who comes forward to accuse." "Paranoia and the Film System," *Screen,* vol. 17, no. 4 (1977): 95.

12. In his interview with Truffaut on the film, Hitchcock explains the paucity of bird cries at this point by saying it is "as if the birds were telling Melanie, 'Now we've got you where we want you.'" François Truffaut, *Hitchcock* (New York: Simon & Schuster, 1967): 224.

13. Bergstrom writes, "When Norman, impersonating his mother, kills Marion, it is as the mother killing a rival for her son's affection" (p. 57).

14. Bellour writes, with regard to the gull attack on Melanie when she is in the boat, "Her look has been wounded, for it is only metaphorically, and for the sake of the rest of the plot, that the gull does not strike her eyes," in "The Birds: Analysis of a Sequence" (p. 30).

15. In terms of closure, compare how Melanie is stunned after the first gull attack and has to be helped out of the boat by Mitch.

16. The significance of the site of this invasion cannot be overlooked since it is a reminder of Cathy's "culpability."

I thank Michael Renov and Frank Tomasulo for helpful discussions. I am also grateful to Michele McGlade for her critical reading of the manuscript, to Stephen Mamber for useful suggestions, and to Edward Branigan for his encouragement and valuable comments.

CHAPTER TWENTY-TWO

Mark's Marnie

Michele Piso

> It's no accident: women take after birds and robbers just as robbers take after women and birds. . . . What woman hasn't flown/stolen? Who hasn't felt, dreamt, performed the gesture that jams sociality? Who hasn't crumbled, held up to ridicule, the bar of separation? Who hasn't inscribed with her body the differential, punctured the system of couples and opposition? Who, by some act of transgression, hasn't overthrown . . . ?
>
> — CIXOUS

> The flesh is sad, alas! and I have read all the books.
>
> — MALLARMÉ

Marnie's reception in 1964 is notable for the popular press's smug disdain of a film now highly regarded by both journalists and academic film theorists. *Time* magazine dismissed *Marnie* as a straightforward case history of a frigid kleptomaniac. Andrew Sarris pronounced it "a failure by any standard except the most esoteric," and, in a strikingly contradictory sentence, described Mark Rutland as both a rapist and a patient husband.[1] Critics found the sets distracting and phoney; the dialogue banal; the plot congealed more than it thickened. The film-critical events leading to *Marnie*'s current revaluation as a masterpiece of modern cinema have come about in three stages.

The first interpretive system to illuminate Hitchcock's work was the French auteur approach pioneered in the fifties by Claude Chabrol and Eric Rohmer.[2] Behind Hitchcock's Hollywood thrillers they perceived graver themes of sin, guilt, and redemption through confession. Heavily influenced by the auteur method, Robin Wood's later analysis of *Marnie* adopted traditional psychoanalytic concepts in search of the cause of the heroine's disorder and the steps necessary to her cure. In Wood's view the film's world is both bewildering and imperfect, yet in the individual couple a true psychological order and unity may be defined and achieved through the recovery of an unremembered past.[3] A decade later, the more radical social and psychological movements inspired by Louis Althusser and Jacques Lacan challenged the humanism of both auteurist models. This third phase of film interpretation, as practiced for example by Raymond Bellour and Laura Mulvey, foregrounds the material production and consumption of film, criticizes the objectification and fetishizing of the female image, and interrogates the filmic text as a bearer of ideology.[4] Their investigations into the complex ways in which film meaning is socially structured replace the metaphysical interpretations of a film's meaning typical of Chabrol, Rohmer, and Wood. More importantly for our purposes here, recent psychoanalytic theory attends to film narrative as an enactment of the Lacanian version of the Oedipal structure, a tangle of desire, sexual differentiation, and identification: the "family romance."

My primary purpose here is to observe the distance between "therapeutic" and feminist rereadings of *Marnie*. But I will question as well the rapport between feminism and Lacanian theories of film meaning that reduce the film to fixed structures of voyeurism, fetishism, and the repetition of a childhood trauma. To perceive Marnie's marriage to Mark as a cure, in my view, is to deny the social misery in the bleak street and cast-off mother imaged at the film's end. It is to accept a melancholic and merely subjective discovery as the salvation of modern life. Further, to endorse as a fuller, more progressive reading of *Marnie* a voyeuristic relation between film and spectator, or to confine its many riches to the mechanics of the Oedipal plot, deprives the viewer of the film's awareness of another fundamental antagonism. Following Marx, therefore, I shall privilege as the film's central tension and particular pathos the class antagonism between Mark and Marnie, with her mother standing not only for a purely private and hideous past but also as the twisted embodiment of social repression and sexual exploitation.[5]

An adequate description of *Marnie* as a nightmare of social exploitation and violation requires a distinction between commodity exchange and gift exchange. Where capital relations generally insist upon division within the labor forces and the further separation of the worker from his or her product, gift relations encourage an imparting of the giving spirit to the thing given and the establishing of communion among segmented parts of society. Drawing upon Marcel Mauss's gift theory, Lewis Hyde describes how commodity exchange stifles any except the most impersonal and objective contact, while gift exchange draws donor and recipient into a feeling bond. Cold to the touch, the purely economic transaction maintains vertical relations of power and privilege. The gift, however, "moves" in circular relations of community, affection, mystery, leaving a "series of interconnected relationships in its wake, a kind of decentralized cohesiveness."[6] In Hyde's view, then, the gift inhibits the threat of domination and inspires social and erotic acts of the imagination: feasts, dances, entertainment, art, and love. French feminist Hélène Cixous would call these "exchanges that multiply," in the sense that they multiply and incorporate human desires and differences as opposed to "hierarchizing exchange" which involves a "struggle for mastery."[7] If the reciprocal social gift holds us to the familiar and conventional, to the beauty of a world held in common, its more heightened form as an artistic or erotic gift bears us away toward the visionary and unexpected. A social gesture calls forth our similarities, while the more intimate gift—a keepsake of some sort—touches in us what is unique; yet both bind us to others. In Hitchcock's films, however, love is suspect and locked within a house set apart from any neighborhood—there are no meals, no parties, no offerings of wine that aren't preludes to death. Personal gifts are contaminated too. "Money answereth all things," mocks Marnie, giving her mother a mink scarf. With a barb, she acknowledges the spread of money and pierces the spiritual generosity of the gift.

Organized around the sexual combat of Mark and Marnie and the familial strife between Marnie and her mother, the film's most general and unresolved social contradiction turns, not surprisingly, around love and money, giving and acquisition. It is precisely this antagonism between the sensual world and the business world that runs through *Marnie:* the world of capital dominates and chills the erotic and creative aspects of life. The real abjection in *Marnie* lies in the blank streets and fast-food restaurants, the alienation from nature, and the replacement of communal spontaneity with the rational corporate hierarchy depicted by Strutt, Ward, and, more suavely, Mark. Think for a moment of the great crowds and collectives of Renoir, whose members gaily redistribute or wreck the wealth and property of the bourgeoisie. Imagine the circles of Fellini, widening to gather whores and intellectuals, producers and pimps. But in Hitchcock, where personal neurosis stands for a more pervasive social ill, multiplicity scatters into an edgy solitude. The group splinters into isolated individuals: Uncle Charlie, Marion Crane, and Norman Bates, saddest of all. The social rituals that create and continue relations between individuals and groups, in whose light a stranger's features flare into a familiarity and collective rapport, burn out in a breach of faith. In *Psycho,* Norman offers bread to Marion and later stabs her to death; in *Shadow of a Doubt,* Uncle Charlie's keepsake to his niece is the emerald ring of his murdered victim; in *Marnie,* marriage is an abduction consummated in rape. Covenants, vows, and promises are reciprocal exchanges that should weave individuals and differences into nets of social and spiritual accord. Yet in the world of *Marnie* community has already broken down into hierarchies fixed in opposition: family/business; men/women; higher class/underclass; north/south; bosses/workers; daughter/mother. Lacking the communal participation that helps dissolve these divisions, *Marnie*'s characters exist unnaturally as separate entities, antagonistic monads. The convergence of differences that could result in a shared public world occurs instead as private collisions, acts of violation, and invasion. In Marnie's case, the invasion is robbery; in Mark's, the violation is rape.

From a Marxist perspective, then, Marnie's frigidity can be read as a metaphor of an oppressed class and as a reflection of the desensualized and rational sphere of business. Anthropologist Mary Douglas describes the body/society relation in similar terms:

> The human body is always treated as an image of society. . . . [T]here can be no natural way of considering the body that does not involve at the same time a social dimension. Interest in its apertures depends on the preoccupations with social exits and entrances, escape routes and invasions. If there is no concern to preserve social boundaries, I would not expect to find concern with bodily boundaries. The relation of head to feet, of brain and sexual organs, of mouth and anus are commonly treated so that they express the relevant patterns of hierarchy. . . . [B]odily control is an expression of social control.[8]

Marnie suggests the negative power of private interest penetrating and emptying itself into a woman, invading gestures which—privatized, isolated— are at the same time a struggle against that isolation. Marnie's mother also represents a victimized world—as mother, as prostitute, as underclass. In the struggle between Mark and Marnie, hers is the body to be won or lost, and we must ask ourselves why we think it healthy that Marnie abandon her. Viewed within the context offered by Douglas, *Marnie*'s characters and images depict not merely the psychological problems of individual characters but evoke as well the conditions of the larger organization of society—an ebbing away of ceremonial culture, the dissolution of vital collective bonds, the isolation of individual action. These are the modern horrors constituting the social vision embedded below the surface of *Marnie*. By grasping the indirect ways its messages are located in the subtext of the film, we can better understand the plight of Marnie and her mother and what it reveals to us of larger patterns of American culture.

Marnie's most consequential act of degraded reciprocity is the mother's first sexual union. Unlike Marnie's trauma, this key episode occurs offscreen and thus makes more complex and elusive the origin of *Marnie*'s pain. At fifteen, Marnie's mother accepts a sweater for her virginity ("He asked me, would I let him?"); deserting her even before the child's birth, the boy violates their union. In a single act, the bartering of virginity for a commodity unites defloration, prostitution, and conception. Yet, in pregnancy, the victimized womb of the virgin/mother/prostitute reflowers and bears Margaret, whose name derives from the Greek and Latin words for flower and pearl. Later in the film we will learn that the mother still has the sweater, as if it were a keepsake, a token of her inner wish to transform degradation and abandonment into a memory of love. With her imagination, the prostitute attempts to turn a different kind of trick—the trade of her body into a gift of love: "Do you want to know how I got you, Marnie? There was this boy, Billy. . . ." With these words, she begins the recitation of her own lonely and impoverished past. The sweater, together with all other gifts in *Marnie*—the mink scarf; the marital ring; the stone animals of the former wife; Forio, the horse that Mark restores to his new wife—all are symbols passed back and forth between one body and another in the hope of an emotional union. Nevertheless, all gifts fall short of their fullest expression in love. They function instead as bribes or swindles and poison the erotic flow. Distortion of life's emotional dimension is implicit in Mark's marriage for money and the mother's sale of her body to get it. The flow of giving and taking implied in Hyde's description of erotic exchange degenerates in *Marnie* to social transgression: Marnie's theft, Mark's marital blackmail, the mother's prostitution.

*   *   *   *   *   *

Following *Psycho* (1960) and *The Birds* (1963), *Marnie* completes Hitchcock's trilogy of modern despair. As one of America's most rigorously beautiful studies of communal alienation and lost rapport, *Marnie*'s thematic conflicts between reciprocity and exploitation, vulnerability and violation, unfold in a deliberately stiff and rigid *mise en scène*. The mortality of the body itself— suggested by Marnie's rape and attempted suicide, the deaths of Forio and the sailor, the mother's injured leg—differs sharply from the stark invulnerability of train stations and offices, their metallic architecture restricted to a design of horizontals and verticals and to colors in primary hues plus white. There are no rounded or soft forms to connote fruitfulness nor tender colors to evoke warmth and calm. The denaturalized purism of style, all fortuitous and distracting elements eliminated, recalls the geometrics of Mondrian, the cropped chasteness of Bresson, the angularity of Antonioni's techno-world. The image is cold, silent, intense; its restricted framing creates an abstract and disorienting relation to the body, as in the early fragmenting shots of Marnie's hands and legs in the hotel and train station. *Marnie* opens with the credits turning as pages of a text, each curling page removing us from reality and preparing us for a narrative. Throughout, *Marnie*'s visual composition is extremely controlled, its formal stylization heightened by the glaringly artificial rear projections of the horse rides and the exaggerated, painterly sets of the Edgar neighborhood and Rutland office. These distortions of outside space are not careless flaws, as lamented by Donald Spoto in *The Dark Side of Genius*.[9] Rather, they are defiantly airless inventions which underscore and condemn the unnatural quality of the film's depicted world. Thus at the end of the Baltimore street, enfolded in silver clouds, lies a false harbor, a painted ship upon a painted ocean. Just as shallow is the façade of the Rutland Company, the harsh jagged lines of its parking lot suggesting the slashes of lightning linked to the storm and the sailor. These outside places associated with the mother's client and Marnie's employer are hollow fabrications propped up under an unreal shell of sky.

Equally claustrophobic are the interior spaces that function less as havens than as torture chambers. Absent are those happy spaces, those dwellings and shelters that can inspire daily chat or nocturnal intimacy. *Marnie*'s domestic spaces are rather marred by violence and transgression: the bedroom where Marnie has nightmares, the deep-freeze kitchen where she is slapped by her mother, the living room where the child-Marnie murders the sailor, the boat bedroom where Mark momentarily covers Marnie's nakedness and then rapes her. Marnie's mother's home has a depressed, banal atmosphere; Mark's mansion is materially bloated, emotionally empty, the site of the father's inertia and Lil's frustrated desire. The aristocratic "home" is a showcase, a display, a façade, a training ground: "This is a drill, dear. Wife follows husband to door, gives and/or gets a kiss, stands pensively as he drives away. A wistful little wave is optional." In Preston Sturges, the absurdity in turning marital intimacy into a martial drill could be funny. In Hitchcock, Marnie's darkly witty reply, "Mark, I, um, I don't have any money," cynically replaces the erotic with the economic and exposes the love union of marriage as a business affair. *Marnie* is built around the similarities and differences between these uncomfortable and unhappy homes; in each, one parent is missing and one child is an outsider, rivalrous for the attention of the surrogate mother or father, as are Jessie and Lil.

Of Hitchcock's work, *Marnie* may be the most unusually severe, its social implications the most bleak. Gone are the quirky minor characters and little bits of goofiness that lighten the earlier films. The shallow surface of the image evokes the impersonality of an advertisement, the cool pragmatism of the business world, and a visual impassivity that suggests daily physical and emotional repression. The peculiarly austere style heightens the image of the body in whose visibility and mortality, its desires so confused and constrained, Hitchcock ultimately places his tenderness. The colder and blanker the world of buildings and nature, the more desolate and unprotected the flesh, its loneliness increased by the dead silence of earth and space. Marnie's cry, "Help me. Oh God, please, somebody help me," wells up from a woman's body, so easily hurt, torn, betrayed. The sense of humiliating exposure is expressed in the "honeymoon" scene. Mark strips Marnie and then shields her nakedness with his robe, as if this covering, like the boy's sweater and the jacket that Mark will finally give to Marnie in the rain, were the male body's promise of protection. Yet Mark's is the gift that takes. Raping her, he breaks all promises.

The modern-day trap of visibility has been commented upon widely, most acutely by Michel Foucault and Jean-Paul Sartre. In *Marnie* the contemporary body is controlled by the totally administered sphere of the Rutland Publishing Company, a symbol of the twentieth-century workplace's estrangement of self and others and the reduction of reciprocal relations to commodity exchange. The Rutland Company is Foucault's "space of exact legibility," an "enclosed, segmented space, observed at every point, in which the individuals are inserted in a fixed place, in which the slightest movements are supervised, in which all events are recorded, in which power is exercised without division . . . in which each individual is constantly located, examined and distributed among the living beings."[10] At the racetrack, the office, and the Rutland home, Hitchcock combines planar lighting and the alert gaze of the lens to achieve the visual equivalent of Bentham's panopticon plan of "power through transparency" and "subjugation by illumination." Intended for a more general social application, Bentham's architectural plan for prisons arranged living quarters around a tower from which each prisoner could be watched without knowing when or by whom. As described by Foucault, the primary modern technique of force is an institutional "visibility organized entirely around a dominating overseeing gaze . . . which exists to serve a rigorous, meticulous power."[11] Similarly, almost anywhere she is, Marnie's physical and psychological independence is limited by a modern fluorescence that exposes every move. Conspiring with this hostile clarity in a subtle transference of secrecy to visibility, the camera turns from Marnie eyeing the safe to Mark observing Marnie from behind a glass partition. According to Foucault, the anxiety of being observed can be stimulated by anyone; "it doesn't matter who exercises power, . . . or what motive animates him" (*Discipline and Punish*, p. 202). So Lil spies from a window, a stranger spies at the racetrack, Mark stares from a corner, Hitchcock watches in the corridor. The woman who would prefer to turn her body inward and hide from the air itself (covering her legs, sneers Strutt, "as if they were a national treasure") is the most exposed, "pinned by a look," in Sartre's words, "a butterfly fixed to a cork."[12] In the film's opening shot of Marnie's receding back (Sartre's "blind mass" possessed by everyone before it belongs to the woman), the fixed camera stresses detachment between viewer and Marnie, aligning the viewer's gaze with the "rigorous, meticulous" eye of power, seeing but unseen. In this manner the conventional inscription of a woman's unseen face as enigma is challenged by Hitchcock's knowing eye; the camera follows Marnie, observes her routines, appropriates her smugness. Indeed, *Marnie* is a struggle between absolute surveillance and a woman's camouflage and subterfuge. When Strutt barks "Robbed!," the film's first spoken word, we hear the shout of a blinded eye, a man deceived. Mark's father may think that Marnie will merely bring "a little pizazz" to the farm, but her deeper function is to disorder, to make less perfect the operations of money and power.

The shock of transgression and rupture, of degraded and violent reciprocity, is conveyed through visual and verbal metaphors. By intensifying boundary images that segment space into public and private, familiar and foreign, legal and illegal, social and psychological, the threat of invasion is made more sinister. Theft, staring, interrogation, eavesdropping, rape: all suggest hostile penetration of the hidden and covert. *Marnie* is an intricate design of barriers and enclosures, stressing a theme of secrecy: the threshold of the screen where we watch as Marnie recedes along the cautionary yellow line; the sharp narrowness of the mother's street and stair; the hotel corridor where Hitchcock makes his appearance, catching us watching him watching Marnie; the mother's closed bedroom door; the window mysteriously tapped; the office window and cabinet violently smashed; the safes broken into, hurdles not crossed, silences kept, dreams, a veil of hair; the pecans that spill to the floor, something sweet protected by a hard shell to be broken only by a hard tool, like the fire poker that breaks the sailor's body. Each of these boundaries articulates, traces, invokes the most profound barrier of all, the hymenal membrane enclosed within Marnie and broken by Mark.

*   *   *   *   *   *

There is an odd moment in *Marnie,* during the first car ride and after the branch has destroyed his dead wife's pre-Columbian art collection, when Mark explains that the storm has not destroyed all that he had left of his wife. Rather, the art collection was all that he had left "that had belonged to my wife." The distinction Mark makes between what had "belonged" to his wife and what he had "left" of her deepens him. Its disclosure stresses a difference between the material and the spiritual, between encased animals of carved stone and the memory of the invisible (abandoned?) woman enclosed within him. If Marnie has nothing, the wife had almost everything, except perhaps love. Why else would she have died of "heart disease," an heiress and collector of precious objects, whose money has kept the Rutland family business afloat? The repressed guilt Mark feels for this bit of familial whoring surfaces as ennui. Mark's material monotony, a dissatisfaction with rank and money, is the source of his attraction to Marnie. Shattering the stone animal and saying "We've all got to go sometime," Mark destroys part of his legacy of hypocrisy and privilege and takes his place with a criminal. He is to do this again, with greater risk, at the "bash," the reception to honor their wedding. To protect Marnie that evening, Mark drops the illicit suggestion before Lil and the Strutts that he and Marnie had known each other during his first marriage. With a destructive social gesture, he cuts his moorings to convention and begins his unruly adventure.

Marnie revolves around the contradictory notion of "belonging" as a matter of possession or domination on the one hand and belonging as a flow of giving and taking, of affinity with a place or a beloved, on the other. The word "belonging" is uttered again when Lil, watching the couple depart after their wedding, tells the money-minded Cousin Bob that Mark spent $42,000 ("plus tax") on a diamond so that Marnie could have "something that had never belonged to anyone else." Finally, Mrs. Edgar, never married, always bought, implies the theme of belonging when she confesses that before she gave birth to Marnie she never had anything of her own. To belong to, or to be loved; to be in possession of, or to give; to gather a thing to oneself and hoard it, or to open and empty oneself in the fullness of love—these are *Marnie's* opposing values. The film's crucial moments of birth, marriage, and death press possession and love together in confusion. The emotion possible in each instance is either the stasis of property, like the objets d'art impoverished behind glass, thus deprived of their original mystery, inert and mute, or the pouring forth of feeling that both gathers and liberates.

"To possess is to give," wrote Malinowski. Smashing the useless objects or transforming his capital into the marital ring, Mark, like the Haida Indian tribe described by Hyde, is "killing his wealth" (p. 9). The "furtive little wedding," then, is Mark's freest moment, a flight from the hoarding tribe of Cousin Bob, Ward, and Strutt, a release from his role as client in a market that has no imagination for love. "The man is deranged," snorts the sexless cousin, and indeed Mark is, if, after marrying for money and devoting years to acquiring more of it, he suddenly spends it in a fit of love. "What would mother say?" Cousin Bob huffs, implying that Mark is to be as frugal about money as Marnie is to be decent about sex; his cold hard cash and her body are equally frigid, locked up. Neither are to be circulated outside of an elaborate set of governing social and economic conventions. The falseness of money, its utter uselessness in providing happiness, is the secret of the cousin's social reality; it is what makes that world a rigid and unlyrical place. It chills Marnie and stunts Mark's ability to conceive of the ring as more than a right to power and rape, of marriage not as integration but domination. *Marnie* is as much about a man's inability to free himself from the constraining ideology of his wealth, from the authority and certainty it confers, as it is about a woman's refusal to submit to that ideology.

Mark's first wife was an heiress; the second, a thief. The first gave him the property that the second one steals. Enclosed in the glass cage of the Rutland office, Mark is trapped within what Joan Landes calls "the inherent tension in the bourgeois love match between the demands of the heart and the considerations of property."[13] Mark's marriage of convenience, to save the family business, is an act of prostitution not unlike Marnie's mother's prostitution to save her child from poverty and state intervention. The difference, of course, is that Mark's property identifies him with civil law, while the illegitimate professions of mother and daughter place them at its farthest remove.

That Mark can be tender and arch is evident and attractive. His youth "blighted, dragged down by money, ambition, noblesse oblige," then bored by his corporate interests, a boredom only briefly relieved by his Third World zoology jaunts, Mark's restlessness reflects his desire to escape the bourgeois world. But he is too hemmed in by an arrogant assumption of knowledge, and this assumption, insofar as it is unrecognized and unchanged, is his flaw. Where Marnie has the slyness of an insurgent, Mark merely lacks scruples—as evidenced by his first marriage and his ruthless rebuilding of the Rutland Company. Marnie is the danger zone that Mark enters for a spell, attracted by her parody of the diligent worker ("I want work, Mr. Ward, good, hard, work"), by her mockery of a system that would subject her as it has subjected every other woman in the film, from the secretaries waiting to be called by their boyfriends ("oh, this is the best one you've had"), to the economically dependent Lil, to the waitresses at the roadside restaurant, to the patch-sweatered cleaning woman scrubbing the boss's floor while Marnie, cleverly paralleled in the same frame, cracks the boss's safe. (In the film's trailer, a shot of Marnie breaking into Mark's safe is accompanied by Hitchcock's wry off-screen comment: "Here's Marnie going about her business like any normal girl: happy, happy, happy.") *Marnie* keenly observes a woman's humiliation at job hunting, at having to put out for a job, but to play at being decent. Witness Marnie's rare and wonderful smiles, the calculation and great lies at the interview. With her own private secret, Marnie turns the profession of secretary on its head. Mark wants the outlaw, the criminal, the woman who can jam sociality and ridicule the routine of tea and classy talk, whose glance can foil the snobbery of a spontaneously sprained wrist. He admires the woman who, when asked how she will spend her married days, responds with disdain, "I thought I'd be a society hostess"; the woman who with her wit pierces society's pretensions as well as its safes. He loves her because, tumbling combinations, she dares to challenge the codes, to mimic them in her voice, her dress, her good manners, because perhaps she can smash the glass that surrounds his emotional and sexual desire and free him from the rut that is his life. Unfortunately for Mark, however, he is not Godard's perfect hero, always ready to flee the infinite net of the bourgeoisie. The net is of his own weaving, and with it he captures Marnie. Instead of stealing his property, she becomes it.

Marriage, then, as acquisition. Listen to Sartre on Genet: "The man rarely wishes to seduce by his physical qualities. He has received them, not made them. He makes his woman love him for his power, his courage, his pride, his aggressiveness, in short he makes her desire him as a faceless force, a pure power to do and take" (p. 80). For Mark, marriage is not a reciprocal act transcending the contractual "standpoint from which man and wife are deemed to have property in each other, especially in one another's sexual faculties" (Landes, p. 129). Elsewhere in *Saint Genet,* Sartre tells us that a man's way of making love reflects his economic situation. What then will Marnie have to look forward to, kidnapped by Mark, coerced, raped, broken at the end of the film, unequal to his stallion powers, as was the wife whose heart failed? ("I'm still a little hoarse today, Mama," whispers Marnie, covering the rape with a cough, and identifying herself with Forio, the beloved animal she will later kill, relieving his misery, reliving her own.) Mark's control is everywhere visible, in his secretaries, in the incompetent subordinate Ward, in the business bearing his name, a name emblazoned on the safe and the black worker's uniform and, presumably, upon the books published by his company. The Rutland family name is a remarkable condensation of trade (a trade name known in the nineteenth century for its roan leather bindings) and periodic sexual excitement, of property and pleasure, money and sex, power and phallus. Mark's unquestioned view of himself as owner and as a man of property leads to the heinous rape. So accustomed is he to owning, so synonymous is his sexuality with social power, that he assumes he can possess Marnie too, violate her, break her down, and then build her back up (in his image, his language, in the image of the "normal" female) in much the same way that he rebuilt the Rutland business. In the most literal and terrible way, Marnie is Mark's.

Viewing himself as "criminally and morally responsible" for Marnie, Mark's morality is, finally, inseparable from the ethics of the State. Just as his authority is rooted in the Rutland property, his property is bounded by bourgeois law, a civil preserve from which neither Marnie nor Mark can escape. In the beginning of *Marnie,* Mark makes his first appearance directly on the heels of the police investigating Marnie's robbery of Strutt. His attitude is ironic, detached. At the end of the film he becomes the Law: when the police hear what Mark has to tell them, Marnie won't be arrested. Hitchcock's *Marnie* is about the encounter between Mark, whose name means money and implies the tracing of boundaries, observation and inscription, and Marnie, whose name plays on a virginal Mary and a sexual Mark and also suggests to mar, to damage, to go astray. Mark rapes, Marnie steals; the film's title links and locates both Mar/k and Mar/nie in transgression. Yet at the film's close, he embodies legal authority, while Marnie loses all autonomy.

Mark's space is full of people and possessions and fixed in place, property, and address; Marnie's is hidden, hymenal, and fluid, like blood, like the water of the port at the edge of her town, the rain of the murder night. Moving from one city to another (mimicking the sailor?), Marnie travels through a no-man's land, without dwelling or love. This lack of place encompasses all of America, its lonely geography characterized by hotels and roadside Howard Johnsons where, recalling Marion Crane, Marnie doesn't eat. Placelessness is crucial to *Marnie,* identifying woman as wanderer, the one who, crossing borders and thresholds, merely expands a territory of desolation. To be without place is to be without identity; Marnie has had several, none sufficient.

*   *   *   *   *   *

Genet wrote of the criminal: "I shall so bedeck him with flowers that, as he disappears beneath them, he will himself become a flower, a gigantic and new one."[14] Marnie is the Genet figure in reverse; the unbroken hymen, a symbol of alienation and unhappiness rather than criminal frigidity, is hidden by a thief from a world that renders nearly everything visible. "To escape the eyes of hungry birds," Mark tells Marnie during their honeymoon, "insects disappear in the illusion of a beautiful flower." Escaping within so many aliases, the virgin disappears in the persona of a thief. "Are you called Margaret?" asks Mark, his English accent turning "called" into "cold": "Are you cold, Margaret?" Mark had asked earlier. Margaret, from the Greek "margarites," means pearl, precious gem; from the Italian "margherita," it means flower, the pearl-flower that is her sex, unbroken, ungiven, buried within the thief.

At the center of *Marnie* is the virginal hymen, "tainted with vice," says

Mallarmé, "yet sacred, between desire and fulfillment."[15] Alluding to Simone de Beauvoir's discussion of adolescent female sexuality, Sartre described the virgin's resistance:

> Girls often force themselves to touch repulsive insects and sometimes put them to their mouths. . . . We know the reason for these exercises. Out of a mixture of hatred, curiosity and defiance, these adolescents are making an effort to perform symbolically and through their own initiative the act of deflowering, the obscure presentiment of which is sufficient to fill them with horror and which they know will be imposed upon them. . . . Since they are unable to escape the future in store for them, all they can do is refuse to *undergo* it. Sentenced to death, they demand the right to give the order to fire that will kill them.(p. 57)

The shot that kills the beloved Forio appeases the death of the sailor and jars Marnie's memory of the murder's unleashed violence. "There, there, now," she murmurs, repeating the words that bind the deaths, her love for Forio purifying the contamination of the murder. Contrasting with the fox hunt's hypocritical display of killing as recreation, the death of Forio is both an atonement for murder and a surrender to marriage. Forio has a direct relationship to Marnie's sexuality, and the violence of his death on the Rutland property is linked to the violence of her abduction and rape. The divergent meanings of the scene stem from Marnie's as yet unconscious desire to clear up the past, made more apparent later when she can no longer steal, and her dismal realization of her entry into the permanent enclosure of the Rutland world. That this territory is bounded and closed off, that there are thresholds here that she cannot cross, is made perfectly clear by the stone wall, the guarded doorway, and the lack of compassion in the tenant from whom Marnie demands the gun. Shocked by the cruelty of the sport, she has fled the upper class hunt but cannot clear the stone wall of the Rutland property upon which Forio is fatally harmed.

We know that Marnie can jump hurdles; she has done it before with ease. But now she hesitates, and it is her indecision that causes the accident. Her loss of Forio is a loss of self, and perhaps this loss could be a gain, an emotional clearing in which she could be free from the past and anticipate the future. But numerous and cheerless signs — the disgust of the hunt; the rawboned hostility of the Rutland tenant, ingratiating to Lil and repellantly small-minded and mean toward Marnie; Marnie's desperate isolation as she kills Forio — warn against too facile a reading of the scene as a fruitful breakdown of Marnie's resistances. The way to full consciousness is not through rape and the enforced subjugation of marriage. Like an animal, Marnie has been hunted down and broken; her remorse for past crimes is not easily distinguishable from the exhaustion and sorrow which result from the crimes presently visited against her. The blood of the terrified and violated body, the blood of women, of murder and rape, mingle in the famous red suffusions, the red of suffering. Over the twisted limbs of Hitchcock's defiled Pietà rise the screams of the mother and her child, crying for an entire world, not lost but never gained. Love is degraded, a caress becomes a slap, a marital embrace ends in rape, a drunken attempt to comfort a child leads to murder. A rape, a hunt, prostitution, and murder—these are Hitchcock's forlorn instances of violation in marriage, community, and love, where all that should be held sacred is torn apart.

In a film in which all relationships are characterized by cash, it is misleading, then, to read *Marnie* merely as a psychological narrative slashed by the blade of the Oedipal guillotine. To see in the familial trauma only the gash that separates the daughter from the Imaginary and inserts her precariously on the edge of the Symbolic is to suppress Marnie's poverty ("We were poor, grindingly poor," she tells Mark at the racetrack) and the mother's prostitution as the social origins of psychological illness. Marnie's problems are both Oedipal and Capital—her world inhabited by those who can be entertained by suffering, like the hunters swarming around the wounded fox, elite dinner guests by night and, we might infer, corporate executives by day. Threatened by poverty, Marnie's mother sells her body and numbs it in a denial of sexual love. But what is the mother to do, her prostitution not freely chosen, as Marnie's marriage isn't? What is Jessie's mother to do, away all day, working to support her daughter but unable to sustain her life with love? What is Lil to do, also motherless, lying around the house all day, taking handouts from Ward? "I thought I'd stick Mark for lunch and you for cash," says Lil, her play on "stick," connoting both "stick up" and knife thrust, linking her to robbery and murder.

After the sailor's murder, the effect of the state's threat to take away the mother's child is an absolute freezing of even the maternal love she bears for her daughter, all she ever loved. The mother's body stiffens in pathetic imitation of social propriety, of an enforced "decency" (a word emphasized throughout) that she must impose on her daughter to save her. Marnie's thievery becomes the mother's economic support, but while the mother had to forfeit sexual love for sex and money, the daughter drops the sex and just steals the money. Prostitution and frigidity, then, are state products. In Marnie's blank stare, which closes so many of the film's sequences, are the dead eyes of the woman whose sexuality is raped, prostituted, and censored by an authority that is markedly male.

Marnie negotiates the rift between the realm of the mother's prostitution and the Rutland Company's realm of capital. That both places are houses of prostitution is suggested by Mark's first marriage to save the company. The mother's product is private and nominally denounced; Mark's is public, the literary or scientific books (similar, we might assume, to *Sexual Aberrations of the Criminal Female*) respectably bound and distributed. Marnie represses her memory of the murder, but she also represses knowledge of the "work" hidden behind the mother's closed bedroom door, linked to the closed doors of the Rutland office. Marnie's nightmares contain the truth of her mother's secret profession as prostitute: she dreams that she is sleeping on the sailor's "aloha" pillow, sign of the victim/client; she dreams the mysterious taps of the men in white shirts and feels the "cold" of her dislocation from the mother's bed to the couch, where later, during her honeymoon, she will cringe from Mark as if he too were a sailor. The bed, described by Heidegger as childhood's "hallowed site," serves repeatedly in *Marnie* as the location of bad dreams, rape, prostitution—yet, most movingly, as the place where she free-associates and calls out for help. In the brilliant closing of the film, the mother tells two stories, the one of a psychological trauma of murder, the other of her first act of prostitution as a young girl. Yet the dismal material conditions of her mother's early life and Marnie's own origins remain concealed within a psychological "revelation" of the repressed murder. Seduced by psychology, itself coextensive with social control and normalization, with scientific certainty and the certainty of the Law, Mark hears only one of the narratives, his head turned by his own capital interests.

Mark forces his way into the memories of Marnie and her mother, just as he had earlier penetrated Marnie's body, now forcing confession as before he had caused shame. It's terrible to be a lie and a cheat; not to know the fulfillments of desire, dwelling place, or identity; to be without laughter and unresponsive in erotic love. But what kind of love is this that goes from bad to worse, this submission that claims to represent marriage? "Will I have to go to jail?" asks Marnie in the dazed voice of a child. "I'd rather stay with you." One wonders, a woman wonders, if there is much difference between going off with Rutland or going to jail. For aren't they part of the same undifferentiated social space, the Law and psychiatry, the Law and business, widening now to enclose Marnie, to domesticate her, this once cagey woman? "Had you, love?" he responds, framing the film's last spoken words in a fearful ambivalence. The question disturbs, swerves us toward a future more ominous than the past. "The little witch," snaps Strutt at the beginning of the film, "I'll have her put away for twenty years." Instead she marries Mark.

To summarize, *Marnie* entwines two contrasting narrative threads. One weaves the story of a woman who compensates for a traumatic past and need for her mother's love by stealing but is brought to a breakthrough by a man who helps her confront her past and unlock the repressed truth. That is to say, transference occurs in the last scene, when Marnie's head moves from the mother who cannot touch her hair to the man who can and does. On this level, the filmic text projects a therapeutic resolution of social and psychological conflicts, as it allows Marnie to pass from the emotionally troubled domain of the mother to the rational and affluent shelter of the aristocratic male. Unquestioned, however, are Mark's authoritative relation to power and his possession of Marnie-as-child. "I want to know what happened to the child," he asks the detective, "the little girl, the daughter." He has her now.

At this point, a second narrative unravels the Utopian resolution. From the perspective of class (and race, as well, but this requires a future consider-ation of the Hitchcock production), Marnie's project is to undermine the power of money; yet in the end her class is crushed, her mother is marginalized, and Mark's capital and aggression are victorious. Marnie, who has in effect married the boss, is now a young girl, not a sexually mature woman. She doesn't know what will happen to her, nor how to protect herself, nor how to face the world. Regressing, she returns to the past so that she may retrieve herself and start out anew from the lost place. But the film gives us no hope that this can be so, for even though Marnie is no longer frigid, the world is still dead. In the film's final image, the car slowly moves hearse-like toward the fateful ship; it does not clear the frame but intersects with the edge of the false harbor. "Mother, mother, I feel worse," sing the children, frozen on the sidewalk. Like Mark, Marnie leaves with a partial truth, while its entire burden weighs upon the mother, defeated in her last struggle to hold on to her child.

  Marnie's climax is thus multiple and leads the viewer in several directions. Mistaken in thinking that the mother was the murderer, Mark is equally mis-taken in presuming that Marnie is healed by the knowledge of her trauma. And if we follow him in thinking that we have found in the murder the secret truth of Marnie's sexuality, we too, like Marnie, are led astray. The presump-tion of certainty that allowed Mark to misperceive Marnie's mother extends to all who see her as the gloomy figure on the staircase rather than as the woman forsaken once by the child's father, always by her clients, and then, finally, by the daughter Mark takes away. "I'll bring Marnie back," he rules, always the owner. "When a child can't get love," he intones, "it takes what it can get, any way it can get it; it's not so hard to understand." His explanation of Marnie's sickness falls far short of understanding her mother, damaged by the self-hatred of exploitation and prostitution. Mother, daughter, sailor—all are de-filed by a history of human misery, its material conditions concealed in psycho-logical mists.

  Marnie reveals a woman's pain but cannot heal it, cannot, in the words of Cixous, " 'realize' the decensored relation of woman to her sexuality." Hearing her cry, the film cannot "give her back her goods, her pleasures, her organs, her immense bodily territories which have been kept under seal . . . [or] tear her away from the superegoized structure in which she has always occupied the place reserved for the guilty (guilty of everything, guilty at every turn: for having desires, for not having any; for being frigid, for being 'too hot'; for not being both at once . . .)" (p. 250). Buried deep within *Marnie* is, not the single trauma of the murdered sailor, but the several wounds of a mother and daughter oppressed by poverty and violated in prostitution and marital rape, of the female body drawn into the categories of illegitimacy and frigidity and supposedly reconstituted in marriage. For Marnie, marriage is not salvation but subjugation, less a recuperation and recovery than the deepening of a wound that won't close.

Finally, *Marnie*'s narrative levels are inconsistent, in tension with one another. While one promotes Marnie's happiness, the other perpetuates pain. In this way, the suspense of the "thriller" is transformed into textual doubt about the unity of a couple linked in violence and the betrayal of social consciousness by a psychological insight that maintains class power and privilege, these wrecking the existence of those who have neither. *Marnie*'s conflicting ideologies delay the resolution of questions about the control of erotic and communal relations by class domination and money. Yet if *Marnie*'s contradictions hinder a lasting solution to the segmentation and exploitation of class struggle, they do not repress knowledge of its miserable tyranny and destruction.

Notes

1. Sarris's *Village Voice* review is reprinted in *Confessions of a Cultist* (New York: Simon & Schuster, 1970), 141–44.
2. Eric Rohmer and Claude Chabrol, *Hitchcock: The First Forty-Four Films,* trans. Stanley Hochman (New York: Frederick Ungar, 1979).
3. Robin Wood, *Hitchcock's Films,* 3rd ed. (South Brunswick and New York: A. S. Barnes, 1977).
4. For references to Bellour and Mulvey see the editors' introduction to Part V of this volume — "Hitchcock and Film Theory: A *Psycho* Dossier."
5. See Karl Marx and Friedrich Engels, "The Communist Manifesto," in K. Marx, *On Revolution,* ed. and trans. S. K. Padoner (New York: McGraw-Hill, 1971), 81: "Freeman and slave, patrician and plebeian, lord and serf, guild master and journeyman — in a word, oppressor and oppressed — stood in constant opposition to one another, carried on an uninterrupted, now hidden, now open fight, a fight that each time ended either in a revolutionary reconstitution of society at large, or in the common ruin of the contending classes."
6. Lewis Hyde, *The Gift: Imagination and the Erotic Life of Property* (New York: Vintage Books, 1983), xiv.
7. Hélène Cixous, "The Laugh of Medusa," in Elaine Marks and Isabelle de Courtivron, eds., *New French Feminisms* (New York: Schocken Books, 1981), 264.
8. Mary Douglas, *Natural Symbols* (New York: Pantheon, 1979), 70.
9. Donald Spoto, *The Dark Side of Genius: The Life of Alfred Hitchcock* (New York: Ballantine Books, 1984), 505.
10. Michel Foucault, *Discipline and Punish: The Birth of the Prison* (New York: Vintage Books, 1979), 197.
11. Michel Foucault, "The Eye of Power," in *Power/Knowledge* (New York: Pantheon Books, 1980), 152.
12. Jean-Paul Sartre, *Saint Genet* (New York: George Braziller, 1963), 49.
13. Joan B. Landes, "Hegel's Conception of the Family," in Jean Bethke Elshtain, ed., *The Family and Political Thought* (Amherst: Univ. of Massachusetts Press, 1982), 136.
14. Jean Genet, *The Thief's Journal* (New York: Grove Press, 1964), 91.
15. Stéphane Mallarmé, "Mimique," in Mary Ann Caws, ed., *Selected Poetry and Prose* (New York: New Directions Books, 1982), 69.

THE END

PART FIVE

Hitchcock and Film Theory: A *Psycho* Dossier

In recent years, film theory has drawn from a number of comprehensive philosophical systems—chief among them Marxism, linguistics, and psychoanalysis—in its attempts to account for the institutional and cultural workings of the cinema and for the relations between viewers and the projected image. A number of the essays in this volume take up such questions in their analyses of Hitchcock's films, though often in a richly metaphoric vocabulary which, like Freud's, is especially attuned to the almost uncanny analogies which exist between the realms of economic and psychic experience: desire in each is a matter of "power and freedom," as *Vertigo* so forcefully reminds us, though whose power, and whose freedom, and at whose expense are questions repeatedly posed.

Nowhere are those questions posed more thoroughly or more provocatively than in the work of Raymond Bellour whose essay on *Psycho* stands here as a crucial example of the interests which advanced film theory currently pursues. The essays by Barbara Klinger and Leland Poague which follow—though clearly different in their appropriation of Bellour—leave little question that coming to terms with Bellour's Hitchcock, and through him with a certain conception of the psychosocial function of "the classical narrative cinema," is absolutely necessary to an understanding of latter-day Hitchcock criticism, regardless of the problems Bellour raises.

"Coming to terms" here can be taken quite literally, in the sense that reading Bellour depends upon mastering a fairly elaborate vocabulary drawn ultimately from Jacques Lacan's rewriting of Freud along lines suggested by the linguistic theories of Ferdinand de Saussure. The summary remarks which follow are but the briefest sketch of what might be termed the "Lacanian scenario." Readers wishing further assistance are urged to consult, in ascending order of elaboration and difficulty, the following items from the appended bibliography: Charles Altman's "Psychoanalysis and Cinema," Malcolm Bowie's "Jacques Lacan," Annette Kuhn's *Women's Pictures,* Christine Gledhill's "Recent Developments in Feminist Criticism," Janet Bergstrom's "Enunciation and Sexual Difference," Kaja Silverman's *The Subject of Semiotics, The Imaginary Signifier* by Christian Metz, Stephen Heath's *Questions of Cinema,* and, for critique, Noël Carroll's "Address to the Heathen," and William Cadbury and Leland Poague's *Film Criticism: A Counter Theory.*

Central to Lacan's project, as to those of Freud and Marx, is the question of the relationship between consciousness and experience. For different reasons all three reject the Cartesian model which (in this general view) posits an individual subject existing somehow *prior* to his or her experience of a world of objects. For Marx, class experience and the alienation which results determines consciousness; for Freud and Lacan consciousness is determined by the unconscious, which is itself determined by the experiences of early childhood, chiefly by parent/child relationships. Lacan's indebtedness to Freud involves his reliance on language as symptomatic of the unconscious. In therapy it is through language, the patient's dream reports, for instance, but also through plays on words, free associations, etc., that the analyst acquires access to the unconscious and its primary processes of condensation and displacement by which the latent becomes manifest, and vice versa. Lacan's swerve from Freud is to assert that language not only allows access to but actually forms the unconscious, which is structured like and by language. Hence the "self," for Lacan, is no longer a free-standing "ego" which uses language but is rather a "subject," in the grammatical sense, someone who only exists *in* language, as an "I," and is thus subject *to* language, i.e., to an endless process of linguistic difference, deferment, and substitution. "Selfhood" is no longer a cause of meaning (in the intentional sense) but an effect of meaning.

The experience by which this "subjugation" to language (hence to society) occurs is generally taken to have two phases, a "mirror phase" and an "Oedipal phase," both of which happen "at the expense" of women. In the mirror phase a child (typically conceptualized as male) identifies with an image beyond himself, either a literal "mirror" image of himself, or its analog, his mother's face or body. Involved here is an essential illusion or misapprehension: that child and image, that mother and child, are unified, that each is fully "present" to the other, "as" the other. "That's me!" The mirror phase is thus "imaginary" in two respects, in that it depends on "images," and in its aspect of falsity, of being "imagined" or "projected." The Oedipal phase, then, is taken to shatter that illusion, only to reconstitute it at a higher level of abstraction, the level of language, of "the law."

In one version of the Oedipal story the father is seen to intervene between mother and child, to "absent" one from the other. In Freud this Oedipal moment involves the "primal scene" wherein the (apparently absent) child overhears or surreptitiously witnesses the sexual union of mother and father. In Lacan's rewrite of Freud the father's intervention is less physical than metaphorical. As a rival for the mother's affections and attentions, as a representative of the social world outside the domestic space of the home, the father comes "between" mother and child, "absents" one from the other, an absence which both requires and provides the basis for symbolization: requires it, because the child needs a way of referring to the absent mother, of "representing" her; provides the basis for it because language, as Ferdinand de Saussure described it, is nothing but a system of arbitrary differences to which meaning can be attached. We recognize "hit" by means of its phonemic difference from "bit" or "kit," and upon that recognition of difference all subsequent meaning depends.

Indeed, in another version of the Oedipal scenario the absence/presence antinomy which grounds our use of language is tied specifically to anatomical fact, as figured in the moment when the (male) child discovers his mother's lack of the phallus, at which point the illusory unity of mother and child breaks down, to be replaced by the child's identification with the father. Thus sexual difference, of mother from father, is causally related to the symbolic difference which grounds our ability to speak. And the illusion here is that in acquiring language we acquire a kind of freedom—the freedom to speak "for ourselves." But such freedom is bought at the expense of the mother, who loses her only social power in giving up her child to the linguistic rules which govern the paternal realm of "The Symbolic." And, moreover, we are less the possessors of language than its possessions: "Language speaks, not man," as Heidegger put it. Identity is not a matter of individuality but rather of "identifying with" the language which speaks us and with "The Father" who first initiates our speaking.

Lacanians generally apply this picture of psycholinguistic development to our experience of cinema—especially "the classical narrative cinema"—in two regards, along two axes of interest or desire. At the level of "enunciation," the moment-by-moment flow of images, our experience is taken to be a matter both of *regression,* in that our "scopic" (visual) relationship to the "specular" screen is an analog of our relationship to the mirror of the mirror phase, and of *repression,* in that our perception of images which seem "present" before us requires a willed forgetfulness of their "absence," of the sense in which the objects "represented" are not really there at all. Film viewing thus partakes of that "illusoriness" which characterizes an individual's earliest "view" of himself and his subsequent view of "himself." And the greatest illusion of all is that which takes the entire process to be natural, inevitable, as if the world we see, on screen and off, is the only world imaginable. But, as the words of Jean-Luc Godard should remind us, "It's not a just image; it's just an image." And the corollary urging, especially among feminists, is that we need to change those images, which can only begin to happen when the process of image formation (on screen and off) is foregrounded and questioned.

Another application of the Lacanian scenario to the question of our experience of film involves the question of narrative, the overall shape of a film as opposed (quite literally) to the moment-by-moment flow of its images. Here it is more the realm of the Symbolic (rather than the Imaginary) which comes into play. Images invite regression, to childhood. But the work of Bellour and others suggests that we see all narratives as versions of the Oedipal fable where the son's maturing into the Symbolic is figured in his taking the place of the father, either literally, by killing the father and marrying the mother, or meta-phorically, through a process of investigation which brings him to a comparable knowledge. The process is "psychotic," as Bellour suggests in his discussion of *Psycho,* involving a rampant play of the "id." But this play, akin to the regressive aspects of indulging the Imaginary, is finally contained by the "closure" of the narrative, what Bellour calls "le blocage symbolique," where the dead father is resurrected in the son who takes his place, a place-taking typically confirmed by his taking a wife whose primary function is to reproduce, if not by having children, at least by marking the sexual difference upon which the entire linguistic/social system rests. Indeed, much of the interest of *Psycho,* for both Bellour and Klinger, involves its foregrounding of this pattern by displacing it into a paradoxically feminine yet also matricidal register. In "speaking" for mother Norman finally "becomes" mother.

This Oedipal scenario is not limited, we should note, to the narrative trajectory of the film story. Criticism has a trajectory, a story, too. And Bellour has suggested in his interview with Janet Bergstrom that the critic also undertakes a kind of investigation, also seeks after a knowledge of the film in question which will displace the father, the film's "enunciator." The catch is that in *dis*placing the father one *re*places him, as if in trying to solve the mystery of "le nom du père" via an investigation of sexual difference Bellour were in the process of becoming the father—as Scottie becomes Elster in *Vertigo* via his dehumanizing investigation/re-creation of Judy. In "speaking" (for) Hitchcock, Bellour "becomes" Hitchcock. Moreover, this temptation to murderous speaking is hardly limited to Lacanians: David Thomson's condemnation in *Overexposures* of the "incipient hostility" aroused by *Psycho* is itself a remarkably hostile critical performance, as if Thomson too had become a version of that which he condemns. Whether such Oedipal transformations are necessary or inevitable is open to question, as Leland Poague demonstrates in our concluding essay, but the answer most current within advanced film theory is one of profound skepticism regarding our conscious ability to wrest any real measure of psychic freedom from the realm of social necessity as Lacan has described it. Psychosis. Neurosis. Perversion. Indeed.

References and Suggested Readings

Film Theory

Altman, Charles F. "Psychoanalysis and Cinema: The Imaginary Discourse." *Quarterly Review of Film Studies,* vol. 2, no. 3 (1977): 257-72.

Andrew, Dudley. *Concepts in Film Theory.* New York: Oxford Univ. Press, 1984.

Bergstrom, Janet. "Enunciation and Sexual Difference (Part I)." *Camera Obscura,* no. 3-4 (1979): 32-69.

———. "Alternation, Segmentation, Hypnosis: Interview with Raymond Bellour." *Camera Obscura,* no. 3-4 (1979): 70-103.

Bowie, Malcolm. "Jacques Lacan." In John Sturrock, ed. *Structuralism and Since: From Lévi-Strauss to Derrida.* New York: Oxford Univ. Press, 1979, 116-53.

Cadbury, William. "Story, Pleasure, and Meaning in *The Scarlet Empress.*" In Syndy M. Conger and Janice R. Welsch, eds. *Narrative Strategies.* Macomb: Western Illinois Univ., 1980, 115-27. A reply to Mulvey's "Visual Pleasure and Narrative Cinema" (cited below).

Cadbury, William, and Leland Poague. *Film Criticism: A Counter Theory.* Ames: Iowa State Univ. Press, 1982.

Carroll, Noël. "Address to the Heathen." *October,* no. 23 (1982): 89-163. Review of Heath's *Questions of Cinema* (cited below).

———. "A Reply to Heath." *October,* no. 27 (1983): 81-102.

de Lauretis, Teresa. *Alice Doesn't: Feminism, Semiotics, Cinema.* Bloomington: Indiana Univ. Press, 1984. Discusses *Rebecca* and *Vertigo* in her remarks on "Desire in Narrative."

Eberwein, Robert. *Film and the Dream Screen.* Princeton: Princeton Univ. Press, 1984.

Gledhill, Christine. "Recent Developments in Feminist Criticism." *Quarterly Review of Film Studies,* vol. 3, no. 4 (1978): 456-93.

Heath, Stephen. *Questions of Cinema.* Bloomington: Indiana Univ. Press, 1981.

———. "Le Père Noel." *October,* no. 26 (1983): 63-115. Reply to Carroll.

Kaplan, E. Ann. *Women & Film: Both Sides of the Camera.* New York: Methuen, 1983.

Kuhn, Annette. *Women's Pictures: Feminism and Cinema.* London: Routledge & Kegan Paul, 1982.

Lacan, Jacques. *Speech and Language in Psychoanalysis.* Trans. Anthony Wilden. Baltimore: Johns Hopkins Univ. Press, 1968. Only 84 of more than 300 pages are by Lacan; in the rest Wilden attempts "to introduce the English-speaking reader to Lacan." Hence the "brevity" of our own summary account.

Lovell, Terry. *Pictures of Reality: Aesthetics, Politics and Pleasure.* London: British Film Institute, 1980. A Marxist-feminist critique of Lacan.

Metz, Christian. *The Imaginary Signifier: Psychoanalysis and the Cinema.* Trans. Celia Britton et al. Bloomington: Indiana Univ. Press, 1982.

Mulvey, Laura. "Visual Pleasure and Narrative Cinema." *Screen,* vol. 16, no. 3 (1975): 6-18.

———. "Afterthoughts . . . Inspired by *Duel in the Sun.*" *Framework,* no. 15-16-17 (1981): 12-25.

Rosen, Philip. "'Screen' and the Marxist Project in Film Criticism." *Quarterly Review of Film Studies,* vol. 2, no. 3 (1977): 273-87. Especially useful for its bibliography.

Silverman, Kaja. *The Subject of Semiotics.* New York: Oxford Univ. Press, 1983.

Turkle, Sherry. *Psychoanalytic Politics: Freud's French Revolution.* New York: Basic Books, 1978.

On *Psycho*

Braudy, Leo. "Hitchcock, Truffaut, and the Irresponsible Audience." In Albert J. LaValley, ed. *Focus on Hitchcock.* Englewood Cliffs: Prentice-Hall, 1972, 116-27.

Corliss, Richard. "*Psycho* Therapy." In Philip Nobile, ed. *Favorite Movies: Critics' Choice.* New York: Macmillan, 1973, 213-24.

Crawford, Larry. "*Psycho*-Analysis: A Textual Perspective in Film Study." In Rene Jara et al., eds. *The Paradigm Exchange*. Minneapolis: Univ. of Minnesota, College of Liberal Arts, 1981, 77–84.

———. "Subsegmenting the Filmic Text: The Bakersfield Car Lot Scene in *Psycho*." *enclitic*, vol. 5, no. 2/vol. 6, no. 1 (1982): 35–43.

———. "Looking, Film, Painting: The Trickster's In Site/In Sight/Insight/Incite." *Wide Angle*, vol. 5, no. 3 (1983): 64–69. Bakersfield revisited.

Giannetti, Louis D. *Godard and Others: Essays on Film Form*. Rutherford: Fairleigh Dickinson Univ. Press, 1975. See 118–25.

Naremore, James. *Filmguide to* Psycho. Bloomington: Indiana Univ. Press, 1973.

Telotte, J. P. "Faith and Idolatry in the Horror Film." *Literature/Film Quarterly*, vol. 8, no. 3 (1980): 143–55.

Thomson, David. "*Psycho* and the Roller Coaster." In *Overexposures: The Crisis in American Filmmaking*. New York: William Morrow, 1981, 202–14.

———. "Salieri, *Psycho*." *Film Comment*, vol. 21, no. 1 (1985): 70–75.

Wollen, Peter. "Hybrid Plots in *Psycho*." In *Readings and Writings: Semiotic Counter Strategies*. London: Verso, 1982, 34–39.

Zita, Jacquelyn N. "Dark Passages: A Feminist Analysis of *Psycho*." In Jara et al. (cited above), 85–90.

CHAPTER TWENTY-THREE

Psychosis, Neurosis, Perversion
Raymond Bellour

TRANSLATED BY NANCY HUSTON

Barthes said to me the other day: basically, when you give someone
something to read, you give it to your mother.
— PHILIPPE SOLLERS

I.

Psycho is undoubtedly the most obscure of Hitchcock's films. Obscure,
first of all, in a literal sense, because in none of his other films does night seem
so black and day so somber. There is, of course, *The Wrong Man:* exactly like
Psycho (inscribed between the colorful symphonies of *North by Northwest* and
The Birds), it left a trail of shadow, three years earlier, between *The Man Who
Knew Too Much* and *Vertigo*. The two films do have in common a kind of
nocturnal excellence which permeates the gestures, faces, and image tones:
Hitchcock sought, in one case, to endow them with documentary value, and
entrusted them, in the other case, to a television cameraman. However, this
material obscurity—fuller and duller in the realism of *The Wrong Man*—
seemed eventually to dissolve away, or at least be balanced out by the exemplary linearity of the screenplay and by the ultimate resolution of the error,
restoring to Christopher Balestrero the certainty of his identity, and to his wife
the hope of a fragile mental balance{ In *Psycho*, on the contrary, to the extent
that a surrender to the codifications of romanticism and horror is always possible, the role of shadow grows incessantly, according to the interplay of ordering
and disruption that guides the film from its beginning to its end.)

The principle of classical film is well known: the end must reply to the
beginning; between one and the other something must be set in order; the last
scene frequently recalls the first and constitutes its resolution. *Psycho*'s opaque-
ness is contradictory in this respect: the end, apparently, in no way replies to
the beginning: the psychiatrist's commentary on the case of Norman Bates has
little to do with the love scene between Marion and Sam in the Phoenix hotel.
The specific obscurity of *Psycho* is thus, above all, a rhetorical obscurity. It
denotes the fact that the film, in a sense, contravenes the classical model of

narrative—as well as that more singular model which is both an eccentric and exemplary version of it: the Hitchcockian system. Obviously, it does so, not in order to elude the system, but rather—through a greater degree of abstraction—to determine its regime(s): the system here performs displacements with respect to itself, designating with extreme clarity the mechanisms that govern its operation.

II.

The first sign of this is the radical displacement of the investigation. In the Hitchcockian fable, investigations conform to two major modalities, complementary and interchangeable, in which the relationships of identification are established by the position of knowledge that Hitchcock reserves for himself (and thus for the spectator as well), as opposed to the various subjects (supports) of the fiction. The inquiry represents, first of all, an ideal testing-ground for the hero (or the heroine as mirror-image, or the couple-as-subject), who, constrained by chance and necessity, learns to acknowledge a certain truth about his own desire after a dramaturgy of violence based on the search for the secret. To achieve this the riddle must be solved, and the mistaken identity in which it was cloaked revealed; these two questions may then be traced back to their common origin, resulting in a final equilibrium between desire and the law. This renders possible, through the inclusion-exclusion process of the terms of the destructive drive, the ultimate integration (whether successful or not) of the imaginary into the symbolic by means of a general dovetailing of the textual operations. Such is the exemplary itinerary of *North by Northwest,* but the same model is used in *The 39 Steps, Saboteur, Foreign Correspondent, To Catch a Thief,* and, in a slightly different form, in *Strangers on a Train* and *Rear Window.* In *Notorious,* by displacement, it is the hero, the man of the couple, who is the secret agent invested with the knowledge and initiative usually paradoxically divided up between the police and the false culprit. In *Spellbound,* of the two characters which make up the couple, it is the woman who leads the investigation of which the other is the object. And in *Shadow of a Doubt* the investigation is led by both the woman and the policeman, who eventually make up the final couple. Thus, most of Hitchcock's films can be seen as multiple variations or distortions of this same basic model.

Conversely, the second modality consists of denying the hero (or heroine or couple-subject) access to the truth of the investigation: even though they may share its diegetic benefits, they are dispossessed of this knowledge by some external factor. Take, for example, *Dial "M" for Murder,* in which neither the husband nor the wife leads the investigation of which both are the object; or *Under Capricorn,* whose highly improbable plot follows the same model; or even *I Confess,* in which the presumed culprit is, paradoxically, the only one who knows the secret, but can say nothing. However, these narratives in which the hero is deprived of the truth-seeking initiative are, in general, all the more constrained by a uniform dynamic leading from the riddle to its solution (*The Wrong Man,* for example). In addition, they often depend, very naturally, alongside the main couple, on a third important character: in *Under Capricorn,* Charles Adare, the outsider and friend; in *Dial "M" for Murder,* Chief Inspector Hubbard, who unravels all the elaborately tangled threads of the plot.

Psycho, however, apparently conforms to this second model, while breaking the system apart at its very core. Neither of the two main characters is invested as subject during the progression of the investigation; its indices of truth are divided up among Arbogast, the sheriff, Sam, Lila, and the psychiatrist. The former two, a private detective and a policeman, share the partial and misleading truth that is so often allotted them in Hitchcock's films: Arbogast succeeds in tracing Marion but gives credit to the fiction of the mother; the sheriff denies this fiction without being able to account for its effects. Sam and Lila, for their part, seem to fulfill—amidst the scattered functions of the second model—a function proper to the first, that of the couple whose action solves the riddle and opens the way to truth. This is actually due to a displacement, since the solution brings about nothing that concerns them directly (thus Sam and Lila merely mimic the diegetic couple, marking out its absence). In addition—and as a result—their solution is only a half-truth; it immediately requires the mediation of a superior truth. This is provided by the third important character, here embodied in the psychiatrist, with the significant difference that in this case he intervenes, very deliberately, as deus ex machina, a stranger to the action, strictly exterior to what is at stake. This is why the final explanation has sometimes been considered a useless appendix, whereas it is the ultimate result of the work of displacement that has taken place thoughout the film. Thus, from an original dispersion of truth and its diegetic effects, a veritable split occurs between the materiality and the awareness of experience: the division of the investigation merely reproduces the central division organizing the film and determining, at all levels, its regime.

III.

Psycho contains two narratives, slipping one under the other, one into the other. This relationship must be conceptualized in order to penetrate to a structural perversion to which Hitchcock opened the way by deciding to "kill the star in the first third of the film."[1] There is, first of all, the story of Marion. The opening scene in the hotel room calls attention to the problematic: marriage; the ensuing theft produces its dramatic effect. This is a weakened version both of *Strangers on a Train* (as regards marriage, Marion and Sam occupying the place of Guy Haines and Ann Morton, with the third person being a first wife, not yet divorced in *Strangers,* already divorced in *Psycho*) and of *Marnie* (as regards the theft). The story could have various outcomes along its own axis: one of these, the meeting between Marion and Norman, has the ambigu-

ous function of ending the story in order to transform it. The second story, that
of Norman, might thus be said to begin when Marion arrives at the motel and
to continue, slightly altered (because of the persistent pressure of the first
story), to the end of the film. Such, indeed, was the case in the novel by
Robert Bloch used as a pretext for the film: Hitchcock immediately broke up
the overly simple structure of the book, and later justified this in a singularly
underdetermined way.[2]

> In fact, the first part of the story was a red herring. That was deliber-
> ate, you see, to detract the viewer's attention in order to heighten the
> murder. We purposely made that beginning on the long side, with the bit
> about the theft and her escape, in order to get the audience absorbed with
> the question of whether she would or would not be caught. Even that
> business about the forty thousand dollars was milked to the very end so
> that the public might wonder what's going to happen to the money. . . .
> The more we go into the details of the girl's journey, the more the
> audience becomes absorbed in her flight. That's why so much is made of
> the motorcycle cop and the change of cars. When Anthony Perkins tells
> the girl of his life in the motel, and they exchange views, you still play
> upon the girl's problem. It seems as if she's decided to go back to Phoenix
> and give the money back, and it's possible that the public anticipates by
> thinking, "Ah, this young man is influencing her to change her mind."
> You turn the viewer in one direction and then in another; you keep him as
> far as possible from what's actually going to happen.[3]

This statement focuses on what constitutes, properly speaking, the center
of the narrative, its moment of extreme fascination. However, it denies the fact
that, from this very moment onwards, the constitution of the "first story" is
supported by its inscription within the "second," both at the level of narrative
identifications and at that of the logic of its occurrences. Denied, too, is the
subtle movement by which the narrative both masks and accentuates the division constituting its paradoxical unity. The singular genius of the film consists
of indissolubly mixing together the two narratives that it is composed of by
using the meeting of the two characters as the means of their substitution.

Everything contributes to this.

1. The time allotted to the meeting, which by itself takes up, strictly
speaking, one-fifth of the film (more, in fact: a third, counting the rather short
sequence that leads Marion, caught in the storm, to the Bates Motel, and the
much longer sequence between the murder and the disappearance of Marion's
car in the marsh).

2. The violence that concludes the meeting, which is so incredible that it
obfuscates its own secondary effect: namely, the determining fact of the passage, in a sense, from one character to the other.

3. A major rhetorical shift contributes to this displacement and facilitates
the reversal. Whereas the segmentation of the rest of the film systematically
employs, in a highly classical manner, the three criteria of segmental demarca-

tion, the scene of the meeting (in the extended sense) is devoid of all punctuation: there is not a single fade-out between the moment Marion abruptly leaves the garage where she has traded in her car and the moment her new car sinks into the marsh.[4] This does not mean that thirty-five minutes of the film make up a single segment; the two other criteria of demarcation do intervene, although much less distinctly than in most classical films. It is as though the sudden absence of punctuation were responsible for creating the illusion of segmental continuity, isolating the time of the meeting within the construction of a whole in order to give it a greater fluidity and the logical evidence necessary to carry out the substitutive shift.

4. Finally, "naturalness" acts like the musicality of a fiction, integrating with misleading obviousness the elements of the first narrative which contribute to the construction of the second.

IV.

The perfection of the ternary composition both conceals and reveals the binary division between the narratives and the characters. Three movements, reiterated to harmonize term-to-term in coupled oppositions, reinforce the unfolding of the fiction and its organic cohesion by establishing a very stable hierarchy of repetition and difference. All three involve an itinerary leading to the motel, and all three end in a murderous aggression punctuated by strident music. The first takes Marion Crane from her room in Phoenix to the motel room, where she is assassinated by "the mother"; the second takes Arbogast from Sam's store in Fairvale to the motel and then to Norman's house, where he in turn is assassinated by "the mother"; the third takes Sam and Lila from Sam's store to the motel and then to Norman's house, where Lila only escapes aggression by "the mother" thanks to the intervention of Sam, who recognizes Norman through the disguise.

It is immediately clear, limiting the discussion at first to murder, what movements 2 and 3, 1 and 2 have in common, respectively and by pairs: the aggression is a response, in the two latter cases, to an intrusion into the house, first by Arbogast, then by Sam and Lila (whereas Marion's assassination takes place at the motel); but—conversely—in the first two cases the murder is accomplished, whereas its failure in the third case lifts the veil of mystery and carries the film to its resolution. Thus, with the benefit of an equivalence by pairs ($1 = 2, 2 = 3$), the third movement recalls the first, thus accentuating the repetitive circulation.

Nevertheless, on closer examination it can be seen that an intrusion into the house is suggested during the first movement, though in unlike manner, when Norman invites Marion to share his meal, provoking the indignation of "the mother" and, eventually, the murder and everything that ensues. Thus, by a regulated difference, the circularity of the fiction is ensured—what might be called its narrative (dis)similarity. In the same way, just as movements 1 and

3 are organized around the repeated motif of the rooms rented first by Marion, then by Sam and Lila, the second movement includes Norman's very natural proposal of his room to Arbogast (and later, failing that, his less natural proposal that Arbogast come and help him change the beds).

Again, one could evoke the three scenes of shot–reverse shot, identically distributed throughout the three movements, in the small motel office (with Norman on one side of the counter, Marion, Arbogast, Sam, and Lila on the other, reflected in the mirror). However, in the third case, there is a repetition: Sam is later seen alone with Norman in the office (while Lila is on her way up to the house). Thus, the third movement constantly doubles back on itself to emphasize, within the regulated difference, the progression and accomplishment of the narrative. It has been seen that movements 2 and 3 are defined by an identical trajectory: from Sam's store to the motel and then to the house. However, in the third movement this trajectory is split in two by the emergence of the mystery, which constitutes a turning point.[5] When Sam goes to the motel the first time to look for Arbogast, he sees "the mother." He undertakes the same visit with Lila in order to initiate her fully into the secret; thus they follow, together, the whole itinerary leading from their rented room to Marion's, and then, separately, from Norman's office to the mother's room, and from Norman's boyhood room to the cellar where his mother is concealed. The (dis)similarity ensures the circular identity of the narrative by guaranteeing its unpredictable advance toward a final result.

Within this regulated succession, this elaborate interplay of identities, separations, intimations, and revelations that correlatively ensure the superimposition and interchangeability of the two narratives, the second movement, much shorter than the first, has a specific transitive value: following Marion's disappearance, it emphasizes the role of Norman, progressively establishing him as the new hero of the narrative before making him the center of the mystery. The latter is accomplished by the third movement, for which Hitchcock cleverly reserves the sheriff's revelation concerning the mother's death — since, logically, if Sam and Lila were only preoccupied with Marion's fate and the stolen money, the spectator could only expect, and dread, the solution of the undoubtedly horrendous mystery hidden within Norman.

V.

This circular orchestration, by the very progression of its three movements, has a secondary effect: it sets off all the more plainly the segments bordering it on either side (the opening and closing scenes), and, within these segments, rigorously heterogeneous and yet connected, the speech of the psychiatrist and the love scene in the Phoenix hotel.

The speech of the psychiatrist, in the course of which those parts of the mystery still remaining obscure are finally illuminated, is the logical consequence of the radical exclusion of the first narrative. The speech concerns

Norman; it is a commentary and explanation of his case: it says nothing about Marion, who has become the pure object of a murderous desire, and even less about Sam, who can only listen, at Lila's side, to an analysis that excludes him from the diegesis of which he too, through Marion, had been the subject.

This raises a series of questions. Why is this film about psychotic dissociation organized with respect to an original plot which, while supporting it to the point of appearing indispensable, nevertheless remains, in a sense, totally foreign to it? In this highly classically orchestrated film, whose three movements recall the hermeneutic tripartition of *North by Northwest,* how is the internal principle of classical film satisfied — namely, that the end must always reply to the beginning? In what way does the last scene provide a solution, or even an echo, to the first? I think it is necessary, here, to conceive of Hitchcock as pursuing, through fiction, an indirect reflection on the inevitable relationship, in his art and in his society, between psychosis and neurosis, inscribed respectively in narrative terms as murder and theft. These are general instances, fictional rather than clinical, those of a civilization in which a certain subject, who is both a singular subject and the collective agent of enunciation, finds a way to structure his fantasy and determine his symbolic regime. What appears from the fact that the subject of neurosis is offered up in the logic of the narrative to the violence of the subject of psychosis, man or woman, mutually interchangeable throughout the course of the narrative, is the obscure numinous point of a fiction which carries to a vertiginous degree of duplication the fascinated reflection on the logic of desire.

This position is a familiar one within the twists and turns of Hitchcock's labyrinthian scenarios. It is already enunciated with incredible precision in *Shadow of a Doubt* by the doubling of uncle and niece, manifested in the Christian name they share as well as in the repeated motif of the bedrooms (the uncle's hotel room and the niece's family room: both characters are revealed, lying in bed, by a single movement of the camera; and, in a pure mirror-effect, there appears in the first shot, from the left, the woman who runs the hotel, and in the second, from the right, the young girl's father; thus is prepared the substitution that will later place the uncle in the niece's room). On the one hand, there is Charlie's — the niece's — profound, inexpressible dissatisfaction, the neurotic lack which she hopes will magically disappear thanks to Uncle Charlie; on the other, there is the uncle's psychotic split, the return of his childhood trauma that is compulsively acted out in the murder of widows, and that ultimately, due to the progression of the inquiry, turns upon the young girl as the logical object of its deadly desire. Thus, as in *Psycho,* woman, the subject of neurosis, becomes the object of the psychosis of which man is the subject. This is a fundamental aspect of the Hitchcockian constant according to which, given a certain order of desire, it is above all women that get killed.

That is not to say:

1. That women do not kill. But the murder they commit is always the

reverse side of the "psychotic" aggression of which they are the object. It is thus that, in *Shadow of a Doubt,* the uncle, in his struggle, falls off the train from which he had tried to throw his niece; in *Blackmail* the young woman kills the painter who had tried to rape her; and in *Dial "M" for Murder,* the husband's murderous desire having replaced, as in so many of Hitchcock's and other films, the psychosis he conceals, the woman kills to defend herself from the assassin he has hired. This is why, in a rigorously complementary manner, women may—or must—seem in the position of symbolic murderers: thus, in *North by Northwest,* Eve's fictitious murder of Thornhill is woman's response to the murderous desire she awakens in man—if only metaphorically, as a sexual object.

2. That women cannot "manifest psychotic tendencies" (as can be seen in *The Wrong Man* or in *Under Capricorn*). But that they do so only to the extent that the hero has suffered a loss of identity, and never from the same demented object-desire as he. This is why women can only tolerate madness in men if they can save them from it (*Spellbound:* even at the cost of awakening their murderous desire; or, in a totally different way, *Rebecca*). This modality may also be that of men (*Marnie*), but it then involves only, so to speak, a semimadness, and this at the price of a fetishistic position that reinforces love and is related, through scoptophilia, to murderous desire, of which it is the mitigated, possessive form.

Vertigo constitutes, in all respects, a marvelously complex counterexample. The woman is the object of an illusory psychosis; she is an image of psychosis, turned toward death in a twofold manner, through the image-painting of Carlotta Valdes. She awakens a passion in the man: the desire to see, mesmerized by death; this is the moment when Scottie tears Madeleine away from what fascinates him. Later, after the false-real death of Madeleine, the man wanders on the borderline of madness (between neurosis and psychosis: narcissistic neurosis, mourning, and melancholia). Still later, when the false living woman reappears, the desire to kill reemerges: an image must be modeled so that the "real" can at last be transferred onto it, thus accomplishing— with the help of God if necessary (the appearance of the nun diegetically motivating the second fall)—the subject's desire, sublimated in the scopic drive that transfixes the male subject.

3. Finally, this is not to say that men cannot be the subject of neurosis. Such, indeed, is their most common lot. Neurosis is what occurs when an encounter with the extraordinary, by way of the inevitable ritual testing of murder-psychosis, determines for the hero the resolution of the symbolic. There is always a "madman" who kills for the hero, turning the subject of neurosis into a false culprit, and thus inciting him—through a displacement in which neurotic guilt is resolved in the reality of action—to rediscover a certain truth of his desire. Here again, the itinerary of *North by Northwest* is exemplary.

So, in another manner, is that of *Strangers on a Train,* through the meeting of the characters and the fiction of the exchanged murders. The issue of marriage, or in this case remarriage (elsewhere it is the question of stabilizing or restabilizing the couple: *Suspicion, The Man Who Knew Too Much*), serves to sustain what can be called Guy's "neurosis": the basic neurosis of American cinema. By a diabolical twist, this issue — in the interests of its own resolution (final marriage) — provides psychosis with its object. Because of the exchange of murders, Miriam, Guy's wife, comes to occupy the place of Bruno's father, whom Bruno has vainly appealed to Guy to murder. As a part of the fantasy of the murder of the father, necessary to the symbolic resolution of neurosis, Miriam thus embodies the complementary fantasy that indicates, for Hitchcock, the psychotic's access to the real: the murder of a woman (and through her, of the too-well-loved mother; such films as *Shadow of a Doubt, Strangers on a Train,* and *Frenzy* are directly connected around this motif).

These, then, are the terms that *Psycho* sets into play, frontally, through a reversible effect of the articulation between the two psychic structures, grasped in a doubling relationship carried by sexual difference. The criterion used here to associate and dissociate neurosis and psychosis remains, overwhelmingly, the one used by Freud: both are avatars of desire which bring about an unsettling of the subject's relationship to reality.[6] But whereas in psychosis the Ego is at the service of the Id and eludes what it finds intolerable in reality, in neurosis the Ego is the stage of a conflict between the Id and the Superego, such that the loss of reality "affects precisely that piece of reality as a result of whose demands the instinctual repression ensued."[7] This is Marion's situation in *Psycho:* the theft which draws her into this loss is her response to the sociosexual aggression on the part of the "millionaire" in Lowery's office, of which she was, metaphorically, the object. But on a much deeper level, it is her response to Sam's aggression, of which she feels herself to be the object, in the sordid clandestineness of the hotel room, when the conflict between the intensity of her sexual demand and her wish to have it legally sanctioned by marriage (continually postponed due to Sam's financial position) comes to a head.[8] This explains the focus, just as later on in *Marnie,* on money, that polyvalent signifier of desire (sexual or social) which also serves, even better than hysterical conversion and perhaps with greater conformity to unconscious logic, the logic of the fiction.[9] This is what Marion's theft attempts to resolve, magically, "by a sort of flight," as Freud says of neurosis, dodging the fragment of reality that psychosis, for its part, simply denies in order to reconstruct a better reality.

VI.

The long segment during which Marion and Norman are face to face in the small reception room of the motel thus places face to face, fictitiously, two psychic structures: man and woman, the latter destined to become the prey of the former. The mirror arrangement that organizes their dialogue in a regulated alternation of shot–reverse shots ensures, between the two characters, the interchangeability necessary to their future substitution. It is here that Norman's family romance is presented, in the deceptive form in which it has been restructured by his desire, by the truth of his delirium, thus echoing the more disparate elements of Sam's and Marion's family romances, scattered throughout their dialogue in the hotel room.[10] Thus, the two mental forms are brought together by similarity and exclusion: Marion grows aware of her own derangement because of the much more absolute derangement she senses in Norman. Their differential assimilation is concentrated in a metaphor with endless ramifications. "*Norman:* You—you eat like a bird." The metaphor is no sooner spoken than it is denied. "Anyway, I hear the expression 'eats like a bird'—. . . it—it's really a fals-fals-fals-falsity. Because birds really eat a tremendous lot."[11] Marion has to be a bird, in order to be constituted as a body potentially similar to that of Norman's mother, object of his desire, stuffed just like the birds who survey their exchange. But Marion cannot really be a bird, because the bird's "psychotic" appetite has been reserved for Norman, as the body transformed into the mother's body (even if, by a remarkable reversal, Norman eats nothing during the entire scene: "It's all for you. I'm not hungry").

The reception room scene is meticulously organized to lead up to the murder scene. After an opening shot during which Norman appears amidst the stuffed birds disposed about the room, there are four shots showing Marion, standing, in alternation with the birds: the order of these shots (bird *a*—Marion—bird *b*—Marion) denotes her feeling that she is seen by the birds as much as she sees them, and that this disturbs her. After a repetition of shot 1 (Norman standing), there is a shot showing Norman and Marion together, seated on either side of a tray of food prepared by Norman. Then a classical alternation is established, dividing the shot between the two characters to distribute their dialogue. At the same time, a formal opposition emphasizes the fact that Norman, in this second alternation, has come to occupy, with respect to Marion, the place of the birds. In the various ways in which Norman is framed, he is associated with the outstretched beaks and widespread wings of one or several of the stuffed birds. Conversely, Marion is defined successively in two framings: she is beneath an oval painting whose theme was clearly visible during the second bird shot of the preceding alternation. The painting distinctly shows a band of angels, or, more precisely, a group of three women in which the central figure seems to be rising up to heaven, wings outspread. Next to the painting, in the same shot, the menacing shadow of a crow is projected onto the wall, penetrating the picture like a knifeblade or a penis. It is this complex whole that rivets Marion's attention, then splits apart when she takes her seat beneath the painting and becomes—through a double, metaphorical-metonymical inflection—defined by it, just as Norman is later emblematically defined by the birds. Thus the differential assimilation is continued: Marion, angel-woman-bird; Norman, bird-fetish-murderer. And thus is prefigured, in the intertwined motifs of alternation, the aggression of which she is soon to be the object (announced, when she rises, half concealing the painting, by the black beak of the crow that reappears inside the frame).

A few shots later, the alternation between Norman and Marion recommences, this time through an apparatus that mimics the cinematographic apparatus itself. Norman is concealed, significantly, by a painting which prefigures the effect he is to produce: *Susannah and the Elders,* virtually at the moment of the rape. Beneath the painting is a large hole that reveals, in the wall itself, the tiny luminous hole to which Norman puts his eye, creating—just like the projector's beam—an image which is for us virtual and for him almost real: Marion undressing, once again in the proximity of two birds, the portraits hanging on the wall of her bedroom near the bathroom door. The alternation then continues, obsessively marking the insert of the bulging eyeball, and shifting from the relationship between shots to the relationship between segments (or subsegments).

The next double series of shots, postponing voyeurism, intensifies it to the extreme:

(a) Norman, under the influence of what he has seen, goes back to shut himself up in the house in order to imagine what will happen next—or better yet, what will happen metaphorically for him, given the premises that catalyze his desire.

(b) Marion, in her room, soon gets into the shower: the spectator, by this advance intrusion, is witness to the scene for which Norman's obsession has prepared the way.

The moment of the murder marks the invasion by the subject (hero and spectator together) of the constituted image of his fantasy. Here, alternation must be abandoned; it is ruptured by the brutal inscription on the image of the living body-knife-bird of Norman–the mother, the reiterated fragmentation of Marion's body, the insert of her mouth agape in a horrendous scream and that of the dead eye that answers—at the opposite extreme of this very long fragment—the bulging eye of Norman given over to the inordinate desire of the scopic drive.

VII.

That only men are subjects of psychosis (or that women are psychotic only by default, or by reflection) here implies, above all, something else: that only men are subjects of perversion (here and elsewhere, given a certain regime of fiction, and a certain order of civilization).

It should be recalled that the manner in which psychosis and perversion can both be defined—although not in the same way—is by their difference from neurosis, through their common allegiance to the wishes of the Id: the former, as has been seen, by its indulgence in a form of delirious reconstruction, through an infinitely more radical loss of reality than in neurosis, implying a lesser subservience to repressive mechanisms; the latter, in the sense of the famous formula: neurosis is "the negative of perversion." Though it must not be taken literally — as its reversal (perversion is the negative of neurosis) would tend to define perversion as nothing but the raw manifestation of infantile desire — Freud's formula does imply, however, that perversion provides a more direct access to the object of the drive, according to its own defense mechanisms (denial of reality, splitting of the Ego), which in some ways link it to those of psychosis.[12]

More specifically, it can be seen how this twofold difference is articulated here with respect to the inscription of the scopic drive and its destiny. To go back to the beginning of the film: there is the first, continuous shot during which the camera wanders down from a high angle over the rooftops of a city, progressively closing in on a window with half-raised blinds, then going beneath these blinds to reveal, in a bedroom, a couple that has just been making love. Thus, from the start, emphasis is placed on the voyeuristic position, which deliberately constitutes the position of enunciation.[13] It is highly remarkable that this opening shot, quite common in Hitchcock's films (cf. *Shadow of a Doubt*), is especially reminiscent of *Rope,* in which the first interminable shot focuses — having passed through a similar window / screen — on the cold fury of a murder.[14] In this interplay of forms based on an endless interchangeability between murder and the sexual act (cf., for example, the scene of the kiss in the train in *North by Northwest*), it is clearly the "unseen" of the primal scene in the hotel room which, at the level of the enunciating instance itself (Hitchcock – the camera), is displaced from neurosis to psychosis, from the hotel room to the motel room.[15]

Thus, Norman obviously comes to occupy, with respect to Marion, the place of Sam (whence the resemblance, for some striking, between Sam and Norman, particularly during the scene of their confrontation across the counter in the motel office).[16] However, the substitution occurs at the price of a displacement, imputable to the respective identifications between Hitchcock and the two male characters. In the first scene, the camera almost always remains at a distance from Sam: he is held, like Marion, and usually with her, within the frame, that is, within the neurotic field that the two of them circumscribe. An essentially diegetic identification is thus set up (for the male spectator, who is *primarily* addressed), at the level of the sexual possession of which Marion has been the object, when Sam renews his demand and hears it refused.[17]

Conversely, in the shots preceding the shower scene, the camera reduces to an extreme degree the unforseeable effect of the distance separating it from what is being filmed: it virtually coincides with the insert of Norman's bulging eye, due to the metaphor of the apparatus thus constituted. This is the point of maximal identification between the character and the instance of the *mise en scène;* it can only be surpassed by its own excess, when the eye-camera becomes a body-knife, entering the field of its object and attempting in vain to coincide with it.

However, in order to go from one man to another, and from one position to another, the camera must also embody the woman and adopt her look, conserving a strong identification—diegetic, of course, but more specifically specular, determined by the organization of the point of view—with the subject it has taken as its object. (The latter can be maintained in a position of fundamental subjection through a series of carefully planned relays—the policemen, the service station attendant—that reiterate the question of which she has been the object from the start.) In conformity with its basic path, that of perverse structuration, the transformation from neurosis to psychosis is brought about by woman, who is both its foundation and its indispensable form.

This explains the lengthiness of the first half of the first movement, organized around theft and escape. It also explains the systematic series of shot-reverse shots which mark Marion's itinerary up until the moment of blindness (a mixture of fatigue and hypnosis) that causes her to turn off the wet highway and head for the motel. It explains, finally, the resumption and redoubling of these shots as a preparation for the moment of reversal, during the confrontation between Marion and Norman. In this manner, the diegesis participates directly in the aggressive potential, carried to an extreme by the reciprocity of the looks in the alternation of shot-reverse shots. The effects of this cinematographic code par excellence evoke the structure of the cinematographic apparatus, and thereby of the primitive apparatus it imitates, namely, the mirror wherein the subject structures himself, through a mode of narcissistic identification of which aggressivity is an indelible component.[18] However, this reference only makes sense—here very specifically (as in all of Hitchcock's films, and classical cinema in general, particularly American)—within the global system in which the aggressive element can never be separated from the inflection it receives from sexual difference, and the attribution of this difference to the signifier that governs it. In other words, it is directed from the man towards the woman, and that difference which appears due to woman is nothing but the mirror-effect of the narcissistic doubling that makes possible the constitution of the male subject through the woman's body, ordered by a double play of differentiated identity, based on an effect of imaginary projection subjected to the constitutive pressure of a symbolic determination.[19]

Between man and woman, through woman's look as appropriated by the camera, this mirror- or doubling-effect (hence also one of denial and splitting) serves to structure the male subject as the subject of a scopic drive, that is to say, a subject who imaginarily attributes to woman the lack he himself has been assigned, in response to the anxiety created by the fantasized threat of this lack within his own body. This is the classical dialectic—as described by Freud and Lacan—of the phallus and castration; its implications with respect to perversion (the conjugated motifs of voyeurism and fetishism) have been astutely analyzed by Guy Rosolato.[20] Lacan refers this dialectic, particularly as regards the scopic drive, to the lack—unevenly divided between the two sexes—of the signifier that structures it; it is this signifier, castration, which determines "the gaze as *objet a*."[21] In a different perspective, the same dialectic has been relativized by Luce Irigaray, who denounces the fact that in men (that is, in Sam, Norman, Hitchcock, Freud, Lacan, the subject writing these lines in an attempt to fissure the system that holds him) "the scopic drive is predominant."[22]

This is why, theoretically, there are no women fetishists; nor even, more broadly speaking, women perverts: either because, in psychological terms, "perverse" as applied to women connotes perversity rather than perversion, or because theory—elaborated or directed by men—has avoided acknowledging perversions in women, not having discovered *perversion* itself.[23]

This explains the fact that Norman's psychosis, his inordinate object-desire that rushes headlong into murder, is entirely structured by a fetishistic aim carried to the point of madness. Psychoanalytically, it might be said, Norman is a collage (which neither confirms nor denies his clinical possibilities, which are not in question—simply because, for me, that is not the question). He seeks to construct a chain in which the excessiveness of the psychotic-perverse desire of the male subject can be structured—from the man to the camera, his true measure—during the scene where he establishes his presence at a distance, fascinated, in vertiginous mastery. This chain may be written: phallus-bird-fetish-mother-eye-knife-camera. A terrifying play on words (suggested, rather than made explicit, in the film) connects this chain to the omnipotence of infantile desire turned towards death: *Mommy, mummy:* the mother's body, fetishized to death, so to speak, becomes the body that murders, in keeping with the desire awakened in the eye of the subject possessed by it.[24] Through the incredible incorporation of a metaphor-become-reality, Norman's fascinated look carries within it the phallus immemorially attributed to the mother. But he can acknowledge it in himself only on condition that he ceaselessly encounter it in his mirror-image, namely, in the body/look of woman (which engenders the mirage), and as an absolute threat to which he must respond; otherwise, it is his own body that will desert him. Such (to complete the psychiatrist's speech) might be the motivations behind the genealogy of the case: the reiterative passage from the former murder (that of the mother) to the murder of Marion of which Norman–the mother is the agent, emphasizing in both cases, given an original identificatory fantasy, the literally impossible desire for possession and fusion that is at stake.

This allows us to describe the distribution of the three terms (psychosis, neurosis, perversion) within the logic of the process of enunciation. These terms define the primordial relationship between the two scenes which most closely circumscribe this process (the hotel and the motel), through a "breathing space" during which the subject is presented as such. The possessive form used in the credits—"Alfred Hitchcock's *Psycho*"—is a mark of enunciation which may be said to have a double meaning: this film belongs to me; this psychosis is mine, or would be mine if . . . if it weren't, precisely, for this film, which both involves me in and frees me from psychosis, positioning me elsewhere. A special lettering effect (something like the bulging eye during the credits of *Vertigo*) contributes to the singularization of this relatively common signifying arrangement: a vibrato twice causes the center of the letters to shift back and forth, first for the title *Psycho,* and then for the name in the final enunciation: "Directed by Alfred Hitchcock." In addition, the opening scene immediately reiterates the interplay of black and white lines that had striated the credits from top to bottom: the camera must pass under venetian blinds to enter the room at the end of its movement, and it is on the background of these horizontal lines, in the second half of the scene, that Sam and Marion are seen in reverse shot, separately or together. Thus, by displacement and metaphor, what is inscribed in this space communicates an implied relationship between the title and the name.

In the first scene, the camera's power is intrinsically expressed by the bird's-eye view of the city and its rooftops, then emphasized by its concentration on the voyeuristic point of reference: the couple in the bedroom after lovemaking. The "after" is important, since, in a sense, the camera intervenes in place of what happens between man and woman at the literally mythical level of the primal scene: it is a continually withdrawing instance, collecting— at the purified level of vicariousness—what is fundamentally perverse and psychotic, given the logic of this perspective, in man's desire for woman, even within the neurotic configuration that is its most common destiny. The camera becomes, it might be said, the eye-phallus, projected and reprojected from one sex to the other, but [one which,] on the basis of a signifying privilege assigned to only one sex, transforms the camera into pure eye, look, dissociated from the scene, in proportion to the lack of the phallus of which it circumscribes the representation so that—and because—it is represented in it.[25] It is this dialectic, in slightly different terms, that emerges during the second scene, through a temporal actualization: "that which may not be seen" seeks to show itself, to break into awareness (into reality), but displaced from the act. The camera must still, obviously, remain outside its object. Yet it is also doubly inscribed within it, as has been seen: firstly by the mediation of the apparatus set up around Norman, and secondly through the invasion, by the subject of the apparatus, of the tableau of his own vision. From its perverse situation, already enhanced by an identification with the subject of the diegesis, the camera thus fully assumes the psychotic function that was potentially circumscribed during the first scene. However, it can of course attain only a more extreme perversion, since it is filming its metaphorical invasion of its own field. It thus reaffirms all the more strongly, by its very division, the unforseeable effects of distance, lack, and denial that make it up—everything that psychosis (Norman—the camera) is at that very moment attempting to exorcize by presenting as real, through a rape ending in murder, the imaginary and ungraspable relation of the primal scene.

Within this configuration, one thing seems to me to be essential, namely, that it is through woman's pleasure (*jouissance*) that the perverse projection and psychotic inscription are carried out (just as it is through her actions, her body, her look, that the film moves from one scene to the next). The emphasis on Marion's pleasure in the shower goes well beyond all diegetic motivation: close-up shots of her naked body alternate with shots of gushing water; she leans into the stream, opens her mouth, smiles, and closes her eyes in a rapture that is made all the more intense because it contrasts with the horror that is to come, but also because the two are linked together. By a subtle reversal, the pleasure that Marion did not show in the opening love scene at last appears. However, the pleasure is for herself (even if it can only be so for the camera, because of the image-nature assigned to her by the camera); it takes the form of narcissistic intimacy which poses, for men, the question of sexual pleasure itself, with woman's body instituted as its mythical site. The masculine subject can accept the image of woman's pleasure only on condition that, having constructed it, he may inscribe himself and recognize himself within it, and thus reappropriate it even at the cost of its (or her) destruction.[26]

VIII.

Briefly, to resume and strengthen what has been said by considering several points in a spiral-like movement, i.e. together, as a text does whenever one tries to make it appear as what it is, that is to say, as what it becomes, virtually, always in analysis: a *volume*.

1. The first scene(s) is (are) programmed as a matrix whose elements are distributed throughout the whole text by effects of dispersal, rebound, and repetition. This is one of the laws of classical film (see, in particular, the analyses of Thierry Kuntzel).[27] In *Psycho,* this process is at first carried out at a very general level. The first scene, through the shift in the screenplay, primarily serves as a preparation for the succession of scenes between Marion and Norman: their tête-à-tête in the reception room, the series of shots setting up Norman as apparatus, the murder in the shower. From this is derived, at the end, the scene with the psychiatrist, which resolves not only the enigma, but the (psychic) mystery of the murder: this final scene only replies to the first one at the price of the initial displacement caused by the shift in the screenplay.

There is also, however, the way in which the first scene inaugurates the sequence of bedrooms: the motel rooms, Marion's room, Arbogast's room (suggested), Sam and Lila's room, and thence, at the end of the third movement, the intrusion into the bedrooms of the house, especially Norman's and the mother's, under Lila's discovering look.

More subtly, there is a thread which leads from the first shot, to Norman as apparatus, to the next to last shot. Norman – the mother is seen in a medium shot against the naked wall of his cell, smiling, while on his face is gradually superimposed the skull which will make of him, irremediably, the mother. Her voice is heard: "I hope that they are watching, they will see, they will see and they will say, 'Why she wouldn't even harm a fly'."[28] This circular play on words goes from the fly to the bird, to the body-fetish of Norman – the mother. But it goes further still: to the omnipotence of the scopic drive. Norman's words are addressed to all the guardians of the law (policemen, judges, psychiatrist), presumably gathered on the other side of the door and peering at him through the keyhole. However, through them, his words are addressed to the spectator, who is trapped in the mirror by Norman's eyes, staring right into the camera as though to conjure away the power it exerts. The spectator is thus confronted, from within the shot itself, with the "non-authorized scoptophilia" that places cinematic voyeurism "in the direct lineage of the primal scene."[29] Thus, all of the opening shots have been condensed into the body-look of Norman – the mother, revealing the reflective structure of the apparatus, before the final shot, with an ultimate effect of resolution, brings the film to its close (in a single sweep, using a very long dissolve to link the last and next to last shots through the superimposition of the skull). In this way, two screenplays intermingle: male (Sam, Norman, and – in both – Hitchcock) and female (Marion, the mother); and the end, after a monstrous detour, replies to the beginning. Marion's dead body reappears in the white car dragged from the marsh only because it has been, from the beginning, the object of the conjugated desire of a man and the camera.

2. The apparatus is therefore present in the film, though not – as in *Rear Window* – by a mirror effect. Here, a certain rhyming effect of two images strikes me; firstly, on the roadside at dawn, the close-up of the policeman coming upon Marion asleep in her car; and secondly, in the cellar, the close-up of the mother's skeleton. The latter is seen twice, once when Lila puts her hand on Mrs. Bates's shoulder and the draped skeleton slowly swings around toward her, and again at the end of the segment, after Norman's intrusion. There is a similarity between these two faces, sustained by a striking reversal: the eyes have disappeared; in the second case they are nothing but hollow sockets, and in the first they are totally hidden by dark glasses. This is a way of signifying, by its very absence, the unbearably excessive nature of the look. The dark glasses especially (like Mitch's binoculars in *The Birds*) suggest a metaphor of the photographic lens: super-vision of the law, symbolized by its representative; excess of the symbolic itself, which triumphs at the end "in the prolixity of the psychiatrist."[30] Film, both as discourse and as an institution, is subject to an order that is marked by the monolithic power of its ruling signifier. However, this super-vision is also that of disorder, the breaking of the law, of which

fetishistic psychosis is the most inordinate form. Moreover, the signifier is perpetually imaginary, subject to denial and splitting. The hollow eye sockets of the mother are the verso of an apparatus whose recto is the policeman's dark glasses. There is an endless circularity between desire and the law, both of which, taken to an extreme, inspire terror (in Marion, in Lila).

Here, I cannot resist associating more or less freely. When Lila enters the cellar she sees, from behind, a woman seated. In the foreground to the right, in the upper part of the frame, there is an electric light bulb so alive, so enormous, and disposed in such a manner that it seemed to me — at first sight and at each successive viewing, despite critical distance — to simulate a spherical screen, casting a blinding light onto the brick wall across from Mrs. Bates. The mother occupies, in this virtual image, the place of the spectator, thus evoking the real spectator, and even more so his mirror image (the fetish inhabited by the death wish) when she looks at him directly during the next two close-up shots. This is particularly true the second time, when Lila's terror causes her to knock against the light bulb, making it swing back and forth. The vacillation in the lighting thus produced is repeated and amplified later (when Norman bursts in, unmasked and overcome by Sam): the skull seems to be animated by this vibration — this play of lights and shadows which also designates the cinema itself.

Following this, representation dissolves into the very image of the law (a metaphorical reappearance of the policeman): a general shot of the courthouse introduces the psychiatrist's speech.

3. That everything in *Psycho* seems immediately doubled must be seen as the effect — with repercussions in concentric waves down to the microsystematic level of the smallest signifying units — of the two main rhetorical axes that organize the film, namely, its ternary composition and its two screenplays. Other of Hitchcock's films also manifest, by their very structure, the specific pressure of the doubling process that underlies all his films: *Shadow of a Doubt*, with the determining superimposition of the uncle's and niece's names (Charlie); *Strangers on a Train*, with the exchange of murders; *Vertigo*, with the mirror-effect of the double heroine (Madeleine-Judy). However, this doubling process is, so to speak, exacerbated in *Psycho* by the crisscross effects of substitution, division, and echo among characters. The first couple, Sam and Marion, engenders the second, Norman and Marion: Norman has thus taken the place of Sam. Yet he has actually, diegetically speaking, taken the place of Marion, given the mirror dialectic between the sexes and their psychic structurations. Lila's appearance at the beginning of the second movement causes this network of transformations to double back on itself: she represents the return of the indispensable heroine, Marion's reappearance (like Judy's in *Vertigo*) in the form of her sister. Thus, the film could be said to be organized in yet another way with respect to woman's body-look, because of the long

sequence taking Lila from the motel to the cellar where she discovers—with an absolute horror that obviously recalls that of Marion in the shower—the stuffed body of the mother. Thus the diegetic couple disjoined at the end of the first segment is reconstituted as a shadow: Sam and Lila, pretending to be married—as Sam and Marion were intended to be—approach the motel where Marion first met Norman on the path that was supposed to lead her to Sam. The function of this shadow-couple reveals in an exemplary way, through repetition and mimed (undermined) resolution, the deep structural subversion of sameness that is here carried out.

4. To conclude, we might point out the constellation of signifiers that disseminate and recenter the differential doubling between men and women to which the fiction is continually and completely subjected.

* *Norman-Marion:* Christian names in mirror-relation to one another, interchangeable but for a single phoneme (Marion was chosen instead of the Mary of Bloch's novel).

* *Nor-man:* he who is neither woman . . . nor man, since he can be one in the place of the other, or rather one and the other, one within the other.

* *Marie Samuels:* the name used by Marion to sign the motel register, derived from Sam's first name.

* *Phoenix* (superimposed on the first shot to situate the action): again, a bird; the bird that dies only in order to be transformed (as is here the case, through murder, of one character, one sex, one story) into another. In fact, there is a double metamorphosis: a diegetic one (Marion becoming Norman) and a formative one (Norman becoming a living bird-mother) which renders possible the former.

* *Crane:* Marion's last name; once again a bird's name. It marks her body with the signifier that appears, to Norman, as a lack or an excess. But the word "crane" also means something else: the machine that embodies above all others, in the image-taking apparatus, the omniscient power of the look, what might be called the bird's-eye view. This is to say, once again, but here with an element of humor, that the camera becomes one with woman's body, and that in this sense it is itself the fetish, adopting the forms of the bird and of Norman—the mother, going through the whole circuit of the fiction, only to be immediately acknowledged as the enunciating index, at the level of the apparatus that makes fiction possible.

Whence, indissolubly, here, it can be said of film and cinema, that they are the very institution of perversion.

Notes

1 François Truffaut, *Hitchcock* (New York: Simon & Schuster, 1967), 206.
2. Cf., on the relationship between the film and the original narrative, James Naremore,

Filmguide to Psycho (Bloomington: Indiana Univ. Press, 1973), 23–24, 33–34. I found in this
short essay, after having written a first, summary version of the present article ("Psycho,"
Dossiers du Cinéma, Films II [Paris: Casterman, 1972]), several observations along the same
lines as my analysis. Some of the elements organized around Marion during the first section of
the narrative appear, in Bloch's novel, as mental flashbacks to scenes that comprise, in Hitchcock's film, the second section.

3. Truffaut, 206.

4. Syntagmatic change, punctuation, diegetic unity. Cf. Christian Metz, "Ponctuations et démar-
cations dans le film de diégèse," *Essais sur la signification au cinéma,* II (Paris: Klincksieck,
1972), 126–28. Cf. also on this point my study of Minnelli's *Gigi,* "To Analyze, To Segment,"
Quarterly Review of Film Studies, vol. 1, no. 3 (1976): 331–53.

5. Sheriff Chambers expresses this in two sentences, the second of which closes the scene on a
note of horror: "Norman Bates's mother has been dead and buried in Greenlawn Cemetery for
the past ten years." "Well, if that woman up there is Mrs. Bates, who's that woman buried out
in Greenlawn Cemetery?" Richard Anobile, ed., *Psycho* (New York: Avon, 1975), 193, 195.

6. S. Freud, "Loss of Reality in Neurosis and Psychosis" (1904), *Complete Works,* Standard
Edition, XIX.

7. Freud, "Loss of Reality," 183.

8. Marion: Oh, Sam, I hate having to be with you in a place like this.
Sam: I've heard of married couples who deliberately spend an occasional night in a cheap
hotel. They say it's very exciting.
Marion: Oh, when you're married you can do a lot of things deliberately.
Sam: You sure talk like a girl who's been married.
Marion: Sam, this is the last time.
Sam: Yeah? For what?
Marion: For this. For meeting you in secret—so we can be secretive. You come down here on
those business trips and we steal lunch hours and—Oh, Sam, I wish you wouldn't even
come. . . .
Sam: I sweat to pay off my father's debts and he's in his grave. I sweat to pay my ex-wife's
alimony, and she's—living on the other side of the world somewhere!
Marion: I pay, too. They also pay who meet in hotel rooms.
Sam: A couple of years and—the debts will be paid off and—if she ever remarries, the
alimony stops and—
Marion: I haven't even been married once yet!
Sam: Yeah, but when you do you'll swing!
Marion: Sam, let's get married! (Anobile, 15–16, 19–20)

9. It might be added, for the pleasure of the "intertext," that the amount of money stolen by
Marion ($40,000) is the same as the amount spent by Mark, in *Marnie,* on the wedding ring he
offers Marnie. Moreover, this money was intended by the millionaire, who shows it off to
Marion, for the purchase of a house as a wedding gift to his daughter.

10. *Norman's version:* Father's death when he was five. Some years later, his mother falls madly in
love with a man who encourages her to build the motel. When he dies, the mother goes crazy.
    Sheriff's version (emergence of the mystery in the middle of the third movement): Nor-
man poisons the lover. The mother, in turn, poisons herself.
    Psychiatrist's version (solution of the mystery): Norman poisons the lover and his mother.

11. Anobile, *Psycho,* 77.

12. J. Laplanche and J. B. Pontalis, *The Language of Psycho-Analysis* (New York: Norton, 1973),
309.

13. Hitchcock: "It also allows the viewer to become a Peeping Tom" (Truffaut, 204).

14. No contradiction is implied by the fact that in *Rope* it is a man who is being killed. Men, too,
are killed in Hitchcock's films—and often—in more or less direct or displaced reference to the
murder of the father. In *Rope,* the object of the murder may also be referred, in a complementary manner, to the virtually manifest homosexuality of the two murderers.

15. Cf. my analysis, "Le blocage symbolique," *Communications,* no. 23 (1975): 251–256.

16. Cf. Naremore, *Filmguide to* Psycho, 66.

17. Sam: We could laze around here a while longer.
Marion: Checking out time is three p.m. Motels of this sort—are not interested in you when
you come in, but when your time is up—. (Anobile, *Psycho,* 15)

18. Jacqueline Rose, "Paranoia and the Film System," *Screen*, vol. 17, no. 4 (1976–77): 85–104.
19. Cf., for an historical perspective on the symbolic constitution of the male subject, my study "Un jour, la castration," *Alexandre Dumas, L'Arc*, no. 71 (1978).
20. Cf. in particular "Perversions sexuelles," *Encyclopédie médico-chirurgicale* (Paris: 1968), 37392 CIO: 8–9.
21. Jacques Lacan, *Les quatre concepts fondamentaux de la psychanalyse* (Paris: Seuil, 1973). English translation by Alan Sheridan, *The Four Fundamental Concepts of Psycho-Analysis* (London: The Hogarth Press, 1977).
22. "Misère de la psychanalyse," *Critique*, no. 365 (October 1977): 900. Cf. also *Ce sexe qui n'en est pas un* (Paris: Minuit, 1977), 25.
23. Rosolato: "This perversion [fetishism] is practiced exclusively by men," *Encyclopédie médico-chirurgicale*, 9.
24. I owe this to the friendship of Thierry Kuntzel.
25. On the eye-phallus relationship, cf. Lacan, *The Four Fundamental Concepts of Psycho-Analysis*, 101–4.
26. *Marnie*, in this regard, deals with the reappropriation of the image, whereas *Psycho* deals with its destruction. Cf. my article "Hitchcock, The Enunciator," *Camera Obscura*, no. 2 (1977): 69–94.
27. "Le travail du film, 1," *Communications*, no. 19 (1972); English translation, *enclitic*, vol. 2, no. 1 (1978): 39–64. "Le travail du film, 2," *Communications*, no. 25 (1975); English translation, *Camera Obscura*, no. 5 (1980): 6–69. Cf. also my article "Hitchcock, The Enunciator," and similar themes in my articles "Les Oiseaux: analyse d'une séquence," *Cahiers du Cinéma*, no. 216 (October 1969): 38; "Le blocage symbolique," 349; "To Analyse, To Segment."
28. Anobile, *Psycho*, 255.
29. Christian Metz, "Le signifiant imaginaire," *Communications*, no. 23 (1975): 45. English translation, *Screen*, vol. 16, no. 2 (Summer 1975): 14–76.
30. Roger Dadoun, in the few suggestive lines devoted to *Psycho* in "Le fétichisme dans le film d'horreur," *Objets du fétichisme, Nouvelle Revue de Psychanalyse*, no. 2 (Autumn 1970): 238.

PSYCHO (Paramount, 1960). *Producer:* Alfred Hitchcock, *Assistant Director:* Hilton A. Green, *Script:* Joseph Stefano, from the Robert Bloch novel, *Photography:* John L. Russell, *Editor:* George Tomasini, *Sets:* Joseph Hurley, Robert Claworthy, George Milo, *Music:* Bernard Herrmann, *Costumes:* Helen Colvig, *Titles:* Saul Bass, *Players:* Anthony Perkins (Norman Bates), Janet Leigh (Marion Crane), Vera Miles (Lila Crane), John Gavin (Sam Loomis), Martin Balsam (Arbogast), John McIntire (Sheriff Chambers), Lurene Tuttle (Mrs. Chambers), Frank Albertson (Tom Cassidy), Simon Oakland (psychiatrist), Patricia Hitchcock (Caroline). 109 minutes.

CHAPTER TWENTY-FOUR

Psycho: The Institutionalization of Female Sexuality

Barbara Klinger

The narrative structure of *Psycho* (1960) is marked by a particularly disjunctive topographical shift in centering; the original narrative, focused on the exploits of Marion Crane, is suddenly and irrevocably eclipsed by the undertakings of Norman Bates. While this shift resides on a rather elemental level in the narrative trajectory in that the narrative allegiance appears to simply switch from one protagonist to the next, there are substantial ramifications of the shift in both the structural and thematic-symbolic configuration of the text. The Marion-centered narrative is not merely replaced by that concerned with Norman, it is forcibly rejected from representation and rearticulated in terms of a "new" story; this presents exactly the structural situation of displacement. The displacement of the first narrative by the second cues an examination of the underlying principles and effects of this subordination within the textual system of the film — that is, how the first narrative is structurally and thematically refigured within the film.

An exposition of the terms and ramifications of the dislocated structure of *Psycho* has been offered by Raymond Bellour in his essay "Psychosis, Neurosis, Perversion."[1] One of Bellour's projects there is to account for the two narratives of *Psycho* — in particular, to account for the dynamic of the displacement from the first narrative to the second. Bellour distinguishes the logic of this displacement (from the Marion-centered to the Norman-centered narrative) as psychoanalytic, a confrontation of "two psychic structures: man and woman, the latter destined to become the prey of the former" (VI). Significantly, the displacement in narratives is necessitated by sexual difference: "the articulation between the two psychic structures [is] grasped in a doubling relationship carried by sexual difference" (V). Marion's neurosis will be absorbed by Norman's psychosis: "woman, the subject of neurosis, becomes the object of the psychosis of which man is the subject" (V). Hence the dynamic informing the transition in narratives is rooted in an opposition (neurosis/psychosis) whose terms (Marion/Norman) are determined by sexual difference (woman/man) and by the aggression inherent in the difference (man on woman). The whole constitution of the narrative then springs from an articulation of sexual difference.

The effects of this inscription of difference in *Psycho* are for Bellour those characteristic of displacement; the first narrative is "radically excluded" from consideration in the closure of the second narrative. This exclusion is readily evident in the speech of the psychiatrist toward the end of the film. This speech centers almost entirely on the psychotic evolution and activities of Norman and treats Marion as of only incidental psychoanalytic interest as an accessory-component of the crimes (V). The effacement of the first narrative exercised in this pivotal moment of narrative closure in the film problematizes, in Bellour's account, the principle rule of classical Hollywood narrative construction which demands that unity be achieved in closure. Bellour asks (in section V): "Why is this film about psychotic dissociation organized with respect to an original plot which, while supporting it to the point of appearing indispensable, nevertheless remains, in a sense, totally foreign to it. In this highly classically orchestrated film . . . how is the internal principle of classical film satisfied—namely, that the end must always reply to the beginning?"

Bellour finally indicates the relationship between the two narratives as being contracted through the presence of the primal scene in relation to voyeurism in both narratives and, ultimately, in cinematic signification itself. The "non-authorized" scopophilia which instigates the film (under the hotel window) and the scopic obsession of Norman–the mother correspond, thereby structurally welding the two stories together and symbolically reflecting the condition of viewing in the cinema. Bellour writes: "Thus, all of the opening shots have been condensed into the body-look of Norman–the mother, revealing the reflective structure of the apparatus . . . and the end, after a monstrous detour, replies to the beginning. Marion's dead body reappears in the white car dragged from the marsh only because it has been, from the beginning, the object of the conjugated desire of a man and the camera" (VIII). Hence the entire narrative of *Psycho* accelerates toward a usurpation of woman-image by diegetic and extradiegetic (the camera and the spectator) scopophilia.

Though the first narrative which poses Marion as a subject of hermeneutic inquest is, as Bellour suggests, radically excluded from full address in the hermeneutic finale provided by the psychiatrist's speech, there are close structural and thematic-symbolic links between the first and second narratives, forged precisely by the logistics of displacement in the textual system, which remain largely unexplored in Bellour's account. Initially, it might be observed that the psychiatrist's speech does not formally close the film; the series of shots which do so affords a formal connection between the beginning and end of *Psycho*, wherein the symbolic legislation of sexual difference in this displaced structure can be reexamined.

In further testing, then, of how the end of the film replies to the beginning, it is necessary to consider the punctual position occupied by the image of Marion in this reply. The narrative of *Psycho* is generated out of the body of Marion (the shots which travel over the city settle on her) and returns to her body in the car for the last shot. It is in this "book-ending" of the narrative through the figure of Marion that a certain project of the narrative can be traced.

This project is formulated specifically in terms of Marion's spectacle, which is perceived immediately at the outset of the film as representation of her sexuality. In the two vastly different presentations of Marion's body which characterize the beginning and end of the film, a definitive term marking the narrative progression is furnished. Marion is transformed in this progression from an overt erotic spectacle (semiclad, in postcoital embrace) to a figure shrouded entirely from view (a body in the trunk of a car); a figure initially manifested strongly as spectacle becomes an almost complete visual nonentity. A major project of the narrative then can be conceived of as a processing of this image. The image of Marion poses a problem to the narrative, a problematic sexuality, which is generally apprehended as such in the first scene by the friction articulated between her sexuality and the demands of the family (Sam's various familial debts which prevent marriage and perpetuate Marion's "renegade" sexual status outside the strictures of the family). The narrative of *Psycho* can be seen to function in its movement to present this problem, to repress it (the switch in narratives) and restate it (Norman–the mother), and finally to contain/solve it in the name of the family and the law. The terms of the resolution of the film as they reidentify Marion, simultaneously the missing family member and fugitive from justice, suggest that the symbolic circuitry through which the female body moves in the course of the narrative works on the representation of that corpus to efface its difference, to transfigure it according to a phallocentrically defined sexuality.

The question of sexual identity as a major impetus of the textual system is initially raised within the credits of *Psycho*. The title, *Psycho,* connotes a genderless identity, and as it does not refer to a condition (as in "psychotic") but to a person, a hermeneutic question arises which explicitly involves sexual identity—the sexing of the "psycho." One design of the narrative will be a designation of sexual identity for the psycho; this designation itself is problematic, as the psycho-murderer (Norman) is "gender-confused," a cross between mother and son. The title, as it presents this nascent hermeneutic question of sexual identity, also embodies the inevitability of its resolution. That is, while the word "psycho" is an inciteful word, intimating excess, the disposition of the title within the credits—Alfred Hitchcock's *Psycho*—suggests a function of containment to the narrative; the authorial signature, in the possessive case, guarantees that the represented psychosis will not exceed the limits of the signed artwork. Thus the "law" of the discourse is posed against an unlawful subject, the opposition insinuating containment as a narrative function.

In *Psycho,* then, the narrative system is inextricably bound up in questions of sexuality, specifically of sexual identity, and the orchestration of its containment. Though Norman is narratively valued as the crucial instance of switched and confused sexual identity (at the end of *Psycho* there is the sexually disjunctive relationship between his body, masculine, and his voice, feminine), on a symbolic level in the film this deviation in identity can be understood as centering significantly on the question of female sexuality. Just as there is an overt collision of male/female in Norman, there is a similar and equally violent reconception of the sexual identity of Marion (and the mother—the other sexual term in Norman's schizophrenia) which provides a symbolic logic to the formal perimeters of the film.

The first figure structured as a response to the enigma formulated by the title *Psycho* ("Who is . . .?") is Marion. She will be deferred as the actual psycho in favor of Norman, but her appearance in the beginning of the film, a result of a searching camera, is on a symbolic axis in partial answer to the question posed by the title. That Marion is initially symbolically identified as central to the narrative inquest is manifested by the mechanisms through which the space from the Phoenix, Arizona, city-scape to hotel room "body-scape" is articulated; the succession of pans and successively closer dissolves and tracks enforce a condition of expectation on the destination of the shots (Marion, as she appears in the first shot and as she is compositionally central in the rest of the sequence). In addition, the move from scenographic space to an obscenographic space declares, retroactively, the emphatic sexual orientation of the hermeneutic code. This first sequence of shots, then, (city to woman) begins to formulate a statement in answer to the antinomy expressed by the *Psycho* title: the law of the discourse versus the unlawful subject. Marion is established as unlawful through the representation of her sexuality, which is depicted in the hotel room as simultaneously erotic and outside familial jurisprudence. Her aberrance is, ironically, exacerbated as, in her desire to legitimize her sexual status through marriage to Sam, she becomes a thief. The adversary relationship between female sexuality (presented as lawless) and the family (presented as lawful) will be resolved in the workings of the narrative system. The family in league with the law is distinguished as an institution, first against which and then within which female sexuality is treated. This trajectory can be charted in the formal strategies which figure Marion in the beginning and end of the film, and then examined in the logic of the displacement which transforms a female sexuality exiled from the family to one organized totally within the family.

In the first shots of the hotel room the representation of Marion is rather rigorously conveyed in terms of sexual difference. The question of sexual difference in the first shot of her is displaced onto a difference in power: male/ female, active/passive. To this effect, the visual discourse (composition, editing) carefully composes her erotic display. In the first shot Marion is in a prone position gazing upward at an erect male, Sam, who, vertical and bare-chested, appears hypervirile. The characters' faces are not fully disclosed in the first glance, so that character individuation does not intrude upon an emphasis on sexual posturing. Sam's vertical stance echoes the edge of the frameline, while the position of Marion invades center-frame in an unmitigated erotic spectacle. Compositionally, she is meticulously inscribed in the space; the edge of the mattress sags down to "invite" the viewer into her space and the black bedposts over her body rivet attention back downwards to her body. Her gaze is apparently engaged with Sam's off-screen look, furthering her image's inscription in space (Sam as a diegetic analogue to the compositional components which capture Marion as "vision"). The first shot of Marion and Sam dynamically binds Marion into the composition; the second shot, an insert of an uneaten lunch, echoes the way in which the image of Marion is composed—literally sandwiched in space, consumable as a carefully laid-out still life. A function of the composition and editing in this first sequence in general is to maximize the spectacle of sexual difference, especially as it legislates hierarchically different positions for male and female characters.

Hence, in this first few minutes of the film, Marion is bound as an erotic object in space, virtually clenched in the composition. In this relation of composition to woman's body, this initial panorama finds its logical outcome in the shower murder which serves as a veritable visual dictionary of possibilities of framing and fragmentation. In this way the shower murder scenario is an acceleration and termination of this spectacle as it has been posed visually. In addition, the abrasive relation of Marion's sexuality to the family, established in the first scene, here comes similarly to fruition. Her sexuality is seen as overtly problematic to the family (Norman's desire for her against the mother's wishes) and is subsequently effectively "regulated" by the family which it threatens.

The last series of shots in the film, which depict the return of Marion, reply in several ways to the initial shots which introduced her. The process of dissolves at the beginning of the film is telescoped in the final two shots to a superimposition and dissolve from Norman–the mother to the car being dragged from the swamp. The formal logic from opening to closing shot is also satisfied as the tracking-in of the camera is "answered" by the motion of the chain which withdraws the car from the swamp. The symmetry from the first to last shots then is one of reversal. The development in terms of the representation of Marion corresponds to this formal pattern: the progress is distinctly from a rather emphatic full vision of her image (in the hotel room, at the Bates motel) to absolutely no visual access at all (in the car trunk). Finally, the question of Marion as presented in sexual versus familial terms at the film's start is closed off here, as Marion is restored to the family (through her sister Lila's efforts), her erotic representation entirely reconstituted and her difference annulled.

The progression suggested in this comparative analysis of the beginning and end of the film, in which the female character established outside the family is constructed within the family domain, is supported in the nature and effects of the narrative displacement; this displacement (from first to second narratives) is characterized by an increased investment in family ideology. The sexual overtones of the first hotel room scene (heated kissing, partial dress) are immediately placed in opposition to the family. The orientation toward the family is pronounced in the second narrative, which is mobilized almost entirely by the family quest (to find Marion, to find the mother—the two missing family members). The displacement toward the family is significant, as it signals the terms in which the conflict between sexuality and the family will be resolved. A unit which spans both narratives and signifies the effect of the transition is the couple.

The narrative initially represents a sexualized, romantic couple in Marion and Sam. The reformulation of the couple in the second part, Lila and Sam, is in totally asexual, nonromantic terms. Though Lila resembles Marion, the resemblance effects mainly a distinction; Lila is depicted as prim, a severely restricted counterpart to Marion in terms of sexual iconography. Similarly, though Lila and Sam are potentially a romantic couple in the second narrative, they are portrayed without romantic affiliation of any kind; their motel room behavior never even slightly rivals that of previous scenarios in that location.

The transition in the typage of the definitive couple from the first to second narrative has ramifications for the symbolic trajectory of the film; while Marion and Sam are posed in opposition to the family and the law, Lila and Sam in contradistinction are increasingly associated with both institutions. Their activities find them consorting with Arbogast, a private detective, then with the sheriff, and finally with the psychiatrist and the police. Lila and Sam achieve a respectability (to the point of being asked to breakfast after church by the sheriff and his wife) that Marion desired but was denied. That there begins to be an indissoluble link between the family and the law· in the second narrative is multiply represented. Lila's investigation to find Marion is motivated by familial concerns but serves the legal establishment which has labeled Marion a criminal; the figures of legal authority which she encounters are simultaneously defined familially—Arbogast, as a private detective, is a domestic version of a policeman, the sheriff is domesticized by the constant presence of his wife, and the psychiatrist is a doctor committed to unraveling the family mystery. Perhaps the bond between the family and the law is most concisely presented in the dissolve from the just discovered mother's corpse to the courthouse, which begins the explanatory epilogue of the psychiatrist.

This movement toward familial values and the law via the reformulated

couple is especially interesting as it corresponds to the restatement and intensi-
fication of the opposition of female sexuality and the family found in the
second narrative. This restatement is located in the embedded hermeneutic of
the second narrative which centers on the sexual transgression against the family performed by Mrs. Bates (and her suitor) which is punished through the
family (matricide). This situation rhymes explicitly with that of Marion; both
characters are involved in illicit, outside-the-family affairs, and their fates are
instigated through acts of voyeurism followed by murder at the hand of Norman. Another effect of the displacement in narrative structure resides in this
rearticulation of the problematic of female sexuality from Marion to the
mother.

Though it is the search for Marion which bridges the two narratives, that
search becomes translated into an investigation of the whereabouts and identity of Mrs. Bates (the latter will yield the former). The result of this narrative
equation of the mother's story with Marion's is an erasure, a repression of the
original question of Marion's sexuality, so that it comes to be represented in
terms of the sexual problematic of the mother—a problematic which defines
female sexuality as emphatically and inextricably familial. The restatement in
narratives relegates the question of female sexuality and desire to the explanatory confines of family logic (the Oedipal configuration of relations). That is
the content of the psychiatrist's speech and the only locus in which Marion's
demise is understood. The family then becomes the definitive site for any
comprehension of female sexuality.

There is a structural synonymity engaging the respective representations of
Marion and Mrs. Bates which further indicates their comparison. Both figures
are depicted through a play on concealment and disclosure of their bodies:
Marion's as it is partially revealed either in her various half-clothed appearances
or, especially, in the shower scene; the mother's as the camera works to refuse
disclosure of her in the shower sequence, in Arbogast's murder, and in the
sojourn to the fruit cellar. Again, the dramatic eclipse of the first narrative by
the second produces an interpretation of the enigma of the body which is
almost totally absorbed in the question of the identity of the mother. Hence
the final revealing of the mother stands as the synthetic answer to the desire
continually prescribed by the camera to "see all." The displacement from
Marion to the mother here comes to great effect in terms of the comparative
spectacles provided by the female bodies (a *corpus delecti* instead of a delecta-
ble corpus?). The narrative maneuvers toward a final representation of the
female form as corpse and this designation signals the manner in which the
problem of female sexuality is resolved within the symbolic field of the film.

The conclusion of the film details a twin resurrection of the missing female family members, both literally from the grave, back into the folds of
family and law. Their return is marked by a symbolic transfiguration in the
signification of their sexual identities. Technically the mother is endowed with

a phallus (the fusion of Norman's body with her mind); the corpse-form itself suggests an anatomical correlative to the phallus. The "animation" of the mother's corpse by Norman retains this corpse—a lingering monument to the vicissitudes of a male psychosis—as phallic both by preservation and psychic inhabitation. The logic of the phallocentric order in its extreme state of perversion aims to homogenize sexual representation so as to nullify sexual difference (that is, female sexuality which is aphallic). This order in *Psycho* is aligned with the requirements of the family and the law. The revelation of the psychosexual identity of Norman–the mother coincides simultaneously with the reconstitution of that family and its legal institutionalization (the padded cell).

The return of Marion, represented in the dredging of the car out of the swamp, is linked visually to Norman–the mother through the superimposition of Norman's head, the mother's skull, and the car. Marion's reappearance functions to reiterate and to finish the correspondence between the two narratives. Marion's form has been reconceived in similar terms to the mother. Just as the mother has been preserved and "resexualized" according to male psychosis, so too has Marion been preserved (the shower curtain, the trunk, the bog) and "resexualized." To be reconstituted for the family, she has been visually reduced, transposed into a phallic image—the car withdrawing from the swamp. The narrative, then, in its treatment of female sexuality has reformed it, reconceived the female form so as to disavow difference. The end of the narrative replies to the beginning in this reconceptualization of female sexuality according to the strictures of the family institution as it responds to extreme phallocentrism.

The resolution achieved in the last nonimage of Marion succinctly expresses the results of the narrative displacement as it functions to rearticulate the "female problematic" through familially defined repression culminating in a phallically inflected erasure of difference. The law of the discourse in answer to the presentation of female sexuality contains it by symbolically turning the female body into a phallus. Hence the res-erection of the family members to close off the narrative.

Note

1. Raymond Bellour's "Psychosis, Neurosis, Perversion" originally appeared in *Camera Obscura*, no. 3-4 (1979): 104–32 and is reprinted here. [Klinger's original endnotes have been dropped in favor of roman numerals, cited in the text, corresponding to the subsections of Bellour's essay—eds.]

CHAPTER TWENTY-FIVE

Links in a Chain:
Psycho and Film Classicism

Leland Poague

Advanced film studies have turned increasingly to the question of desire in the cinema, much of this work implying that our desires for certain kinds of films are the result of particular, in some cases essentially negative, psycho-cultural formations. Central to this line of argument is the concept of "the classical narrative cinema," of which Alfred Hitchcock's *Psycho* is often taken to be an exemplary instance.[1] I would agree that *Psycho* is a classic film—will urge that it *earns* its reputation as a landmark of film classicism—but I want also to suggest that the experience of thinking about *Psycho* can serve to test what we *mean* by the notion of "classicism" in the cinema. Put another way, it strikes me that certain important qualities of *Psycho*—qualities of style and implication, let us say—are not well accounted for by reference either to standard readings of the film or to more recently developed paradigms of film-classical style.

By "standard reading" here I refer to the familiar argument, advanced early by Jean Douchet and Robin Wood and later by Leo Braudy and others, that *Psycho* is a film about voyeurism, that in *Psycho* Hitchcock manipulates the conventions of viewer identification, by means of narrative construction and subjective camera, in order to make voyeurs of us all. What we see, in seeing *Psycho,* is a mirror akin to the mirror Lila Crane encounters in the bedroom of "mother" Bates, a mirror wherein our own desires for illicit gratification are imaged, to rebound upon us, as those of Marion and Norman and Lila rebound upon each of them in turn. We are doubles of these characters as they are doubles of each other; and accordingly we must be said to share in the duplicity verging upon madness which characterizes life in the depicted world of the film.[2]

The problems with such an approach to *Psycho* are many—chief among them the contention that audience response to *Psycho* is so completely under Hitchcock's control that an idealized viewer is in fact the film's "central character." The methodological problem is obvious. Upon what grounds can one claim to know how all members of a given audience, much less all members of all possible audiences, will respond to a particular film? More significantly, by what logic is audience response, summed up for critics of *Psycho* by the very imprecise notion of "identification," even *admissible* as evidence of how one *should* read the film?[3] More practically, we can say that this recurrent focus on the primacy of the viewer of *Psycho* turns our attention away from certain important facts of the text by asserting the primacy of "private" or "psychological" experience. (I will return to this point.)

An alternative to such standard readings of *Psycho* is to see the film as an instance of "the classical narrative cinema." To do so (as the notion of film classicism has been developed in the work of David Bordwell, Kristin Thompson, and others) is to focus primarily on the ways in which the classical film narrative alternately effaces or contains the forces and possibilities of the medium — the way continuity cutting, for example, subordinates space to action, subordinates discourse to story; the way the desire for narrative unity or closure "subordinates impersonal or apersonal causes . . . to personal causes," implying thereby that social causes do *not* determine individual actions or narrative outcomes.[4] At its extreme, in the work of Daniel Dayan, for instance, or Laura Mulvey, such subordination even extends to the psychological processes by which the viewer as (the pronominal) "I" is "subjected" to the phallocentric "law" of the Lacanian father, the realm of the Symbolic, the realm of language and acculturation.[5]

An admirable instance of such a reading is provided by Barbara Klinger's discussion of *Psycho* in *Wide Angle,* wherein she traces the means by which the film's first narrative, focused on Marion Crane, is "displaced" or "effaced" by its second narrative, focused on Norman Bates. At issue is the question of sexual difference, especially the question of female sexuality as figured in the person of Marion Crane. "The narrative of *Psycho,*" writes Klinger, "can be seen to function in its movement to present this problem [of female sexuality], to repress it (the switch in narratives) and restate it (Norman–the mother), and finally to contain/solve it in the name of the family and the law."[6] Put another way, Marion is first pictured as an image of erotic spectacle, but by film's end her status has changed to that of missing family member and fugitive from justice. Female sexuality is thus "institutionalized," "contained" in and by the narrative system, particularly by that system's valorization of "the family" as the site of an "homogenized sexuality" wherein sexual difference is denied entirely.

An important advantage of this reading is obvious: it shifts our attention away from private psychology to more public facts of the film's depicted world. I will eventually want to suggest another way in which such public facts may be understood as crucial to any reading of *Psycho*. But there are methodological problems implicit in the classical narrative cinema paradigm which require comment. One of these problems involves what Tony Bennett has called the "metaphysic of the text," the notion that a text (any text) has a "once-and-for-all existence, a once-and-for-all relationship to other texts which is marked and determined by the circumstances of its origin."[7] We see a version of this metaphysic in the standard reading of *Psycho:* Hitchcock as point of origin determines how all readers will read *Psycho* by means of his manipulation of narrative and point of view. But a similar reification of origins and audience response haunts Klinger's reading of *Psycho*. Because the film is, as Raymond Bellour attests, an instance of the classical narrative cinema . . . it *must* function to naturalize the ideology of Hollywood, to contain threats to its hegemony and coherence, to deny them. "Classicism," as Bellour and many others use the term, is thus an historically determined and emergent property of the text which in turn determines how it has, will, and must function.[8]

I would urge, however, that the function of a particular text or film is better understood less by reference to its objective properties (important as those are) than by reference to the manner in which the film is used. One way of using a film is to actively interpret it, to take it as an opportunity for aesthetic experience. Under such a reading the "classical" status of a text is less a matter of its historical origins or generic properties (among which might well be certain recurrent stylistic features) than of its continued centrality and relevance to a critical tradition. We can say on historical grounds whether a text *has* been classical in this sense; we can predict that a given film *will* be classical in this sense. But there is no *test* of "classicism" apart from the ongoing ability of critics and readers to find new ways of interpreting the text in question within the larger context of film culture and the film-critical community. Thus no a priori list of features will determine the "classicism" of a text, however useful such a list might be in heuristic terms. Just the contrary: any feature of a text which contributes to its continuing "readability" will play a part in the critical decision to use a text as a "film classic," whether the film in question is *Psycho* or *Weekend*. The problem with the notion of the classical narrative cinema, then, is that it tends to privilege certain textual features over others, especially those features which are congruent with an a priori model of film's cultural function. Jay Cantor has called this "reading for the already known."[9] Hence the fact that "classicism," as currently used and understood, is so often a pejorative. Let me now point to some facts of *Psycho* only recently known to me in their totality as support for the claim that *Psycho*, a film classic in the older, less restrictive sense of the term, continues to justify and reward critical attention.[10]

Let me begin with the fact of the psychiatrist in *Psycho*—a figure understood by many as an explicit agent of denial and containment who offers us "a way to escape responsibility" by setting up a "screen of jargon to 'explain' Norman," thereby denying "the continuum between [Norman's] actions and our own" (Braudy, p. 126). Such a view of the psychiatrist is itself a species of denial and must be resisted. He makes, it is worth noting, no claim to solve the larger enigma of the film, offers no explanation, for example, of what drove Marion to the act of theft and hence to the Bates Motel, so he can hardly be held accountable for those readings which grant his explanation more credit than it earns. Indeed, the film gives us a kind of second ending, as "mother" soliloquizes down the hall—even perhaps a third ending in the final shot of Marion's car being hauled from the swamp. The psychiatrist's explanation is hardly presented as the last word.

Where the psychiatrist goes wrong—and he does go wrong in one crucial respect—he does so for lack of knowledge. Let us say he hasn't seen *Psycho*. But we have and can specify precisely where he (and with him, I fear, many a film critic) is in error. After the psychiatrist explains, as best he can, Norman's motive and manner of killing, the sheriff asks him about the money Marion stole: "Who got that?" "The swamp," replies the doctor, "these were crimes of passion, not profit." Money, we might say, is another MacGuffin. But money is no MacGuffin at all, I would assert; it is the "public fact" of the film's depicted world (and of our own) which I spoke of earlier as being central to my current understanding of the movie. To miss the importance of the experience of money to these characters in these circumstances is to miss an important part of the experience of *Psycho*.[11]

Money, it can be argued, serves to pollute and distort nearly every human relationship in the world of the film. Sam in the film's opening scene is aroused by the cheapness of the hotel room he shares with Marion—a fact reprised later when he and Lila check in, sans baggage, at the Bates Motel. Sam insists upon getting a room receipt—he's on a "business trip" he tells Norman. Money, or the lack of it, is Sam's excuse for refusing Marion's proposal of marriage. Money, the explicit presence of it, the overt power of it as embodied in the cowboy-hatted Cassidy, baits the trap into which Marion falls—not to mention the way Cassidy boasts of tax evasion or the way his $40,000 wedding present (a house—Sam lives in a back room) is likely to shackle the sexuality of his daughter. California Charlie assumes (wrongly, it turns out) that Marion, like any customer, has "always got time to argue money"; and we subsequently see Marion peel off each of the seven $100 bills she uses to pay for her second car. Money and flesh are invoked as interchangeable entities in Marion's voice-over imagining of Cassidy's response to her theft—he'll replace every lost dollar of it with her "fine soft flesh." The Fairvale sheriff explains the disappearance of Arbogast by reference to greed: "I think he got himself a hot lead as to where your sister was goin' . . . and called you to keep you still while he took off after her and the money." And Lila attributes the same motive to Norman after she and Sam check in as husband and wife at the Bates Motel: "If you had a useless business like this motel, what would you need to get out? To get a new business somewhere else? Forty thousand dollars?" Most crucially, it is arguable that the relationship between Norman's mother and her lover was financially grounded; or at least that it was the lover's ability to persuade Mrs. Bates to build the motel with the money left by Norman's father which pushed the boy over the edge; the motel provided physical evidence of his mother's devotion to another man (Norman: "He talked her into building this motel — he could've talked her into anything").

Another crucial fact of the film is the connection between money, cars, and madness or obsession. Only in a culture obsessed with automobiles would a Bates Motel be built. Only in a culture obsessed with speed and volume of traffic would a main road be moved. Indeed, the connection between cars, madness, Norman, and Marion is made remarkably explicit in the film's visuals. Robin Wood notes in his reading of the film that Marion's decision to switch cars within sight of the highway cop is itself evidence of obsession; it hardly seems likely to throw the law off her track (though, ironically, it does). Her first license plate, furthermore, bears the letters ANL — as if to signify the Freudian equation between compulsive acquisition and the auto culture. And her second car bears another, even more crucial set of letters — NFB. Clearly N and B here can be (often are) taken to refer to Norman Bates. And the otherwise missing middle name is suggested very directly (or at least is implied via the family crest trunk ornament) in nearly every frame wherein the license plate is readable: Norman FORD Bates. The suggestion is most direct, indeed, when it is Norman himself behind the wheel as he drives the car toward the camera, metaphorically shoving the car's FORD logo in our faces. The implied familial relation of crazy Norman and the father of American assembly line capitalism is confirmed by the fact that nearly every major character in the film drives a car or is associated with cars produced by the Ford Motor Company. Marion trades one Ford for another and is framed, while talking with California Charlie, against the grillwork of a 1958 Ford. The highway cop drives a Ford. Lila arrives at Sam's hardware store in a Ford taxi. Arbogast is only partially an exception; he drives a Mercury, another Ford product, as befits his status as messenger. The only major character *not* associated with Ford cars is Sam. He drives a Dodge pickup (as if to signify that he prefers casual, "pickup" sex, or perhaps that his "dodging" of Marion's proposal was a contributing factor in the fate which befell her?). It is also worth noting, in discussing cars, that almost all of the Fords we see have wing-like tail fins, suggesting another connection of a destructive, polluting motor car culture and the mad bird-man of Fairvale. What drove Marion to the Bates Motel? A Ford four-door.

Perhaps in this light the psychiatrist's remark that the swamp got the money bears a measure of truth; we might say that money ("private money," as Cassidy puts it) is a swamp which threatens to engulf us all. Indeed, two of the film's most important visual features reinforce the sense in which capitalism — as represented by the oil-rich Mr. Cassidy and the oil-burning Mr. Ford — is a dark swamp threatening to suck us all, everyone and everything, down. One such feature involves the recurrence of a "twisting" camera movement, usually involving simultaneous panning and craning. We see this movement several times, but two such shots stand out. The first is in the initial hotel scene between Sam and Marion. Marion has expressed her distaste for cheap hotel rooms and afternoon liaisons, Sam refuses to take her seriously ("What do we do instead?"), and Marion pulls away from him; cut on action here to a slightly longer shot, after which the camera cranes slowly back, away from them both, and pans to the left as Marion begins dressing before an off-screen mirror. Let us say the camera here mimes or mirrors Marion's actions—a tentative gesture of rejection, of endistancing. This shot is both mimed and exaggerated in turn, then, by the famous crane shot which accompanies Norman as he goes upstairs to retrieve his mother's corpse prior to depositing it in the fruit cellar. The camera cranes up after Norman, slowly turns to the left, and then pans downward, slowly, to frame the landing where Norman–the mother had attacked Arbogast. Both shots involve a twisting motion, an implicit reversal of direction (the right-to-left pan of the first shot reverses the left-to-right movement of the film's credit sequence; the second shot turns 180 degrees), and both conclude on a downward angle of view. Both, furthermore, involve a species of rejection—Marion of Sam, Norman of "mother's" remonstrances.

A second visual feature of the film involves less a twisting camera than twisting or spinning objects or visual patterns, correlated quite explicitly with money, death, and waste. The first is the fan on the wall in the first hotel room; Sam stands directly beneath it as he complains of the burden of his dead father's debts. Or consider the swirling pattern of the water in the toilet bowl when Marion flushes the scraps of paper upon which she had figured out how to repay the $700 she had spent (after Lila recovers one of the scraps, Sam places it, appropriately enough, in his wallet). Or the blades of the fan on the wall behind the psychiatrist (echoing the one behind Sam in the first hotel scene) while he explains how Norman killed his mother.

The connection between these two visual figures—spinning/swirling objects or patterns and the twisting camera—and the resulting thematic correlation of money, death, and rejection is made chillingly explicit at the end of the shower sequence where the figures are literally *fused*. Marion's blood swirls down the drain with the shower water in a counterclockwise motion, the camera looking almost directly down into the drain pipe; dissolve, then, to an extreme closeup of Marion's eye, as if we were still looking directly downward—at which point the camera now begins to twist slowly outward, as if from the drain, revealing a new angle of vision, horizontal rather than vertical, as we see Marion's body sprawled out of the tub and onto the floor, her head against the toilet which still holds the paper scrap with the figure of $40,000 on it.

Much has been written about the eye motif in *Psycho*—much of it in connection with the voyeurism theme.[12] The connection of twirling objects, money, and death embodied in the dissolve from the drain to Marion's eye, however, suggests a different reading of the vision or sight motif. Let us say that money in the world of *Psycho* serves to twist or limit vision, to turn it back upon itself, and that the visual expression of this limitation is figured in the shot of the bathtub drain as water, life, even sight, is sucked into the swamp-like darkness. The correlation between darkness, money, and obscured sight is seen initially in Marion's drive to Fairvale. The first water hits her car windshield immediately *after* the remark about her "fine soft flesh," a remark accompanied in the visuals by Marion's oddly self-satisfied, self-obsessed grin—which looks forward, as William Rothman points out, to the death's-head expression on Norman—the mother's face in the film's next to last shot. Indeed, the effect of the water on the windshield at certain moments is to fuse the headlights of the oncoming cars into a single circle of light (like the light bulb hanging over Mrs. Bates in the fruit cellar). Normal vision—seeing with two eyes, as it were—thus gives way to tunnel vision, seeing with a single eye, from a singular vantage point.

The importance, the deadliness, of this species of tunnel vision is then reinforced by Norman's one-eyed glance through the peephole into Marion's motel room. The point-of-view shot is masked, to replicate not only what Norman sees, as he sees it, but what he doesn't see. And this sense of limitation is picked up in the shower sequence itself—in the point-of-view shots (Marion's of the peephole-like shower head, for instance; again the connection of water and sight, Marion's, Norman's); in the shots through the shower curtain which obscure our view of "mother"; even in those few frames toward the end of the sequence where the image is again masked briefly, as if it were a Norman's-eye view.

The sense in which money is an agent of destruction that twists vision into a vertiginous tunnel, literally sucking our sight into darkness, is especially evident in a linking of two shots, as noted by William Rothman in *Hitch-cock—The Murderous Gaze;* the first shot a close-up of Norman's eye as it peeks through the peephole, the second a close-up of the shower head seen from the same side-angle view.[13] There are two points to make in this connection. The most obvious is that the pairing equates vision with water, as if lines of sight were now physical, visual (visible) entities which can be captured, directed, pulled down into the swamp (like the taillight "eyes" of Marion's car moments later). Indeed, lines of sight can also be active agents of this process, as Norman's watery eyesight metaphorically engulfs Marion in the shower. Secondly, this correlation of eyesight with entrapment is also arguably a function of "one-sidedness," of partial vision. That is, we see Norman's eye in profile—as we often see characters in profile in *Psycho*—and seeing in profile is only to see (to be seen) partially, to see only half. Let us say that seeing only half of something or somebody is itself a source of danger, for the person seen *and* the person seeing. It is the psychiatrist's partial perspective on things which limits the credit we can grant his explanation of Norman, for example.

It is seeing—or at least hearing—both sides of Norman (mother and son) which enables Marion to "see" the degree to which she has stepped into a trap and encourages her to reclaim her own name, her own whole if problematic identity.

The importance of doubles in *Psycho,* then, is better understood as a matter of perspective rather than in reference to voyeurism or identification. We do not "become" first one character then another in a process which both splits and condemns us as "viewers-in-the-text." We are not cut apart and left for dead to satisfy the possessive fantasies of a money-blind and money-blinded culture, whether we see Norman, Marion, or even Henry Ford as its primary representative. Or at least we don't *have* to be, don't *have* to let it happen. On the contrary, by comparison with every character in the film our vision is remarkably free of limitation, is remarkably "unmasked," remarkably capable of seeing what other characters only see in fits and starts. We *see* the degree to which they mirror each other's actions, for good or ill; we understand—or can if we choose—the degree to which they are victims of a culture which encourages possessiveness and limited perspective. Indeed, the many shots of mirrors in *Psycho* can be taken as images of the potential inclusiveness of our vision; we can see *both* sides of a character or of several characters, can see the degree to which these characters mirror (or do not mirror) each other, can even see the degree to which their actions and values mirror (or do not) our own, without thereby asserting that we *are* these characters. The point, rather, is that we *might* be if we don't work hard enough (as hard as we can) at seeing things in their wholeness.

What I understand as the most ethically charged sequence in the whole film confirms the sense in which we are both to recognize ourselves *in* and thence to distinguish ourselves *from* the characters in the film. As Marion returns to her office after "lunch" with Sam, she passes someone on the sidewalk, a man, wearing a Stetson hat, Hitchcock. We pan inside with her and then, after a few lines of dialogue between Marion and the other secretary, we cut back to the door as her boss and a man, wearing a Stetson, come in. The client is Cassidy, the "oil-lease man." But it could almost have been Hitchcock. And in a way it is—hence the identical cowboy hats. Cassidy gets the film going, as it were—he finances it, is its producer. And so is Hitchcock. But there is also a crucial difference. Hitchcock (more as implicit character than as an empirical individual) knows what he is about, knows the ethical risks involved, knows it in every frame of *Psycho,* in every gesture and image. Indeed, the final images of the film—the "death's head" of Norman–the mother dissolving into the swamp from which Marion's car emerges at the end of a tow chain—amount to a gesture of declaration, an example of the positive role film *can* play in our lives. Hitchcock shows us in *Psycho* how not to use money, how letting money use us condemns us to death; but he also shows us how to use it well, to forge a chain of images, let us say, which pulls from the heart of

Norman's darkness a final image of a truth we would deny, the connection between capitalism, sexuality, and death. Capitalism, we can say with Klinger, *does* threaten to "institutionalize"—but not just Marion nor sexuality alone. Institutions in the film's depicted world, preeminently the Ford Motor Company, threaten everything, even sight itself when characters let those institutions or paradigms delimit their field of vision. I want to call this theme a crucial "fact" of *Psycho;* I understand my construal of it to be an instance of "classicism" in action—an effort, not of constraint or naturalization, but of confrontation and analysis. We might even call it a species of "deconstruction," in a Jonathan Culler sense of the term, in that I have taken what some might deem marginal features—the psychiatrist, Marion's second license plate—as points of textual entry.[14]

However, it should be noted that such a reading depends very little upon a knowledge of genetic circumstances beyond those implicitly connoted by the text itself. Knowledge of the world is involved: one must know something (as much as one can) about people and about films, even something about cars. But that knowledge remains at a relatively *general* and available level and involves no particular knowledge of authorial intent or historical determinants. Indeed, to limit one's construal of *Psycho* to the context of its genesis—to say, for instance, that the presence of all those Fords simply means that Hitchcock colluded with Ford Motor Company to sell cars—is to miss altogether the way those cars *function* in *Psycho* (regardless of how they got there) to help raise the general issue of the problematic relationship between social power (of which capitalism is only an especially resonant instance) and individual freedom. I take the latter construal of the film to be the more relevant for being the more general—for applying to more possible futures. (And who is to say with any certainty which of those futures we will see or suffer, in what sequence or combination—that such certitude might readily serve to guide or limit interpretation?) The film-historical alternative, as currently practiced, always runs the risk of being trapped by the very past it seeks to indict and transcend. We are trapped enough as is.

Notes

1. See Raymond Bellour's "Psychosis, Neurosis, Perversion," for example. For commentary on Bellour see Janet Bergstrom, "Enunciation and Sexual Difference (Part I)" *Camera Obscura,* no. 3-4 (1979): 33–65; and Annette Kuhn, *Women's Pictures: Feminism and Cinema* (London: Routledge & Kegan Paul, 1982).
2. See Jean Douchet (reprinted here); Robin Wood, *Hitchcock's Films,* 3rd edition (South Brunswick and New York: A. S. Barnes, 1977), 106–14, and Leo Braudy, "Hitchcock, Truffaut, and the Irresponsible Audience," in *Focus on Hitchcock,* ed. Albert J. LaValley (Englewood Cliffs: Prentice-Hall, 1972), 116–27.
3. It is worth remarking that even Janet Bergstrom finds Bellour's use of the identification notion problematic: "It is now possible and absolutely necessary to complicate the question of identification as it functions in the classical film, first of all in terms of the realization that spectators are able to take up multiple identificatory positions, whether successively or simultaneously" ("Enunciation and Sexual Difference," 58).

4. David Bordwell, *The Films of Carl-Theodor Dryer* (Berkeley: Univ. of California Press, 1981), 25. See also Kristin Thompson, *Eisenstein's Ivan the Terrible: A Neoformalist Analysis* (Princeton: Princeton Univ. Press, 1981); and Bordwell and Thompson, *Film Art* (Reading, Mass.: Addison-Wesley, 1979).
5. Daniel Dayan, "The Tutor-Code of Classical Cinema," *Film Quarterly,* vol. 28, no. 1 (1974): 22–31; and Laura Mulvey, "Visual Pleasure and Narrative Cinema," *Screen,* vol. 16, no. 2 (1975): 6–18.
6. Klinger's essay, reprinted here, originally appeared in *Wide Angle,* vol. 5, no. 1 (1982): 49–55.
7. Tony Bennett, *Formalism and Marxism* (New York: Methuen, 1979), 69. I discuss the question of the relationship of art work to historical context in the chapter on *Blackmail* in this volume, but see also the "History/Cinema/Criticism" chapter of William Cadbury and Leland Poague, *Film Criticism: A Counter Theory* (Ames: Iowa State Univ. Press, 1982).
8. In a more recent essay Klinger distances herself somewhat from the more static view of "the classical narrative cinema." See her " 'Cinema/Ideology/Criticism' Revisited: The Progressive Text," *Screen,* vol. 25, no. 1 (1984): 30–44.
9. Jay Cantor, *The Space Between: Literature and Politics* (Baltimore: Johns Hopkins, 1981), 5.
10. For a more "art-historical" construal of the concept of "classical" as it applies to film see William Cadbury, "The Classic as a Phase of Style in Renaissance Painting and in Film," in *Proceedings* of the Purdue University Seventh Annual Conference on Film (West Lafayette, 1983), 289–94.
11. On this point I am indebted to Richard Corliss, "*Psycho* Therapy," in Philip Nobile, ed., *Favorite Movies* (New York: Macmillan, 1973), 213–24.
12. See, for instance, Louis D. Giannetti, *Godard and Others: Essays on Film Form* (Rutherford: Fairleigh Dickinson Univ. Press, 1975), 118–25.
13. William Rothman, *Hitchcock—The Murderous Gaze* (Cambridge: Harvard Univ. Press, 1982), 293.
14. See Jonathan Culler, *On Deconstruction: Theory and Criticism after Structuralism* (Ithaca: Cornell Univ. Press, 1982), 139.

A Brief Chronology

Those films marked with an asterisk (*) were directed by Graham Cutts, with Hitchcock writing scenarios, designing sets, and serving (except in the case of *The White Shadow*) as assistant director. All other films or television programs were directed by Hitchcock himself unless otherwise noted.

1922 *Number 13* (unfinished)
1923 *Always Tell Your Wife* (codirected with Seymour Hicks), *Woman to Woman**
1924 *The White Shadow**, *The Prude's Fall**, *The Passionate Adventure**
1925 *The Blackguard**
1926 *The Pleasure Garden* (produced 1925), *The Mountain Eagle* (produced 1925), *The Lodger*
1927 *Downhill, Easy Virtue, The Ring*
1928 *The Farmer's Wife* (produced 1927), *Champagne*
1929 *Harmony Heaven* (part directed), *The Manxman* (produced 1928), *Blackmail*
1930 *Elstree Calling, Juno and the Paycock, Murder!, Mary* (German version of *Murder!*)
1931 *The Skin Game*
1932 *Rich and Strange, Number Seventeen* (produced 1931), *Lord Chamber's Ladies* (producer)
1933 *Waltzes from Vienna*
1934 *The Man Who Knew Too Much*
1935 *The 39 Steps*
1936 *Secret Agent* (produced 1935), *Sabotage*
1937 *Young and Innocent*
1938 *The Lady Vanishes* (produced 1937)
1939 *Jamaica Inn* (produced 1938)
1940 *Rebecca* (produced 1939), *Foreign Correspondent*
1941 *Mr. and Mrs. Smith* (produced 1940), *Suspicion*
1942 *Saboteur*
1943 *Shadow of a Doubt* (produced 1942)
1944 *Lifeboat* (produced 1943), *Bon Voyage, Adventure Malgache*

1945 *Spellbound* (produced 1944)
1946 *Notorious*
1947 *The Paradine Case*
1948 *Rope*
1949 *Under Capricorn* (produced 1948)
1950 *Stage Fright* (produced 1949)
1951 *Strangers on a Train* (produced 1950)
1953 *I Confess* (produced 1952)
1954 *Dial "M" for Murder* (produced 1953), *Rear Window* (produced 1953)
1955 *To Catch a Thief* (produced 1954), "Revenge," *The Trouble with Harry* (produced 1954), "Breakdown," "The Case of Mr. Pelham"
1956 "Back for Christmas," "Wet Saturday," *The Man Who Knew Too Much* (produced 1955), *The Wrong Man*, "Mr. Blanchard's Secret"
1957 "One More Mile to Go," "Four O'Clock," "The Perfect Crime"
1958 "Lamb to the Slaughter," *Vertigo* (produced 1957), "Dip in the Pool," "Poison"
1959 "Banquo's Chair," *North by Northwest*, "Arthur," "The Crystal Trench"
1960 "Incident at a Corner," *Psycho*, "Mrs. Bixby and the Colonel's Coat"
1961 "The Horseplayer," "Bang! You're Dead!"
1962 "I Saw the Whole Thing"
1963 *The Birds* (produced 1962)
1964 *Marnie*
1966 *Torn Curtain*
1969 *Topaz*
1972 *Frenzy* (produced 1971)
1976 *Family Plot* (produced 1975)

Contributors

RICHARD ABEL teaches in the English Department at Drake University. He is the author of *French Cinema: The First Wave, 1915–1929* (Princeton, 1984), and his essays on film have appeared in *Film Quarterly, Cinema Journal, Wide Angle, Quarterly Review of Film Studies, Contemporary Literature,* and others.

RAYMOND BELLOUR is a Chargé de Recherches at the Centre National de la Recherche Scientifique in Paris and teaches also at the Centre Universitaire Américain du Cinéma à Paris. Among his books are *Alexandre Astruc* and *L'analyse du film.* He has also edited two volumes of *Le cinéma américain.*

LESLEY W. BRILL is Associate Professor of English at the University of Colorado (Boulder). His articles on photography, film, and Renaissance theater have appeared in *Journal of American Culture, Modern Language Quarterly, Film Criticism,* and *Literature/Film Quarterly.*

IAN CAMERON founded and still edits *Movie,* has edited books on Robert Bresson and Jean-Luc Godard (among others), and is coauthor, with Robin Wood, of *Antonioni.*

STANLEY CAVELL is Walter M. Cabot Professor of Aesthetics and the General Theory of Value at Harvard University. His books on topics in film and philosophy include *The World Viewed, Pursuits of Happiness,* and (most recently) *Themes Out of School: Effects and Causes.*

VERENA CONLEY has written on contemporary feminist fiction, cinema, and theory. Her book *Hélène Cixous: Writing the Feminine* has recently been published by the University of Nebraska Press.

MARSHALL DEUTELBAUM, formerly an historian on the staff of the George Eastman House, currently teaches film in the English Department at Purdue University. He is the editor of *"Image" on the Art and Evolution of the Film,* a member of the executive council of the Society for Cinema Studies, and the author of film articles in *Wide Angle, North Dakota Quarterly, Literature/Film Quarterly,* and *Cinema Journal.*

JEAN DOUCHET began writing film criticism for *Cahiers du Cinéma* in 1957; his *Alfred Hitchcock* (Paris) was published in 1967. Between times he wrote monographs on Minnelli and Mizoguchi and made films, including a segment in *Paris vu par. . . .* which also featured contributions from Jean-Luc Godard, Eric Rohmer, and Claude Chabrol.

MARGARET M. HORWITZ is a doctoral candidate in Motion Picture/ Television at UCLA, and is currently completing her Ph.D. dissertation. She lives in Los Angeles with her husband and their son.

NANCY HUSTON is a Canadian, a writer, and a feminist. She lives in Paris, writes her books in French, and translates as seldom as possible (exclusively for friends).

THOMAS HYDE has studied and taught film at the University of Oregon. He currently resides in Paris where he is writing a study of the films of F. W. Murnau.

MARIAN E. KEANE is a Ph.D. candidate in Cinema Studies at New York University and is currently completing a dissertation on film acting which takes John Barrymore as its central subject. She was a Teaching Assistant at Harvard University in the Department of Visual and Environmental Studies from 1978 to 1984.

BARBARA KLINGER currently teaches film in the Comparative Literature Program at Indiana University. She has published in *Wide Angle, Camera Obscura,* and *Screen.*

LEONARD J. LEFF, Associate Professor of English at Oklahoma State University, teaches courses in film history and screenwriting. The author of *Film Plots* (Pierian Press, 1983), he has published essays on film in *The Georgia Review, Western Humanities Review, Quarterly Review of Film Studies, Cinema Journal,* and *Film Quarterly.* He is presently completing a book entitled *Hitchcock with Selznick.*

JAMES McLAUGHLIN has studied at Columbia University and at the University of Paris. He is currently completing his Ph.D. in the Department of Communication Studies at the University of Iowa.

ROBERTA PEARSON is a graduate student in Cinema Studies at New York University.

PATRICE PETRO is a doctoral candidate in the Division of Broadcasting and Film at the University of Iowa. She has recently received a Fulbright grant to research a dissertation on issues of gender and mass culture in the Weimar cinema.

MICHELE PISO, a teacher in migrant education programs and an editor of *Northwest Review,* is currently at work on a dissertation on exchange relations in the films of Alfred Hitchcock. She lives in New York City and teaches at Solidaridad Humana on Manhattan's lower East Side.

LELAND POAGUE teaches theory and criticism in the English Department at Iowa State University. A regular contributor to *The Journal of Aesthetic Education* and *Film Criticism,* his most recent books are *Howard Hawks* and *Film Criticism: A Counter Theory* (with William Cadbury).

WILLIAM ROTHMAN received his doctorate in philosophy from Harvard University and has taught film theory, criticism, and history at New York University and Harvard. His book *Hitchcock — The Murderous Gaze* was published in 1982 by the Harvard University Press.

CHARLES L. P. SILET teaches film and American literature and culture at Iowa State University. He has written widely on literary and film subjects, including books on Lindsay Anderson and the images of American Indians on film. He is currently editing a collection of Anderson's writings on film and is thinking about a book on Hitchcock.

ROBERT STAM teaches in the Cinema Studies Department at New York University. He is the author (in Portuguese) of *The Interrupted Spectacle* and coauthor (with Randal Johnson) of *Brazilian Cinema*. His *Reflexivity in Film and Literature: From Don Quixote to Jean-Luc Godard* has just been published by UMI Press.

ELISABETH WEIS is Associate Professor of Film at Brooklyn College, CUNY, and Executive Secretary of the National Society of Film Critics, for whom she has edited two anthologies, *Movie Comedy* and *The Movie Star.* Her other books include *Film Sound: Theory and Practice* (Columbia University Press) and *The Silent Scream: Alfred Hitchcock's Sound Track.*

ROBIN WOOD coordinates and teaches in the film study program of Atkinson College, York University, Toronto, where he lives with Richard Lippe. His latest book is *Hollywood from Vietnam to Reagan* (Columbia University Press). He is currently working on a much enlarged and updated version of *Hitchcock's Films.*

MAURICE YACOWAR is Dean of Humanities and Professor of Film Studies at Brock University, St. Catharines, Ontario, Canada. He is the author of *No Use Shutting the Door* (poems), *Hitchcock's British Films, Tennessee Williams and Film, I Found it at the Movies, Loser Take All: The Comic Art of Woody Allen,* and *Method in Madness: The Comic Art of Mel Brooks.*